Political Clientelism
and Democracy in Belize

Political Clientelism and Democracy in Belize

From My Hand to Yours

Dylan Vernon

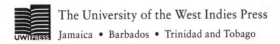
The University of the West Indies Press
Jamaica • Barbados • Trinidad and Tobago

The University of the West Indies Press
7A Gibraltar Hall Road, Mona
Kingston 7, Jamaica
www.uwipress.com

A catalogue record of this book is available from the National
Library of Jamaica.

ISBN: 978-976-640-896-1 (print)
978-976-640-898-5 (ePub)

Printed in the United States of America

Contents

Figures

Tables

Preface and Acknowledgements

It was the last week of feverish campaigning before Belize's sixth post-independence general election of 7 February 2008. The daily local news was dominated with stories about thousands of people swarming constituency offices of incumbent politicians across the country for a chance to get a piece of the "Venezuela money". A few weeks before, in January 2008, the then administration of the People's United Party (PUP) announced that Venezuela had donated BZ$20 million to Belize, ostensibly for housing support. Almost all of these funds were rapidly and chaotically "disbursed" through PUP candidates in the month before the elections.[1] Some persons waiting in the overflowing queues publicly threatened to vote for the PUP "only if they got some". In at least one constituency the police had to be called in to keep the peace. Elements of the United Democratic Party (UDP), the then official opposition party, urged voters to "tek di money but vote dehn out". As a seasoned governance reform advocate, I was cognizant of this unspoken and informal "handout politics" through which so many Belizeans transact with their politicians from day to day.[2] But it was its widespread, open, flagrant and shameless display before that February election day that triggered my determination to take a forensic look.

Not limited to any one political party nor to just election campaign periods, such scenes of blatant *political clientelism* have become commonplace in post-independence Belize – as well as across the Caribbean region. In Caribbean societies, political clientelism (the term social scientists use to describe the ubiquitous relationships in which politicians provide resources and services to people in return for political support) is colloquially known as benefits politics, handout politics, patronage politics, and "rum and roti" politics among other terms. Using Belize as a case study of the rapid expansion and entrenchment of political clientelism in the Caribbean, I explore its origins and its manifestations with the central goal of assessing the implications it presents for democratic governance and sustainable development in states like Belize.

Due to its tendency for informal and secret transactions, its overall nefarious reputation and the fact that much of it is illegal, political clientelism is undeniably a sensitive topic to explore – more so in small states like Belize characterized by personal and visceral styles of partisan politics, and where many of the subjects are recent or still active political actors. I trust that any such sensitivities are tempered by the knowledge that the PhD process that informed this book demanded the highest levels of academic rigour and objectivity, and that my temporal coverage spans governance administrations of both of Belize's major political parties. Indeed, I was able to access a wealth of new information, conduct sixty-nine key informant interviews with mostly willing political leaders and operators, and gather valuable insights from over one hundred citizens across partisan lines. I am especially privileged to have interviewed the first prime minister of Belize, George Price, just months before his passing in 2011, as well as all other former prime ministers of Belize: Sir Manuel Esquivel, Said Musa and Dean Barrow. Additionally, the current prime minister, John Briceño, was also one of my interviewees in his former capacity as a leader of the opposition.

For reasons I explain in the Introduction, my political research focuses on the recent historical period from 1954 to 2013 – just after the 2012 general elections when my focused research concluded. Even as this book is being published after 2013, I have opted to preserve my core study to the original research period and to engage in selective comparative analysis of subsequent years (2014–21) by means of a substantive Epilogue. In essence, my book is about political clientelism in the modern history of Belize. For topics as sensitive as political clientelism this is not only prudent but also avoids the risk of analysis with incomplete and evolving information. Indeed, material from the post-2013 period, which would have had to be based on similarly comprehensive and rigorous research as with the prior period, would quite easily yield another complete volume.

I owe many debts of gratitude to colleagues and friends. First and foremost, I acknowledge the sound, rigorous and meticulous academic guidance provided by Kevin Middlebrook, my PhD supervisor at the University College London. After dissecting my first essays and listening closely to my defence, he advised early and correctly that my core angle was the "politics of the poor" and from there it all flowed. Katherine Quinn, my second supervisor, gave invaluable overall input, especially on modern Caribbean comparative history. Victor Bulmer-Thomas not only provided sagacious advice on improving the work, but also kept up the pressure for its publication. I am especially grateful to my parents – Lawrence Vernon, who invaluably assisted with document research from afar, and Crystal Vernon, who always keeps me grounded. For archival research support, special thanks to Michael Bradley of the National Heritage Library, Elsie

Alpuche (formerly) of the George Price Archival Collection, Herman Byrd and the then staff at the Belize National Archives, and Clarita Pech at the Office of the Clerk of the National Assembly.

My passion for improving the quality of democracy in Belize would not have been fully fired without the exciting and irreplaceable decade of work done with Assad Shoman, Diane Haylock, Dennis Jones, Dean Roches, Adele Catzim and all my comrades at the Society for the Promotion of Education and Research (SPEAR). I must acknowledge the support received along the way from Karen Vernon, Marlon Vernon, Ashley Williamson, Charles Gibson, Anna Rossington, Steve Cushion, Anne Macpherson, Mary Turner, Emily Morris, Paul Sutton, Jean Stubbs, Lisel Alamilla, Robert Pennell, Shaun Finnetty, Leonie Jordan, Phil Westman and Debra Lewis. Judy Lumb provided timely editing advice that contributed to advancing my book project. The book cover was creatively designed by the progressive Belizean graphic artist, Carlos Quiroz. Most importantly, this book would have been impossible without the input of all my interviewees – both politicians and citizens alike.

Note to Readers

All dollar figures ($) are in Belize currency, unless otherwise stated. US$1 = BZ$2 (fixed rate).

All interviews that were conducted in Belize Kriol and Spanish have been translated by the author to English. Some Kriol words have been kept in cases where the meaning is clear to English-language readers.

The positions of the interviewees are those at the exact date of the interviews, and some of these have changed over time. Where relevant for clarity, these changes are noted in the text.

The names of constituents and political brokers interviewed are anonymized based on mutual agreement with the author.

Key Acronyms and Abbreviations

ACB	Association of Concerned Belizeans
ANDA	Association of National Development Agencies
BCCI	Belize Chamber of Commerce and Industry
BNA	Belize National Archives
CARICOM	Caribbean Community
CCT	conditional cash transfer programme
CEO	chief executive officer (formerly permanent secretary)
CPA	Country Poverty Assessment
CPI	Corruption Perception Index
CSO	civil society organization
EBC	Elections and Boundaries Commission
EBD	Elections and Boundaries Department
FPTP	first past the post
FY	financial year
GC	Gini coefficient
GDP	gross domestic product
GNI	gross national income
GoB	Government of Belize
GPAC	George Price Archival Collection
GWU	General Workers Union
HDI	Human Development Index
House	House of Representatives
HSD	Human Services Department
IMF	International Monetary Fund
Katalyst	Katalyst Institute for Public Policy and Research
MP	member of Parliament
NCP	Non-Contributory Pension
NGOs	non-governmental organizations
NIP	National Independence Party
NTUCB	National Trade Union Congress of Belize
OAS	Organization of American States
PNP	People's National Party
PRC	Political Reform Commission

PSC	Public Services Commission
PSU	Public Services Union
PUP	People's United Party
SHIE	Samuel Haynes Institute of Excellence
SPEAR	Society for the Promotion of Education and Research
TI	Transparency International
UB	University of Belize
UDP	United Democratic Party
UNDP	United Nations Development Programme
VIP	Vision Inspired by the People
WGI	Worldwide Governance Indicators

1.

Introduction

Belize, Democracy and Clientelism

Belize's seventh general election on 7 March 2012 made post-independence political history with hardly much publicity: for the first time a losing political party refused to accept the official results. The People's United Party (PUP), the then official opposition, accused the incumbent United Democratic Party (UDP) of winning the election through blatant voter bribery and would not concede.[1] Such cyclical allegations of vote buying and election buying have become all too predictable; but these are only the more dramatic and visible indicators of a much deeper political trend in the modern politics of Belize and of the Caribbean: the rapid expansion and deepening entrenchment of political clientelism in the daily relations between politicians and citizens. Based on rationale explained later in this chapter, I define political clientelism as *an informal and dynamic political exchange between individual or collective clients, who provide or promise political support, and patrons, who provide or promise a variety of targeted and divisible resources and favours.* It is a universal political phenomenon that all countries experience in some form and to some extent. As such, my core research query is not *if* political clientelism exists in Belize and in the Caribbean. More substantively, my focus is on *how* its prevalence and specific contextual manifestations affect democracy and development in Commonwealth Caribbean states such as Belize.

Comparatively, I present the small state of Belize on the Caribbean coast of Central America as an illustrative and critical case of political clientelism in similar independent states in the Commonwealth Caribbean, hereafter, also referred to as "the region" or "the Caribbean".[2] Situating this study in a Commonwealth Caribbean political context does not ignore that Belize is simultaneously Central American and that its continental location is highly relevant to its history, development and key aspects of its politics. Yet Belize's political history, political identity and political system are decidedly more Commonwealth Caribbean than Latin American, and my subregional focus on the Caribbean facilitates comparative political analysis. However,

I do address Belize in Central America where this has significance for the manifestations of political clientelism in Belize – for example, for the issue of immigration. With regard to temporal coverage, I begin with the colonial period and particularly in 1954 when Belize achieved universal adult suffrage under a new constitution that, in effect, launched the Westminster political model and its competitive party system. I then proceed to examine (in two phases) the post-independence period up to 2013 when my in-depth research period concluded. A full chapter is dedicated to examining the case of Belize from a Commonwealth Caribbean comparative perspective. In an extensive Epilogue, I provide comparative commentary on selected developments in the 2014 to June 2021 period as they relate to my principal conclusions.

In this introductory chapter, I situate political clientelism in Belize in the wider framework of the modern political context of the Commonwealth Caribbean and then unpack the concepts of democracy and political clientelism as relevant to exploring the case of Belize. Finally, I outline my research queries, summarize my research methods and present the layout of this book.

The Other Side of Westminster Democracy

By the time Belize achieved its delayed independence from the United Kingdom on 21 September 1981, the Westminster parliamentary model of governance was firmly rooted as the defining feature of its political identity. As is the case for the other independent states of the Commonwealth Caribbean, this model in practice has had a mixed and often contradictory record of progress in consolidating aspects of formal democracy, on the one hand, and in contributing to worrying challenges to substantive democracy, on the other. As "Caribbean", Belize is undoubtedly in a grouping of states that scores positive assessments and high rankings for democracy. Rosy observations such as "no other region, in what has been called the Third World, has had, for so long so many liberal polities" and that "the Caribbean's capacity to sustain liberal democratic politics is impressive"[3] have been so often repeated as to become both too oversimplified and too superficial.

Favourable assessments have come largely, but not exclusively, from the findings of quantitative studies that attempt to correlate aspects of democracy with specific independent variables. Commonwealth Caribbean democracy has been positively correlated to the level of economic development,[4] to former British colonial status,[5] to small-state status[6] and, especially, to the presence of the Westminster parliamentary system.[7] This narrative of flourishing democracy is further corroborated by the results of most cross-national rankings. One of the most cited and comprehensive of these, the Worldwide Governance Indicators, has consistently ranked the twelve independent states of the Commonwealth Caribbean region above all other developing world regions for all six of its aggregate indicators: voice and accountability, political stability and absence of violence/terrorism, government effectiveness, regulatory quality, rule of law, and control of corruption.[8]

Belize has a valid claim to a share of this overall positive record of formal democracy in the Caribbean. Between 1981 and 2013, there were seven free and fair general elections with a high average voter turnout of 76.9 per cent, five peaceful alternations of parties in power and the free growth of an active civil society sector.[9] Unlike other multi-ethnic states in the region, such as Guyana and Trinidad and Tobago, Belize has avoided ethnically divisive party politics.[10] An extensive political reform debate, led largely by civil society groups, resulted in constitutional amendments and legislative initiatives with the objectives of enhancing civil liberties, access to justice, formal democratic participation, and transparency and accountability in government. Between 1981 and 2013, Belize had at least twenty-five separate governance reform initiatives (both from civil society and from government) that resulted in dozens of constitutional amendments as part of eight amendment acts.[11] Such governance achievements contributed to the positive assessment of the Commonwealth Secretariat in 2008 that "Belize enjoys a mature democracy and a well-functioning electoral process".[12]

On the other hand, there is a more dubious and perturbing picture of Commonwealth Caribbean democracy. After a tumultuous and divisive transition to independence in 1966, Guyana's elections under Forbes Burnham (1964–92) were notorious for systematic rigging of ballots. In 1979, Grenada became the first independent Commonwealth Caribbean state to change governments by coup d'état – albeit that this was near bloodless and to overthrow a corrupted authoritarian leader. In 1990, a Muslim group (Jamaat al Muslimeen) attempted a coup d'état in Trinidad and Tobago in which the then prime minister and most of his cabinet were held hostage for six days. Several general elections in Jamaica, especially in the 1980s and 1990s, were marred by high levels of partisan political violence. Qualitative studies that look beyond formal democracy argue that there has been a clear and worsening trend in much of the post-independence period. In 2001 the prominent political scientist Selwyn Ryan warned that "liberal democracy is in grave danger in the Anglophone

Caribbean" and unless there is a renewal of democracy, the region's states "will be lumped with other states that are negatively classified along the governance continuum".[13]

Lack of popular participation in the construction of the Westminster political system gave rise to critical questions about its relevance to the political culture of small Caribbean states.[14] For instance, due to the limited number of constituency seats appropriate for smaller populations, more than half of the elected representatives in parliament are often appointed to cabinets. Side effects of this fusing of executive and legislative powers include rubber-stamp legislatures, the absence of effective legislative oversight, invariably weak backbenches as well as the added propensity for personality-based and particularistic politics. Several studies have exposed the unfairness of first-past-the-post (FPTP) systems in which winning parties control all; opposition parties are virtually powerless; and party politics are divisive, personal and unregulated.[15] A recurring theme is that electoral democracy in the region "has not led to either broader participation in national decision-making within formal institutions and in wider society" nor to substantive democracy.[16]

Belize exhibits most of these worrying challenges to liberal democracy. Along with Jamaica and Guyana, Belize received the lowest Worldwide Governance Indicators governance scores for 1998–2008 compared with those of the other states in the region. Overall, there was a worsening trend in this ten-year period, with 2008 scores below the 50 percentile rankings for control of corruption, government effectiveness, regulatory quality and rule of law.[17] Further evidence of challenges to Belize's democracy appears in several qualitative studies and governance reports on Belize's political system and practice.[18] In 2000, the Belize Political Reform Commission highlighted core problems related to the lack of effective separation of executive, legislative and judicial powers; the absence of legislative oversight; the inadequacies of the FPTP electoral system; the prevalence of divisive party politics and political tribalism; the pervasiveness of political corruption; the lack of campaign finance regulation; the poor record of political participation (outside of elections); and growing voter bribery.[19]

It is against this contrary backdrop of simultaneous democratic advance and democratic decay that political clientelism comes into sharper focus as a particularly persistent challenge to mainstream notions of democracy in the Commonwealth Caribbean, including Belize. Except for the groundbreaking works on party-based clientelism in Jamaica by Carl Stone and Charlene Edie,[20] and its secondary treatment in some studies, there has been no comprehensive and dedicated research on political clientelism in any other state in the region.[21] Cynthia Barrow-Giles's astute reflection is shared by many observers of politics in the Caribbean: "vote buying and related practices" occur in the region but are "not openly discussed".[22]

In Belize, political clientelism has been referenced, mostly secondarily, in the context of a few academic studies, official reports and media stories. Assad Shoman, for example, identified the growth of party-based clientelism as an element related to the emergence of political parties after the 1950s. One study demonstrated how party-based patronage spread to rural villages in southern Belize.[23] Another exposed the deep penetration of clientelism in the execution of international development projects since the 1990s.[24] In 2000, the Political Reform Commission noted with concern that the "practice of political parties and candidates giving monies and gifts for votes . . . while illegal is rampant" in post-independence Belize.[25] In 2008, Commonwealth Secretariat election observers reported that there were allegations of votes being exchanged for land, loans and money, and for facilitating access to Belizean citizenship in the lead up to the 2008 general elections.[26] In an AmericasBarometer survey conducted in 2010 on the incidence of citizens being offered benefits for votes in twenty-two Caribbean and Latin American countries, Belize ranked fourth highest overall, second of all Central American countries and the first of four Commonwealth Caribbean countries polled.[27] A scan of political news stories in the local media over the past two decades reveals an increasing number of allegations and counter-allegations directly related to political clientelism. In short, despite a modern political history characterized by an overall positive record of formal democracy, concerns about the expansion of clientelism in Belize's politics have grown louder since independence.

What Is Democracy For?

Studies of political clientelism are rife with observations that "an overwhelmingly negative image of clientelism permeates scholarly analysis"[28] and that political clientelism is usually seen as "lying at the far end of the institutional spectrum from democracy".[29] As such, it is necessary to understand first what we mean by democracy. The term "democracy" is used so widely and often so loosely by so many that it is critical to agree what we mean by it at the onset. For this book, democracy includes but goes beyond what is often denoted "formal democracy" – a term used, hereafter, to refer to the existence of a set of political institutions and basic civil liberties that facilitate the selection of leaders who make governance decisions on behalf of citizens.[30] Juan Linz and Alfred Stephan limited their conceptualization of democracy to its formal elements when they argued that it is consolidated when "it is the only game in town" and meets basic criteria, including the existence of an active civil society, rules and laws to allow individual rights and the exercise of "control over public power and the state apparatus".[31] The ongoing process towards the goal of deepening democracy is generally denoted as "democratization". However, this process is seldom straightforward and often messy, for, as Guillermo O'Donnell noted, "formal rules about how political institutions are supposed to work are often poor guides to what actually happens" in new democracies.[32] Once procedures for the selection of leaders to facilitate decision-making, based on democratic values, are institutionalized in a state, what is democracy for?

As essential as formal political institutions, rule of law and elections are for democracy, they are not sufficient. A more substantive and useful approach is to view democracy as a context-driven goal that is strived for through processes that are evolving, dynamic and participatory.[33] Huber et al. persuasively argued that the overall goal can be construed as "social democracy" characterized by "increasing equality in social and economic outcomes" and which is only achievable when there is both formal democracy, as well as what they denote as "participatory democracy": "high levels of participation without systematic differences across social categories"[34] As David Hinds puts it, "The presence of formal democratic institutions and practices are indispensable to democratisation", but they must "involve substantive elements such as the broad participation of the masses of people in decision making and an absence of group dominance" and "also be rooted in the quest for equality and social justice".[35] There are, arguably, normative and interpretivist elements in defining the goal of democracy, and as Whitehead contented, democracy is like a boat at anchor: "There is both a core of meaning that is anchoring and a margin of contestation that is floating."[36]

Accepting that precise outcomes are contextually determined, I employ "social democracy" as a core analytical concept for exploring political clientelism for Belize. It assumes that democracy should facilitate sustainable development and contribute to the achievement of a more equal and just society. This is not to say that all decisions will lead to these goals or that the process is a direct and flawless one, but that the decisions should, in the longer term, contribute to movement towards these goals. The failure to address problems of economic inequality and lack of access to social goods cannot only curtail participation in formal democracy by determining how many and who get involved but can also be factors for people to engage in informal activities such as clientelism.

From a formal democracy perspective, political clientelism – "another game in town" – is broadly seen as an undemocratic and nefarious informal activity that corrupts formal modes of participation, but that should gradually wither away or be restrained as new democracies become consolidated, liberal values predominate and regulatory frameworks improve. However, its persistence, in advanced and emerging democracies alike, suggests that achievements in formal democracy do not, alone, mitigate clientelism. Taking a more substantive approach and viewing democracy as social democracy allows one to more practically view the expansion and persistence of political clientelism as one element of the "messiness" characteristic of democratization processes.

Unpacking Political Clientelism

The study of clientelism originated largely as part of anthropological research in traditional rural communities in the first half of the twentieth century. In this context clientelism is broadly defined as a "form of particularistic, personal and dyadic exchange, usually characterized by a sense of obligation, and often also by an unequal balance of power between those involved".[37] This conceptualization focused earlier studies of clientelism to the micro-analytical level of dyadic relationships, especially in small communities. Since the 1960s, a new generation of social scientists has theorized clientelism from a more macro-political perspective as a "form of behaviour that becomes rational for people to pursue, given particular external conditions" in any political context, rather than only as "behaviour characteristic of particular [traditional] cultures".[38] This approach led to a spate of studies on "political" clientelism in the wider literature on democracy, especially in the context of the emergence of new nation states as colonialism waned and as formal democracy spread in Latin America, Africa, the Caribbean and Eastern Europe.

Overall, definitions of political clientelism depict an informal relationship in which political actors (patrons), with access to demanded resources, exchange these for political support from citizens (clients) in need of resources. Patrons and clients can have direct relationships, but as the volume of these expand, exchanges tend to be mediated by brokers. Daniel Sabet's definition of *brokers* is sound: those community leaders who fill the "structural holes" between the network of clients "who have the right to vote but lack resources" and the network of patrons "who have access to resources and require political support".[39] This critical liaison role of brokers makes them powerful clientelist actors who can significantly influence who gets what and when. Although the term "patron" generally refers to individual political actors, it can also extend to organizations such as political parties, which can also function directly as patrons.[40] Similarly, clients are mostly presented as individuals in their relationships with patrons, but exchanges between a patron and a collective of clients, for example in village or neighbourhood, also classify as political clientelism.

Clientelist relationships can exist based on either direct exchange of resources for political support or in the form of promises. Apart from not always being verifiable (for example, if a client did vote as promised for a patron), clientelist relationships operate over time and can exist without the actual delivery of either resources or political support. As Allen Hicken rightly noted, "clientelism is at its core an iterated interaction, with each side anticipating future interactions as they make decisions about their behaviour today".[41] It is largely for this reason that patrons eventually tend to establish elaborate mechanisms to monitor compliance of clientelist agreements. This element of "promise" in the conceptualization of political clientelism introduces three important assumptions for this book: political clientelism does not have to be legally proven to be denoted as such; it is not always possible to verify if promises are indeed kept by clients or patrons; and clientelist transactions are not always immediate. Consequently, there is a built-in element of unpredictability inherent to clientelist exchanges.

Another significant definitional distinction relates to how the actual content of the clientelist exchange is conceived by some and not by others. I concur with the view that "what matters is not so much the content of the exchange, but the fact that the benefit must be divisible and targeted towards clients in order to gain their political allegiance".[42] This element of resource divisibility is true both for the distribution of resources directly to individual clients, as well as for the division and distribution of resources to a collective of clients. An example of the latter is when incumbent politicians divide development funds for road construction among a number of client groups based in particular communities in return for political support. It is also important to acknowledge that the resources provided or promised can be more or less tangible. One study on Jamaica, for example, demonstrated how the comfort and personal security that derive from belonging to a clientelist political party can be in high demand in violence-ridden urban communities.[43] In terms of what clients provide, some scholars focus too narrowly on electoral support and voting, whereas others envision a much broader set of support activities under the banner of "political support". I adopt the latter approach which better allows for the exploration of political clientelism as an ongoing political relationship that necessarily includes, but can also transcend, election campaigns proper.

A clear elitist bias can be detected in studies that only approach clientelist relationships hierarchically from viewpoints of politicians or political parties (patrons) and not from the vantage point of citizens as clients. Javier Auyero criticized this bias and correctly argued for more research based on the viewpoints of clients and intermediaries. His groundbreaking research on Argentina illustrated that, from this analytical angle, clientelist relations should also be construed as "constructive problem-solving networks meant to ensure material survival and of shared cultural representations".[44] This nuance is important because analyses that exclude or minimize either the viewpoints of patrons or of clients can overlook relevant manifestations and implications of clientelist politics, as well as minimize the importance of the non-structural and more cultural dimensions of clientelism.[45]

Because clientelist exchanges are not legally enforceable and are theoretically breakable by the patron or client at any time, they have been generally conceptualized in the scholarship as voluntary. The contestation that does exist around this issue is invariably around the degree of voluntarism inherent in the client's participation. Clients are, in principle, "free to choose their patrons and free to exit the relationship should it not be to their satisfaction".[46] However, in contexts of economic inequity, clients are often exploited by patrons and can become dependent on the resources exchanged for support to the extent that exiting the relationship can be difficult. Studies on shantytowns in Brazil and Argentina, for example, indicate that poor clients often feel compelled to remain in patron–client relationships for fear of losing needed benefits.[47] Tina Hilgers got it just right: "The degree of voluntarism is, thus, probably related directly to the size of the client's resource base or access to alternative patrons – that is, to his relative power vis-à-vis the patron."[48]

Tellingly, there is little academic discussion of voluntarism on the part of the political patron. The conventional wisdom is that patrons voluntarily choose to give or promise clientelist inducements to an individual, and in so doing commence or continue a clientelist relationship. Yet several studies have shown that once clientelism becomes established as dominant in a political system, politicians and political parties may feel obligated or pressured to engage in clientelist activities. For example, it has been illustrated that opposition parties in Latin America and the Caribbean states with high incidences of poverty have great incentive to use clientelism as an electoral strategy to enhance competitiveness against incumbent clientelist parties. As with clients, voluntarism is also a matter of degree for political patrons. In competitive party contexts, the degree of patron voluntarism is no doubt directly related to the extent of inequality of access to resources and the extent of systemic entrenchment of clientelism. In short, although clientelist exchanges at the dyadic level are theoretically voluntary for both patrons and clients, the degree of voluntarism may be less so in practice. It is for this reason that I decided not to refer to political clientelism as a purely voluntary relationship on the part of clients and patrons in my definition of the phenomena.

This discussion on voluntarism raises the critical question as to whether political clientelism is a mode of political participation for clients. Such is, indeed, the case if political participation is conceived beyond just voting and more broadly as "behaviour influencing or attempting to influence the distribution of public goods" and as inclusive of informal participation.[49] Not surprisingly, most studies on informal participation focus on conventional modes, such as civil society advocacy, social movements and community organizing, and exclude political clientelism. This exclusion is mainly the result of the negative and dubious reputation surrounding political clientelism. However, as Lauth convincingly argues, "clientelist structures are based upon a relationship of exchange, which justifies our understanding of them as forms of participation, even when the personal connections are [or can be] asymmetrically structured".[50] As such, I approach political clientelism as a mode of political participation in that some citizens voluntarily, and even proactively, barter political support to political actors so as to influence the distribution of resources in their direction.

The decisions that citizens make on whether to participate in clientelist relationships are brought into sharper focus when viewed from a "rational choice" approach.[51] From this conceptual angle, potential clients decide to enter clientelist agreements only when the benefits of resources received or promised are assumed to outweigh the costs of promising or providing political support.[52] Of course, one of the much-discussed practical flaws in this approach is that not all potential clients have equal access to the contextual information required to make such rational decisions. It has been argued, for example, that citizens who trade votes for benefits tend to be those who are more politically involved and informed. Despite this caveat, in the particular political and social contexts of some developing states, the individual decisions of citizens to engage in clientelist relationships to access needed resources are often highly rational indeed.

On Supporting Conditions for Political Clientelism

As conceptualized earlier, political clientelism has long been present in some form in all states, regardless of size, stage of development and system of government. But how does it develop, and what conditions make it thrive in a "new" democracy? The discussion thus far and a review of the literature on this particular question point to three broad categories of supporting conditions: poverty and inequality, control of political and resource allocation institutions, and the consolidation of competitive party politics. The relevant premise is that the particular nature and incidence of political clientelism in Belize are determined largely by the interplay of these supporting variables over time.

With regard to poverty and inequality, the core argument is decidedly rational: poverty and unequal or ineffective resource distribution make political clientelism more attractive to both clients, who need resources, and to patrons, who find "buying" political support cost-effective as part of their electoral strategies. Not surprisingly, the 2011 AmericasBarometer survey on vote buying in the Americas reported that "the results affirm the importance of individual-level poverty and, as well, country-level income inequality in predicting offers of vote buying".[53] Moreover, ineffective or inadequate alternatives to address poverty, such as state welfare institutions and civil society interventions, can facilitate political clientelism. As Philip Keefer argues, in some contexts of high incidences of poverty in young democracies, "the inability of political competitors to make credible promises to citizens leads them to prefer clientelist policies: to underprovide nontargeted goods, to overprovide targeted transfers to narrow groups of voters".[54] From the vantage point of clients, Auyero is particularly percipient in conceptualizing political clientelism as the "politics of the poor" to emphasize how the poor do proactively barter their political support to access much-needed resources.[55]

There is also the converse implication that a reduction in poverty and a more equitable distribution of wealth should theoretically contribute to dampening clientelist behaviour. As Carl Stone suggested, political clientelism is usually more "muted and restrained by contrary forces" in richer and more developed states.[56] In this regard, one study used a quantitative model of electoral competition in Latin America to illustrate that economic development and improvements in the distribution of non-targeted resources "undermine[s] the incumbent patron's advantage over any challenger" and can diminish clientelism.[57]

However, several scholars have demonstrated that the use of political clientelism to gain electoral advantage can also persist in developed states with low levels of poverty and high levels of economic development, such as Japan and Italy. And some studies on developing countries have found that middle-income citizens can also become clients. Jorge Domínguez, for instance, noted that "patronage did not just benefit the poor" but that elements of the middle and business classes are also clients in Caribbean states.[58] Other scholars have argued that, in some countries, people in poor communities can hold strong anti-clientelist tendencies.[59] The implication is that, in practice, the extent to which poverty and inequality are relevant depends not only on their particular manifestations but also on their interplay with other supporting conditions in a particular country context.

The logic for "the control of resource allocation institutions" as the second core-supporting condition for political clientelism is straightforward: newly democratized polities are generally more conducive to clientelist behaviour when political leaders have more and dominant control over institutions of state that can disburse goods and services as favours.[60] Simply put, when political control over resources and benefits is high, more discretionary and subject to low levels of accountability, opportunities for clientelist exchanges are maximized. The level of institutional control needs to be such that enough politicians and citizens alike believe that which candidate or party is in control has the capacity or the potential to directly benefit favoured individuals and groups.

It is well established that political clientelism can be equally prevalent in states with quite different systems of governance, for example, the presidential or parliamentary models. Yet, because Westminster's parliamentary model relatively allows for faster policy decision-making, fewer legislative bottlenecks and generally stronger governments than presidential systems, it will be useful to explore whether these characteristics can facilitate political clientelism. The extent of control exercised over electoral management and regulatory institutions by incumbents is also relevant to the prevalence of clientelism. As Susan Stokes argues, it is de facto practices of electoral institutions in any system that may "encourage the personal vote . . . and also clientelism".[61] The pertinent point here is that although most electoral systems, including those in the Caribbean, do have legal institutions and procedures to ban or discourage the bribery of voters, these rules are often ignored by government officials, political parties and voters.

The identification of competitive party politics as the third supporting condition for political clientelism is perhaps the most obvious. A party system can be described as "competitive" when partisans "have strong incentives to try to win supporters at the margin for one or the other partisan camp" and that a key indicator of such competition is when elections results are close between partisan blocs.[62] Conceptually, party–citizen relationships in a context of competition can take variants of two broad forms at different points in time: programmatic or clientelist.[63] Generally, programmatic relationships are characterized by the dominant distribution of non-targeted and non-contingent resources through public institutions and are normally more ideological and civic based in orientation. On the other hand, clientelist party–citizen relationships generally feature transactional distribution of targeted and contingent resources. Whereas programme-oriented political leaders tend to be more public service oriented in motivation, clientelist politicians tend to be more motivated by getting political support and gaining political power through providing whatever is demanded by their constituents. Both forms of political relationships with citizens can exist simultaneously within one party or politician, and both require the establishment of party and constituency machines to organize voter support. Importantly, because particular contextual conditions contribute to determining the degree of prevalence of either relationship, both can be approached analytically as being potentially path dependent.

The usual narrative is that of smaller or weaker political parties adopting the clientelist "machine party" tactics of the larger and better-established parties, with the goal of becoming more competitive and of controlling the powers of government. Across the Commonwealth Caribbean, the rise of party politics in the decolonization period and after independence was generally accompanied by increasingly divisive competitive politics as opposition parties plotted to unseat the original parties of the nationalist movement.[64] Studies on particular states in the region have also linked the emergence of political clientelism directly to the emergence of competitive party politics. Overall, much of the literature approaches political clientelism as a party-based political strategy that is utilized by competing politicians and parties with the objective of enhancing the predictability of electoral performance – especially in contexts where political parties are ideologically similar.

Even though intense party competition and political clientelism are not specific to particular systems of governance or electoral models, it has been illustrated that Westminster's FPTP electoral system, in which two or more politicians compete for the same voters in the same constituency, can be more conducive to the development of competitive clientelist practices by politicians than those in certain proportional representative systems that do not feature single-seat constituencies.[65] Highly familiar politician–citizen relationships in FPTP electoral systems, particularly in small-state contexts, are also likely more conducive to the expansion of clientelism.[66]

Other Contextual Variables for Belize

While the relative mix of these three central supporting conditions (or independent variables) for political clientelism are essential for flavouring its particular manifestations in a specific political context, there are other contextual ingredients that can also contribute. Gender, for example, although receiving but negligible focused consideration in the political clientelism literature, has obvious relevance, as it does for every social and political relationship. A number of studies have explored gender constructs in the broader context of research on informal institutions. For example, Mackay, Kenny and Chappell highlighted country studies that show that "male-dominated political elites have shifted the locus of power from formal to informal mechanisms in order to counteract women's increased access and presence in formal decision-making".[67] In her studies on male dominance in informal political institutions (in Thailand) Elin Bjarnegård is convincing in her demonstration that clientelism is also gendered and that leadership roles (patrons and brokers) are even more dominated by men than is the case in formal political institutions.[68] She argued that the underrepresentation of women in the highest hierarchical levels of clientelist networks translates into underrepresentation in parliament because it is through these networks that candidate recruitment and selection most transpire.[69] Although men dominate the leadership roles of clientelist networks in most contexts, several studies indicate that women often participate more in the lowest hierarchical level as clients.[70]

Issues related to gender and clientelism have also been highlighted in several assessments of conditional cash transfer programmes (CCTs), especially in Latin America.[71] Within the broad goal of poverty alleviation, CCTs have targeted women predominately and are often highly susceptible to politicization and clientelist politics.[72] In a study on CCTs in Argentina, for example, findings "suggest that women regularly found themselves in a subservient role to men with more power, resources and social status in the client–patron relationship" and that "the CCT may be transforming the traditional patron–client relations into genderised relations of domination".[73] Gender-related abuses regarding clientelism recorded in CCTs in Latin America have included extortion of CCT monies by patrons, conditional requirements for recipients to participate in party events and even sexual violence.[74] Clearly, the gender dimensions of political clientelism are of great relevance to explore for this study.

For the Commonwealth Caribbean, it is also clear from the discussion thus far that small state size is another unique contextual feature to consider. State scale and population size have received marginal attention in the political clientelism literature, and there is still little international consensus on how to define a small state. The Commonwealth Secretariat, an international leader in promoting small-state studies, once defined small states as those with populations of less than 1.5 million, but strictly applied, this would, for example, exclude the small state of Jamaica. The Commonwealth Secretariat also popularized the understanding that, apart from small populations, small states possess unique special development challenges, including openness, income volatility, poverty, limited diversification and capacity, and susceptibility to natural disasters and environmental change. Such features, which in effect result in high levels of state vulnerability, are part of what defines a small state. With Belize's 2010 census counting a population of 312,698 in a territory of 22,966 square kilometres (second only to Guyana in the Commonwealth Caribbean), Belize is by every definition a small state – as is every nation in the Caribbean.

Although little studied, some insights into the relationship between political clientelism and state scale can be derived from observing the impact of small size on other political phenomena. On the one hand, small states have been identified as being "among the more democratic of developing states" and in which political parties find it less challenging to inform and mobilize people, given the smaller populations and geographical spaces.[75] Most significant for this study, small states generally allow for a type of highly personalized politics that is likely very conducive to the fostering of dyadic clientelist relationships. As suggested by one study, the attraction of clientelism is greatest in electoral systems that are more familiar, in part, because monitoring of clients' compliance with clientelist agreements is more cost-effective "where the numbers of voters is small – hundreds or thousands rather than tens of thousands".[76]

One other contextual feature that warrants some attention is that of the possible interplay between ethnicity and political clientelism in multi-ethnic states such as Belize. (Based on the ethnic categories selected by the 2010 Belize census, six ethnic groups were identified with at least 3 per cent and up to 50 per cent proportions of the total population.) A few studies have explored whether multi-ethnic societies can facilitate the construction of clientelist networks. Stokes and Medina found that ethnicity was a key factor in distribution decisions and that "ethnically divided societies may be more prone to clientelism than are ethnically homogeneous ones".[77] Kanchan Chandra examined the relationship between high levels of political clientelism and ethnic favouritism in India and found that ethnic similarity facilitates clientelist exchanges.[78] A few studies have examined the issue of ethnicity and clientelism in Trinidad and Tobago and in Guyana, both of which have experiences with ethnically divisive party politics. For example, Ralph Premdas explored, among other things, ethnic inequalities in Trinidad and Tobago's public service and found that, because political parties are ethnically identified, parties in power tend towards distributing a large portion of public service jobs and public services by ethnic criteria.[79]

Receiving less attention in the political clientelism literature is the issue of migration, and, in particular, immigration. With the foreign-born population making up almost 15 per cent of Belize's population in 2010 and with this having a significant demographic impact on the "ethnic mix", Belize is among the few Commonwealth Caribbean states (the others being the Bahamas, and Antigua and Barbuda) that have had notable rates of immigration since the 1980s. In the case of Belize, the vast majority of the new immigrants have come from Belize's Central American neighbours of Guatemala, El Salvador and Honduras through largely open land borders. As can be gleaned from the literature reviewed, the incidence of political clientelism in Latin America, which includes these three Central American states, is comparatively high among developing regions.[80] It is therefore interesting to explore, even if preliminarily, whether any interesting relationships can be observed between immigration and the manifestations of political clientelism in Belize, including, for example, how immigrants from Central American states with high incidence of political clientelism have interfaced with the consolidation of Belize's version of political clientelism since independence.

On the Implications of Political Clientelism

As Eisenstadt and Roniger rightly contend, the "full institutional implications and repercussions [of political clientelism] are only seen when they become a part or manifestation of the central mode of regulation of resources . . . and are best understood in relation to the broader, often macro-societal, setting in which they take place".[81] Yet comprehensive research on the macro-political and governance consequences for new democracies is sparse. Most studies focus exclusively on particular consequences for individuals, small communities or political parties at the expense of broader systemic consequences. This is due, in no small part, to the complex analytical challenge of inferring national political implications from relationships that are mostly dyadic, informal and often illegal in nature. Not surprisingly, most studies focus on the negative implications of political clientelism.

One cross-national study found that governance reforms "often fail because they tend to threaten existing power relations: the patronage systems through which political advantage is maintained, and the patterns of collusion through which public resources are diverted to favoured groups".[82] Politicians therefore weigh reform measures by the "risk that they will lose patronage resources, such as public sector jobs and rents, and also lose popular support".[83] Seen from this perspective, political clientelism is a disincentive to long-term policy development as well as to governance reforms that can threaten the allocation of resources through clientelist networks. As such, pervasive clientelism can encourage short-term fixes and risky decisions based more on the demands of election cycles and patron–client relationships than on the national and collective good of states.

In some contexts, political clientelism can also contribute to both conflict and violence in communities in which it is entrenched. As noted, quite a few studies have examined political clientelism as a primary cause of the highly divisive and violent nature of constituency-based politics in Jamaica in the 1990s. In particular, they demonstrated how some politicians' use of drug dons (drug lords) as a source of clientelist resources resulted in a situation in which some drug dons themselves became patrons in several Kingston constituencies.

Importantly, the link between political clientelism and public corruption has received much attention.[84] Paul Hutchcroft examined the relationship between clientelism, rent-seeking and corruption, on the one hand, and economic development, on the other, and demonstrated that clientelism overlaps with corruption when patrons use public office, or access to office holders, to direct state resources and services to themselves, clients and party financiers.[85] Similarly, Alfredo Rehren noted that "when political parties control the bureaucracy and behave as virtual patrons, dispensing public resources and positions in exchange for partisan allegiance, and eventually allow party members to enrich themselves, clientelism facilitates corruption".[86] A study on why corrupt governments maintain public support found that "people in countries where government institutions are weak and patron–client relations are strong are more likely to support a corrupt leader from whom they expect to receive tangible benefits".[87] It additionally contended that such public support is more likely in states that exhibit higher levels of poverty and inequality. Generally, these studies highlight the reality of the very thin and grey line between political clientelism and corruption and how they feed each other in practice.

However, a few studies do point to possible positive effects for both clients and the macro-political system. Generally, they focus on distributive benefits and the enhancement of the political engagement of clients. Poor people and poor communities, especially in a context of socio-economic inequality, can receive needed goods and services that may not have been otherwise available to them.[88] It is largely because of these redistributive and problem-solving arguments that some contend that political clientelism may even help to preserve democracy and social stability in young democracies.[89] There is, therefore, significant merit to the argument that practices related to political clientelism may best be seen as "neither good nor bad in themselves . . . what matters are the outcomes, and those are varied".[90]

The existence of high and pervasive levels of clientelism alongside formal democracy in young democracies led Stone to coin the seemingly oxymoronic term "clientelist democracy" for Jamaica.[91] It is quite similar but broader in usage to the concept of "patronage democracy" developed later by Chandra to depict a state in which clientelism is systemic and elected officials enjoy "significant discretion in the implementation of laws allocating jobs and services" and the public sector is a major "source of jobs and provider of services in comparison to the private sector".[92] However contradictory the terms "clientelist democracy" and "patronage democracy" may appear, they acknowledge the reality that developing states can exhibit features of formal democracy simultaneously with significant levels of political clientelism.

On the Analytical Approach

Based on the preceding conceptual discussion of political clientelism, I formulate the following definition for my analysis: *an informal and dynamic political exchange between individual or collective clients, who provide or promise political support, and patrons, who provide or promise a variety of targeted and divisible resources and favours.* This definition subsumes two key elements that are widely associated with political clientelism: political patronage and vote trading. I use the term "patronage" to denote those clientelist exchanges that are more directly related to the discretionary allocation of state resources, including public sector jobs.[93] Political patronage or patronage politics more specifically refers to "the proffering of public resources (most typically, public employment) by office holders in return for electoral support".[94] "Nepotism" is approached as a form of political patronage in the sense that it is patronage given to family relatives that is not based strictly on merit. I use the term "vote trading" to refer to the exchange of votes for resources, inclusive of "vote buying" and "vote selling". Implicit to my definition of political clientelism are the assumptions that it can transcend voting, can take both legitimate and unlawful forms, can be more or less voluntary, and can be justifiably explored as both a form of informal participation and a mode of resource distribution.

Departing from my core research query on how the rampant expansion, level of prevalence and specific contextual manifestations of political clientelism in Belize affect its democracy and development, I organize my analysis around five specific questions:

1. How did political clientelism emerge in the formative period of Belize's modern politics?
2. What are the principal manifestations of the expansion of political clientelism in Belize in the post-independence period?
3. What factors have contributed to this high rate of expansion of clientelism at the same time as formal democratic advances in Belize?
4. How has widespread clientelism affected the quality of Belize's democracy and its social and economic development?
5. How does the Belize case compare to experiences of other independent states in the Commonwealth Caribbean?

At the macro-analytical level, I situate political clientelism (in effect, my dependent variable) within the broader conceptual framework of democracy and democratization, and I centre the examination of the expansion of political clientelism around the three broad independent variables identified in the preceding conceptual discussion: the degree and nature of competitive party politics, the extent of centralized and politicized control of resource allocation institutions, the extent and nature of poverty and inequality. Additionally, I explore the relevance of three other features that are more distinct to the Belize context: small size, multi-ethnicity and immigration. Gender is fully integrated in the overall analysis as a thematic thread. To examine the core question on the implications of political clientelism for Belize, I focus on the possible consequences for formal political institutions, policy development and reform, political corruption, political participation, resource distribution, and people's livelihoods.

This analytical framework facilitates the examination of the various levels of relationships between and among a variety of political actors within Belize: citizen–politician relationships, clientelist network relationships, political party relationships and relationships within the wider macro-political system. These possible interactions between and among the various actors (citizens, politicians, political parties, government, private donors and civil society groups) are depicted in a basic influence and resource flow diagram designed to help frame the examination of clientelist flows (figure 1). With 1981 established as the baseline year to explore the post-independence expansion and manifestations of political clientelism, I use nine tracer markers, as listed in table 1, to facilitate a comparison to changes that occurred up to 2013.

I employ an overall qualitative research methodology for studying the Belize case due largely to the limitations of quantitative research in relation to political clientelism. Quantitative studies have proven useful for cross-national analysis of political clientelism, but they are generally limited in their ability to meet the research challenges identified by Luigi Graziano: "how to observe relationships that are amorphous and ill-defined, latent rather than explicit, and often disreputable if not illegal."[95] This is, indeed, true for most studies of democracy that enquire into relationships that go beyond its formal and procedural features. Quantitative methods are also

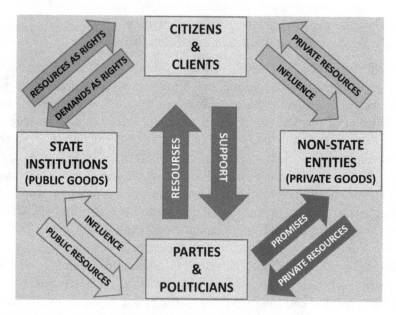

Figure 1. Influence and resource flows among political actors

Table 1. Tracer Markers to Track Changes in Clientelism between 1981 and 2013

Tracer Markers
1. Numbers and geographical spread of political clinics[a]
2. Numbers and profiles of clients
3. Types and volume of goods and services going to clients
4. Monetary value of goods and services going to clients
5. Types of political support going to patrons
6. Extent of distribution of public resources for party/clientelist purposes
7. Ratio of permanent vs temporary/contractual public service jobs[b]
8. Extent of references to clientelism in news stories and public documents
9. Number of alleged cases of voter bribery taken to court

[a]In the Belize context, a "political clinic" is the node of clientelist operations at the constituency level, where constituents can visit with representatives, candidates and their staff.
[b]Since independence, governments have used a provision in the public service regulations to expand the hiring of "open vote" public officers – a category of non-established contract officers. They are not part of the permanent public service, not budgeted for, and can be easily hired and dismissed.

less useful for exploring my core query on the political and socio-economic implications of entrenched clientelism for a particular state.

Within the wider qualitative approach, I employ a comparative historical method to document and compare the evolution of Belize's political clientelism and its characteristics at various critical historical points, as well as to analyse the Belize experience in the wider Commonwealth Caribbean region. Elements of ethnographic methods were used to allow for close-up observation of personal relationships and political processes as they happen. Within this mixed methodological approach, my primary research techniques included the comprehensive review of secondary and archival material, semi-structured one-on-one interviews of carefully selected key political actors, informal interviews with a sample of citizens in selected political constituencies, and observation of political events and processes at the constituency level.

Apart from the ongoing review of the relevant secondary literature and archival materials (which took place from 2009 to 2013), the on-the-ground fieldwork in Belize occurred over the eight-month period from September 2010 to April 2011. Importantly, this research period coincided with the intra-party convention "season" in which candidates for the 2012 general election of both major political parties were being selected. In September 2010 when the fieldwork commenced, Belize's total population was

312,698, and the total number of registered voters in Belize was 162,150, with a 50.7 per cent to 49.3 per cent male-to-female breakdown.[96] Since 2007, when the number of constituencies was increased, there have been thirty-one constituencies spread across six districts (see figure 2).[97] The number of registered voters per constituency ranged from 3,131 to 7,125, with an average of 5,231. The breakdown of the constituencies by political parties in 2008, which was used to select constituencies for targeted fieldwork, is illustrated in the electoral map in appendix 1.

Figure 2. Political map of Belize showing six administrative districts

At the time of the fieldwork, the Belize district had thirteen of the then thirty-one constituencies. Fourteen of the thirty-one constituencies were in predominantly rural areas. The then governing United Democratic Party held twenty-five seats, and the opposition People's United Party held six seats, for a four-to-one seat advantage. For in-depth research, a purposive sample of four electoral constituencies was selected for more focused attention and as areas in which to conduct citizen interviews and event observation. The four constituencies were selected based on five criteria: the political party holding the seat, balance in geographical location, urban–rural breakdown, ethnic make-up and the incidence of poverty. Table 2 summarizes the basic features of these constituencies, and a more detailed description of each constituency appears in appendix 2.

The fieldwork execution included four overlapping parts: archival and library review, a phase of elite interviews, an overlapping phase of citizen interviews and event observations. As the principal research technique, the interviews produced the most plentiful and useful information. In the "key actors" interview phase, sixty-nine semi-structured interviews were conducted with carefully selected past politicians, active politicians, political operatives, senior public officers and key "non-partisan" informants. These included all the elected representatives of the four constituencies selected, as well as most of their challengers. Of the sixty-nine key actors interviewed, forty-six were past or active politicians: twenty-three were affiliated with the PUP, twenty-one with the UDP and two of the interviewees were leaders of other parties. Ten of the forty-six politicians were active in the pre-independence period. The politicians included all four former prime ministers of Belize, including the prime minister during coverage of the study (Dean Barrow), and ten sitting ministers of government. The current prime minister (John Briceño) was interviewed in his former capacity as leader of the opposition during the fieldwork phase.

The second phase of interviews constituted focused discussions with constituents and accounts for what was referred to earlier as "elements of ethnographic" methodology. I spent an average of three to five weeks in each of the four electoral constituencies, and in each I conducted informal interviews and discussions with constituents and brokers, and I observed a variety of partisan political events and processes. The key objective of this phase was to gather in-depth information and perceptions from the viewpoints of citizens and brokers about the nature, operations and implications of political clientelism. One hundred and fourteen such informal interviews and discussions were conducted. The average number per constituency was 28.5: Pickstock (27), Orange Walk Central (26), Toledo

Table 2. Basic Profile of the Four Constituencies Selected for Focused Research by Selection Criteria (at August 2010)

Division (No. of Voters)	District (Location)	Urban/Rural	Ethnic Make-Up	Poverty and Inequality (2009)	Political Party
Pickstock (3,168)	Belize (Central East Belize)	Urban	Vast majority Creole	District poverty is 28.8%[a] and GC is 0.41	UDP
Orange Walk Central (6,139)	Orange Walk (Northern Belize)	Urban with some rural villages	Vast majority Mestizo	District poverty is 42.8% and GC is 0.36	PUP
Toledo East (6,183)	Toledo (Southern Belize)	Rural and urban mix	Creole, Garifuna, Maya, Mestizo, East Indians	District poverty is 60.4% and GC is 0.46	UDP
Belmopan (6,733)	Cayo (Western Belize)	Mostly urban with some rural	Mestizo, Creole, Maya, Garifuna	District poverty is 40.6% and GC is 0.41	UDP

Sources: Elections and Boundaries Department (2010) and the Country Poverty Assessment (2010).

Note: Voters = registered voters. National poverty was measured at 41.3 per cent, and the national Gini coefficient (GC) was 0.42 in 2009. Poverty is defined here as the percentage of individuals with incomes below the national poverty line. The GC is a measure of income inequality and varies between 0, representing a wholly equal distribution, and 1, representing a wholly unequal distribution. PUP is People's United Party, and UDP is United Democratic Party.

[a] Although district level poverty in the Belize district was the lowest of all districts, the Pickstock constituency is in an area of high urban poverty in Belize City.

East (35) and Belmopan (26). Six of the total 114 interviews were conducted with brokers from both political parties: five males to one female, and four affiliated with the UDP and two with the PUP. There was also one focus-group type session with a group of undergraduate university students. All respondents in this second phase of informal interviews were assured of confidentiality and anonymity before the interview.[98] In addition to ongoing general observation in each constituency, a total of fifteen separate political events were observed, including political party conventions, political clinics in operation and neighbourhood meetings held by political parties. In summary, my findings are based on the triangulation of information from secondary literature, key actor interviews, citizen interviews, news reports, official documents and event observation.

Chapter Organization

In the next seven chapters, I follow the trajectory of political clientelism from its pre-independence rooting phase (1954–80), a transitionary but still formative phase in the first decade of independence (1981–91) and the phase of rampant expansion (1992–2013). In doing so, each of the five main research questions are addressed in sequence.

Chapter 2 addresses how and why political clientelism took root in Belize's nascent politician–citizen relationships, and what relative salience competitive party politics, the control of public allocation institutions, poor socio-economic conditions, small-state scale and multi-ethnicity had in this formative period. As such, the chapter covers the trajectory of political clientelism in the formative period of Belize's pre-independence modern politics from 1954 to 1980–81 and summarizes the state of play at the time of independence, based on the nine tracer markers selected. Chapter 3 explores the transitionary but still formative period represented by Belize's first decade after independence (1981–91), in which there were important political developments with significant implications for the expansion of political clientelism in the 1990s.

Chapters 4, 5 and 6 all focus on the "rampant" phase of political clientelism from approximately 1992 to 2013. Chapter 4 addresses the second research question: What are the principal manifestations of the expansion of political clientelism in Belize in the post-independence period? As such, this chapter builds the empirical foundation required for tracking the trajectory of political clientelism and for in-depth analysis of its implications for Belize's democratic governance. It pinpoints the late 1990s as a pivotal surge period in the upward trajectory of political clientelism and it details the critical features of the ongoing clientelist relationships among the state, political parties, politicians, citizens and financiers.

Chapter 5 focuses on the third research question: What factors have contributed to this high rate of expansion of clientelism at the same time as formal democratic advances in Belize? It examines the explanatory salience of developments in the political–institutional context, with a focus on political control of state institutions and party competition. It also addresses the relevance of socio-economic developments for the expansion of political clientelism, with a focus on poverty and inequality, neoliberal economic policies, and on alternatives to clientelism in the formal and informal sectors.

Chapter 6 brings the spotlight on the principal and fourth research question: How has widespread clientelism affected the quality of Belize's democracy and its social and economic development? It explores the implications for electoral processes; public institutions and political parties; and participatory democracy beyond elections, including those for informal political influence and problem-solving, day-to-day relationships between citizens and elected representatives, the work of civil society organizations, resource distribution and social welfare, public policy and reform, fiscal management, and political culture.

Chapter 7 examines the fifth and most important research question: How does the experience of Belize compare to experiences of other parliamentary democracies in the Commonwealth Caribbean? Chapter 8 highlights the book's key findings and concludes with a discussion on the prospects for mitigating political clientelism in Belize. Finally, in the Epilogue, I discuss key developments in Belize related to political clientelism since 2013 and assess the relevance of my findings and conclusions for the seven-year period from 2014 to mid-2021.

2.

Helping the People

1954 to Independence

By the middle of the twentieth century, colonial Belize (called British Honduras until 1973) had long been characterized by inadequate national responses by the British imperial authorities to poor living conditions for most Belizeans. The fledging colony also lacked at least two other basic conditions critical to the growth of political clientelism in emerging democracies: dominant control of public resources by local leaders and competitive party politics. These were both gradually consolidated after universal adult suffrage in 1954 and full internal self-government a decade later. By the eve of independence in September 1981, when Belize's Westminster model of governance was all but totally formalized, political clientelism had begun to take good root.

Although studies of Belize's modern political history now have considerable coverage of party politics and legislative governance,[1] there has been but passing treatment of the role of political clientelism in the pre-independence period. This chapter aims to fill this gap. I illustrate how and why political clientelism took root in Belize's nascent politician–citizen relationships, and examine the role played by competitive party politics, the control of public allocation institutions, responses to poor socio-economic conditions, small-state scale and multi-ethnicity. I argue that Belize's evolution from colony to independent state reflects a process of uneven democratization in which informal political relationships, such as political clientelism, emerged and expanded asymmetrically alongside the formal transition to sovereign democracy.

Clientelism before Self-Government

As was the case with British imperialism across the Caribbean, the colonial authorities invested in but limited social and infrastructural development in Belize, and most economic activity in the colony up to the middle of the twentieth century was focused on extracting forestry wealth and on entrepôt trading. As labourers and then unions began to organize to protest terrible living conditions and authoritarian rule, British governors employed patronage as one of several tools to diffuse local opposition to colonialism and so further maintain the status quo until the granting of political independence became unavoidable. These included the practices of dispensing food, land, short-term work and public office jobs to targeted individuals and groups so as to quell periodic uprisings and curry political favour. As such, some types of clientelist behaviour pre-dated the commencement of Belize's modern politics in the 1950s and of self-government in 1964.

Nigel O. Bolland illustrated that one tactic the colonial establishment used to respond to Belizean workers' resistance was "providing (or sometimes just promising) relief to assuage a proportion of the working people . . . this was part of the Colonial Development and Welfare programme used across British West Indies".[2] Anne Macpherson demonstrated how working women involved in the nationalist movement were treated by the British and the local elite "as politically disordered", and there were also attempts to "transform them from militant wage-earners to clients of state social services" through the use of short-lived social welfare work programmes.[3] Since the central objective of these tactics of the British was to maintain authoritarian power and so "buy" colonialism more time, they represented a form of "state clientelism" practised by a small British and local political elite, and directed at both individuals and narrow groups.

Belizean nationalist leaders would later adopt and adapt similar approaches as they gained more control over the powers of state and the distribution of public resources. Yet, before the onset of the nationalist movement in the 1950s, the occasional patronage practised by the colonial state did not belie the general and persistent unresponsiveness of the colonial authorities to the numerous petitions and demands by "British Hondurans" for more political rights and socio-economic relief.

Nascent Party Politics in Hard Times

The top-down patronage strategies of the colonial elite were employed in a wider societal context of colonial authoritarianism in which the general population had minimal opportunity for electoral participation. From 1871 when Belize became a Crown Colony to 1931, there was a Legislative Council that was wholly appointed. Thereafter, some members were elected by a small number of registered voters who met salary, property and other criteria, and after 1959, there was a totally elected Legislative Assembly.[4] Just a decade before full adult suffrage in 1954, property and gender restrictions limited registered voters to only 1.3 per cent of the population.[5] One central objective of nationalist movements across the Caribbean was to erase such disparities. As in other British colonies in the region, political parties in Belize emerged from a nationalist movement born out of working-class and labour resistance to economic and political exclusion. A series of protest activities sparked by a monetary devaluation in 1949 led to the formation of the nationalist PUP in September 1950. Thereafter, a PUP and union alliance organized a spate of strikes and civil unrest that helped push the colonial establishment to give in to demands for a new constitution with universal adult suffrage in 1954. This constitution represented the formal introduction of the Westminster political system and competitive party politics, with a two-party adversarial model evolving as an essential feature.

In 1956, conflicts among the original PUP leadership led to the formation of a splinter party that would evolve into the National Independence Party (NIP) in 1957.[6] As the then second major party, the NIP was the official opposition until 1973, when it morphed into the UDP after an alliance with two other small parties – the Liberal Party and the People's Democratic Movement. Although the PUP won every general election up to independence, the NIP and then the UDP opposition competed in each and gained increasing proportions of the national vote. In 1961 the NIP won 23.2 per cent of the vote, and then 39.4 per cent and 39.8 per cent of the vote in 1965 and 1969, respectively.[7] In 1974 the UDP won 38.1 per cent, and in 1979 its support increased to 46.8 per cent. As such, Belize's competitive party system was being consolidated along two party lines by the time of internal self-government in 1964, and this was well advanced by the time of independence. No other political party posed any serious threat to the evolving two-party variant. In the 1961 election, the Corozal Democratic Party, a district-based party, won 11.4 per cent of the vote, the highest percentage by another party in the electoral history of Belize. Except for a 4.7 per cent showing by the Corozal United Front in 1974, other alternative parties polled below 1 per cent in all other pre-independence elections.[8] Even as the opposition won larger percentages of the popular vote, the PUP held disproportionate seat majorities in the House of Representatives, and consequently on every public sector body it had the authority to appoint.

During this period, the citizenry had clearly distinguishable party and national visions and positions on which to assess the PUP and the NIP and then the UDP. The PUP's central goal was national unity and full political independence as a means for addressing poor socio-economic conditions and achieving national development. Although embracing the historical ties with the British Caribbean, the PUP also actively promoted Belize's Central American identity. The NIP, on the other hand, espoused a less anti-colonial stance, emphasized Belize's British Caribbean identity and pitched a more overtly patriotic "no Guatemala" message as part of its political identity.[9] After its formation in 1973, the UDP presented itself as more free-market oriented and sought to downplay the colonialist tendencies of the old NIP elements. At the same time, it argued that independence should be delayed until the British had resolved the Guatemalan claim and until Belize was more developed economically.

Along with this expansion of competitive party politics, the achievement of internal self-government in January 1964 was also of critical significance for the emergence of political clientelism precisely because it gave elected local politicians more control over resource distribution. Except for defence, internal security, external affairs and specific senior-level public service appointments, Belize's elected representatives gained control over all other public institutions and home affairs, allowing for greater influence over the distribution of key public resources. Full control of the powers and resources of the state was delayed for seventeen more years, but the British colonial authorities no longer exercised total political power.[10] As part of the political tutelage taking place, the PUP government could propose national budgets, develop socio-economic policies and programmes, and exercise growing control and discretionary influence over public service resources, some public service jobs and most local government matters.

The new 1964 self-government constitution also further consolidated additional formal features of the Westminster model, manifested by an expanded House of Representatives of eighteen members based on first-past-the-post electoral rules, an appointed upper chamber called the Senate, and the establishment of the offices of premier and leader of the opposition. As local leaders increased their participation in these formal political structures of the young democracy, so did the Belizean people. In addition to joining political parties, attending party activities and volunteering for party campaigns, they enthusiastically exercised new voting rights. Whereas only 2.8 per cent of the population was registered to vote in 1948, this share had increased tenfold by 1954 (after universal adult suffrage) and to approximately 35 per cent by 1979.[11] Between 1954 and 1979, an average of 72.8 per cent of the registered electorate voted in seven general elections. Importantly, voter participation in local government elections also grew as candidates of the two major parties expanded their competitive participation to include the evolving and expanding system of municipal and village governance. By 1958, in addition to Belize City, elections were being held in six municipalities, and this increased to eight just after 1981.

By the end of the 1970s, the party tentacles of the PUP and UDP had begun to reach almost every community in every district, and it was through them that most formal and informal political participation transpired in the colony. Although party membership was not as high as in the mid-1950s, it remained significant. The PUP had house-to-house membership drives in the 1950s to build working-class support, and in the 1960s there was a concerted effort to broaden the membership base to "all classes and sectors of the society".[12] However, people's participation after self-government was not just limited to formal voting and to political party activity. Non-party political activity, such as union action, petitions to the governor and civil protests, continued, albeit with decreasing frequency and numbers. After the establishment of political parties, the leadership of the unions and parties merged for a time, and then the parties took over most of the mobilizing role of the unions. One of the most graphic indicators of this quick demise of the union movement is that membership in the largest union, the General Workers Union, fell from 10,500 in 1954 to only 700 in 1956.[13]

In the late 1960s and early 1970s, a number of radical groups, inspired by the international civil rights movement and frustrated by the slow pace of change in the colony, sought to challenge the political dominance of the PUP and UDP. These included the United Black Association for Development, led by Evan X Hyde, and the People's Action Committee, led by Assad Shoman and Said Musa who organized anti-British and anti-political party demonstrations and public meetings to promote social justice, black power and immediate independence.[14] These were short-lived and posed no credible electoral threat to the two dominant parties – and, indeed, this was not their original intent. By the mid-1970s, some of their key leaders, including Musa and Shoman, were co-opted into the PUP. Friendly and charity-based societies such as the Black Cross Nurses and the Women's League remained important, albeit weakened, forums for women on such issues as social justice, employment and political participation.[15]

The emergence of political parties, the establishment of formal democratic institutions and increased political participation were transpiring in a small country with a fragile economy and a tiny multi-ethnic population, the majority of whom were poor. The forestry industry, on which the economy of Belize had been based since its settlement, had collapsed by the time of self-government in 1964, and policies for economic diversification, with a focus on agricultural production, had finally become more sustained. Although there was an increase in agricultural exports, "it was not fast enough to compensate for the decline in forestry and unemployment remained a serious problem".[16] Combined with the poor state of infrastructure, the inadequacy of the revenue pool in a tiny population and the loss of bilateral preferential treatment of forestry exports to the United Kingdom, this situation resulted in "an unimpressive macroeconomic performance in the last decades of colonialism".[17]

During this formative period of the nationalist movement, "conditions of the working people were terrible – low wages, intermittent employment and under-employment, atrocious housing, hunger, and bad health, poor education or none at all".[18] These legacies of two centuries of colonialism were exacerbated in 1961 by Hurricane Hattie, which had devastating effects on the economy and on the infrastructure of several coastal towns and communities. As evidenced by the early victories of the nationalist PUP, the impetus for Belizeans to expand and utilize their voting rights lay, in large part, in the hope that these harsh social and economic conditions would improve with self-government and with independence.

Belize's population (90,505 in 1960, 119,645 in 1970 and 145,343 in 1980) represented a small and personalized political playing field on which politician–citizen relations unfolded.[19] The total number of registered electors in any one constituency was tiny, averaging only between 1,500 and 3,000 over this period,[20] which contributed to the evolution of highly familiar electoral politics. By the time of self-government, Belize's diverse multi-ethnicity had been long established by a history of settlement, resettlement, forced migrations, and the influx of political and economic refugees. The last pre-independence census of 1980 revealed that Creoles were 40 per cent of the population, Mestizos were 33 per cent, Maya groups were 10 per cent, Garinagu were 8 per cent, East Indians were 2 per cent and others 7 per cent.[21] At the time, these groups clustered geographically and around distinct economic activities, and there was always a particular ethnic majority in almost every political constituency.

In a society with such diverse and dynamic multi-ethnicity, it is remarkable that support for political parties did not become ethnically based, as it did in the sister states of Trinidad and Tobago, and Guyana. Like the unions before them, neither of the two major parties actively and publicly sought political identification based on ethnic allegiances for any sustained period, and both parties received relatively balanced support from all demographic and ethnic groups.[22] This is not to deny that there were ethnic dimensions to the nascent phase of political party emergence before independence. For example, it has been argued that during this time the NIP and then the

UDP received more support from the Creole elite than did the PUP, which received more from the black working class. Also, because the PUP was opposed to the West Indian Federation and more open to relationships with Belize's geographic neighbours in Central America than the NIP, the PUP was perceived by some as more "Latino" friendly. Yet overt ethnic-based party identification did not feature in the electoral strategies of the two major parties. This relatively exceptional feature of Belizean politics is due largely to the early efforts by the PUP to implement its goal "to achieve and preserve for the people of Belize national unity and political and economic independence".[23] This "national freedom and unity" of the PUP imperative translated into seeking support across geographical, gender, class and ethnic lines – a strategy that the NIP and then the UDP sought to emulate to remain nationally competitive. Its success is reflected in the findings of a 1974 survey on the political perceptions of university students: "There is no strong relation between ethnic identity and party preference . . . there is also a surprising consensus that the two major ethnic groups [Creoles and Mestizos] are influential in politics . . . this consensus may be a major factor dampening ethnic polarisation as long as people feel that ethnicity does not determine access to politics and government, they are less likely to base political attitudes on ethnic identity."[24] However, and as will be illustrated, the absence of open ethnic politics did not preclude a role for ethnicity in the development of political clientelism in Belize.

The Early PUP: Working for All the People

Almost all political actors interviewed endorsed the popularly held view in Belize that party-based political clientelism was initiated by the PUP, and in particular, by George Price, the PUP's co-founder, and long-time populist leader, first prime minister of Belize and the "Father of the Nation".[25] However, there were important caveats, not all attributable to party affiliation. Among these is the proposition that, if there was political clientelism before independence, it was inevitable in origin, innocent in intent and mild in manifestation. What does the record show?

Fredrick Hunter, a member of Price's first cabinet, recollected that in the 1950s and 1960s, people who made personal requests of PUP politicians were generally satisfied with the campaign pitch that "our job is to help you help yourself".[26] In the 1960s and part of the 1970s, the PUP government attempted to direct much of the new legislative and budgetary powers of allocation towards ameliorating some of the long-standing socio-economic problems. These early efforts focused largely on the preparation and implementation of development policies, infrastructure projects, and social and economic programmes. Practical achievements included the construction of roads, a new international airport, housing developments, land reform, the promotion of agriculture and fisheries to replace forestry, strategies to promote foreign investment, and the further expansion of local government. Albeit bringing much death and infrastructural destruction, Hurricane Hattie in 1961 sparked a short-term influx of capital for other development initiatives, including the visionary decision of Price to build a new capital city, Belmopan, from scratch in a rural and underpopulated location on higher land near the geographic centre of the country.

In exploring the relative prevalence of clientelism as formal democracy takes hold, some observers contend that there is a phase in the early processes of state and party formation when appeals to an expanding electorate are based more on ideology and programmatic promises because the state patronage system is not fully established.[27] The implication is that new political parties, which have only just achieved control of a state's bureaucracy, tend to be less clientelist until they evolve into more established parties. This is a credible approach for assessing a party like the PUP that benefited from the momentum of working-class and anti-British voter support for decades after the heydays of the nationalist movement in the 1950s. In this regard, the early national programmes and initiatives of the PUP government, which were also used to appeal to voters, are examples of resources being collectively directed at the citizenry at large and not primarily targeted at individuals or narrow groups of voters. Indeed, in the formative political period up to the 1970s, the PUP as a political party was decidedly more policy-oriented and progressive in its actions in government than it was a party of patronage. Although never holding formal political power, the then main opposition NIP was also more policy differentiated. As such, pre-independence party–citizen relationships in Belize were, for some time, more programmatic and nationalistic than clientelist.

After self-government was achieved in 1964, the majority of the people, especially the poor, felt profoundly dissatisfied with the performance of the government "despite the improvements made in infrastructure development, education, health, and other areas".[28] With limited state resources, the PUP manoeuvred to fulfil its promises of better living conditions, to maintain popular and middle-class support against colonialism, and to compete against a gradually strengthening opposition party during the period of delayed independence. During this seventeen-year delay, the record shows that the PUP gradually began to use some of its new powers of allocation to influence voters through more targeted and individual approaches. In these circumstances political clientelism was too tempting an electoral strategy to ignore in the context of unmet needs, an increasingly frustrated and impatient citizenry, and the long struggle to maintain popular support for political independence.

Innocent Beginnings: Price and the Launch of the Clinics

A reconstruction of this pre-independence phase of modern political clientelism reveals a limited and loose set of informal operations that emanated from Price and gradually became more institutionalized, widespread and publicly acceptable. As PUP party leader (1956–96), first minister (1961–64) and premier (1964–81), Price set a precedent of personalized politician–citizen relationships and became the original, if inadvertent, "national political patron". Price, who had given up on his training to become a priest during the Second World War, was not new to dealing with direct personal requests. As the personal secretary (1942–55) for Robert Turton, an influential and wealthy local businessman, Price himself interacted, on Turton's behalf, with an almost daily flow of loan-seekers and supplicants.[29]

Upon entering municipal politics in 1944, Price honed a highly familiar, hands-on and paternalistic campaign and leadership style. After the enactment of the 1954 constitution, Price was elected to the Legislative Council, beginning a thirty-year stint of consecutive national election victories. In addition to interactions with citizens in their homes and on streets, Price's primary mode of monitoring the needs of citizens and dispensing targeted assistance was through the operation of an increasingly popular political clinic in the then capital, Belize City.[30] Price recounted that he needed to "appoint a day and specific place to facilitate people" in his constituency and from all over the country to come to him with their concerns and needs.[31] So began the iconic Price weekly "Wednesday clinics" where people from every district came to him for "any personal need", including jobs, medicines, money for food, and, as he said with a chuckle, "even their love affairs".[32]

After self-government in 1964, Price's political clinics became more institutionalized and truly national in scope as citizens from across the colony began to show up. First conducted from PUP party premises, an office next to the Supreme Court in Belize City became the permanent site for clinics for most of Price's career. After the establishment of Belmopan as the new capital in 1970, Price established a second weekly Monday clinic from his executive office there. Although anyone could also come to these Belmopan clinics, their central geographic location meant that Price became more accessible to citizens from the western and southern parts of the country. For those who could not afford to come to the national clinics due to distance or cost, Price occasionally took his clinic on the road to every part of Belize.[33] V.S. Naipaul accompanied Price on one of these in 1969 and colourfully captured the personal and paternalistic approach of Price in his book of travel essays.[34] Seeing Price to make a personal or collective request basically meant getting to a clinic and queuing – without need for an appointment – and many Belizeans did so.

Price recalled that he "helped", at first, with small amounts of cash from his own official salary and then from a small government stipend that was allocated to all elected representatives for their constituency work. The original intent of this official constituency stipend was to assist elected representatives with the direct administrative costs, such as rent, office supplies and utilities, of meeting constituents to hear concerns and share government developments.[35] At some point, Price and other representatives began using part of this money as handouts to constituents. As this practice expanded, the stipend amount was gradually increased from some $200 per month per representative in the 1960s to some $900 in the 1970s.[36] Yet most targeted assistance came directly through existing public service opportunities and through referrals to a growing network of official and private contacts.

As Price recollected and as corroborated by some of his compatriots, his more popular modes of "helping" were to write untold numbers of letters of recommendation and to make "on the spot" phone referrals to cabinet ministers, public officers, business leaders, church leaders and others, who felt compelled to follow up. A member of Price's first self-government cabinet, who served until 1974 and received hundreds of such letters, stated: "If the head of government asks you to do something, you do it."[37] A review of a sample of these letters reveals that they addressed a wide variety of resources and services, including appeals for houses, land, jobs, and social and educational assistance; business loans; and detailed requests such as the repair of leaking toilets, fixing water meters and providing fence paint.[38] In addition to being visited at his clinics, Price also received daily letters requesting direct personal assistance, especially from people in communities outside Belize City and Belmopan.

Ministers who served with Price in the pre-independence period recall that, as premier, he also encouraged other ministers and representatives to follow his example and set up regular clinics for their constituents as a way to monitor and respond to personal needs and to assess the effectiveness of the government's work.[39] Although not at the same frequency as Price, some other political leaders established clinics, especially during election campaigns.[40] In this way, the clinic system gradually began to spread across the nation with the weekly Price clinic being in a dominant category of its own. So deep was this dominance that some of his own ministers and elected representatives wrote to him or even attended his clinics to follow up on requests for their constituents.[41]

Accounts from Price and other politicians of the period indicate that, even as infrastructure and programmatic developments continued to feature on the road to independence, there was a gradual increase in individualized allocations through these informal clinic mechanisms. In particular, the Price clinics came to be seen as the primary place to get almost any type of need met and problem solved. Some citizens began to believe that to get anything done, one had to join lengthy clinic lines to see Price personally. An example, related with some embarrassment, is of a citizen who went to Price in the mid-1960s to request a visa to enter the United States. He said that Price did write a letter on his behalf to the US Embassy, but that the letter was neither required nor helpful in his endeavour.[42]

Although predominant, the clinic system was not the only means of dispensing assistance to individual citizens or groups of citizens. Grant contends that Price awarded and juggled senior official posts to maintain the personal support of the party elite and that political patronage became "the main determining factor for advancement in the civil service".[43] Even if not the main determining factor (in light of a still permanent public service), patronage was certainly on the rise. Price, his cabinet ministers and senior government appointees also began using some of the new powers of their elected offices to target public resources preferentially. As an example, an examination of village politics in southern Belize in the 1960s found that "selective employment in public works projects" was "among the earliest and most divisive forms of patronage administered through village councils nationwide".[44] Such allocation strategies emanated from the central government's ministries and resembled earlier colonial work programmes. For instance, "Aided Self-Help, a works program first introduced in 1963, was ostensibly intended to reinforce village cooperation by providing nominal payment to people who contributed labour to local projects", but "while politically active supporters of the ruling party [PUP] were well paid for their labour contributions to the program, others received no payment or merely a token amount".[45]

Party-based clientelist activities, apart from the Price clinics, then began to spread from Belize City to constituencies across the country. As a retired

UDP politician from the northern town of Orange Walk recounted, "this new handout thing got started with the PUP in Belize City" and then "they expanded it to the out districts because it worked in Belize City".[46] In this regard, he recalled that "in early days, the PUP used sugar quotas in Orange Walk as handouts . . . they would divide quotas into individual amounts of a few tons and give them to their people as a way to get support, and the same thing happened in Corozal".[47] Although generally agreeing with such accounts, Hunter (one of the former ministers from the pre-independence era) added that there were also a small number of powerful politician patrons apart from Price. In particular, he alleged that Florencio Marin Sr, a powerful Corozal politician and a former deputy prime minister, "used his authority as minister of lands to get people to become PUP" with the mantra "you only get land if you join the party".[48]

Court Cases on Voter Bribery before Independence

As in other British colonies in the Caribbean, laws to arrest some manifestations of political clientelism were already transplanted and enacted as part of the formalization of the new electoral institutions that accompanied universal adult suffrage and competitive party elections. A section in the British Honduras Representation of the People Ordinance of 1953 deemed the practice of trading or promising money, favours or support for votes illegal and indictable, with penalties of fines or prison time, and debarment from future election participation applicable upon conviction.[49]

Of the politicians interviewed, ten were active in the 1954–81 period, and they recollect just a handful of allegations of acts of political clientelism in general, and even fewer of direct voter bribery. Newspaper stories from this era demonstrate that, in a trend that would expand, the allegations cluster largely around election periods. It is useful here to assess one of the tracer markers selected for this study: the number of allegations of voter bribery that were taken to a court. News accounts, secondary sources and research at the national court registry show that there were five court cases related to voter bribery during the nationalist period. All five relate to instances in which prominent incumbent PUP politicians were accused of violating the voter bribery law, and, collectively, they provide an insightful angle from which to view the early manifestations of political clientelism.

The first court case in modern Belizean history alleging voter bribery was *The Crown v. Louis Sylvestre* in 1961, just after the general election of March of that year and before internal self-government was achieved.[50] The charge was that Sylvestre, who was appointed minister of local government, social services and cooperatives by Price after the 1961 election, had directed that pens, pencils and small pouches with a nail file and a comb, all inscribed with the words "Vote for Honourable Louis Sylvestre, PUP All the Way", be distributed to voters in his constituency just days before the election.[51] Sylvestre was charged and tried in the Supreme Court, under the Representation of the People Ordinance (1953), on nine counts of bribing citizens to vote on his behalf in two villages of his Belize Rural South constituency.[52] One reporter called the scheme a "giveaway programme" and insinuated ill intent.[53] The Crown argued that the set of four items given to voters was valued at more than 25 cents and thus over the limit of individual gifts legally allowed, and that the inscription represented deliberate intent to induce voters.[54] The defence did not deny that Sylvestre initiated the distribution of the items, but argued that these were advertising material – and in any case were not bribes, but gifts valued at less than 25 cents.[55] In July 1961, the jury found Sylvestre not guilty, and he was acquitted of all charges in the widely followed case.[56] It should not be lost on anyone that in 1961 the British colonial authority was still actively attempting to undermine the Price-led PUP and likely saw an opportunity to so do in the Sylvestre case.

The other four cases were all part of a set of election petitions taken up by UDP candidates (not the British Crown) after their defeat by PUP candidates in the November 1979 general election. In all four cases heard before the Supreme Court in January 1980, the UDP's allegations were that the PUP candidates had bribed voters and so committed corrupt acts that warranted that their victories be revoked under the revised Representation of the People Ordinance (1978).[57] One case was thrown out for lack of proper filing, and another two were dismissed on preliminary objections. In one of these, the allegation was of a $20 bribery of a voter in Orange Walk.[58] In this set of four cases, the one that received the most court time and press coverage was triggered by an election petition against Jane Usher (a sister of Price), the PUP victor, by Paul Rodríguez, the losing UDP candidate in the Pickstock constituency. The petition alleged that Usher "was personally guilty of the corrupt act of bribery" and so had violated the law by giving a voter $60 and facilitating two loans (in her capacity as manager of a credit union) valued at $600.[59] The petition was eventually thrown out by the judge on the assessment that the voter, Norris Garcia, had lied under oath and was therefore not a credible witness.[60]

The relatively small monetary values and petty nature of most of these charges may contribute to explaining why some observers, with the benefit of hindsight, characterize handouts in the pre-independence period as "small fry stuff"[61] and use the descriptive labels of "innocent" and "benign". That these pre-1981 allegations reached the Supreme Court at all and attracted significant public attention suggest that voter bribery was viewed by many as both novel and scandalous. In effect, however, Belize's voter bribery laws had been tested. The fact that the cases were all unsuccessful illustrated to both political parties and to some in the electorate that legal proof of voter bribery is exceedingly difficult and that it was relatively easy to evade punitive measures. This difficulty lies in the fact that a judge must be able to establish that there is sufficient evidence from both the alleged bribe giver and the alleged recipient that an exchange happened which was intended and received as a bribe. Overall, the five pre-independence court cases support the contention that some politicians in this early period were beginning to actively engage and experiment with clientelist practices of dubious legality.

Helping the People!

Price and most other politicians of the pre-independence period explain or excuse their early clientelist actions as simply helping people in need.[62] Price himself, who pointed to colonialism as the cause of the colony's poverty, contended that "there was great human need, we were a poor country, everybody had to help each other" and politicians were there "to help the people".[63] Disassociating himself from the bribery of voters, he conceded:

> It goes on, it's a human thing . . . they came [to my clinics] for help and even tell you that [they will] vote for you if so and so . . . I have told them, no, you don't have to do that. So, you have to be careful how you do it . . . don't let them believe that it is so easy to get, but at the same time you help them.[64]

A UDP politician active in the post-independence period agreed: "Giving money in those days was not so much to get out votes as to help people."[65] A retired PUP politician reflected that pre-independence handouts "were minor but always there . . . as part of campaigning and assisting the people . . . but also part of what you need to compete and get votes at elections".[66] Similarly, a younger politician repeated a popular view in some UDP circles that it was the Price clinics that "opened the flood gates for the entrenchment of patronage politics and now we can't close the gates".[67] He added, however, that the clinics also helped "to fill a gap in the formal welfare system".[68] One political operative suggested that Price used his clinics as a way of monitoring both the mood of the nation and the work of his own ministers.[69] Another assessed that the clinic system was one of the only mechanisms through which people in rural areas accessed resources for their communities and themselves.[70]

Assad Shoman, who joined the PUP in 1974 and served in several ministerial posts, did not think that Price himself "was engaging in the same kind of clientelism or handout politics that we are witnessing today . . . his was much more a benign version".[71] He interpreted Price's helping poor people as part of his wider national vision: "Price did not deliberately, purposefully, openly use it as a way of bartering for support . . . Yes, he would hint that it would be good to support the PUP because it was for independence, because it was for development, but he didn't have that direct exchange that we have now."[72] When asked about the 1961 and 1979 legal allegations of bribery, Shoman opined that while Price was "a clean man, not an avaricious man, not a greedy man, not a thief . . . some of his ministers were corrupt and Price tolerated some of this in the interest of party unity and the goal of independence".[73]

Former prime minister Dean Barrow, although agreeing that Price and the PUP planted the seeds for modern political clientelism, observed:

> It was at a very basic level, he [Price] would give a small $5 or $10 dollars . . . but I say that not to be judgemental. It was going to happen anyway . . . as numbers grew and poverty deepened and conditions became more difficult, it was a natural thing for people to turn to politicians in a more personal way, not so much in terms of fixing my street, improving my infrastructure, do a low-cost housing scheme . . . but on a daily basis, a personal basis. It was inevitable.[74]

Barrow related this inevitability to the reality of state scale, noting that in a smaller, more personal society, people assess you less on the record of delivery of public goods and more on the expectation that "you [the politician] have to take care of people on a personal basis if you are going to be successful".[75]

The essence of the small-size argument is that it facilitates a familiar form of politics in which "governing and opposition elites know each other personally", citizens have a high degree of access to political leaders, and patronage is a very attractive political strategy.[76] Indeed, most Belizeans over sixty-five years of age have stories of some direct personal contact with Price or one of his senior ministers during this pre-independence period. Queuing at clinics in Belize City or Belmopan practically assured one of communicating directly with the leader of the state. Additionally, because the numbers of registered voters in a constituency averaged less than three thousand before independence, it was feasible for politicians to meet each of their constituents and to win elections by just a couple hundred or even dozens of votes. As such, Belize's small size and highly personalized politician–citizen relationships increased the relative allure of political clientelism as an electoral strategy for politicians and as a mode of informal political participation for citizens. This style of familiar politics also helps to explain recollections from interviewees that most politician–citizen bargaining in the pre-independence period was handled directly by politicians themselves and not via brokers.

An Inevitable Path?

An objective explanation of the emergence of political clientelism in pre-independence Belize lies somewhere along the spectrum of accounts that judge the actions of the PUP and Price as deliberate and damning in the pursuit of political power, and those that excuse them as normal and expected in the struggle for independence. The former view is hardly surprising when we consider that the PUP, as the only political party in government until 1984, bore the brunt of any accusations of bad governance and inadequate social interventions. However, there is little to disagree with former prime minister Barrow's observation that the development of clientelist politics was inevitable and would have happened to whoever was in power. Indeed, the record indicates that the roles of the PUP and Price were initially more context-driven than they were pre-meditated and deserving of singular personal or partisan historical blame.

The gradual increase in use of individual handouts and favours was one reflection of the inability of new middle-class political leaders to maintain working-class voter support by adequately meeting socio-economic needs through formal and programmatic approaches. The fact that the new parties and politicians were still operating in a colonial context, in which much still depended on the permission and financial support of the British, cannot be discounted as a factor in the failure to meet needs and in the decisions to use clientelist handouts and patronage to appease an impatient electorate. Belize's small size and the highly personal style of the charismatic Price certainly contributed to the emergence of the clinic system and its individualized politician–citizen relationships. Price's populism and his genuine desire to help people were further contributing factors.

Undoubtedly there was some point at which Price and the PUP began to leverage the potential electoral advantage of this informal option, the eventual result being a gradual blurring of two lines: that of personal handouts as primarily "helping" with that of exchanging them as inducements just for political support. As one politician from the period summarized, "remember what the term 'handout' means . . . from my hand to yours – and you owe me something personal . . . a vote is expected".[77] Moreover, the constitutional achievements of universal adult suffrage and self-government, which had granted politicians new electoral power and greater control over resource allocation, simultaneously gave citizens the vote, the most essential bargaining tool in negotiating influence with their political leaders.

Shoman is on target when he argues that

> in the case of the PUP in government . . . many from the working-class would offer their unflinching allegiance in the expectation that they would personally be accorded certain material benefits – a job, a house, a piece of land, a scholarship, and even a recommendation. The clientele or patronage system, which won the PUP the support of members of the middle class as well as the working class, also served to swell ranks of the opposition, since there was simply not enough to go around.[78]

Indeed, it was not long before the opposition UDP gradually began to give small handouts to constituents as an added tactic to compete against the PUP's electoral dominance. Interviewees indicated that in this pre-independence period, the UDP's sources of funding were largely personal funds and small private donations from individuals and businesses.

Dean Lindo, the first leader of the UDP (1974–79), told of an incident in his constituency in the 1979 elections when a voter came up to him and said that "Musa [Lindo's opponent] gave me $10. If you give me $15, I'll vote for you".[79] He recalled that in pre-independence elections, the UDP only used this tactic in a limited way "because we did not have money . . . or we would have done more of it".[80] He too opined that the UDP would have gone along a similar path as the PUP in similar historical and political circumstances – with or without Price. Manuel Esquivel, UDP co-founder and Belize's second prime minister, contended that the pre-independence manifestations of handout politics were likely negligible before 1973 because the NIP was never a credible competitive alterative to the PUP.[81] However, he believed that UDP electoral advances in 1974 and 1979 "scared the PUP . . . into using more tactics of patronage to win future elections".[82] Although it is more than likely that the UDP would have eventually employed clientelist tactics if it were in government before independence, the unbroken PUP victories before independence and Price's own longevity accelerated the rate at which the PUP evolved to become the dominant clientelist party.

Belize's multi-ethnicity cannot be dismissed as a factor in how political clientelism emerged before independence. Ethnic majorities in every constituency facilitated self-selection, and then party selection, of most constituency candidates based on ethnicity. It was highly likely that voters were represented by candidates of the ethnic majority in their constituency.[83] This, in turn, gave a politically useful multi-ethnic flavour to national party leadership and to the membership of the House of Representatives. In the pursuit of national unity in a multi-ethnic state, ethnicity began to factor slowly into how Price and the PUP distributed the more visible spoils of power, such as ministerial appointments, senior public office positions, land, roads and social assistance funds. It was no coincidence that Price's first cabinet in 1964 included two "Afro" Creoles, one "white" Creole, two Mestizos and a Garinagu. The original intent was, in part, to avoid any public perception of favouring one ethnic group over another. Importantly, geographic clustering by ethnicity further facilitated political clientelism by providing politicians with easily definable avenues for communicating with voters and for dispensing resources and favours.[84]

Various circumstances contributed to the Creole ethnic group being most exposed to nascent clientelist practices before independence. The geographic location of the original Price weekly national clinics made them more accessible to urban Belize City residents, where Creoles made up more than three-quarters of the population in the 1970s. Creoles had formed the majority of the workforce in the forestry industry, the collapse of which in the 1950s left working-class Creoles among the most economically vulnerable of Belizeans.[85] Whereas middle-class Creoles already made up the majority of the middle and lower levels of the public service, working-class Creoles competed more intensely for the other jobs and for handouts, over which local leaders now had some influence. For these reasons, Belize City and the urban Creole became more associated with the formative manifestations of political clientelism.

The State of Play on the Eve of Independence

At the time of the last pre-independence general election in 1979, the PUP had been in power for a quarter century, the population was nearing 145,000, the Guatemala claim still lingered, and the economy was beginning another downslide triggered by the global recession and depressed sugar prices. After capturing 38.1 per cent of the vote in the 1974 elections and winning its largest number of House seats to date (six seats, compared to twelve for the PUP), the electoral competitiveness of the UDP had continued to improve, with significant victories in the 1977 Belize City municipal elections and in the majority of municipalities across the country.[86] Indeed, the UDP felt highly confident about its 1979 chances and, under the theme "time for a change", campaigned on positions of national and economic security, on delaying independence (until the Guatemala claim was settled), and on allegations of PUP patronage.

Yet the PUP, which appealed to Belizeans to stay united for the prize of independence, was once again victorious in 1979, polling 51.8 per cent of the vote to 46.8 per cent for the UDP and winning thirteen of eighteen parliamentary seats.[87] Apart from the dominant factor of divergent party positions on the timing of independence, this 1979 general election played out in the era when outright requests for individual handouts were still outweighed by those relating to collective needs such as job creation, housing, education, streets and support for agricultural projects. Yet clientelist politics was on the rise. As Belize went through the final two tumultuous and divisive years to independence, a snapshot of the political clientelist landscape captured the state of play that would carry over into the post-independence period.[88]

In terms of numbers and spread of political clinics, the two weekly Price clinics in Belize City and Belmopan dominated, and only a handful of representatives, mostly ministers of government, held other clinics in other districts with any degree of regularity. Except for the Price clinics, most clinic activity clustered around election campaigns proper. By 1980, however, a few other politicians had begun to operate other political clinics, albeit irregularly. A handful of UDP opposition candidates also had constituency offices, which can be viewed as emerging clinics, in operation in the few weeks just before elections. Overall, Price's clinics aside, political clinics were few in number and largely temporary in operation.

Because the politicians informed that they had no records of numbers of citizens visiting their clinics, it is not possible to accurately assess the proportion of total constituents who participated then. However, the Price clinics were always overflowing and waiting times were generally long. Although anyone in the entire colony could attend, these clinics were based in Belize City and Belmopan, and the proportion of the entire voting population that could actually visit a Price clinic was likely modest and generally urban-based. Even as clientelist politician–citizen relationships had begun to spread to other towns and rural areas, it was still concentrated in Belize City – and so mostly Creole in client profile. Even as client numbers gradually increased, most people still expected a "start" through programmatic approaches rather than a handout. And although the majority of citizens visiting the Price clinics were poor, citizens in the middle and business classes also queued for a chance to make appeals to Price.

It is difficult to estimate the numbers of each type of good and service being provided to citizens in the pre-independence period, but the types themselves are clear. Price's letters and information from other politicians active during the period show that the major individual requests were for jobs, agricultural land, house lots, house construction and repairs, healthcare and educational assistance, and microcredit, as well as small amounts of money for basic daily needs. In terms of cash exchanges, the amounts requested and given were largely to supplement other income rather than to take responsibility for most needs. The amounts ranged from cents to rarely above $10–15. For example, no politician interviewed could remember paying an individual's entire utility bill or paying constituents' bills on a monthly basis before independence. Overall, handouts to voters were mostly confined to campaign periods and to special times of the year.

The financial values of handouts around this last pre-independence election are also challenging to assess. Without the expense of radio and television advertising, the costs of election campaigns were relatively low. A retired politician recalled that his last election in 1974 cost $2,000, a campaign manager noted that the 1979 campaign in the Collet constituency cost $5,000[89] and a candidate in a Belize Rural constituency in 1979 revealed that his campaign cost under $10,000.[90] In 1979, cash payments to party supporters for campaigning were almost unheard of in both political parties. On the contrary, some citizens actually made financial donations to their parties and candidates, providing most food, drinks and advertising supplies.[91] However, a small number of politicians were already giving handouts and doing favours for voters between elections.

Apart from beginning to barter their votes, it can be deduced from politicians' accounts that those voters who participated in clientelist exchanges also provided political support through party membership, volunteering for party activities such as campaigning, posting campaign posters at their homes and participating in public partisan rallies. Both the PUP and UDP could attract huge crowds to listen to their differing positions on the timing of independence and on resolving the Guatemala claim. For instance, one informant noted that the most popular request in the Collet constituency in Belize City in 1979 was for PUP campaign posters to be put on houses to show support for the party.[92] Because a significant proportion of the population at the time was still basing political support for the PUP or UDP on national and issue-based party positions, many voters would have used similar means of expressing support for the candidates they favoured, based on party-based policy differences. In particular, most campaign and other support work for both the PUP and UDP was done voluntarily without expectation of a payment.

Although politicians of the time indicate that their clinic and campaign costs were partly self-financed or from small private donations, the record indicates that the practice of allocating public resources with partisan overtones was increasing by 1980.[93] Not only were elected representatives already redirecting monthly constituency stipends as monetary handouts to constituents, but the practice of dispensing public sector resources and favours to citizens through partisan clinics and partisan contacts was becoming more common and more national in scope. In terms of the use of public sector resources, one interviewee shared the view that the PUP's 1979 electoral success victory in the Collet constituency was due, in part, to the popularity among voters of a major new low-cost housing development.[94] At that time, projects of this sort could still be construed as part of the PUP's identity as a programmatic party.

Public service jobs, although not yet under the full control of the PUP government, were in high demand, and letters of recommendation from Price and other ministers to senior public officers carried much weight in this regard. In the year leading up to independence, public service jobs numbered some 1,736 and made up a significant proportion of the national workforce.[95] Even though there was some partisan influence over who got certain jobs, hiring was generally done by established process and through the filling of permanent posts. Temporary contract worker categories already existed, but they were not yet significantly exploited for job patronage. In 1981, at the most, two of every one hundred public service jobs were in the open vote (non-established) category, and the regulations on public service hiring were strictly applied.[96]

Before independence, the number of news stories on political clientelism activities was negligible and largely related to reporting on cases that were in the court system. As noted, some studies have made passing references to patronage and clientelism in writing about Belize's pre-independence politics. Five court cases alleging voter bribery were identified in the period between 1961 and 1979 – in effect, a testing of sections of the electoral law that made voter bribery illegal. Because none of these five cases led to a conviction, both politicians and voters were becoming cognizant of the relative ease of breaking the voter bribery law.

Conclusion

Although the essential elements of Belize's political system were in place since 1954, it was not until independence that Belizeans became fully responsible for all the powers and the challenges of the new state. Ironically, as much as the introduction of elections based on universal suffrage, the emergence of party politics and the control of public resources by local leaders were critical prerequisites for the consolidation of formal democracy in the soon-to-be independent state, they were also critical for modern political clientelism to take root.

After early attempts at programmatic approaches to address deep-seated social inequities and maintain broad-based voter support proved inadequate, the nationalist PUP slowly began to integrate clientelist practices into its repertoire of party strategies. The personalized, populist and paternalistic style of Price, in the context of Belize's small territorial size and tiny population, was a key but not sufficient contributing factor to the emergence of particularized politician–citizen relationships. Diverse multi-ethnicity, although not a direct causal factor, was beginning to add a unique Belizean flavour to the bargaining among politicians, communities and citizens for the distribution of public resources.

Overall, the account provided in this chapter found that the primary and driving forces for the emergence of political clientelism in this formative period were the consolidation of increasingly competitive party politics and the continuing reality of unmet livelihood needs of a significant proportion of the Belizean people. The inherited social and welfare institutions of the colonial state were simply unable to meet most people's needs and expectations. As the opposition UDP improved its electoral performance and slowly entered the handout game, the PUP stepped up its direct appeals to individual voters and communities through the clinic system and through the targeted allocation of public goods. With the benefit of hindsight, the pre-independence manifestations of political clientelism were indeed limited and often quaint. But by the time of independence, politicians were beginning to move beyond nationalist appeals and to provide or promise a variety of discretionary resources and favours to citizens with some expectation of voter support. Belizeans, now more aware of the bargaining value of their vote, were beginning to access this "novel" clientelist option with the knowledge that their political support was expected. However, the extent to which political clientelism could be used by local leaders was still limited by the reality that the British authorities still controlled central elements of political and economic power – including state patronage.

3.

Fertile Ground

The First Post-Independence Decade

Belize's first decade after independence was characterized by a gradual transition in the upward trajectory of political clientelism as political leaders and citizens alike adapted to independence, and as political parties developed new identities and advanced new strategies for winning ever more competitive elections. The decade witnessed the first two post-independence elections in a political context of Belizeans controlling the full powers of state and in which the PUP and the UDP were challenged to redefine themselves beyond binary positions, especially on the timing of independence. Importantly, it was in the 1980s that developments in the international economy, as well as national decisions made by governments, were harbingers of the era of political clientelism that was to come. In this chapter, I identify this 1981–91 period as a short but critical formative bridge from the pre-independence phase of the emergence of party-based clientelism to the phase of intense expansion of clientelist practices that would follow in the 1990s.

Independence in Challenging Economic Times

Economically, Belize's birth as a new nation coincided with the global recession of the late 1970s and early 1980s, and its worst macroeconomic performance since the collapse of the forestry industry in the middle of the twentieth century. By the end of 1984, after registering a gross domestic product (GDP) growth rate below 1 per cent in 1982 and a 25 per cent decline in the total value of exports and huge budget deficits, Belize entered a belt-tightening stand-by arrangement with the International Monetary Fund (IMF).[1] Mercilessly, the birth of Belize as a nation was quickly followed by the baptism of fire of neoliberalism, which was spreading rapidly across the globe – championed then by Ronald Reagan and Margaret Thatcher. Social sector spending freezes, triggered by the recession and the IMF medicine, tied the hands of government administrations seeking to deliver the national and human development that independence had, with such hope, promised to bring. Along with the easing of the global economic recession in the last years of the 1980s, increasing foreign investment, economic stabilization support from the United States Agency for International Development and some further diversification of the national economy, the IMF measures contributed to the short-term improvements in fiscal and GDP performance by 1989 but not in the basic social conditions of the people.[2] Pushed by conditionalities from IMF and the United States Agency for International Development, Belize began to adopt neoliberal economic policies that would gradually decrease the "size" of the state, further limit its capacity to address social problems – and also facilitate political clientelism.[3]

Demographically, the national population had increased from 145,343 in 1980 to 189,392 in 1990, representing a 30.3 per cent jump in intercensal population growth, compared to 21.3 per cent in the 1970s.[4] The harsh socio-economic conditions of most of the 1980s contributed to a new post-independence wave of economic emigration of an estimated twenty thousand to thirty thousand Belizeans, mostly Creoles and mostly to the United States.[5] Around the same time, an estimated thirty thousand political and economic immigrants were flooding into Belize from Guatemala, Honduras and El Salvador, further taxing the already stretched institutions and services of the new state.[6] These mostly Latino immigrants (some likely exposed to clientelist politics in their home countries) contributed to increased population growth and represented a pool of potential new voters in the 1990s. Because new immigrants need to attain Belizean citizenship (after residency for a minimum of five years) before becoming registered voters, their potential effect on the 1984 and 1989 elections was still minimal. Yet, just before the 1984 elections, elements in the opposition UDP criticized the PUP government's refugee and immigration policies as too liberal and as aimed at "Latinizing" the electorate for political gain.[7]

Key Changes in the Political Context

The Independence Constitution, which expanded the number of seats in the House from eighteen to twenty-eight, enshrined the Senate and confirmed the British monarch as the head of state (represented locally by an appointed governor general), also gave Belizean governments total control over national security, foreign affairs, all fiscal matters and public services. Another major step along the road of consolidating the Westminster model of formal democracy occurred in the 1984 general election with the first and seamless change of party in government since the first election under adult suffrage in 1954. In that first post-independence election, the UDP won a general election for the first time, with over 53.3 per cent of the vote and a "supermajority" of twenty-one of twenty-eight House seats, under the leadership of Manuel Esquivel.[8] George Price himself lost his constituency seat in the UDP landslide. Most assessments of the PUP loss in 1984 point to the PUP being a worn-out party with no new ideas after thirty years in power, to an ideologically divided leadership and to an inability to step up development programmes sufficiently due to the hard economic times. It was indeed a sea-change election and the full arrival of the UDP as the "other" credible political party signalled the ongoing consolidation of a "two-party dominant" variant of the Westminster model, heightened the competitive level of party politics and launched a twenty-year span (1984–2003) of the PUP and UDP alternating in power at each of the four general elections during the period.

With independence no longer an issue and with a defence guarantee secured from the United Kingdom in case of a military threat from Guatemala, the political parties were beginning to lose their key traditional and distinctive policy profiles. For a short period up to the 1989 general election, there were some serious intra-party debates about ideology and development visions. For its part, the UDP had made it clear that it was right of centre and decidedly free enterprise and anti-communist in orientation, and it governed as such in the 1984–89 term. The PUP, although never publicly against free markets, held on to its working-class origins for some time, and Price identified the PUP as a progressive party that strived for a mixed economy. After a brief and failed attempt by left-wing elements to win control before the 1984 elections, the PUP started to present itself more as a centrist and business-friendly party. When the PUP returned to power in 1989, it embraced, and then expanded on, the UDP's free-enterprise model and policies.

In this period, party politics in Belize continued to develop in such a manner that no one party dominated in terms of geographic, class or ethnic advantage. As argued by the former United Black Association for Development leader and well-known Belizean newspaper publisher, Evan X Hyde, "The two-party system played a major role. . . . Politicians from different ethnicities and administrative districts have to work together over long periods of time to establish the national credibility a political party requires in order to win elections."[9] Consequently, the PUP and the UDP, without any strong distinguishing national visions, continued to consolidate identities as multi-class, multi-racial, multi-gender and multi-ethnic parties, and to receive support from all these groupings across urban and rural communities.

Another relevant change in the country context was the significant spike in the number and scope of work of civil society organizations (CSOs) in the last half of the 1980s. One study by Herman Byrd related this growth both to the inability of governments to adequately address socio-economic needs and to the greater availability of international development funding and found that by the turn of the decade, non-governmental organizations (NGOs), community groups and charity groups were working in all districts of Belize and in almost every thematic area, including community development, political reform and social policy.[10] Byrd found that the spate of new CSOs was partly related to "new" international development financing triggered by independence and to the investments in the NGO sector made by the United States Agency for International Development. Overall, the CSOs were beginning to help fill economic and social development gaps not adequately serviced by state institutions, and so provide Belizeans with alternative opportunities to participate and receive benefits outside of political party relationships.

Political Clientelism in the 1980s

After independence in 1981, and in the lead up to the PUP's first loss in 1984, Price's weekly political clinics continued unabated and the clinic practice continued to spread gradually to the constituency level.[11] A review of inter-ministerial communications from this period, although showing that the types of requests remained similar, indicates a further institutionalization of clientelism in the first decade of independence. Representative examples from the George Price Archival Collection include:

- A letter from Price to Minister of Lands Marin requesting house lots be allocated to sixteen specific citizens in Belize City.[12]
- Minister of Housing Shoman to Price requesting assistance for $10,000 housing loan for a constituent.[13]
- Price to Deputy Minister for Housing Usher requesting assistance to procure a house for an individual.[14]
- High school principal to Price requesting paint.[15]
- Citizen to Price requesting help with loudspeakers for an event.[16]
- Price to Shoman requesting repair of a roof.[17]
- Price to Minister of Energy Briceño requesting action on a complaint that a utility bill is too high.[18]

- Price to Attorney-General Courtenay requesting assessment of prospect of reducing the length of a prison sentence.[19]
- Price to Minister of Sports Musa requesting that an individual be given a job.[20]
- Price to a housing agency requesting that a loan be written off for individual.[21]

Assessments of the first PUP defeat in 1984 generally fail to explore the angle that macroeconomic constraints in the first three years after independence restricted the PUP's opportunities to maintain or expand its clientelist appeals to the electorate. Although not making a direct connection to clientelism, Shoman did suggest that the economic crisis "caused significant loss of support for the PUP" because it was unable to maintain its land reform and infrastructure development programmes, especially in rural parts of the country.[22] For sure, diminished clientelist opportunities from the state were at least one factor in the PUP's defeat in 1984.

Accounts from politicians also paint a picture of a gradual but not dramatic increase in clientelist activity in the UDP's first term of office from 1984 to 1989. This inaugural stint in power gave the UDP its first experience of both the challenges and advantages of incumbency in terms of the distribution of public resources and favours. Former prime minister Esquivel recalled that after the election and on becoming prime minister in 1984, he was "unbelievably naive to be surprised that campaign volunteers began coming to collect, saying . . . we helped you to win so we deserve something".[23] Esquivel, albeit not as natural a clientelist politician as Price, continued the Price tradition of holding weekly Wednesday national clinics at his office in Belmopan and occasionally in Belize City.[24] The use of political clinics by other UDP politicians expanded, but they were still clustered around election campaigns. Esquivel recounted that in the late 1980s most handouts were in-kind and that monetary gifts were still quite rare.[25] A UDP political insider supported this view: "After its first election the UDP had tasted power and the flow of public money . . . by 1989 there was vote-influencing . . . not so much with money then, but more so with government resources like land lots and land leases."[26] Esquivel estimated that, by the end of 1990, the constituency stipend had increased to about $3,000 and that the cost of a constituency campaign was around $15,000–$20,000.[27]

Although "helping" was still seen as the primary motive for handouts by politicians, changes in the political context did affect the evolving relationships between politicians and citizens. By the late 1980s, "bigger money" began to trickle slowly into Belize's political parties. This had some direct relationship to the spread of neoliberal economic policies during this decade. On the demand side, Esquivel related the increase of money in politics in part to the advent of television advertising and expanded radio advertising in Belizean politics.[28] In addition to the growing costs of campaigns, parties and politicians also began to spend more on improving the organization of national and constituency-level canvassing and on particularistic appeals to voters.

This was especially noteworthy and precedent-setting in the 1984 campaign of the young businessman Derek Aikman, who had dealt Price his historic first general election defeat. As former prime minister Said Musa (1998–2008) noted, "There was the Aikman phenomenon . . . he took campaigning to another level of glitz, propaganda, communications, organization . . . and money, and, to compete, others followed that lead."[29] Several interviewees also pointed to the 1984 big money contest in the Queen's Square constituency of then newcomer Dean Barrow, who was financially supported by one of Belize's richest local businessmen at the time, in a contest against a wealthy PUP newcomer and businessman, Ralph Fonseca. Fonseca, who was defeated by Barrow in 1984, went on to win in another constituency in 1993 and became one of the chief architects of rebranding the PUP in his capacity as its national campaign manager and financial czar.[30] Fonseca noted that he had come away from his 1984 loss with the lesson that "people don't care what you know until they know that you care" (by receiving resources and favours), and he set out to create a national party machine based on a business model.[31] Fonseca attested that he had observed how modern political parties operated and campaigned while studying and living in Canada, and he applied some of these basic business principles to the PUP.

Musa, who took over as PUP party leader after Price and was a key architect of the new PUP, recounted, "After independence we could not identify clear aspirations that grabbed people's minds . . . before it was freedom . . . how can you top that?"[32] A senior political operative contended that a key aspect of the rebranding was the deliberate "paradigm shift to a new PUP political strategy in which a more centrist and capitalist approach was accompanied by more money in campaigns and the move from volunteerism to payments . . . and one result was that street campaigning began a shift from 'what does your constituency need?' to 'what do you want?'"[33] Expressing similar views, another senior PUP operative marked the 1989 election as the political moment the PUP "stopped being a movement and began its transition to a commercial entity".[34]

With the gradual diminishing of distinguishing party identities and visions in an increasingly competitive electoral context, both parties also had added incentive to raise more private money to strengthen and expand particularistic politician–citizen relationships. This not only facilitated the entry of more wealthy candidates into electoral politics but also led to both parties competing to make larger appeals to big business for donations. As the first party leader of the UDP reflected, "Handout politics grew in the 1980s as more money flowed in and as the electorate realized that they could get more out of the game."[35] And even though volunteering for parties continued, payments to party and campaign workers were creeping into party operations. By the time campaigning for the 1989 general election commenced, it was clear that any hopes that may have existed that the first UDP government in 1984 would break the trend of gradually expanding clientelist politics (began by the PUP) were all but dashed.

The UDP's Foray into Clientelist Politics

In addition to continuing the PUP's practice of weekly clinics, expanding the monthly constituency stipends to representatives and continuing party-based patronage with government resources and programmes, the UDP government of 1984–89 spearheaded several developments that facilitated the future growth of political clientelism. Significantly, in its first stint in office, the UDP raised the bar for the open use of publicly funded resources for targeted programmes for party purposes before a general election. In the year leading up to the 4 September 1989 election, the UDP government launched a large "community development projects" programme, in which each of the then twenty-eight constituencies was targeted for the allocation of a portion of the funds.[36] Although the opposition PUP alleged that over $8 million was disbursed, the records of the House of Representatives show that $1.8 million of Capital II funds was allocated for small constituency projects, such as electrification, water supply, streets and drainage, and housing.[37] The opposition PUP accused the UDP of using public funds for its campaign and alleged that accounting officers in the public service were either being bypassed or pressured by UDP candidates to break accounting rules.[38]

A post-election Commission of Inquiry appointed by the PUP government (1989–93) into the use of the funds found that "the community development funds were driven primarily by a political agenda at the expense of public accountability for expenditures borne by taxpayers".[39] Even as it conceded that some funds were used for targeted community-level projects such as roadworks in the constituencies, the commission claimed to have unearthed evidence of significant misappropriation and waste. Esquivel, the prime minister at the time, strongly refuted all allegations of misappropriation and insisted that no funds were allocated directly through UDP candidates.[40] Yet it is clear that the allocation of funds via established public sector channels does not negate the possibility of direct influence by politicians of which particular groups or individuals are targeted to benefit within a constituency.

Another key development relates to amendments made to election laws that would have significant implications for the management of future elections, in general, and for the control of political clientelism, specifically. An amendment to the Constitution in 1988 (Second Constitutional Amendment of 1988), in effect, allowed the majority party to appoint three members, including the chair, and for the official opposition to appoint two members of the Elections and Boundaries Commission (EBC), de facto giving the party in power access to majority control of the five-member EBC if it so desired. Prior to this amendment, appointments to the five-member EBC and of the chief elections officer were made by the governor general, and there was no allowance for direct political party appointments. Further legal changes in 1989 shifted the power of staff appointments from the EBC to the public service and re-established the formerly autonomous EBC secretariat as a regular department within a government ministry.[41]

In practical effect, the amendments split the responsibility for election management into two bodies, both of which could be directly controlled by the incumbent party. A key consequence would be that incumbent parties now had added legal cover to influence election administration, including the responsibility to investigate allegations of voter bribery. As Myrtle Palacio rightly argued, "Instead of more autonomy for the election management body, its relative independence was literally snuffed."[42]

A third development likely seemed unrelated to political clientelism at the time. In 1987, Michael Ashcroft, British billionaire and international investor, had made one of his first major investments in Belize with the purchase of the Belize branch of the Royal Bank of Canada during the first government of the UDP.[43] By 1990, he had negotiated a thirty-year tax holiday from a newly elected PUP government for all his then and future business interests in Belize, which he placed under the then umbrella of Belize Holdings Inc. The salient point here is that it was around this time that Lord Ashcroft's[44] role as one of the single largest financial contributors to both Belize's major political parties,[45] and, by implication, his oversized and controversial role as a major contributor of private funds to the parties' clientelist operations, was beginning. In short, Ashcroft had commenced a strategic and contentious journey in which he would successfully fashion himself into Belize's foremost business oligarch across elections, economic cycles, political parties, administrations and prime ministers.

As significant as these developments were, most politicians of both parties, making comparisons to later years, still view the 1980s as a time when offers and requests for handouts were still minimal. Apart from the national clinics, most clinics were still clustered around elections campaigns, even as clinic numbers grew. The types of goods and services remained basically the same, even though the amounts of money spent on clientelist operations increased. Party membership, volunteering as canvassers, attending party rallies and wearing party colours were still dominant as ways of manifesting support for a political party.

On the other hand, several politicians suggest that the parties had both become more adept at using public resources, including jobs, as clientelist rewards and inducements. Even as allegations of corruption by the two parties increased, few news reports made the direct connection to clientelism, and no case of voter bribery was brought to the courts in this bridging decade.

Conclusion

In this first post-independence decade of the 1980s, full national control of resource allocation, partisan alternations in government, more vulnerable economic conditions, significant immigration and an expanding population favoured the growth of political clientelism. Belize was also unfortunate that its delayed decolonization coincided with the emergence of neoliberal globalization that constrained the capacity of the first two governments of the post-colonial states to deliver on the lofty promises of independence. On the other hand, the temporary "escape valves" of financial stabilization and of emigration to the United States, and the alternatives for participation provided by CSOs, collectively represented a temporary counterweight.

The UDP's introductory foray into clientelist politics during its first term in government did not prevent an exceedingly narrow victory by a rebranded and combative "new" PUP in 1989. The PUP, which was not short on financing, had run a modern and well-managed campaign marked by persistent accusations of UDP corruption and aloofness. It won fifteen of the twenty-eight House of Representative seats with just 50 per cent of the popular vote, compared to the UDP's 48.2 per cent.[46] Reflecting on the UDP failure, a UDP minister opined, "One reason we lost the

1989 elections was because we did not do enough benefits politics . . . and we could have."[47] Overall, the 1989 election marked a turning point, but not yet a sea change, in the trajectory of political clientelism. As former prime minister Musa stated, by 1989, "The era of 'bashments' and of more open financial incentives for voter participation was beginning."[48] Although not a candidate in the 1989 elections, the master of operations was PUP campaign manager Ralph Fonseca, who was rewarded with a key ministerial appointment. Significantly, the man who would become Lord Ashcroft of Chichester had installed himself as a major financial and political actor.

As Belize commemorated its first decade of independence in 1991, the PUP and UDP had begun to espouse near-identical national positions on many issues, to devise new tactics for utilizing public funds to dispense programmes to targeted areas and to attract larger sums of private money. Despite there being no major threats to formal democracy, it was becoming clear that the seedlings of political clientelism rooted in the nationalist period were finding fertile sprouting grounds in the newly independent Belize.

4.

Clientelism Entrenched

The 1990s and Beyond

If 1954–81 marked the planting of the seeds of modern political clientelism in Belize and the first decade after independence chronicled a slow but determinative transition in its trajectory, the period thereafter witnessed its rampant expansion and deep entrenchment. The UDP regained power from the PUP in another close general election in 1993 (sixteen to thirteen seats in the House of Representatives), but the PUP won the 1998 election in a landslide (twenty-six to three seats). In this chapter, I argue that by that 1998 election, political clientelism had vaulted from the "innocent" phase of offering pens, coins and five-dollar bills to, as one observer put it, "a new normal of guiltless and shameless trading of political favours for political support".[1]

After a repeat PUP victory in 2003 and a lopsided UDP victory in 2008, episodes of blatant vote bartering and the informal distribution of public funds through partisans were no longer limited to election campaigns. By the 2012 general election, these had become permanent features of the daily political relationships of exchange and influence between citizens and politicians. I now chronicle this rapid expansion of political clientelism in Belize and deconstruct its machinations. Particularly, I trace the post-1990 changes in the magnitude, nature, political actors and operational features of clientelist activity, and present the empirical evidence proving that Belize is an illustrative and critical case of clientelist democracy.

Indisputable Evidence of Rampant Expansion

Given the paucity of written records, the oral recollections of past and current politicians and political operatives of both major political parties are critical for confirming the post-independence expansion of clientelist activities and for constructing a detailed picture of their operational features. There was unanimous concurrence among key actors interviewed that clientelist politics expanded rapidly in the 1990s and thereafter. One former politician recounted, "By 2008, there was a massive difference, a massive increase compared to my first election in 1993 . . . people now believe that politicians have drawers of money ready to give out."[2] In a similar vein, a party operative said, "In 1989 it was limited to small amounts for fewer people for such things as help with uniforms and favours to get scholarships. By 2008, it was everything, everything! Paying house rents, electricity bills, school fees . . . everything!"[3] A party executive recalled witnessing the chaos of hundreds of people waiting for some of the "Venezuela money" in front of the Housing Department in Dangriga (a coastal town south of Belize City) just before the 2008 elections and remarked that, by that time, "causes and issues" were "almost irrelevant" and that the practice of paying campaign workers had settled in.[4] Another politician lamented, "In the 1980s I was expected to pay a part of a power bill but now they want you to pay the whole bill . . . and others too!"[5]

If there was a symbolic pivot point when handout politics spiked sharply and then consolidated quickly into a day-to-day phenomenon, it was around the 1998 national election. Former prime minister Esquivel opined that a distinguishing feature in this election was "the huge increase in direct cash handouts".[6] In that election, a well-funded (opposition) PUP dislodged the incumbent UDP with a supermajority of 90 per cent of House seats (twenty-six of twenty-nine) and 59.3 per cent of the vote.[7] Informants from both parties confirm that it was by far the most expensive election in Belize's electoral history at the time and that the PUP, even while in opposition, outspent the UDP significantly. One (unverified) estimate from a UDP insider placed PUP campaign expenditures at some four times that of the $5 million the UDP claimed it spent.[8] Key PUP party officials did not deny the conventional view that Lord Ashcroft (introduced in the last chapter) was a primary financial donor to the party and to selected PUP candidates in the election. A PUP party executive member observed, "The party's campaigns became commercial operations in the early 1990s and this came to a head in 1998."[9]

This narrative of expanding clientelism described by key political actors is absolutely reflected in the spike in the number of news accounts related to allegations of political clientelism in the lead-up to the 1998 general election. An article headlined "PUP Insider Trading in Land", in the *Amandala* of 5 July 1991 alleged that the governing PUP used land to gain partisan political influence. In "Esquivel Gives Howell $700,000 to Buy Votes", the *Belize Times* of 3 March 1996 claimed that the UDP candidate intended to buy votes in a by-election in Belize City. In "Immigration Racket in Voter Fraud", the *Belize Times* of 22 February 1998 alleged that the UDP government was registering new immigrants illegally so as to give the UDP an electoral advantage in the 1998 election. In "Crazy Land Give Away", the *Belize Times* of 16 August 1998 alleged that the UDP government was facilitating land grants and leases to influence the 1998 election.

This pattern continued after 1998, with reporting of clientelist practices especially prominent in the months before and after elections. For example, in "PUP Area Reps Got $100,000–$150,000 Each, UDP Got Nothing", the *Amandala* of 5 February 2008 reported on an interview with the financial secretary that revealed that much of the Venezuela grant was distributed through incumbent politicians of the PUP prior to the 2008 election. In "75 Families in Collet Receive Housing Grants", *7 News* of 28 August 2009 reported on the representative for the Collet constituency handing out grants of up to $3,000 per person to seventy-five constituents for housing repairs, as part of the recovered second tranche of the Venezuela grant. In "Christmas Crush at Finnegan's Office", *7 News* of 17 December 2009 reported on a crowd of some three hundred citizens queuing for pre-Christmas handouts at a constituency political clinic. In "PM Barrow Defends Firings at Ministry of Works", the *Amandala* of 11 April 2008 reported on an interview it conducted with then prime minister Barrow, in which he defended particular post-election dismissals of people, who were hired during the previous PUP term and replaced by persons favourable to the UDP. The review of media reports also suggested an increase in handout politics at the level of party conventions. For example, in "Blue Notes for Blue Votes", the *Independent* of 6 July 2007 alleged that the PUP paid voters to attend a PUP party convention. In "Joe Blames Dirty Politics and $$$!", the *Amandala* of 15 April 2011 reported on the allegations by a losing candidate of vote buying by his opponent in a PUP convention. In "Tom Morrison Alleges Vote Buying in UDP Albert Division", the *Belize Times* of 17 April 2011 reported on the losing candidate's allegations of vote buying by his opponent as the reason for his loss in a UDP convention.

However, the more detailed and plausible substantiations of the growing scope of clientelist activity are the reports of commissions of inquiry, independent governance assessments, government audit reports and court documents. Nineteen such reports and documents dealing directly or indirectly with some aspect of clientelism were identified (between 1981 and 2013), and six examples are selected that cover the administrations of both the PUP and UDP. The first example relates to the issue of politicians targeting new Central American immigrants for political support. The *Report of the National NGO Consortium on the Granting of Belizean Nationality and Implications for Voter Registration* found clear evidence of official abuse of the nationalization process to fast-track citizenship for Central American immigrants during the 1989–93 PUP government.[10] The report details how, on the intervention of incumbent politicians, various departments of government compressed the time frame required for processing nationality claims and waived various requirements, including the $200 fee, so as to "accommodate larger number of applicants as the 1993 election drew near".[11] Whereas 492 nationality awards were made to Guatemalans, Salvadorians and Hondurans in 1991, the number of awards increased to 1,127 in 1992 and to 1,221 in 1993, and there was a corresponding spike in the number of naturalized Belizeans who registered to vote, from 239 in 1991 to 505 in 1992, and to 953 in 1993.[12] The consortium considered that, because elections can be won by small numbers in Belize, "any registration of illegal persons as voters could be a major factor in deciding individual races and perhaps determining party control of the government".[13] It was implied in the report that those immigrants being fast-tracked for nationality and voter registration were expected to boost political support for particular PUP candidates.

The second example is the first Supreme Court case of alleged voter bribery brought to court after independence.[14] Dr Amin Hegar (PUP), who had lost the 1998 election in the Cayo West constituency by just ten votes even as his party had won, accused his opponent and then incumbent Erwin Contreras (UDP) of distributing some four hundred house lot leases on the very day of the election, including to people who were queuing to vote. Hegar was able to get signed affidavits from ten constituents who all stated that they had been given leases for house lots from Contreras on the day of the election, with the direct or indirect understanding that their vote was expected.[15]

Before the case was fully heard, Hegar's court application was thrown out in January 1999 based on technicalities related to the filing of both the affidavits and the court petition. When asked about this incident, Contreras did not deny that land leases were being distributed in his constituency before and on election day: "That happened because I had requested 500 housing lots for people in my division and got them late . . . some on election day. I had to give them out that day."[16] There was speculation that Hegar was asked by his own party to abandon the case because there were fears that it would draw unwanted attention to similar allegations against the PUP itself.[17] However, Hegar doggedly pursued the case until it was dismissed by the Supreme Court.

The third example highlights the alleged distribution of publicly funded educational assistance for political support. In February 2003, after various news media had been reporting improprieties, the opposition UDP held a press conference alleging "officials in the Ministry of Education have been simply running a scholarship scam. They have been approving tuition grants to students at universities at home and abroad and these [persons] have never been enrolled in the schools. We have proof of several persons who have been receiving scholarship funds and who were not enrolled in institutions for which they are receiving the grants."[18] The charges, which were corroborated by a non-student recipient of such funds,[19] were the subject of a special audit performed by the Office of the Auditor General in 2004. The audit found that an initial review pointed to gross irregularities and misuse of public funds: "Some 1,337 individuals who were not registered students . . . received financial assistance totalling some \$666,192 during the period April 2001 to March 2003."[20] Once recipients had been selected by the ministry, the funds were apparently transferred through the ministry's usual financial system and payments were made normally by government vouchers.[21] Again, and apart from the prospect of public corruption inferred, the relevant implication was that targeted recipients included constituency supporters of the then minister of education, Cordel Hyde, who denied all allegations.

The fourth case focuses on a variety of vote trading concerns raised in a report of the Commonwealth Secretariat's election observers about the 2008 election. The report stated that the observers received accounts of

> accusations of hurried large-scale granting of citizenship to Guatemalans; the granting of loans and land titles in return for loyalty to the PUP at the polls; and the outright buying of votes, with payment to be made upon proof of how people cast their ballots. This last was exacerbated by a heated debate over the possible use of cell phone cameras in polling booths to record how a vote was cast.[22]

The report pointed to three of the more popular resources that are bartered for political support in Belize: land, immigration assistance and money. On the day before the 2008 election, the Elections and Boundaries Commission ruled that there was no law that allowed it to ban cell phones from voting booths, as had been formally requested by the Association of Concerned Belizeans (ACB).[23] Importantly, the account of the observer team marked the first time that accusations of vote trading in Belize were highlighted in a credible international report.

The fifth example highlights the well-known use of land as clientelist inducement in Belize. A special audit of land issuance in the lead-up to the 2008 election found that there were numerous procedural violations and irregularities in an accelerated spate of land titles and leases issuances from September 2007 to February 2008, just before the 2008 general election.[24] Although the Auditor General did not comment directly on the partisan incentives of the transactions, the audit implied that the large number of titles and leases approved in the months just before a national election represented attempts to influence individual voters. This was indeed the allegation made repeatedly in sections of the press. In one newspaper article the then PUP minister of natural resources was accused of distributing land to friends and PUP supporters outside of established procedures.[25] Again, the conventional view was that some citizens received land as either inducements or rewards for political support.

The sixth case selected is the now infamous saga of the Venezuela money that was referred to earlier. Just one month before the general election of 7 February 2008, the PUP government informed the nation that a grant to Belize of $20 million, mostly for low-income housing, from Venezuela could be accessed through its thirty-one constituency-based candidates.[26] In similar scenes in political constituencies across the country, huge crowds gathered outside party-constituency or government offices to receive or lobby for a share of the Venezuela money.[27] Some citizens made their anger publicly known to the media, as reflected in the threat of one voter: "I am waiting for a check they promised me from one month time . . . they have to bring that check to my house for me to go and vote."[28] The opposition UDP alleged that the Venezuelan grant funds were being abused to buy the election, but there was acknowledgement that some of its supporters also encouraged voters to take the PUP handouts but to still vote for the UDP.[29] The $20 million Venezuelan grant all but disappeared in the four-week period before the election. A post-election special audit of the funds revealed that disbursement decisions were made at the discretion of politicians, that transfers ranged between $500 and $1,000, that there were no criteria to define "low-income" and that there were numerous financial irregularities, including the failure to account for over $7 million.[30]

Two weeks after winning the 1998 election, the new UDP government learnt that the Venezuelan grant was not $20 million but actually $40 million and that the former administration had secretly used the other half towards settling a government-guaranteed loan held by Ashcroft's Belize Bank Limited on behalf of a private local business group.[31] Using the courts, the then UDP government recovered the second $20 million from the Belize Bank in August 2008 and then moved quickly in early 2009 to itself commence disbursement of some $18 million as housing grants to citizens through constituency-based representatives.[32]

Emerging Trends and Threads

Within the overall upwards trajectory of political clientelism in the late 1990s, several emerging trends are readily observable. First, it was obvious that both the PUP and UDP were equally implicated as engaging in similar types and measures of clientelist practices. After its victory in 1984, the UDP could no longer justifiably paint the PUP as the sole perpetuators of handout politics – even if the then conventional wisdom was that the PUP was more adept at the clientelist game than the UDP. Both parties adopted clientelist practices that had proven successful for the other. For example, after elements of the PUP fast-tracked the registration of immigrants for electoral advantage in 1993, some UDP candidates ran similar schemes in 1998. In particular, the saga of the Venezuela money stands out for the conspicuous disbursements of large amounts of funds from the same source by both political parties in rapid succession. In short, by 1998, political clientelism had become a characteristic feature, indeed dominant feature, of the electoral strategies of both major parties and, by extension, of Belize's political system itself.

The body of evidence also illustrates that even as there are spikes in clientelist activity during election campaigns, the phenomenon has become more and more characteristic of day-to-day political relationships between elections. For example, the scholarship scandal, the "Christmas Crush" story, several of the land scandals and the disbursement of the second part of the Venezuela money all happened outside of campaign periods. Another clear indicator of this new normal is that allegations of direct voter bribery have become regular occurrences even within the intra-party contests of both parties. This is evident in the aforementioned pre-2012 elections stories "Joe Blames Dirty Politics and $$$" and "Tom Morrison Alleges Vote Buying in UDP Albert Division". Additionally, and as indicated by the 2008 controversies related to having cell phones in voting booths, politicians have also sought to employ more novel tactics to monitor individual voter compliance. Although such tactics are in no way unique to Belize, the 2008 cell phone episode was another indicator of the pervasive levels of political clientelism.

The examples described also suggest that the goods and services traded in clientelist exchanges were multiplying in both types and numbers since independence. The primary resources continue to include land, houses and housing repairs, jobs, education assistance, and money. With regard to land, both parties perfected the art of dispensing land for political gain when in power. Notwithstanding that one-third of Belize's territory is under some level of environmental protection and much of the remainder is privately owned, the government of Belize can still access land to use this much-demanded resource as a preferred inducement for votes.[33]

Immigration assistance also emerged in the 1990s as a new and highly demanded tradable. The NGO Consortium Report of 1993 was the first to provide independent confirmation that a political party was targeting Central American immigrants as potential clients. Every election thereafter would witness one party accusing the other of registering immigrants illegally by falsifying and/or fast-tracking nationality applications. Whereas the incentive for the political party and politicians is to gain electoral advantage, that for the immigrants is to gain access to work permits, residency or nationality so as to facilitate legal access to such resources as jobs, land scholarships and social welfare. The lead-up to the 2012 election was a case in point, as several UDP candidates were accused of fast-tracking nationality awards. In one television interview, a UDP representative actually admitted that he was paying up to half of the application fees for some one hundred potential "new" Belizeans at a total cost of some $15,000, personally handling and filling in the forms to pass on to the immigration office. When asked if he was expecting votes from this activity, he responded, "Well I believe that if I'm working day and night for them, and they are out here seeing it, I don't think that they would turn their backs on me."[34]

There was also evidence that those citizens and potential citizens being assisted were beginning to master the art of the clientelist game. A case in point is the nationally televised views of an immigrant waiting for application assistance in a line outside the house of a UDP political operative in Belize City: "We are a people who are living in a foreign country and we would like to exercise our rights, but we cannot do so without our papers . . . we will get our papers in exchange for our votes, because that is what he is asking right now. If we get our nationality, then we get to vote for him."[35] In a one-month period just weeks before the March 2012 general election, over one thousand new immigrants were naturalized and registered, some in one day, when the average number of naturalizations per quarter before was below one hundred.[36]

Several of the examples also suggest that politicians quickly became more adept at manipulating informal modes of transferring resources to citizens. These include both direct transfers, such as gifts at Christmas and money for votes, and indirect transfers through government offices, such as vouchers for educational assistance and residency permits. A noteworthy example of transfers through party representatives is the $1.4 million

Christmas Assistance Programme of December 2011, in which $40,000 was "distributed" to each of the thirty-one constituencies to allow UDP representatives and aspirants to deliver additional Christmas goodies to constituents.[37] This tradition of politicians handing out Christmas baskets of turkeys, hams, other foodstuffs and gifts had long existed, but the funding used to come largely from private sources or from the constituency stipend. In this instance, public funds were used in a new and temporary handout scheme in which constituency-based politicians made the decisions regarding recipients and personally handed out gift packages, often with full media coverage.[38] Opposition party representatives complained loudly, but this was also about their exclusion from this popular scheme.[39] Just three weeks later, the government announced yet another "special assistance" scheme in which each constituency received another $50,000 of public funds to be disbursed at the discretion of the UDP's thirty-one candidates for the general election.[40]

Regarding indirect transfers, the 2002–03 scholarship scandal highlighted one of the common strategies that politicians have used when in government to transfer funds as incentives or pay-offs for political support. In short, lists of names of recipients of a resource or service are received informally from constituency representatives or party candidates. These are then approved by the relevant minister or senior public officer, then formally processed through a ministry's financial system before being disbursed to the recipient. The end result is similar to that of a direct transfer from the politician in that it is the politician who influences which individuals receive public resources – and the recipient is made to know this. Middle-class citizens were not left out of such "special" pre-election programmes, as the examples of loan and mortgage write-offs in 2011 and 2012 attest. In October 2011, the UDP government wrote off 9,200 of what were described as non-performing loans valued at $60 million.[41] In January 2012 and less than two months before the 2012 election, the government wrote off another 780 mortgages, each under $50,000, and valued at $17 million and held by the Belize Social Security Board.[42]

Another clear trend is that even as news media outlets increasingly reported on incidents and allegations related to political clientelism, they have done so with negligible commentary on possible illegality or on implications for democratic governance. Clientelist activities tend to be increasingly presented as a normal, even cultural, part of daily political activity. This was remarkably clear in the 2008 news reporting around the Venezuela money. Statements from citizens, which left no doubt that vote trading was taking place, were broadcast to a national audience with negligible critical comment on the legal prohibition against exchanges of money for votes. Both this blatant and open sharing of such sentiments by citizens, and the normalcy that characterized the news reporting, would have been near unimaginable three decades earlier. In a period of expanding clientelism, of high frequency of public allegations of vote buying, and even of numerous official confirmations of some allegations via audits and inquiries, the Hegar case of 1998 was the only one to be taken to the courts between 1981 and up to the 2012 general election.

Inside a Political Clinic

As a consequence of population growth from 189,392 in 1990 to 312,698 in 2010 and of boundary revisions, the number of political constituencies in Belize increased from twenty-eight to twenty-nine in 1993 and to thirty-one in 2007.[43] In November 2011 there were, on average, some 10,090 citizens and 5,530 registered voters per constituency.[44] An analysis of the party constitutions illustrates that the PUP and the UDP have similar institutional structures at the constituency level, generally led by executive committees.[45] Special conventions in each constituency elect or endorse candidates to contest the next general election. With varying levels of organizational sophistication, representatives and candidates generally divide their constituencies into zones with a fixed number of streets, each usually having a zone leader and other operatives. However, there are nuances to this approach. For example, instead of zoning by streets, a former PUP representative for the Albert constituency subdivided his constituents into some sixty sets of thirty persons, each set being the direct personal responsibility of two or three operatives. He argued that this facilitates attending to the needs of individual constituents and allows for more direct personal attention to constituents who do not reside in the division.[46]

Constituency operations, anchored by political clinics, are most often administered on a day-to-day basis from the constituency-based offices of elected representatives or aspirants. For members of the House of Representatives, these constituency offices ostensibly have the key functions of allowing them to share government developments and programme information with constituents and facilitating constituents to raise their concerns directly with representatives. The line between these key functions and clientelist activities has become so blurred that most constituency offices are denoted as just "clinics" by politicians and citizens alike. Indeed, one of the most significant indicators of the rapid expansion of political clientelism is the major increase in the number and scope of work of political clinics since the first Price clinic in the 1950s. Clinics became the year-round nodes of clientelist politician–citizen relationships.

Although Belize City and urban areas generally have larger and more regular clinic operations than rural areas, political clinics have become countrywide phenomena. At least two ongoing clinic operations are identifiable in most constituencies – one PUP and one UDP. When all thirty-one constituencies have some level of up-and-running clinic operations, especially before general elections, there are sixty-two clinics countrywide. However, allowing for periods of clinic inactivity in some constituencies over an average year, triangulation of information from politicians suggested (in 2010) that there were at least fifty-five clinic-type operations at any one time, most of which were operated by politicians of the incumbent party.[47]

Most politicians conduct personal clinics from their constituency offices at least once weekly, and some politicians do so even more regularly. Former prime minister Barrow was the only incumbent politician interviewed for this study who did not personally hold a weekly constituency clinic on a regular basis. Instead, his trusted sister discharged clinic duties on a daily basis on his behalf.[48] Although fixed office-based constituency clinics are the most frequent venues for such operations, there are also other arrangements for citizens to access clinics. A few candidates in constituencies that are spread out over larger geographical areas, such as Stann Creek West, Toledo East and Toledo West,[49] have multiple constituency offices and/or conduct mobile clinic operations.[50] It is not uncommon for incumbent politicians who have ministerial portfolios to conduct party-constituency and clinic business from official government offices or from community centres located in or near their constituencies.[51] Most representatives who have ministerial portfolios also conduct clinics from their official offices in Belmopan or elsewhere on a regular basis. The audiences for these clinics are mostly persons seeking resources or assistance related to particular ministerial portfolios, but these can also be open to the ministers' own constituents. As another carry-over from the Price era, prime ministers have also continued to conduct national-level clinics from offices in Belmopan and Belize City.

Although some constituents can visit political clinics on a daily basis to pursue individual requests, most clientelist activity occurs on the set weekly clinic days. On these days, citizens either arrive on the advice of brokers or other constituency operatives or just show up for a chance to see their politicians. Representatives of the governing party, particularly those with ministerial portfolios, generally have more extensive operations than backbenchers, opposition party politicians and new aspirants. Elected representatives from the official opposition tend to have larger clinic operations than their unelected counterparts in most constituencies, but it is not unusual for a well-financed constituency standard bearer, constituency caretaker or constituency aspirant of either major party to have an elaborate clinic operation.[52] On an ongoing basis, but especially on clinic days, brokers and office staff monitor the needs and requests of constituents, and provide the politicians with information on past requests, responses and the status of disbursements. In constituencies with larger clinic networks, it is not unusual for politicians to attend to long queues of constituents for up to five to eight hours on weekly clinic days, especially during campaign seasons.

On those days of the week when politicians are not present to conduct personal constituency clinics, their offices receive and screen requests from constituents, dispense pre-approved resources and services, and gather information on constituents. The majority of the offices now have full-time employees and monitoring systems to keep track of requests, responses to requests, partisan affiliations, numbers in households and other such data on constituents. In the case of incumbent party politicians and most opposition party operations, the average full-time constituency office is operated by paid staff and/or part-time workers. Staffs can include an office administrator, a secretary, a messenger and temporary outreach workers, who are all invariably trusted partisans and fluctuate in number depending on the election cycle. If a constituency office also doubles as a community centre with educational programmes, or if the constituency has a separate community centre, there can be additional paid workers. Additionally, most politicians employ part-time helpers to assist in day-to-day outreach to constituents and to serve as their ears on the ground. These party workers also fluctuate in number with the cyclical highs and lows of clinic activity.

Party Operatives, Brokers and Clients

Most party workers receive a monetary stipend and, in some cases, the privilege of primary access to their politicians and to the discretionary handouts and favours they provide.[53] One politician complained, "By 2008 I had to pay campaigners . . . getting indebted in the process. I had to lobby more businesses for donations. Some of my campaigners actually mutinied for more pay! They went on strike!"[54] Another related that even when persons give free time, it is not true volunteerism because they expect the privileges of having first access to the goods and services that are disbursed.[55] By 2012, the payment of brokers, office staff, zone workers, street campaigners, signature gatherers and agitators was the norm.

Whereas the overall increase in the number of paid party workers is a lead indicator of the level of organization of clientelist networks in Belize, the expansion in the numbers and influence of brokers is particularly telling. The use of brokers, variously denoted as "bosses", "sidekicks", "captains", "street captains" and "bagmen", as trusted go-betweens has increased since the 1990s. Politicians, especially incumbents, who have access to more resources and are subject to more demands from constituents tend to use multiple brokers. Politicians who have large constituencies with many small communities, such as Toledo West and Stann Creek West, tend to use more brokers to facilitate reaching constituents. Brokers in the Belize context are generally the overall managers of constituency operations, including the office and its staff, the administration of zone workers and communications with citizens. A notable feature of broker–politician relationships in Belize is the high proportion of brokers who double as the drivers and personal assistants of politicians. Of the twenty-three active politicians from the major political parties who were interviewed for this study, most employed broker-drivers, even if they used multiple brokers. At times when their politician bosses are in power, these broker-drivers often become the official drivers and trusted personal aides of elected representatives, as paid public officers.

Brokers, the vast majority of whom are male, have attracted public attention for their levels of political access and for the possessions they acquire over a short period of time. Brokers are highly aware and can even be boastful of the influence they wield.[56] As one shared, "I am the chief cook and bottle washer . . . driver, security, lead campaigner, confidant, liaison and overall zone commander for the boss. I know the voters better than him. I even do clinics on his behalf."[57] Another stated, "I am his right-hand man, his main contact with the people and without me he couldn't operate. I get 80–90 [phone] calls a day from people wanting something. People know my role as having his ear and come to me directly."[58] Yet another confessed, "People flock me everywhere like I am Santa. I have the power to decide to take up a case or not. The people have high demands and sometimes they accuse me of blocking them. It's hard work."[59] Brokers confirmed that their politician bosses gave them varying degrees of authority to dispense cash, resources or favours on their behalf. Overall, they indicated that the amount of responsibility a politician delegates depends on the personal style, time availability, the geographical spread of the constituency and the availability of resources to dispense.

As much as the increased use of brokers has accompanied the overall expansion of political clinic operations, the majority of Belizean politicians still maintain a high personal profile in their constituencies. Not only do they want to ensure that their constituents are aware of "who" exactly is helping them, but their constituents also expect direct personal communication with them in the context of Belize's small size. Although the average numbers of voters per constituency had increased from around two thousand in 1981 to over five thousand in 2011, it remained relatively easy for a politician to maintain a high degree of visibility and operate a highly personalized political clinic network. Indeed, the conventional wisdom is that politicians circumvent regular, visible presence in their constituencies at their own peril.

That being so, most politicians interviewed for this study complained of being overwhelmed and often frustrated by the time and resource demands of dealing with constituents' requests for assistance, and indicated that they devise ways to cope, including creating excuses. Many, especially outside of election time, avoid public places such as restaurants and clubs, or go to ones far from their constituencies. Some grumbled that some clients gather outside their homes in early mornings or late evenings, and that they design ways to dodge them. One politician kept a second "secret" office outside his constituency in order to avoid such harassment. Another lamented, "It all makes the work of politicians distasteful . . . you have a constant flow of requests and people wherever you are. In my last stint, my motto was 'high visibility but minimal contact'. It is frustrating! I used to leave my house before 6:00 am just to avoid people who would come there . . . and I sometimes hide out for long hours with friends or family before going home at night."[60]

In the months leading up to general and local elections, politicians increase their presence in the constituencies and hold more clinic days, hire more party workers, and disperse more money and handouts. A common feature of constituency-based handout politics around election time is that politicians host special events in which large-value items such as house lots and loans are distributed publicly or raffled at gatherings of constituents. Outside of election campaigns, there are also spikes of higher clientelist activity in the normal course of a year. The key periods are around Easter holidays, the start of the school year, Mother's Day and Christmas. It has become the norm for politicians to deliver gift packages (such as food, toys and school supplies), throw constituency parties and organize special vacation or shopping trips around these dates. These "bashments" generally include free transportation, raffles, gifts, and free or subsidized food and drinks, and tend to be more elaborate in Belize City and other urban areas than in rural areas. The annual Christmas party in the UDP Mesopotamia constituency of the former representative, Michael Finnegan, became so well known for its generous handouts that it even made the national news. In December 2010 a television news station reported on the lavish Christmas party in Mesopotamia at which seventeen hundred gift packages (including hams and turkeys) and seventeen hundred plates of food were given out.[61] The figure 1,700 represented 47.1 per cent of the then 3,610 registered voters (as at August 2010) in Mesopotamia, and above the total number of households in that constituency.

Additionally, and as noted, intra-party candidate conventions, which were once mostly uneventful and predictable "crowning of the chosen" affairs, have evolved in the past decade to become extremely competitive and expensive contests. For example, the 2001 contest for the PUP Pickstock division to replace the retiring George Price is often singled out for being one of the most expensive intra-party fights since independence to that time. Godfrey Smith, who defeated a nephew of Price at the convention, revealed that his campaign cost approximately $500,000 in the six-month period leading to the convention.[62] It is at the level of party conventions that aspiring politicians are baptized into the game of handout politics. Aspirants who are challenging incumbents of the party in government and do not have ready access to public resources and political clinic networks are disadvantaged. Yet there has been a gradual trend in the past decade of more incumbents facing increasingly aggressive challenges from new, and sometimes well-funded, aspirants. Some constituents welcome hard-fought party conventions in their constituencies as they know that opportunities for handouts will spike. As one Pickstock resident put it during the 2011 UDP convention season, "I hope somebody run against Sedi [the incumbent] for UDP [convention] so that blue notes could flow. Or else we have to wait for 'general' [elections]."[63]

The process of constituents communicating needs to politicians of either party, albeit informal, is now well institutionalized. Most citizens gather information on what is available and can be requested from politicians through neighbours, the politicians' offices, brokers and other party workers, government offices, and through the media. Thereafter, the most established way to communicate the need is to see a politician personally through the weekly clinic system or to communicate with a broker. If the politicians are representatives whose party is in power, they may be visited at their official government offices. On occasions, but especially around election time, politicians and their staff do house-to-house visits, providing opportunities for constituents to communicate requests directly. Other means of communication include zone meetings, letters, emails, telephone calls and, increasingly, text messaging. Indeed, active politicians indicate that cell phones are increasingly used by some constituents to make and follow-up on requests.

One novel request mechanism since the late 1990s is through the now ubiquitous live morning call-in radio shows, most of which are also televised. Citizens who feel they are not getting a need or want met, especially after failing through the clinic system, call these live radio shows to make personal requests for goods and services of specific politicians. This is akin to a public calling-out and shaming of politicians by constituents, which, in a small country context, increases the pressure to respond. Indeed, politicians have increasingly responded – especially if persons call repeatedly to multiple talk shows. Politicians or their staff monitor these call-in talk shows on a regular basis and assess if responses are needed. Sometimes, the politicians' staff or the politicians themselves call the radio shows either to make denials, give advice to the complainant on how to get assistance or publicly commit to "fix" particular personal situations.

A flip side of this public mode of communicating individual needs and wants is that, in some cases, a politician may stop or decrease a handout that a complaining caller is already receiving, in effect, using the radio as a means of monitoring client compliance. For example, one woman expressed fear that if she called the radio station to complain about not getting promised funds for housing repairs, her representative might stop the regular payment of her electricity bill.[64] As such, the call-in show has become a novel and more public forum for the playing out of the handout game.

Numbers and Profiles of Clients

It is always a difficult challenge to estimate total numbers of citizens engaged in political clientelism with a high degree of accuracy, especially in a qualitative study. Even in quantitative surveys, polling past or future behaviour on an informal and, often, illegal activity is problematic, as some respondents may not be forthcoming or honest about such behaviour. Additionally, not only do politicians and clients negotiate exchanges of resources, favours and support in numerous and often secretive ways, but most politicians in Belize claimed to keep no records or did not allow access to them.[65] Yet, while acknowledging the limitations, it is possible to roughly assess the numerical extent of political clientelism based on both the limited polling available and on estimates from politicians themselves.

A survey by the Society for the Promotion of Education and Research (SPEAR) in 2005 included a question related to political clientelism: "Would you vote for a political party because of monetary and other financial benefits?" SPEAR reported that 31.8 per cent of the 387 persons polled said yes.[66] In the AmericasBarometer regional poll of 2010, 17.1 per cent of 1,504 Belizeans surveyed answered "sometimes" to the question: "Has a candidate or someone from a political party offered you something like a favour, food, or any other benefit or thing in return for your vote?"[67] Apart from these being different questions, vote trading, as conceptualized for this study, is also only one sub-category of political clientelism. Yet these poll results do indicate a significant level of incidence of vote trading and vote-trading intent in 2005 and in 2010.

Another approach to assess numbers is to ask the politician patrons themselves how many (different) constituents come to them on a weekly basis to make or follow up on an individual request, including visits to clinics, official offices, homes and/or other contact. The twenty-three active politicians interviewed for this study gave estimates that ranged from one hundred and eighty to two hundred and seventy persons per week, with an average of around two hundred per week. This would be the equivalent of approximately eight hundred and sixty persons per month per constituency (200 × 4.3 weeks in an average month). With an average of 5,231 registered voters per constituency in August 2010, 860 clients represented approximately 16.5 per cent of all registered constituents. Clearly, this estimate would only capture those persons who interact with politicians in a constituency clinic situation, and, as illustrated, there are some citizens who do not go to clinics to negotiate favours from their politicians. Interestingly, when asked to directly estimate the proportion of their constituents who participate in handout politics in some way, the responses from the active politicians ranged from 25 to 30 per cent – likely an estimate that better captures more of those who do not attend clinics.

With the caveats and challenges of estimating client numbers acknowledged, the available poll numbers combined with estimates offered by politicians provide some insight into the number of clients as a proportion of total numbers of registered voters. My analysis of political clientelism in Belize will proceed from a likely cautious but reasonable estimate that around 20 per cent and up to 25 per cent of the electorate was involved, to some degree, in clientelist politics around 2010 and going into the

2012 general elections. Just using the lower range of 20 per cent of the total electorate of 162,150 in August 2010, would be approximately 32,430. With an average of 5,231 registered voters per constituency at that time, 20 per cent would be approximately 1,046 persons per constituency. Considering that constituency elections can be won by margins of hundreds and even tens of votes, client numbers of 1,046 per constituency are highly significant for all matters related to clientelist politics, and especially for election outcomes.

What of the characteristics of the "political clientele"? Client age ranges seem to generally mirror the structure of the age demographic in the 2010 population census: 20.2 per cent in the 15–24 age range,[68] and 40 per cent in the 25–64 age range.[69] However, in terms of gender, there was unanimous agreement among interviewees that women, who make up 49.5 per cent of the population, utilize the clinics in larger numbers than men. Estimates provided by interviewees ranged from 55 per cent to as high as 75 per cent. The responses revealed that, whereas women make more requests for basic and immediate needs and for items with smaller monetary value (such as utility bills, paying the rent, medicines, food for the day/week), men are more likely to request larger-value items and items related to individual needs (such as assistance with getting weed whackers, cars, money for entertainment and so forth). Several politicians related that women are easier to deal with because they ask for less in terms of monetary value, do so in a less threatening manner, and are more likely to accept delays and excuses.

In terms of ethnicity, the majority of clients in a particular constituency tend to be members of the ethnic group that constitutes the majority in that constituency, but general needs and requests were largely similar across ethnic groups. However, there are some noteworthy differences in the kind of requests that persons from different ethnic groups prioritize. Most of these differences derive from geographic location and the economic activities relevant to specific constituencies. For example, Belize City politicians report that Creoles tend to make more requests for money and to meet immediate needs, while Latino immigrants tend to make more request for assistance with residency issues and productive inputs. The examples most often cited of the latter are requests for gardening and carpentry equipment. Mestizo or Maya clients in areas with agricultural activities tend to make more requests for land and agricultural inputs. The active politicians interviewed also indicate that persons with Mestizo and Maya ethnicities, especially new immigrants, are more apt to approach them in organized groups, and not only as individuals.

Apart from the historical geographic clustering of ethnic groups, the major groups (Creole, Garifuna, Maya, East Indian and Mestizo) have all formed ethnic councils, mostly in the post-independent period. Some observers have argued that one of the intended functions of these councils is to improve access to resources for particular ethnic groups. For example, J. Palacio suggested, "The Garifuna and the Maya are using ethnicity as a method of inserting themselves into the new Belizean nation thereby being able to extract socio-economic benefits for themselves and their progeny."[70] The most notable recent example of this is the successful legal claim (based on ancestral rights) of a coalition of Maya groups for communal land rights in the Toledo district.

There was strong consensus among all politicians interviewed that "the poor" made up the majority of the clients who visited their clinics, but also that the number of middle-class clients has been steadily increasing. Most also indicate that middle-class clients are more likely than the poor to use means other than the constituency-based clinic to make requests. For example, they may make direct contact with the politicians outside of clinic days, by letters or telephone calls and visits to the official offices of those politicians who are representatives and ministers. Even though there is agreement among politicians that the number of "opportunistic" clients has been increasing, they concur that most people are genuinely in need of assistance. Indeed, the vast majority of these politicians, as did those of the Price era, sought to justify most of their giving of handouts and favours as helping needy people. The challenge is to be able to distinguish the two types and to minimize the freeloaders, and politicians admit to giving inducements to persons they know are opportunistic, especially around the time of party conventions, national elections and the aforementioned annual periods of heightened demand.

Another insight from the interviews is that seasoned clients tend to be somewhat more active in political activities than non-clients, and seem to be more informed about constituency activities and attend more partisan events. Likewise, the AmericasBarometer poll on vote buying found "strong evidence that, considering the Latin American and Caribbean regions as a whole, the more civically and politically engaged a person is, the more likely she is to report being offered a material benefit in exchange for her vote".[71] In Belize, clientelist politicians clearly target those more likely to vote; and clients and potential clients who are more engaged are likely more successful at maximizing their clientelist opportunities.

Goods and Services Offered and Requested

Since independence, the types and volumes of public and private goods and services that are offered and requested in political clinic networks have also expanded. Politicians and citizens alike indicate that the specific types of tradables now include almost every divisible good and service imaginable. As one politician noted, "By the time I ran in 2003, people wanted almost everything really . . . computers, cement blocks, sand, money for utility bills . . . everything."[72] A collation of these responses, as depicted in table 3, allows for a comprehensive, albeit not exhaustive, listing and sub-categorizing of the types of goods and services offered and demanded around the time of the general election of 2012 and into 2013.

As around the time of independence, the primary resources requested and delivered three decades later were still land, housing, jobs, school fees, healthcare, payment of utility bills and money for various purposes. Whereas a few of the categories, such as durable goods, vacations and immigration assistance, are "new" compared to 1981, the major difference lies in the extent to which the categories are increasingly stratified. With regard to bills, not only have the type of bills expanded, but politicians reported that they now pay a larger proportion of these or even the entire bills. This suggests that the overall volume of the exchange has also expanded significantly alongside the increase in types and number of sub-categories of tradables since 1981.

Although direct cash transfers to individuals and letters of reference remain popular, politicians have devised transfer mechanisms of increasing sophistication. One mode, used when there has to be some semblance of accountability, is to reach agreements with private suppliers and service providers to transfer resources indirectly to particular individuals. Clients may receive letters of permission or supply vouchers from politicians, then take these to the suppliers and receive the agreed resources. As an example, one informant described how a pharmacy provided medicines to constituents on presentation of such letters and then sent bills for payment as directed by the politicians.[73] In this case, monthly bills were sent by this pharmacy to an office in the then ministry of health for payment.

This "voucher" mechanism is used mostly for distributing more expensive and durable items such as building materials, but it is also used for apparently innocuous purposes, such as the daily distribution of tortillas.[74] Some politicians prefer to take personal bills from clients, for such things as utilities, rent and loan payments, and organize for these to be paid indirectly on behalf of constituents. These more indirect means of delivering handouts provide some degree of monitoring control for politicians and can also expand their opportunities to tap into a wider variety of public funds.

Table 3. Categorization of Goods and Services Provided by Politicians, Approximately 2013

Category	Specific Resources
Employment	Permanent government jobs, temporary government jobs, project jobs and private sector jobs
Land	Residential lots, farm land, land for commerce and land for speculation
Official appointments	Official public offices, statutory bodies and foreign postings
Houses and building materials	Houses, housing repair, landfill, cement, construction sand and gravel, lumber, roofing materials, floor tiles and others
Medical assistance	Doctors' fees, medicines, medical travel, medical procedures and hospital costs
Educational assistance	School fees, textbooks, school bags, uniforms, scholarships and transportation
Utility and other recurrent bills	Water, electricity, telephone, mobiles, internet, cable television, cooking gas and house rent
Durable goods	Stoves, refrigerators, washing machines, bicycles, gardening tools and cars
Infrastructure	Electrification, roads and drainage
Staples	Basic staples, grocery bills, one-off meals and gift baskets
Transport	Airline, bus and boat fares
Official loans/grants	For housing, small businesses, projects, social security and loan repayments
Fee exemptions	Import duties, trade licences, liquor licences, tax holidays and land tax
Nationality and immigration assistance	Passports, work permits, residency papers, nationality papers and voters' registration
Legal support	Legal advice, intervention with the police and payment of bail fees
Personal support and advice	Weddings, funerals, baptisms, graduations, birthdays, Mother's Day and relationship problems
Government contracts and other patronage	Supplies, building, roadworks, cleaning and other services, and media advertisements
Entertainment	Alcoholic beverages, concert tickets and sporting events tickets
Recommendations and referrals	For almost every good and service
Other cash transfers	Miscellaneous

Sources: News reports and interviews conducted by author with politicians, brokers and citizens.

Another significant change in the nature of the clientelist exchange since 1981 is the noticeable decrease in requests for collective and non-targeted goods and services as the number of requests for individual and targeted goods and services has grown. One politician captured the overall sentiment well when he said, "In 1989, the people wanted you to assist with things like job creation, health care, education and housing – for the division as a whole. If we fast-forward to 2008, it's a totally different world. People were now asking 'What have you done for *me* lately?' It became all me, me, me . . . the individual."[75] One politician related, "I did do some division-wide community projects such as drains, libraries, a sport field and park. But these were not as appreciated by most people. They wanted to receive things personally."[76] Another told the story of organizing a backyard session to try to get his constituents to apply for technical vocational classes at the vocational and technical institute. He related that people did show up and did listen, but most did not sign up for classes and most queued afterwards for food and drinks and to appeal for cash handouts.[77]

When asked what they expect from their local politicians, most constituents expressed the desire for immediate and individually targeted goods and services. A constituent in Belize City expressed a common sentiment when she said, "Yes, I believe that he [the politician] should give me stuff . . . like pay my rent and light bill. That's why we vote for him. They promise this . . . and they have the money that they thief."[78] Accusations that politicians steal and enrich themselves as justification for them giving back to the people was a common thread in constituents' responses. Overall, appeals for collective goods such as streets, drains, employment generation and skills training were very much in the minority. In addition to straightforward individual handouts at clinics, some politicians do provide various levels of constituency-level community development activities aimed at particular disadvantaged groups. These activities range from the more common one-off training events and irregular workshops to the much rarer comprehensive and longer-term educational programmes.

One of the few notable examples of a longer-term educational programme is the Samuel Haynes Institute for Excellence (SHIE), initiated by a former minister, Wilfred Elrington, who represented the Pickstock constituency in Belize City. At the time of my visit in 2010, the SHIE was conducting a variety of regular educational and training sessions for some 200 children, unemployed youth, women and men in such areas as remedial education, homework assistance, textile arts, computer instruction and gardening. The relatively large complex in a poor neighbourhood was built on public land through private donations and was receiving international grant funding for several of its programmes. Yet one feature that the SHIE shared with similar constituency-based programmes was that it doubled as the representative's political constituency office that hosted weekly political clinics, making it inevitable that partisan and community development work overlapped. The staff of these politician-initiated community programmes often receive salaries or stipends that come from public funds outside of the constituency stipend.

Political Support from Citizens

As noted, this study assumes a broad conceptualization of "political support" that includes activities and political relationships that transcend election campaigns and voting. In the Belize case, the findings show that the ways in which clients promise or provide political support have also expanded. Table 4 summarizes the key types of political support provided by clients around 2013, based on the triangulation of information from interviews, news reports and observation. The fact that most of these seventeen types of political support are "ongoing" activities and not limited to election periods is testament to the year-round and day-to-day nature of the practice of political clientelism in Belize today.

Several of these types of political support were negligible in 1981, including that of transferring to another constituency. The Representation of the People Act requires Belizeans to register in the constituencies they reside and officially transfer constituencies with the Elections and Boundaries Department (EBD) when they move residence. However, it has become common practice for politicians to seek electoral advantage by working around this requirement. In return for transferring to a constituency in which they do not reside or not transferring when they move out of a constituency, voters can receive various forms of compensation from instigating politicians. There is an annual opportunity for official challenges to be made to the voters' list based on inaccurate residency status information. However, such abuses are so widespread that it is challenging for the EBD, with limited resources, to pursue most cases. The onus is therefore on political opponents of the other party to monitor their opponents' registering and transferring activities, and, in this, the incumbent party generally has some advantage. This often leads to allegations and counter-allegations of fraud by politicians. For example, in September 2011 the PUP candidate for Port Loyola charged that the UDP incumbent was "padding the election list . . . [by] the fraudulent transfer of over 140 persons in Port Loyola who have not lived in the division for even

Table 4. Key Types of Political Support Given or Promised to Politicians, Approximately 2013

Types of Political Support
1. Voting or not voting in party, national and/or local elections
2. Promise of voting in party, national and/or local elections
3. Registering to vote
4. Transferring or not transferring to another constituency
5. Providing assistance to constituency-based operators
6. Attending partisan conventions and meetings
7. Attending partisan marches and protests
8. Providing protection and security support to politicians
9. Providing intelligence/information on other constituents
10. Committing acts of mischief against opposing parties/candidates
11. Providing public solidarity and crowd support to politicians
12. Wearing party colours and displaying posters on property
13. Writing letters and making statements to the media
14. Calling in to a talk show to support or oppose an issue or person
15. Campaigning for candidates
16. Collecting signatures for partisan petitions
17. Donating funds to politicians

Sources: Interviews conducted with politicians, brokers and citizens, and newspaper stories.

a single day".[79] He also accused the EBD of not processing the objections in a timely manner, which resulted in them not being heard in court.[80] The candidate for the PUP side laid similar accusations.

Also new to the list of types of political support (compared to 1981) is the recent trend of clients being rewarded to make calls to live radio and television shows to support or oppose a particular politician, party or issue. During periods of heightened partisan activity, this produces a snowball effect as both major parties compete for getting in calls to these shows. The "renting of a crowd" by creating incentives, such as food, drinks, cash and other handouts, to attend partisan rallies or civil protests is also now ubiquitous, and both parties routinely accuse the other of this practice. In one such instance, a 2011 news item reported on allegations that constituents of a particular minister were being rallied to attend a public House Committee consultation to show their support for the government's position on a constitutional amendment.[81] Not denying the allegation totally, the minister pointed to the past assistance he had given to his constituents – suggesting that such political support was, indeed, to be expected in exchange.[82]

The inclusion of "donating funds to politicians" as a type of political support is based on the finding that just as persons of different income levels request different benefits, they also provide different types of political support. For example, apart from votes, middle-class clients may provide technical skills or manage a particular zone for a politician and, in return, receive primary access to scholarship assistance for their children or import duty exemption on a car. Similarly, wealthy individuals who donate funds to a politician or political party may also receive, in return, favours or promises of favours from politicians. One operative used a colourful analogy to describe these various income-based types of clientelist exchanges:

> It's like a feeding frenzy in which there are bottom-feeders, middle-feeders and top-feeders. The bottom-feeders are the majority – the voters, poorer class – who get as much as they can. They compete for the crumbs, and election time is especially their time. The middle-feeders are the middle-class folks who get special favours – like a second piece of land, scholarships, tax-free imports and so on. The top-feeders are the individuals and business donors who fund campaigns and grease the wheels of the feeding frenzy. Of course, they expect a return on their investment many times fold.[83]

The interviews with politicians and clients additionally indicated that, since independence, both have honed their skills at negotiating the content of the clientelist exchange. It was more common for a politician to offer assistance to the family as a household unit in the 1990s, but by 2008, a growing number of households were negotiating with politicians based on the number of individual voters in the home or family. One politician recounted, "One person actually came to me saying 'I have twelve voters in my house. Give us $100 each and you'll have our vote'."[84] On the other side of the coin, a single mother in the Pickstock constituency who claimed not to be getting enough attention from politicians lamented, "The politician they stupid because I have six votes [in my house] that I can deliver for them. If they give me a house and fix up each of us . . . any of them can get the votes . . . but they have to deliver."[85] Such sentiments confirm that citizens know that their votes can be bartered or auctioned to willing politicians in a context in which handout politics is such a big game in town.

A Very Pricey Game

The informal and sometimes illicit nature of clientelist practices complicate assessments of the monetary values of handouts. Clearly, if the numbers of clients increase, and if the types and volume of resources given as handouts increase, then the total monetary value also must grow. One former politician contended, "The bulk of political financing is consumed even before elections roll around . . . on funerals, graduation, textbooks, summer programmes for children, house rent, medical bills, utility bills and home repairs."[86] Examples of amounts that politicians report paying for include $300 per semester for school fees, $40 for monthly cable television, $30 for weekly cell phone top-ups and $100–$200 for birthday gifts. By 2012, politicians reported that the "going rate" for direct cash transfers for miscellaneous purposes averaged $100–$300 per month per client outside of election campaign periods. The interviews also provided some insights on overall costs. Fourteen of the twenty-three active politicians interviewed for this study agreed to estimate the monthly financial costs of constituency clinic operations in a non-election year. The conservative estimates they provided ranged from $6,000 to $15,000 per month per constituency, with an overall average of around $9,000. This figure was derived by adding the estimates from the politicians and dividing by fourteen (the number who agreed to provide estimates). It is likely that some of the lower figures given are deliberate underestimates. For example, one politician claimed to be spending significantly less per month on clinic operations than his monthly constituency transfer from the government for constituency support. Using these monthly estimates to calculate a rough annual estimate, the range could be at least around $72,000 to $180,000 per constituency per year, or a mean average of approximately $108,000 per year.

Clearly, the expenditure for clinic operations expands dramatically in an election year. One study estimated that the average cost of a constituency campaign in Belize increased from $50,000 at independence to over $900,000 in 2005.[87] A former politician estimated that his 2008 election campaign cost over $1 million.[88] When asked what a politician actually expends per vote they received in the course of an average constituency campaign, responses from active politicians ranged from $200 to $400. These estimates would amount to some $500,000–1,000,000 per constituency when an average of 2,500 registered voters (half of the average total in a constituency at the time) is employed.

Apart from the costs of handouts to voters, politicians spend campaign funds on other expenses, not the least of which is advertising. Yet the estimates of election year expenditure figures provide further indication of the huge amounts of funds needed for clientelist operations. Just using conservative estimates that politicians provided for a non-election year ($72,000–$180,000 per constituency per year, or an average of approximately $108,000 per year), and assuming that fifty-five constituency clinics are operational, the total annual expenditures for nationwide clinic operations would range from $3.96 million to $9.90 million per year, with an estimated average of approximately $5.94 million per year.

Demands on representatives and political candidates to procure adequate financing to make their clinic networks competitive are clearly enormous. So, where do the funds come from? Politicians unanimously concurred that there are three usual basic sources: their own personal funds, private financing and public resources. Overall, the interviews suggest that personal financing, which was a key source before the 1990s, has decreased dramatically. Most active politicians informed that use of personal funds was minimal, and several claimed that they never touch their own money. One former politician, who did use his own funds, lamented that "it bled me" and that he considered this one of the key reasons he left electoral politics.[89] A minority of others who conceded that they used substantial amounts of personal funds tended to be independently wealthy or newbies to electoral politics.

On the other hand, there was strong agreement that other private funding of clinic networks has skyrocketed since independence. Not surprisingly, politicians were generally reluctant to discuss specific private funding sources, preferring to use generic terms such as "friends", "business colleagues" and "wealthy supporters". One former politician said, "In terms of private donations, there are two groups of donors: the 'big ten' richest ones and the thousands of smaller donors. . . . Big donors also give to the party, and then the party shares this among candidates at election time based in part on the size of their constituencies."[90] As do many keen observers of Belizean politics, the former politician (referring to the period before 2010) singled out Lord Ashcroft and Sir Barry Bowen as being among the top donors in the "big ten". Bowen, who died in 2010, owned majority interests in Bowen & Bowen Ltd and was one of Belize's richest nationals. Over the years, Bowen & Bowen's business interests have expanded from bottling (soft drinks and beer) to a variety of other areas, including shipping, transportation, real estate, hospitality, automotive, agro-industry and energy.

Apart from Ashcroft and Bowen, the bigger donors included national and foreign owners of the larger companies in import-based merchandising, in the agricultural-export sector, in the tourism sector and in the financial services sector. Smaller business interests, including more recent Indian and Taiwanese investors, also engage in "donations for favours" relationships with political parties. Additionally, there has been speculation that foreign investors in the oil sector (post-2005) have also made campaign contributions and that some proceeds from the drug trade have also entered the realm of political party and politician financing.[91] As to be expected, a small number of business entities are known to be more linked to one or the other political party, but the conventional wisdom is that the majority of larger private donors have contributed to both parties over time. This account of the sources for private funds is corroborated by the finding of a study that found that the millions of dollars required for national campaigns come largely from a small number of big business donors.[92] The pertinent point is that some of these private funds, whether they are donated during or outside of campaign periods, help to fund clientelist politics. In this regard, former prime minister Esquivel was sober in his reflection: "Patronage is dependent on the finances and financial bribery of the very rich few. This was once minimal but is now huge. These unelected few decide much of the actions of government."[93]

Public funds, including those from international grants and loans, have also swelled as a key source of financing to become the primary source for incumbent politicians. The constituency stipend, a constant public funding source, was denoted "Grants to Constituencies" in annual budgets and listed under the Office of the Prime Minister in the national budgets from 2008–12. These funds are allocated on the discretion of the cabinet, and no financial reporting is required once funds have been transferred to the various bank accounts of elected representatives.[94] This is a departure from the normal accounting procedures for disbursements of public funds. For the financial year, for example, 2011–12, a total of $1.57 million was allocated as grants to constituencies in the national budget.[95] The average amount for each of the thirty-one representatives was $50,710 per year or $4,225 per month. Some representatives can receive more than this monthly amount either because larger constituencies generally receive more, certain representatives are favoured or because other budget lines are used to supplement these basic funds. For example, staff of the Collet constituency office in 2011, which doubled as an educational centre, was also on the payroll of the Ministry of Education, and the monthly rental for this centre/office also came from this ministry's budget.[96]

Additionally, since the 1990s there has been a trend towards increasing proportions of the budgets for government ministries being allocated on a discretionary basis through representatives and candidates of the ruling party. A former minister explained how this process generally works:

> The budgets of every government department and every statutory body . . . such as the Belize Tourism Board . . . are targeted and ways are found to use some of

these funds to assist your people. You lobby ministers and send over a list of your people who will get assistance. If you are on a statutory body, you create some credible sounding project for needy people and use it to help "your" people.[97]

The largest pot of such public discretionary funds has been within the budget of the Ministry of Education. The Ministry of Education receives, on average, over 20 per cent of the total annual government budget – for, example, some $192 million in fiscal year 2011–12 – and has the largest proportion of any ministry's budget that is disbursed by ministerial discretion.[98] For example, $3,168,216 was allocated as "Grants to Individuals" for secondary education in fiscal year 2011–12.[99] The cabinet and the minister of education decide how such discretionary funds are to be disbursed. For example, constituency representatives were allocated a fixed share of the ministry's discretionary budget in fiscal year 2011–12. They accessed their portions by sending a list of names to the ministry of the individuals to receive educational subsidies.[100] Although the ministry maintained that recipients were still means-tested, it did not deny that constituents need to visit their elected representatives to get on lists and to be in the system.[101] A few other ministries with smaller budgets, such as those with responsibility for housing, health and human development, also have budget lines reserved for similar kinds of discretionary spending. If not allocated directly to politicians for dispensing to individuals at the constituency level, politicians compete to ensure that they are the ones to make the decisions on exactly who in their constituencies will be on lists to receive such funds.

Assisting individual constituents from public resources comes in forms other than direct or indirect monetary transfers. Politicians from parties in power have significant discretionary influence over the distribution of public service and project jobs, and over a wide array of government resources, benefits, services, licences and fee waivers.[102] For example, the minister responsible for lands has total discretionary authority in deciding exactly who will receive land grants and leases; and the entire land distribution system, at the levels of the public service, constituencies, municipalities and villages, is influenced by appointees of the party in power.[103] Similarly, the minister of immigration can grant waivers related to certain nationality matters, the minister of local government can veto decisions on the granting of liquor licences, the minister of finance can grant certain categories of import duty exemptions and the minister of public works can influence exactly which street will get paved in a particular village or neighbourhood.

In terms of jobs, the public sector, including employees in the public service, security services, education, statutory bodies and public sector projects, is the single largest employer. In 2011, the public sector as a whole employed over 15 per cent of the total labour force, or some 20,000 workers.[104] In 2004, the public service portion (excluding 3,648 teachers)[105] had approximately 8,123 employees, of which 2,148, or 25 per cent, were estimated to be open vote workers.[106] (Open vote workers are officially defined as "an employee of any Government Department whose post is not provided for under any Personal Emoluments of any Head of Expenditure" in the annual budget.[107]) As of 31 January 2013, there were 9,031 public officers (excluding some 5,000 teachers) in the public service proper broken down as detailed in table 5.

The 2,327 open vote workers at the time represented 26 per cent of the total number of 9,031 public officers. If teachers are included and the total number of 14,031 public sector employees is used, open vote workers made up 17 per cent of total public sector employees. When the total for other non-established employees (contract plus temporary categories) of 1,155 is added to the open vote workers total, some 3,482 or 38 per cent of the public service was in the non-permanent category.[108] Overall, since the 1990s, incumbent politicians of both parties have expanded the practice of disbursing public service jobs, resources and favours in a manner that enhances their political support from people of all income levels. In particular, the increase of open vote workers as a proportion of

Table 5. Numbers of Public Service Workers by Category (January 2013)

Category	Number
Permanent establishment	5,299
Open vote	2,327
Contract	326
Temporary	829
Stipend (retired rural workers in the health and postal service)	217
National Assembly support staff	33
Total: Public officers	9,031
Teaching service employees	5,000
Total: Public sector (including teaching service employees)	14,031

Source: Chief executive officer of the Ministry of the Public Service (Communication of February 2013).

public service employees is a critical indicator of the expansion of political clientelism and of its expense to the state.

Finally, a relatively new development in the expansion of political clientelism was the gradual formal inclusion of elected representatives of the opposition as fund recipients in a limited, but not insignificant, manner. In addition to being included in the ongoing constituency stipend for all thirty-one representatives, the 2008–12 UDP government added elected PUP representatives of the opposition to at least two other significant public sector programmes. The first is the aforementioned educational assistance quota programme of the Ministry of Education, from which opposition representatives received access to funds for onward distribution to their constituents. The second is the one-off housing grant scheme administered by the Ministry of Housing in 2009–10, which disbursed $18 million of the recovered Venezuela grant funds. The basic process was like that used for educational assistance: opposition representatives received access to housing grant funds roughly proportionate to the size of their constituencies and sent names of suggested eligible recipients to the ministry for vetting and processing.[109]

On the surface, these inclusions of elected representatives of the opposition party (when they were previously excluded) may seem to reflect some degree of democratic maturity in the disbursement of selected public funds, and a small move away from divisive and spiteful partisan politics. However, they are more likely indications of the normalization of clientelist transfers, to the extent that the PUP and the UDP can sometimes reach a gentlemen's agreement to award each other similar treatment of access to some public funds for use in clinic operations when in opposition.

Conclusion

The sea change in clientelist politics from 1981 to 2013 is summarized in table 6 using the nine tracer markers prioritized for this study. In particular, the prevalence of full-time political clinics in all constituencies by both the PUP and the UDP, the high costs of these clinics, the increase in the influence of private financing, the extent to which public resources are being targeted for clientelist purposes, the percentage of citizens who have become clients, and the normality that characterizes clientelist politician–citizen relationships, all chronicle the deep entrenchment of political clientelism.

Importantly, by 2013 the profile of Belizeans as "clients" became more multilayered and overlapping. The poor remain the largest proportion, but

Table 6. Comparative Status of Political Clientelism in 1981 and in 2013

Tracer Marker	Status in 1981	Status in 2013
Number and geographical spread of political clinics	Few regular ones aside from the two Price clinics. Most others were campaign related and temporary in nature.	Some fifty-five regular year-round clinics by both parties in the thirty-one constituencies and sixty-two at election time. Most operate daily and have paid staff and brokers. Clinic activity is a common feature of intra-party conventions.
Number and profiles of clients	Difficult to assess, but relatively few and mostly limited to urban areas and especially Belize City.	Twenty to 25 per cent of a constituency is estimated to be involved in clientelist relationships. Although all groups are represented, the majority are poor and over 50 per cent are women.
Types of and volume of goods and services going to clients	Jobs, agricultural land, house lots, house construction and repairs, healthcare and educational assistance, microcredit, as well as small amounts of monies for basic daily needs.	In addition to the 1981 list, almost every good and service is tradable (see table 3), and there are more categories and sub-categories.
Monetary value of goods and services	Difficult to assess, but estimated to be limited. Direct cash transfers were mostly under $15 per person[a] and election campaign costs were mostly below $10,000.	Per month clinic operational costs in a non-election year are estimated to be at least $9,000. This estimate does not include the value of most resources coming from public sources. Constituency campaigns are estimated to cost around $1,000,000 and cash transfers range from $100 to $300 per person.

(Continued)

Table 6. (Continued)

Tracer Marker	Status in 1981	Status in 2013
Types of political support going to politician	Largely limited to party membership, attending rallies, voting, voluntary support and wearing party colours at election time.	Seventeen options are identified in table 4. The majority are ongoing and transcend election campaign periods. Volunteering is negligible as most party workers are paid in cash or in-kind.
Extent of distribution of public resources for party/clientelist purposes	The practice was clearly observable countrywide, but relatively it was limited in comparison to non-targeted allocation. The constituency stipend was established as a source of handout funds.	This practice became rampant and increasingly institutionalized. Almost every ministry and statutory body has a fund, programme or authority that is used to direct resources and favours as rewards or inducements to constituents of representatives. This practice has also spread to the local government.
Ratio of permanent/temporary public service jobs	Less than 2 per cent were in the open vote category.	Approximately 26 per cent of public service jobs (excluding teachers) were in the open vote category.
Extent of references to clientelism in news stories and other documents	News reports were very rare and mostly focused on reporting on court cases. References in academic studies were scarce.	News reporting is regular and voluminous. Academic references are more numerous but still limited. References in official reports are significant.
Number of alleged cases of voter bribery taken to court	Five cases before independence.	One case between 1981 and 2011. Two cases in 2012.

[a]Based on inflation figures that averaged 3.4 per cent per year between 1980 and 2010, $15 would be worth around $30 in 2010.

the number of middle-class clients has grown. Although clientelist politics have continued to transcend gender, ethnicity, race, religion and geography, Latino immigrants and their children became a significant "new" proportion of clients, and the proportion of women has grown. Moreover, as client numbers have increased overall, the distinction between an inner core of more seasoned, habitual clients and an outer core of more transient clients became more noticeable. As the proportion of the electorate participating in informal clientelist relationships has expanded, so has the sophistication of their "grassroots diplomacy" to barter political support for resources.[110]

By the time of the seventh post-independence election in 2012, it was patently clear that astute politicians in both the PUP and UDP agreed that "a politician would be a fool if he did not feel that, in return for trying to help, he will try to extract loyalty and political support. The fact is that whether he gets that support or not, he has to try."[111] Handout politics had become so entrenched that not playing the game guarantees electoral defeat in a constituency, and by extension, in a general election. In small constituencies, which can often be won by margins of well under one hundred votes, getting at least one thousand of five thousand voters to promise their political support is, on balance, worth all the effort when winning is the core goal of the game. Taken altogether, the evidence narrated in this chapter confirms the rampant expansion and entrenchment of political clientelism in Belize in the 1990s and thereafter. In short, political clientelism shifted from being a quaint and occasional electoral tactic used by pre-independence politicians to an ever-present feature of daily political life.

5.

Fuelling the Expansion

A Perfect Storm

By its thirtieth anniversary of independence, Belize had witnessed a first decade of slow growth of political clientelism, followed by two decades of its exponential expansion and deepening entrenchment. The rapid expansion after the 1990s transpired in a context of evermore striking democratic contradictions. On the one hand, Belize continued to garner international praise for its electoral and procedural successes as a liberal democracy. Free and fair elections in 1993, 1998, 2003 and 2008, with average voter turnout of over 75 per cent, were split equally between the PUP and UDP. Strong civil society organizations initiated intense debate and some legal reforms of Belize's inherited Westminster parliamentary system. Moreover, Belize continued to avoid ethnic-based party politics, while integrating tens of thousands of immigrants, and exhibited a generally sound record on the protection of civil liberties.

On the other hand, several worrying trends in Belize's practise of democracy have intensified since the 1980s. A spate of national assessments of governance exposed growing concerns about democratic practices in Belize.[1] These include concerns about the increasing centralization and politicization of government institutions, the entrenchment of "tribally" competitive two-party politics, higher rates of public corruption, the total absence of laws to regulate campaign financing, weakened public service institutions and, of course, voter bribery.

Having illustrated how political clientelism expanded in Belize since the 1990s, I now turn to exploring the reasons why. In this chapter, I show how the legacies of the pre-independence context converged with new developments in the Westminster political system and in social and economic relations to fuel the rapid expansion of political clientelism since the early 1990s.

Demographic Considerations

Belize's relatively rapid population growth – from 189,392 in 1990 to 240,204 in 2000 and 312,698 in 2010 – had practical relevance for the trajectory of political clientelism. The average population per electoral constituency increased from about 6,750 in 1990 to 10,100 in 2010, and the average number of registered voters per constituency, which was around 2,300 at the time of the first post-independence election in 1984, grew from some 3,000 in 1990 to 5,231 in 2010.[2] This growth does not diminish the fact that even the average of 5,231 is relatively tiny (in international context) and so supportive of highly personalized political relationships. Yet larger constituency populations translate into more potential voters, more potential hands for benefits and, therefore, the need for more money and other resources for clientelist networks.

As the overall population was increasing, Belize's ethnic mix also continued to undergo significant changes, as illustrated in table 7.

The most notable of these shifts was the further proportional decrease in the Creole population (from 40 per cent in 1980, to 30 per cent in 1991, to 21 per cent in 2010) and the concurrent increase in the Mestizo population (from 33 per cent, to 44 per cent, to 50 per cent, respectively). Higher emigration rates in the 1980s, mostly to the United States, and lower birth rates among Creoles contributed to the decrease in their share of the population.[3] However, the other significant reason for the change in the ethnic mix was the surge in immigration from other Central America states in the 1980s and 1990s. Although political immigration slowed by

Table 7. Belize Population Breakdown by Ethnicity, 1980–2010, by Percentage of Population Share

Ethnic Group	1980	1991	2000	2010
Creole	40	30	25	21
Mestizo	33	44	48	50
Maya	10	11	11	10
Garifuna	8	7	6	5
East Indian	2	3	3	3
Mennonite	3	3	4	4
Other	4	2	3	
Mixed Ethnicity				6

Sources: Central Statistical Office (1981) for 1980, Statistical Institute of Belize (2012, 27) for 1991 and 2000, and Statistical Institute of Belize (2011, 2–3) for 2010.
Note: Figures are rounded to match rounded figures from 1991 and 2000 and do not add exactly to one hundred for all years. "Other" includes Caucasian and Chinese, among others. The labels "Creole" and "Mestizo" refer to mixed ethnicities and create some ambiguity in self-identifying during census surveys. "Mixed Ethnicity" was added as a label for the first time in the 2010 census.

the 1990s, continued economic immigration contributed to the increase of Mestizos and new immigrants as proportions of the overall population. The 2010 census found that of the 14.8 per cent (46,000) of the total population that was foreign-born, 62 per cent had arrived before 2000, mostly from Guatemala, El Salvador and Honduras.[4] This figure of 46,000 foreign-born residents did not account for the tens of thousands of children born as Belizeans to the new immigrants and nor for the totality of illegal and uncounted immigration. Most immigrants settled in rural areas, which is partly why Belize stands out as one of the few countries in Central America and the Caribbean that exhibits a near fifty-fifty balance in its urban to rural population and why the rural-based population increased between 1990 and 2000. Indeed, several new communities sprung up in the west and south of the country that were made up largely of new immigrants.

Although almost all thirty-one electoral constituencies are still characterized by a clear ethnic group majority, a review of census figures by ethnicity and district indicates that by 2010 the majorities were no longer as dominant in some areas as in the 1980s.[5] This has been due in large part to internal migration of members of some ethnic groups who seek to enhance access to land, housing and jobs. Also, settlement patterns of new immigrants have resulted in some constituencies with higher proportions of Latino residents. Recent immigrants have increased as a share of the population in every constituency, especially those in the Cayo and Stann Creek districts. For example, by 2010 the Belmopan constituency, which was majority Creole in the 1980s and 1990s, had a near-equal balance between Creoles and Mestizo–Maya residents, due in large part to international and internal migration. The relevant implication for our purposes is that by the 1990s thousands of immigrants could apply for Belizean citizenship and become eligible to register as new voters. Both their numbers and their relative economic vulnerabilities ensured that they quickly became potential political clients for politicians of the main political parties.[6]

As demonstrated in the previous chapter, immigrants have indeed actively engaged in clientelist transactions in Belize, trading political support not only for the usual goods and services as Belizeans but also specifically for assistance to access work permits, residency permits and naturalizations on their way to becoming Belizeans and voters themselves. Because immigrants were not specifically targeted as a group for interviews, any discussion here about whether they were exposed and inclined to clientelist engagements in their countries of origin before arriving in Belize – and how this may have affected the development of political clientelism in Belize – can only be speculative. It is certainly an area ripe for further research. As noted in chapter 1, Guatemala, El Salvador and Honduras – the main countries of origin – all exhibit high incidences of "clientelismo", and it is likely that new immigrants from these countries were not strangers to the practice when they encountered Belizean politicians. Several Belizean politicians did inform that immigrants as a category were more apt than other clients to request assistance in organized groups, and some did speculate whether this was a practice they had brought with them. Of related interest is that politicians from (at least) El Salvador have often organized buses to transport hundreds of Salvadoran immigrants from Belize to go "home" to vote in presidential elections, a clientelist practice well-known in Central America and the Caribbean. In 2014, a president-elect of El Salvador actually made a visit to Belize before his inauguration to "express gratitude to those nationals who went home to vote for him" in a very close election result.[7]

Westminster "Belizeanized"

During the step-by-step tutelage process from internal self-government in 1964 to independence in 1981, we noted that local leaders had gained increasing and then full control of the powers of state, including all public and foreign policy. The change of government in 1984 had given the UDP a first bite at the powers of state. By 1998, after four consecutive alternations in government, the two dominant parties were well-versed in administering the extensive authority granted to political victors in the Westminster parliamentary system. In particular, the parties further perfected the art of using the political institutions under their control for partisan advantage and developed creative strategies of increasing such control at every level of government.

At the macro-political level, the vast powers of the victorious political parties and politicians in Belize are difficult to exaggerate. They include the power to influence public service appointments of key senior managers, the appointment of the majority of the executive leadership of all public institutions and statutory bodies, the administration of departments of government, the use of extensive discretionary decision-making powers, and wide authority to enact new policies and laws. In both design and practice, the electoral and governance systems are based on winner-takes-all models. The official opposition party is virtually without real power – even when winning the popular vote, but losing the election, as the PUP did in 1993. Where the constitution or a law requires that the leader of the opposition make appointments to public bodies, these all have built-in majorities for the ruling party.[8]

Despite these extensive formal powers, successive Belizean governments have devised ways to amplify their control over policymaking and resource distribution. As a case in point, it has become regular practice for the leaders of ruling parties to appoint more than half of the House of Representatives to their cabinets. For example, in 2008 former prime minister Dean Barrow appointed twenty-one of the twenty-five UDP representatives to cabinet as ministers or ministers of state – meaning that the cabinet de facto made up more than half of the thirty-one member House of Representatives.[9] Both major political parties make the convenient argument that the constitutional provision (section 41.2.a) that prohibits the appointment of more than two-thirds of the elected members in the House to the cabinet refers only to ministers and not to ministers of state. However, in practice, ministers of state sit in the cabinet and have official (often separate) ministerial portfolios.[10] One consequence of the practice is an overlapping fusion of executive and legislative powers and the emasculation of constitutionally provided parliamentary oversight. Such concentrated power at the top of the governance hierarchy facilitates wide partisan control over the formal institutions of resource allocation located in the ministries and departments of government below.

Notwithstanding that governing parties already have majority appointment powers over most key posts, parties in power have devised means to augment this authority. An instructive example is the discontinuation of the Westminster tradition of permanent secretaries as the most senior career public officers administering the ministries of government. Constitutional amendments in 2001 eliminated the post of permanent secretary and replaced it with that of chief executive officer (CEO). In practice, CEOs are contract officers serving at the pleasure of the minister and party in power, and they change with transitions of government. As intended, these critically important posts have been increasingly filled by trusted partisans who are more likely to facilitate activities related to political clientelism than were permanent secretaries under the inherited British model.

Additionally, there has been increasing control by incumbent politicians over who gets hired in the rest of the public service. Although the law requires that all permanent public service hiring be approved by the Public Service Commission (PSC), ministers do seek to influence which persons are nominated to fill posts. Such nominations are not often rejected if the persons are minimally qualified.[11] This may be, in part, why the PSC, which is appointed by the prime minister as positions become available, has itself gradually become more politicized.[12] More worrisome is the growth since the 1990s in the number of open vote and other temporary workers as a percentage of total public service officers. In this regard, a former CEO in the Ministry of the Public Service informed:

> The open vote element has, traditionally, been between 2 to 5 per cent of the permanent establishment, up to early 1990s. During this period, the Government Workers' Regulations, which governs the status of these officers, was strictly adhered to; that is, they were recruited for a specific period of time for a particular job and then released. Since the mid-1990s this has changed and the size of this category of officers has seen a steady increase.[13]

As illustrated in the previous chapter, by the end of 2012, open vote workers made up 26 per cent of the public service (excluding teachers) or 17 per cent of the public sector (including teachers).[14] When in government, both major parties have hired such non-permanent workers on short-term contracts, the majority of which are not required to go through the formal PSC employment process. As with the case of the CEOs and other contract officers, open vote workers can be subject to easy dismissal as the party in government changes and seeks to install its supporters in government jobs. Even though both major political parties engage in this practice, they lambast the incumbent party with accusations of rampant patronage and victimization when in opposition, and when in government they vigorously defend the practice. Notably, after a PUP representative in a House meeting accused the UDP government of partisan dismissals after the 2008 election, former prime minister Barrow responded with an appeal to realpolitik:

> Mr. Speaker, there are those supporters of the UDP that have [been] punished for 10 long years. They [PUP] complain that we are getting rid of open vote workers. I want to make clear that our supporters are giving us hell for not getting rid of enough of those workers . . . so that they, who have been in this punitive wilderness for 10 long years, can finally have a chance at a job and at earning a livelihood. So no apologies will be made from this side of the House.[15]

This tactic of rewarding of partisan supporters with public service jobs is also aimed at placing more trusted partisans in control of all levels of the key institutions of resource allocation. As noted, the ministries that have control over the resources that are most traded in clientelist exchanges are those responsible for education, health, housing, land, social development, immigration and public utilities. The levels of control exercised over these ministries by parties in power since independence facilitate clientelist targeting of more services and programmes to supporters and potential supporters. Within existing discretionary procedures, ministers and representatives can make or influence decisions about which constituency, community, group, or individual receives goods and services, fee waivers, and contracts.

The aforementioned immigration example highlights the extent and abuse of control that incumbent politicians have over the issuance of work permits, residency permits and naturalizations, with the aim of gaining political favour with the large immigrant community. Other examples, such as the 2011 Christmas Assistance Programme, point to the deliberate increase of control through the introduction of strategies that further increase discretionary decision-making, which facilitate clientelist practices. Even when the formal allocation systems of the government are used, the decisions on who gets what are increasingly influenced by politicians of the ruling party.[16]

Overall, the extent of control over public institutions that governing political parties exercise in Belize's practice of Westminster is akin to a "political monopoly" over resource allocations by incumbents. In Belize's intensely competitive political context, this monopoly facilitates political clientelism, as governing parties and politicians are incentivized to use or abuse the powers of state to barter public resources for political support.

Intense Party Competition

It is the grand reward of controlling the extensive powers of the state and so avoiding years of political drought in powerless opposition that is central to the competitive impetus to use political clientelism as a strategy to win elections – and to stay in power once there. As a Belizean business leader observed, "For five years one group stands outside in the cold, looking in on the feast at the trough. Come the next five years it's their turn inside and they feast gluttonously, saying all the while 'it's my turn now', and actively avenging themselves on those who once fed while starving them."[17] National control of political institutions was a necessary condition for the emergence of political clientelism, but the increase in intensity of competitive two-party politics was even more determinative in its expansion since the 1990s. As illustrated, both major parties set up increasingly elaborate, permanent and well-funded clientelist exchange networks in the 1990s with clear expectations that these would give them vote-getting advantages over opponents.

Assessments from politicians are instructive with regard to linking party competition to clientelism. A retired politician contended that "it grew because politicians had to pander more to people to win a seat after the UDP began to win elections".[18] Others stated, "I didn't like giving out money, but you have to play the game of the day to get elected";[19] and "Competition among politicians to win by using handouts causes a feeding frenzy before elections . . . and you do it for one reason: to win."[20] Former prime minister Said Musa reflected a popular view: "In increasingly competitive party politics, winning the next election becomes the biggest thing. This leads to promising too much and increasing expectations. Then it snowballs to where we are today."[21]

After the formative phase of two-party dominant politics, competitive intensity increased appreciably after the first changeover of government in 1984, and then especially rapidly after the 1989 election (see table 8). At the general election level, this trend is manifested in close results and the alternation of parties in power. Across the seven elections held between 1984 and 2012, the popular vote share was very close, with PUP averaging winning majorities of 54.4 per cent and the UDP of 52.1 per cent. As the table shows, this near parity in popular vote share was not always reflected in the number of seats won by each party, but in three elections (1989, 1993 and 2012) the seat margins themselves were thin.

There have also been high levels of competitive intensity at the level of constituencies. One study found that in 118 constituency elections for seats in the House of Representatives in the four general elections from 1993 to 2008, 35 per cent were decided by less than 10 per cent of all votes.[22] In some of these constituency elections, seats were decided by less than twenty votes. Examples include the one-vote margin in the Collet constituency in 1993, the ten-vote margin in the Cayo West constituency in 1998, and the eighteen-vote difference in both the Freetown and Corozal South East

Table 8. Post-Independence General Election Results in Belize, 1984–2012, by Winning Party, Vote Share (%), Seat Share and Voter Turnout (%)

Election Year	Winning Party	Vote Share (%)	Seat Share	Turnout (%)
1984	UDP	53.4	21–7	74.9
1989	PUP	51.2	15–13	72.6
1993	UDP	48.4	16–13	72.1
1998	PUP	59.3	26–3	90.1
2003	PUP	52.9	22–7	79.3
2008	UDP	56.8	25–6	75.3
2012	UDP	49.9	17–14	74.0

Sources: M. Palacio (1993, 10–12; 2011, 155–76) and from the Elections and Boundaries Commission of Belize (http://www.elections.gov.bz/).

constituencies in 2008.[23] At the same time, intra-party competition at the constituency level has also been increasing. In the set of UDP and PUP intra-party conventions between 2010 and 2012, thirty-five of the sixty-two contests were contested, including the seats of several sitting ministers.[24] This increase in the number of potential party candidates and the higher levels of competition have been accompanied by more use of clientelist exchanges at both the intra-party and constituency levels, as partisans seek electoral advantage.

Largely because of the penetration of two-party politics to all levels of local government, party competition and political clientelism have also expanded in all nine municipal cities and towns and to almost every village. The Village Council Act of 1999, while formalizing village-level elections and governance and expanding some powers, also spurred on the spread of partisan competition to some two hundred villages.[25] At the municipal level, the competitive intensity is reflected in the general parity in results of elections for municipal councils. For example, of the nine municipal elections between 1991 and 2011, the UDP won five times to the PUP four.[26] Not surprisingly, municipal councils have been experiencing an increase in requests for handouts from citizens, and some councils feel obligated to assist people to the point of diverting funds from core local governance matters of the councils.[27] The central reason for this spread of clientelism to local government is the increasing competition between the parties and politicians at local levels. The decentralization of local government in the past decade, which gave municipal and village councils marginally more authority, inadvertently also increased the interest of the PUP and UDP in competing at these levels.[28]

Alternative or third parties and independent candidates have comprehensively failed to dent the electoral dominance of the two major parties since independence. In the 2008 general election, for example, the combined share of votes received by all other parties and independent candidates was 2.8 per cent.[29] Alternative-party candidates or independents have won occasional seats at the municipal level, but they have not succeeded in winning the majority of seats in any municipality. Theoretically, alternative-party or independent candidates can make a difference in terms of which of the major parties wins at the constituency level in close contests, but Belize's electoral politics, in practice, is indisputably a two-party/PUP–UDP system. The constitution itself establishes the official and adversarial post of leader of the opposition, who commands the majority of the members of the House who do not support the government.

Intense two-party competition does not mean that there are no independent or swing voters. Indeed, there is some evidence that the proportion of these is significantly increasing. For example, in an opinion survey of three Belize City constituencies from the early 1990s, one-third of respondents claimed no party preference.[30] A pre-election 2008 national SPEAR poll indicated that 27.1 per cent of the electorate was undecided,[31] while a pre-election 2012 national poll (by a local newspaper) found that 32.7 per cent of the electorate was undecided.[32] Although several factors can induce voters to support one party or the other, significant numbers of swing voters increase the attractiveness of clientelist electoral strategies to both politicians and voters – especially when elections can be won by very few votes and when other party distinctions are in such short supply.

Dwindling Party Distinctions

Both the post-1990s intensification of two-party competition and the concurrent expansion of clientelism have transpired in a political context in which the PUP and the UDP have had progressively fewer differentiating bases on which to compete for the support of the electorate. With regard to ideology and national visions, the two major political parties became less distinguishable in the 1990s and thereafter. This can be deduced both from observing striking similarities in policy actions when the parties are in power and from policy statements from the parties themselves.[33] For example, former prime minister Barrow clarified that the UDP "is the preacher of no particular 'ism'. We do operate a system that seeks always to empower the private sector as a preferred instrument of stimulation and economic growth. But we are also statist in a sense, in that we do not shirk from a large activist role for government, especially when it comes to protecting the poor."[34] A review of the PUP's party manifestos and speeches by PUP leaders indicate that the PUP has used very similar language to describe its philosophy of governing. For instance, in its 2008 party manifesto, the PUP presented itself as a business-friendly party that also endeavours to spread the wealth of the nation more fairly to the poor through social justice programmes.[35] As one study summarized, "Both political parties espouse party visions that promote the continuation of the formal, electoral and liberal democratic institutions assumed in the parliamentary democratic system."[36]

The growing similarities between the two parties are not limited to overall ideology. Both the PUP and the UDP "boast a similar type of political-economic elite leadership that has the support of fairly equal portions of the electorate".[37] Furthermore, in the 1990s and after, both parties have continued to maintain multi-class, multi-racial, multi-gender and multi-ethnic support across urban, rural and immigrant communities. In particular, the pre-independence pattern of political parties appealing for votes from all ethnic groupings and winning seats in the same constituencies in different elections has continued. For example, in the urban centre of Belize City (which is majority Creole), the PUP won contests in fourteen of the constituencies in the three general elections between 1993 and 2008, while the UDP won sixteen.[38]

The dwindling of ideological differences and policy-based support between the PUP and UDP led Shoman to conclude that they now compete largely on "the question of which can best manage the mutually acceptable capitalist and neoliberal model".[39] One feature of this basis of competition is that the parties differentiate even more on the basis of which can better attract and allocate more targeted resources to more people based on clientelist motivations. In the late 1990s, and with the 1998 election as the likely symbolic turning point, the relative capacity to deliver targeted resources to individuals displaced ideology and policy visions as the primary competitive feature distinguishing Belize's two main parties to many in the electorate.

A More Politicized Election Management Body

Overall, the Elections and Boundaries Commission (EBC), with the support of the Elections and Boundaries Department, is constitutionally mandated to organize the registration of voters, propose occasional changes in electoral boundaries, and conduct national and local elections with impartiality. As noted in chapter 3, the pre-independence election management body, which functioned until 1988, was relatively independent, consisting of one autonomous body with no party-based appointments and with the power to hire its own chief elections officer and staff. However, the 1988 and 1989 constitutional and legislative amendments gave the majority party dominant control over the EBC, moved the power of staff appointment from the EBC to the already politicized public service and downgraded the EBC secretariat as a regular department within a government ministry. The PUP, which had publicly criticized the UDP amendments when in opposition, further amended the election law in 2001 such that the chief elections officer is no longer appointed by the governor general on the advice of the prime minister and the leader of the opposition, but rather directly by the Public Services Commission.

Public officers in the Elections and Boundaries Department have to contend with "political" bosses in both the EBC and in the department proper, with high staff turnover after elections, with being under-resourced and understaffed, and often with the squashing of proposals for improvements.[40] In relation to voter bribery, although the department is aware of allegations, it keeps no regular records of these. One election officer stated: "If we hear of or see possible bribery, we have the right to investigate it or stop it. But we don't have the capacity to investigate and monitor such things. And there is also the issue of the difficulty of proving bribery. It would likely end up in court . . . and that is more time, resources and staff we don't have."[41] Election officers also acknowledged being aware of the practice of politicians inducing voters to transfer (or not transfer) between constituencies, and that some transferees are required to show their receipts as proof to the politician that the transfer to another constituency has happened. Again, they lamented that the department's resources do not allow for comprehensive and effective checking of the veracity of requests for transfers of residence and noted that "politicians have little incentive to change" this situation.[42]

This relative lack of effectiveness and independence of electoral institutions in Belize has facilitated the expansion of political clientelism. When in government, the PUP and UDP have the legal and institutional means to influence election administration, including changing chief election officers and other staff, and how they respond to reports of violations of the voter bribery laws. The revised section of this law prohibits the trading of money or favours for votes, apart from gifts valued under $20, and there are possible penalties (for bribe giver and taker) of up to one year in prison, fines of up to $500 if convicted and debarment from participating in elections.[43] In spite of the spate of public allegations, there have been only a handful of cases that reach the courts and absolutely no legal convictions in Belize's modern political history – a most sobering indicator that the laws as they exist are no deterrent to voter bribery.

Is It "in the Culture"?

An often-cited narrative in Belize is that British pre-independence socialization of the political-economic elite, the experience of peaceful elections and the freedom to exercise basic political rights have fostered a political culture that values territorial integrity, free elections, peaceful changes of government and respect for fundamental rights. A regional AmericasBarometer survey of twenty-three countries on attitudes to democracy found that "support for democracy" in Belize was 71.9 per cent, "support for the right of public contestation" was 76 per cent, "support for political tolerance" was 65.6 per cent and "support for political legitimacy of core institutions" was 55.9 per cent, the highest of all states polled.[44] In short, these results suggest that Belizeans generally view Westminster parliamentary democracy as a key component of their national political identity.

On the other hand, some have pointed to disturbing aspects of Belize's political culture. A policy report described Belizean political culture as featuring "high levels of cynicism and disillusionment about the political system and political leadership, low levels of interest and practice in planning and monitoring, short-term and front-end bias in policy-making and a tendency to look for panacea solutions".[45] A well-known analyst argued that Belize's history of origin (being settled by pirates, a history of illicit trading activity and a lack of political commitment to the colony from Britain) have contributed to a "nebulous societal moral/legal divide . . . characterized by a general attitude of nonchalance towards high risk, but obviously lucrative illicit activity. It is one that has long historical roots, which perhaps also explains the éminence grise existence of seemingly influential 'underground' economic elite".[46]

The extent to which these worrying features are "cultural", permeate political and economic relationships, or to whether they are more historical or recent in origin is debatable. However, such cultural features may help explain the apparent ease with which so many politicians and citizens have embraced clientelist practices. A former PUP party leader was among those to agree that there is a link to cultural values: "There has been a marked erosion of values. Since the 1990s there is a new generation of voters. They are more informed of the handout game and for them, politicians are just an opportunity. But people reflect their parties, too. The PUP was a party of national vision and of social justice values. But that stopped in early 1980s, and no party has had it since."[47] Another former political actor lamented, "People have become shameless [in wanting handouts] due to the breakdown of our society. The value system is going and personal greed is on the rise. It's in the culture."[48] Whether or not the pervasive nature of clientelism is facilitated by the existing political culture, political clientelism is itself becoming an element of wider Belizean political culture.

Poverty and Income Inequality

High rates of poverty and income disparities have persisted in Belize since independence, and a comprehensive study measured overall poverty at

33 per cent in 1995.[49] Standardized country poverty assessment (CPA) reports in 2002 and 2009 revealed a significant increase in individual poverty from 34 per cent in 2002 to 41.3 per cent in 2009, and a disturbing increase in indigent poverty from 11 per cent to 15.8 per cent.[50] The 2009 rate ranked Belize, at the time, as the third poorest country in the greater Caribbean, with only Haiti and the Dominican Republic showing higher rates.[51] Income inequality, as measured by the Gini coefficient, worsened from 0.40 in 2002 to 0.42 in 2009.[52] However, significant expenditure gaps in 2009 reflected high disparities in income: the top quintile accounted for 48.8 per cent of total expenditures, whereas the bottom quintile accounted for only 5.8 per cent.[53] As in the 2002 poverty survey, the 2009 study showed that poverty rates are highest among the Maya of the Toledo district and in pockets of the Creole urban centre of Belize City, but also pointed to significant poverty increases in agriculturally based rural areas and in the Corozal district. Overall, rural poverty was measured at 55.3 per cent and urban poverty at 27.9 per cent.

The 2002 and 2009 CPAs confirmed much of what most other social sector reports had been indicating about Belize's social context for some time. For example, Belize's First Report on the Millennium Development Goals (as the Social Development Goals were then titled), while pointing to isolated achievements, indicated an overall trend of increasing social problems and social vulnerability. The global Human Development Index reports showed that, out of 182 countries, Belize slipped from a ranking of sixty-seven in 2003 to ninety-three in 2009.[54] Several other studies and reports chronicled the deteriorating human security situation, health challenges and excruciatingly slow progress in improving the quality of education.[55] Importantly, the increase in persistent poverty and more skewed income distribution coincide with the post-1990 period during which the most rapid expansion of political clientelism occurred.

The strongest indication that there is a causal relationship between poverty and inequality, on the one hand, and expanding clientelism, on the other, comes from the experiences of politicians and citizens themselves. The client profile presented in chapter 4 revealed that the poor make up the vast majority of client numbers regardless of geography, ethnicity, migratory status or gender. As in the pre-1990s period, the majority of politicians couched their clientelist support in philanthropic and paternalistic tones of "helping" the needy. Indeed, most argue that larger numbers of poorer people fuelled the post-1990s expansion because their demands on politicians for handouts increased exponentially. One former representative contended, "I don't agree that it is the politicians and the parties that caused this [expansion]. I see it the other way around. It is the people whose needs and demands we reacted to. We have to be there every week reacting to their needs."[56]

However, some politicians conditioned this demand-driven analysis of helping the needy with nuanced views on the relative role of poverty. A few examples suffice:

> Poverty is key. It is not and should not be an excuse, but it is certainly an underlying factor. There is greater need now than before independence, more poverty. The national institutions are not providing the answers in a sustainable way.[57]
>
> There has been a growing social need. Some people even can't afford food, much less paying rent. Deficiencies in the state's social and welfare systems have been filled in part by the politicians, clinics and benefits politics.[58]
>
> It [the expansion] was not fully the fault of politicians. It was a symbiotic relationship between politician and voter. Yes, politicians started this handout thing but people played along and their interests merged. The fact that people were indeed poor just made it easier.[59]
>
> Social vulnerability increased at the same time as partisan competition was increasing . . . making it easier for politicians to buy support. People were poor before [independence], but they had more options [for making ends meet].[60]

The majority of constituents interviewed agreed that social need was a major reason for turning to politicians for assistance. A common type of comment was, "The neighbourhood gone down. There are more poor people, more houses falling down, more crime and no help with things like day care. So, some people go [to politicians]."[61] However, some poorer constituents referred to handouts from politicians as entitlements and argued that it was their money anyway being given back to them. Other constituents accused politicians of seeking power to enrich themselves through corruption and argued that it is only right that they (constituents) get a piece of the spoils. As one contended, "We the poor ones get offers from the representatives and a lot of people take them. I don't blame them . . . they are poor and need help. And the politicians are thieves anyway."[62] Some citizens argued that they go to politicians for individual help because it can be difficult and frustrating to get timely assistance directly from the government's departments. This is reflected in the frustrations of one citizen trying to get a residential lot: "I played the game to get a piece of land. I went first to the ministry of lands but got nowhere at all. So, I went straight to him [my representative] and he got a lease for me quick. I would be stupid not to go to the politician when everyone is playing this game. And I would be stupid not to think he wanted my vote."[63]

Yet it is not only the poor, the unemployed and low-income earners who play the clientelist game in Belize. One middle-class constituent, who admitted to not needing financial assistance, told of receiving annual birthday cards with $100 cash "gifts" from the constituency's representative and keeping them because they were free.[64] Several middle-class citizens and small-business owners shared that they too sometimes approach politicians for assistance in return for some kind of benefit. The central justification running through these responses is that the playing field for accessing state-managed resources and services and for doing business is not level, and one has to play by the existing rules or get left behind. For example, one small-business owner attested to being tempted to purchase contraband liquor for his business because so many others were doing it and undercutting his prices. However, avoiding punitive repercussions often required providing "support" to a certain politician, which some are unwilling to do.[65] Some also made reference to the widely used scheme of overbidding for government supply contracts and then, once paid, transferring part of the difference, as directed by particular politicians who had facilitated the bids.[66]

As indicated in chapter 4, political clientelist behaviour emerged first in urban areas, and especially in the Creole centre of Belize City – due largely to it being the fermenting ground for the nationalist movement and party politics. But by the elections of 2003 and 2008, it had spread extensively to all other districts, and by extension to all ethnic groups. Although poverty had increased across all geographic areas, the 2009 CPA found that poverty was almost twice as high in rural than in urban areas, and that as much as 80 per cent of the indigent poor reside in rural parts of Belize.[67] This would suggest rural areas could be expected to have higher incidences of clientelism – in contrast to the perceptions of politicians. However, most politicians suggested that clientelism is somewhat higher in urban than in rural areas. They pinpointed Belize City as having more intense and more overt clientelist practices and perceived the Creole population there as being more familiar with the dynamics of clientelism. However, this does not mean that there is an ethnic proclivity in relation to clientelism.

Although the Belize district had the least poverty of all six districts in both the 2002 and 2009 CPAs, and the urban part of the Belize district (Belize City) was only marginally less poor than rural Belize district, there were interesting variations. The urban south side of Belize City along with the Toledo district were found to have high "concentrations of poverty and other social and development issues".[68] Belize City is the most densely populated part of the country with 17.1 per cent of the total population and seven of its ten constituencies are on the south side and have a majority-Creole demography. The combination of concentration of poverty in a small urban space and the fact that Belize City is the national commercial, financial and media centre contribute to making it the node of political clientelism in the country. The 2009 CPA found that Creole households had the lowest poverty rate of 32 per cent, that the Maya had the highest at 68 per cent, and that there had been significant increases since 2002 for the Mestizo and Garifuna. Apart from the perceptions of some that a larger proportion of Creoles were clients, there is no clear evidence that differences in incidence of poverty by ethnicity significantly affected the relative prevalence of political clientelism among different ethnic groups. Clientelist behaviour is observable at some incidence across segments of all ethnic groups, and political parties target them all for votes. As such, the perceptions of some politicians that Creoles, as members of an ethnic group, are more prone to becoming clients than any other ethnic group are unsubstantiated. This perception is rather more related to the fact that Belize City, with a higher concentration of Creoles than any other part of the country, has the smallest constituencies but the densest populations. As such, they exhibit higher concentrations of political clientelism, and clientelist transactions are more visible and more reported on. The dangers of arguing a direct relationship between any one ethnic group and political clientelism are well illustrated by the example of the Belmopan constituency in the Cayo district. This constituency has a population of near-equal proportions of Creoles and Maya/Mestizos. Constituents from all ethnic groups there participate in the handout game, and some even contend that the Maya/Mestizos, who generally have lower incomes in Belmopan, may be more apt players of the clientelist game.[69]

The 2009 CPA study found a virtual balance between male and female poverty rates at 42 per cent and 40 per cent, respectively. Interestingly, it also showed that "female-headed households, including single-person households, are slightly less likely to be poor than male-headed ones – 29 per cent compared with 32 per cent".[70] These figures suggest that there are other gender-related factors at play in the reporting from politicians that women outnumber men as clients. When asked to reflect on the reasons for this gender disparity in clients, several female politicians suggested that women have more responsibilities to provide for the home and are better managers of resources, that there are large numbers of single mothers as heads of households in some areas, and that women have more time to come to political clinics because men are more apt to have day jobs. The 2010 population census revealed that 22.6 per cent of children under the age of eighteen years were living with their mothers only, compared to 2.5 per cent living with their fathers only and 65.8 per cent living with both parents. In 2010, female unemployment was at 33.1 per cent, more than twice that of the 15 per cent rate for males.[71] The fact that women's requests of politicians were more related to basic needs than those of men points to the presence of a clear socio-economic connection to the uneven gender burden of dealing with the effects of poverty. One astute observer may have it just right: "Women have always been the political foot soldiers. They may go more to politicians but get less from the informal handout system . . . just as they get less in the formal economy."[72]

Linkages to Neoliberal Economic Policies

As was the case across the Caribbean region, Belize was pressured by financial institutions and major bilateral economic partners to adopt "Washington Consensus" neoliberal economic policies in the late 1980s and in the 1990s. By the end of the 1990s, both UDP and PUP governments were enacting and implementing market-oriented reforms, such as foreign investment promotion, trade liberalization, privatization and deregulation. Distinctive perspectives on the role this macroeconomic policy shift played in the expansion of clientelism were provided by two Belizean political actors with diametrically opposed ideological orientations: Assad Shoman, perhaps Belize's most prominent socialist, and Ralph Fonseca, seen by some as its most ardent capitalist.

Shoman, who was a constituency representative and minister, co-led the last unsuccessful attempt in the mid-1980s to move the PUP to the ideological left. Fonseca, who also served as a representative and minister, was the PUP's campaign and finance manager from 1987 to 2008, and a principal architect of the PUP's sharp turn to the right and its embrace of neoliberal economics in the 1990s and thereafter. Both pinpointed the spread of neoliberal policies and programmes in Belize as a central cause of the expansion of political clientelism, but they gave very different interpretations of why and how it did so.

Fonseca argued that neoliberal economic policies have been positive for Belize in that it provided the fuel for the economic growth witnessed in the late 1990s and early years of the 2000s.[73] He contended that, as the two parties competed more intensely for votes in this free-market context in the 1990s, politicians and voters alike began to rationally view votes as commodities that can be bartered: "Voters had more purchasing price for their votes . . . just like everything else in the marketplace. They understood politicians were dependent on their vote . . . because there was no longer this natural affiliation to any party. It's just like market forces – only in this case increased demand for votes. And the politicians and party strategists have to service it [the demand]."[74] By "service", Fonseca meant delivering targeted benefits to people for votes, and he suggested that a political party simply has to have the right machinery to "manage" demand (expectations) and supply. In short, Fonseca, who preferred the term "benefits politics" over handout politics, viewed the expansion of political clientelism as a natural, expected and potentially positive element of neoliberalism in Belize. Fonseca's argument is that in a neoliberal world that places high importance on markets, individualism and consumerism, more politicians view individual votes just as another commodity for which price can be negotiated – and that's just how it is.

From Shoman's viewpoint, the implementation of neoliberal policies, including unbridled foreign investment, privatizations and increased consumerism, contributed to larger sums of money entering party politics as private and business interests sought to "buy" influence. He argued that in a political context of the two main competitive parties having few substantive distinctions and in which social need was high, more politicians began to engage in clientelism as an electoral strategy. Shoman hastened to add that the post-independence embrace of neoliberalism itself resulted in decreased social spending, in more skewed distribution of economic wealth and in increased poverty.[75] In a fragile societal context made worse by neoliberalism, more people logically began to accept and seek handouts to help make ends meet.

Although differing strongly on the merits and impact of the neoliberal economic policies adopted in the 1990s, the views of Fonseca and Shoman overlap on the point that political clientelism became more attractive to politicians and citizens alike as more private money entered electoral politics. Based on the available evidence, Shoman is on target about the further impact that the sharp swing to neoliberalism had on poverty and political clientelism. Whereas the poverty that contributed to the pre-independence emergence of political clientelism had its roots in the mid-twentieth century economic collapse of the forestry industry and in the inequities of the colonial system, the kind of poverty that fed the post-independence expansion had some "new" features. Not only did the poverty brought over from the colonial period persist, but a widening income gap and a smaller welfare state apparatus severely stressed the capacity of the new state and its leaders to systematically and adequately address growing poverty and unemployment. This, in turn, facilitated conditions conducive to the development of clientelist options in circumstances of heightened electoral competition.

After a first decade of independence marked by a slow recovery from the macroeconomic downturn, Belize's small and open economy continued to be characterized by high volatility in GDP growth, overall fragility and skewed distribution of economic resources over the 1980–2010 period.[76] David Gomez illustrated that the GDP slumps and booms can be nicely matched with alternating periods of contractionary and expansionary fiscal policies, which themselves tended to coincide with election cycles.[77] Although GDP grew by an average of 4.9 per cent per year over the 1980–2010 period, it dipped to below 1 per cent in several years.[78] As measured by GDP per head at constant prices, in 2010 Belize remained at its 1980 rank of twenty-two out of twenty-eight countries in the wider Caribbean.[79] The Belize economy had also changed significantly in terms of the sectoral share of GDP. Between 1980 and 2008, primary activities (sugar, citrus, banana, marine and forestry products) decreased from 27.4 per cent of total GDP to 12.2 per cent, whereas the share related to services, especially tourism, increased from 41.7 per cent to 65.1 per cent.[80] Central to Belize's neoliberal economic policies and to its GDP growth was the mantra to promote foreign investment, and the majority of new investments, especially in services, were, indeed, foreign in origin. The generous concessions granted to attract these investments resulted in less immediate revenue for government coffers, which in turn increased the need to borrow internationally to help meet national development needs. The evidence is strong that growth in GDP since 1990 has had limited effect on social development, and, indeed, the manner in which it was achieved contributed to some negative results.

In terms of employment, Belize's economy performed generally poorly in the 1990s and 2010s. A Belize Central Bank study of economic performance since independence confirmed that "high unemployment has been enduring, registering in double digits in fifteen of the twenty years between 1990 and 2009".[81] Unemployment was 15 per cent in 1990, 14 per cent in 1998, 11.6 per cent in 2004 and 13.1 per cent in 2009.[82] As demonstrated by various poverty assessments, the human impact of the economic growth generated was also skewed in terms of distribution. The revenue leakages related to profit repatriation by foreign investors have also contributed to fiscal deficits in almost every year since the 1990s.[83] These deficits, in turn, resulted in significant increases in public debt, and especially external debt, as a percentage of GDP since the 1990s. This debt-to-GDP ratio peaked in 2004 at over 100 per cent of GDP ($2.2 billion), and economic disaster was only averted by a crippling external debt restructuring package negotiated with private debtors, referred to as the "super bond". This $1.1 billion bond required that Belize must pay increasingly huge amounts of its annual revenue to service this debt until 2029.[84] In March 2013, and following a lengthy negotiation process, the government of Belize announced that it had been successful in restructuring the super bond.[85] In effect, the restructured deal extended the repayment period to 2038 and should have resulted in a saving of $494 million in debt-servicing payments over the 2013–22 period. (The super bond was restructured again twice before being converted into a debt-for-nature "blue bond" in 2021.)

Another core plank of the neoliberal swing in Belize was the divestment of several major state-owned assets and services. Starting in the late 1980s, there was a spate of privatizations, including all of the "big three" utility companies responsible for telecommunications, electricity and water.[86] By 2002, all of these utilities were not only out of government hands but also out of Belizean hands, as parties in power sold off more and more shares to foreign investors. Although partly driven by external forces, including the policy prescriptions of the IMF, the World Bank and the Inter-American Development Bank, the privatizations were also undertaken by Belize's government as a "panacea to the budget deficit situation" in the short term, but ended up leaving government with little control and a long-term loss of public revenue.[87] Proceeds from divestments were often used to service commercial loans repayments that were urgently due or to improve a weak fiscal situation before an election. In short, misguided and poorly implemented neoliberal policies not only contributed to skewed wealth distribution, but they also decreased public revenue that could have been used for social spending to alleviate poverty.

The linkages between neoliberal policies and the expansion of clientelism can be further illustrated by exploring particular business relationships. The example of Lord Ashcroft is particularly telling. Although Ashcroft has not been the only major foreign investor, his investments have been among the largest, and their relevance for Belizean party politics is difficult to overstate. As noted earlier, Ashcroft made one of his first investments in Belize with the purchase of the Belize branch of Royal Bank of Canada in 1987 under a UDP government and was granted a thirty-year tax holiday for all his business interests by the 1989–93 PUP government. As a harbinger of things to come, the International Business Companies Act of 1990, the instrument through which the investment concessions were granted, was actually proposed by Ashcroft's own lawyers.[88] It has also been recounted that Ashcroft's then Belize Holdings Inc played a key role in drafting

Belize's Off-Shore Banking Act and Money Laundering Prevention Act in the mid-1990s.[89] Of great importance is that the UDP government that won the 1993 election continued the various tax concessions enjoyed by Ashcroft's investments. Over the two decades after the International Business Companies Act, these investments would spread to numerous companies, including an off-shore banking business, majority ownership in the privatized telephone company, one of the largest hotels, a national television station, the shipping registry and the off-shore business registry.[90]

It is not a coincidence that Lord Ashcroft's role as the likely single largest financial contributor to Belize's political parties began around the same time as the "negotiations" to draft the International Business Companies Act. As was confirmed in interviews with key leaders of both political parties, Ashcroft has featured "prominently and sometimes controversially in Belizean politics as a financial contributor to both the PUP and UDP".[91] Donations by Ashcroft and other big donors have been a significant part of the "big money" that began flowing to the parties in the 1990s as both dominant parties evolved into commercial entities that competed to outdo the other on the neoliberal policy front. The key implication here is that the amount of private money in party politics increased dramatically in the 1990s and thereafter, as a function of increased demand as both parties modernized and as sources of campaign donations from wealthy business interests expanded. It will never be known what proportion of such private funds finds its way into the realm of handout politics, but such funds are a major source of resources for the clientelist operations of both major parties. Indeed, the extent of private funding exhibited suggests that some politicians and political operatives themselves became "clients" of wealthy "donor patrons" such as Ashcroft to help finance their own downstream clientelist networks.

On the surface, the policy of divestment of government-controlled entities in the 1990s and 2000s appears to represent a significant exception in the narrative of politicians' increasing control over resource allocation institutions as a supportive condition for growing political clientelism. However, even as privatizations took away some ability to dispense patronage in one regard, they increased the opportunities for clientelism in another. This view is argued cogently by a long-time civil society leader:

> In part, the big jump of handout politics in the 1990s was facilitated by the privatisations. This was in effect a transfer of government resources to the private sector and a way for more money to end up outside government and in the unregulated private coffers of parties and politicians. This actually increased

the peddling of influence through the promises of favours for campaign contributions by large investors. The money trail is harder to trace than if government still controlled these entities.[92]

The pertinent argument is that government control over public utilities, which was lost because of the privatizations, was counterbalanced by new opportunities for clientelism gained by political parties through unregulated financial transfers from large donors, who benefited from the divestments. In this regard, political parties and politicians then had access to two sets of funds after the privatizations. One is the immediate revenue from the divestments, some of which was used to influence elections via "piñata goodies".[93] The other is the direct financial contributions to political parties from business interests, some of which have been used for discretionary handouts to clients. It is difficult, for example, to convince the astute Belizean that Lord Ashcroft's purchase of the majority of shares in Belize's telecommunications monopoly and the other generous concessions he had negotiated at the time were unrelated to his campaign donations to both major political parties.

Since 2008 there has been a reversal of some of the major privatizations for reasons unconnected to principled stands against neoliberalism. With differing rationale, but with significant public support, all three major public utilities have been, in effect, re-nationalized and a constitutional amendment enacted to ensure permanent majority state control. The water utility was repossessed by a PUP government in 2007 after the private owners gave up the company for reasons related to low profits – in effect, a rescue. The telecommunications company, then owned once again by Ashcroft, was nationalized by a UDP government in a hostile takeover in 2009, ostensibly over the issue of an obnoxiously generous tax concession agreement negotiated by the previous PUP government and Ashcroft. The electricity company was re-nationalized in 2011 by a UDP government after repeated and costly government bailouts of the company – in effect, a state rescue.

The overall impact of these three major re-nationalizations on political clientelism in Belize is another area ripe for further research. It is likely that governing political parties, now fully seasoned in the art of wily clientelism, still have opportunities to use the increased control of the utility companies for targeted clientelist purposes in a context of growing client demands.[94] One preview was that just months before national and municipal elections in early 2012, the UDP government made quick decisions to lower both electricity and water rates – an obvious attempt at appealing to "collective clients" for votes.[95] In step with the trend of diminishing party distinctions, the PUP, which had originally criticized the nationalizations as dictatorial and bad for the foreign investment climate, committed in its 2012 manifesto to "maintain majority control of all public utilities" for the state.[96]

Inadequate Social Alternatives

A key assumption underlying much of the discussion thus far is that formal public institutions of allocation have generally not succeeded in delivering goods and services adequately and fairly so as to meet the needs and demands of many citizens. In relation to clientelism, the relevant argument is captured well by a former politician: "Our national institutions that are supposed to provide for our people and develop the nation are failing. They have not changed much since the 1960s. More and more people go to the political frontlines. They go straight to the offices, clinics and homes of their representatives. Politicians have become the main social providers for too many."[97] Former prime minister Barrow shared a similar analysis: "[Handout politics] reflect a huge failing of the system. People don't go to the Immigration Department or the Lands Department, and pretty much departments across the public service, on their own because they get absolutely frustrated. Either they are not treated well, or they don't get what they need from government . . . so of course they'll go to their area representatives. Nature abhors a vacuum."[98]

There is ample evidence to validate these views. Belize's key social welfare institutions are located in departments of government with responsibilities for social and human development, health care, education, land, housing and job creation. Overall, the coverage of welfare safety nets directly aimed at disadvantaged Belizeans, although gradually expanding since the 1990s, can be described as limited, inadequate and ad hoc. These include a public hospital system with basic but national coverage, educational assistance through the Ministry of Education, and small monthly and emergency stipends for some of the very poor through the Ministry of Human Development. In the case of compulsory social insurance, the Social Security scheme, established in 1981, is the only national mechanism that covers contributing employees and retirees with basic allowances.

Outside of these, most other welfare assistance programmes at the time were project based and of limited coverage. A pilot National Health Insurance plan, with very limited geographical coverage, was launched by a PUP government in 2005, and several "pro-poor" programmes with limited access were introduced by post-2008 UDP governments.[99] These latter programmes include a pilot CCT programme launched in 2010, a small food pantry programme for very poor households launched in 2011, and various youth employment schemes. The Belize version of the limited CCT was called BOOST at the time, and like CCTs elsewhere it targets poor households through cash transfers to women. After a shaky start, it received fairly positive initial reports. For example, a 2012 World Bank document noted that after "a little over a year in operation, it already reaches 3,177 households (12.5 per cent of all Belize poor households) and over 8,600 people, which represents about 6 per cent of the poor population".[100] However, as will be discussed in the next chapter, these targeted social welfare programmes were not immune from attempts by politicians to use them for clientelist purposes.

In a context of increasing poverty and economic hardships, several recent social assessments indicate that social benefits arrangements do not satisfy needs adequately and are also not effective in distributing what is available in a fair and transparent manner. For example, in its analysis of the social sector, the 2009 CPA found that social spending as a percentage of GDP expenditure fell from 14.5 per cent between 1992 and 1994, to 10 per cent in 2001, and to 7.5 per cent in 2006, with only negligible increases since then – a trend not unrelated to neoliberalism. It also showed that 70 per cent of social spending continues to be on education and much of the remainder on health, leaving little for much else. For instance, spending on social protection by the Ministry of Human Development was under 0.4 per cent of GDP in 2008. Although no examples were provided, the 2009 CPA also raised a key concern: "Political interference in the identification of beneficiaries for targeted programmes".[101]

With regard to the alternatives to clientelism provided by non-state organizations, the record is mixed. After a period of rebirth in the 1980s, the spike in the number and the broadening of coverage of civil society organizations (CSOs) continued into the 1990s, followed by a period of reduced, but still significant, levels of activity in the following decade.[102] A 2005 directory, with just a partial list of CSOs, identified over 150 NGOs, unions, community-based groups, cultural groups, religious groups, business associations, professional associations and international development agencies.[103] CSOs have lobbied for and won significant public policy space. One study found that "participation of CSOs includes membership on a wide range of policy-related bodies such as the National Human Development Advisory Committee, the National Aids Commission, the Advisory Council on the Guatemalan Claim and the Social Security Board".[104] By constitutional amendment, membership in the Senate was increased from nine to twelve in 2001 with the three new members being representatives (one each) from NGOs (shared by CSOs and unions), business associations and religious institutions. In 2016 and after much lobbying, CSOs were awarded their own full seat when the membership of the Senate was expanded to thirteen. CSOs have successfully used this political space to lead initiatives that have directly influenced political reforms enacted by government.[105] It is also generally accepted that that these non-state organizations have helped to fill some of the socio-economic development gaps of state institutions, as well as provide Belizeans with additional informal opportunities to participate and receive benefits outside of political party relationships.

If the expansion of CSO activity and the provision of alternative modes of informal resource allocation and participation had any diminishing effect on political clientelism, it either has been insufficient to counterbalance the expansion of clientelist activity or clientelism has expanded in spite of more CSO activity. A former director of a large CSO suggested that there is truth to the interpretation that the work of CSOs has not dented the expansion of clientelism: "I do not agree with the hypothesis that CSOs have been credible alternatives to clientelism. Belize does not have the kind of broad-based-membership CSOs that provide a real alternative space to people."[106] Similarly, the director of a large national NGO stated: "CSO organising has not been a deterrent to political clientelism in terms of ongoing choices for solving problems. Too many of these groups come and go or have short-term projects. In a small country people catch on to this quickly. The politician is always there and doesn't ask a lot of questions."[107] These views suggest that, although CSO interventions have benefited some citizens, their localized focus, temporary nature and inconsistencies dampen the potential for longer-term impact as credible alternatives to clientelist relationships with politicians. Indeed, there is an argument that "some CSOs have themselves become clients of the state" because some depend on government support for subventions and exemptions, for participation in development projects, and for other favours.[108] In a small society, in which most societal relations are influenced by political parties and in which governments can use discretionary powers to reward or to punish CSOs, it is challenging for CSOs to maintain non-partisan credibility.

Overall, the evidence suggests that some citizens do engage simultaneously in political clientelism and in civil society activities as part of a rational assessment of maximizing opportunities. Yet it appears that most citizens do not perceive CSOs as credible alternatives to political clientelism and see political clientelism as an easier and more predictable mode of accessing needs and wants. As former prime minister Esquivel summed up, "An innocent explanation [for the expansion of clientelism] is that the area representative is most able to identify constituents' needs. He is closest to them and best able to deliver. People begin to believe that that's the politician's job."[109]

Non-Clientelist Voter Motivations

This chapter on what fuelled the rapid expansion of political clientelism in Belize would be incomplete without some discussion of a critical question implied by my estimate that some 20–25 per cent of the electorate has engaged in clientelist transactions in their constituencies: why most Belizeans do *not* engage in such transactions? Even after accepting that the estimate is undoubtedly conservative, the clear implication is that most Belizeans have voted for politicians for reasons other than clientelism or in addition to clientelism. Due to a lack of pertinent and credible quantitative data, and due to the complexity inherent in analysing voter intent, it is challenging to disentangle the motivations of the electorate. One aspect of the challenge is that voters can have overlapping motivations to vote for a candidate or party. For example, a 2005 SPEAR poll showed significant overlap among the polled voter motivations of "party vision", "gifts", "candidate" and "family influence".[110] However, some trends are observable. On a broader and comparative historical level of analysis, this chapter demonstrated how voters have had to choose between candidates of two parties that have become less programmatic and more clientelist since the 1950s. Yet both parties still maintain some programmatic features that likely have had some influence on voting decisions of some in the electorate. This was suggested by a SPEAR poll conducted before the 2008 election that found that most respondents (52.8 per cent) would still vote based on issues.[111]

Interviews with politicians indicated that they too are of the view that both the PUP and the UDP had a smaller and decreasing proportion of the electorate as core supporters in 2010 compared to 1980. These politicians' estimates of core party support ranged from 20 to 25 per cent of the total electorate in 2010. Indeed, SPEAR polls (2008 and 2012) – asking about support for the PUP and UDP – found that no party polled over one-third support of respondents. These same polls suggested that some 30 per cent of the electorate was undecided and without core party preferences. The pertinent implication is that a significant portion of the electorate was potentially open to other voting motivations – including non-clientelist ones. The 2008 SPEAR poll found that 52.8 per cent of respondents said they would vote on "issues" and that 20.6 per cent would vote for the "candidate", 12.6 per cent based on "party loyalty" and 8.2 per cent based on "family influence". As discussed earlier in this chapter, the issues of corruption and economic hardships – all reasons to be dissatisfied with the incumbent – are among the more significant influences on swing voters' decisions.

However, some of the reasons why some voters do not participate in clientelism are related to the nature of clientelism itself. Chapter 3 demonstrated that citizens in higher-income brackets were less likely to engage in clientelist transactions than low-income earners. Interviews with citizens also indicated that there are some in the electorate who view the exchange of political support for resources as distasteful or immoral or both. Several interviewees stated that they would never tarnish their names and reputations by joining or being seen in clinic lines – especially in a small country where such actions are difficult to hide. Another reason is related to the frustrations (expressed by politicians and clients alike) that there are just not enough clientelist handouts to meet the demand and recruit more clients. The finite nature of resources and favours available for clientelism may indeed have a "ceiling" effect on client numbers. For sure, a better understanding of why some citizens choose not to engage in political clientelism will be critical to developing approaches for its mitigation.

Conclusion

After Belize's independence in 1981, higher levels of political control over resource allocation institutions provided the PUP and UDP with additional opportunities to dispense state patronage. By the early 1990s, these two closely competitive political parties already offered little in terms of substantive differences, amplifying party distinctions and appeals for votes based on clientelist inducements. The legal and institutional framework for the management of elections proved generally ineffective in regulating practices related to voter bribery.

At the same time, increasing poverty and inequality of access to resources between the political elite and the majority of citizens provided fertile ground for political clientelism to expand. Neoliberal economic policies, including generous fiscal concessions to foreign investors and extensive privatizations, transformed the features of poverty and curtailed government revenue and social spending. While the privatizations provided short-term discretionary financial resources, including for clientelist operations, the "smaller" state was less able to address people's needs, and clientelist approaches subsequently filled some of the void. Neither public sector programmes nor civil society interventions have proven adequate to diminish preferences for clientelist options. For an increasing number of citizens, personal visits to politicians hold more promise, more predictability and more immediately positive results than these alternatives. Diverse multi-ethnicity and the presence of immigrant communities have provided readily identifiable "networks" through which politicians target resources to individuals and small groups in exchange for possible political support. Small size has facilitated and magnified the relevance of almost every other causal variable in the Belize case.

In the 1980s and much of the 1990s, clientelist transfers were still mostly supply-driven, as political parties experienced the major influx of private funds and perfected the art of directing public resources to influence individual political support. However, sometime in the late 1990s, and after decades of unmet expectations and the failure of state institutions and civil society to meet socio-economic needs, demand-driven motivations increased as more citizens mastered the "clientelist game". For at least one in five citizens, clientelism became a preferred alternative to engage the state and influence allocations. For poorer clients, the imperative was to solve immediate social needs and wants. For middle-class clients, it was to gain advantages in the context of an unlevel playing field.

Over time, the bartering power of clients has been flexed such that it is as likely for voters to tell politicians what they want for their political support as it is for politicians to make offers of bribery. There was a pivotal point around the 1998 election at which more citizens began to view handouts as entitlements and clientelism evolved from a top-down political relationship to one of mutual and self-enforcing dependency between people and their political leaders. The accompanying reliance on more private money to fund handout activities brought another critical element to the dynamics of clientelist politics in Belize: the dual role of politicians as patrons to many citizens but themselves clients to wealthy financiers.

6.

Tek di Money

Distorted Democracy

How, then, has the rapid expansion and entrenchment of political clientelism affected Belize's democracy and development since independence? I now approach this principal question of the book by assessing implications for elements of the two overlapping pillars of democracy as presented in the first chapter: formal democracy and social democracy. In the first half of this chapter, I highlight the troubling impact entrenched clientelism has on electoral processes, political parties, public institutions and political participation in Belize. The second half focuses on the thorny implications for Belize's sustainable development and, in particular, for people's livelihoods. To do so I assess how social welfare, resource distribution, public policy, economic performance and public accountability have been affected.

Tarnished Votes and Suspect Elections

By 2012 more citizens in Belize than ever before were making voting decisions or voting promises based on clientelist exchanges with politicians, and a portion of these constituted a part of the significant proportion of swing voters in the electorate. Overall, the implications for Belize's positive record of formal and electoral democracy are highly worrying. Evan X Hyde was on target when he argued that pre-independence election results in the 1950s and 1960s were more "authentic" from the viewpoint that the majority of people supported the PUP in issue-based elections and "you couldn't buy votes in those days".[1] Hyde lamented that by 2011, due largely to the prevalence of handouts and the need for tens of millions of dollars to run an election campaign, Belizeans have watched "democracy being bought out".[2]

Indeed, widespread political clientelism can cast an ominous shadow over voting motivations and suspicions over the authenticity of election results. Assessments of post-independence elections in Belize must consider that (as cautiously estimated in chapter 4) at least one-fifth of the electorate is voting based on clientelist inducements. It begs the question of how many constituency elections – and, by extension, general elections – have turned on vote trading in particular and on political clientelism more broadly. Most politicians believe that they have or that they can, as indicated by the existence and continued growth of their elaborate clinic operations and by the increase in the number of allegations of the buying of elections at every level. The relative success of clientelism in securing votes is clearly visible in intra-party conventions and constituency elections. There is now a direct relationship between those constituencies characterized as "safe seats" and those known to have the most effective clientelist operations. Examples include the Belize City constituencies of Fort George, Queen's Square and Mesopotamia, which returned incumbents in every election between 1984 and 2012 with winning majorities averaging over 70 per cent, and the Corozal South East constituency, which is the only constituency that has remained continuously in the hands of the same political party. The incidence of clientelism now needs to be added to other key indicators (such as personal popularity and party affiliation) of such instances of homogeneous voting in Belize's elections.[3]

Accounts from politicians illustrate that it was after the 1998 election, and the spike in the incidence of political clientelism, that the vote as a tradable commodity began to increase in proportion to the vote as a true indicator of the voice of the majority. Although the game of negotiating the exchange of resources for political support is now year-round, it is in the heat of election campaigns that the degree of acceptance of the vote as a commodity can be most nakedly observed. One indicator is the open way in which politicians of both parties have, at some point, encouraged the electorate to accept money and other resources from political opponents, but not vote for them. For example, in the 1998 election, elements in the opposition PUP encouraged voters to "tek di blue note [from the UDP government], but vote blue [PUP]".[4] In 2008, after accusing the PUP of trying to buy the elections with the Venezuela grant, a host on the radio station of the opposition UDP advised people to "go get some of the money".[5] One e-poster issued by elements of the PUP before the 2012 election encouraged voters to "tek di passport, tek di ham, tek di money, tek di land. But stick to di plan. Vote PUP" (see appendix 3 for copy of this poster). At the same time opposition party elements were sharing such messages, its politicians were also engaging in the handout game.

The entrenched acceptance of the vote as a commodity among a significant segment of the electorate is further illustrated by the failure of one of the few public education initiatives to discourage it. A group calling itself the Association of Concerned Belizeans (ACB) launched an information campaign in 2006 under the theme "No sell yu vote, Vote yu mind" to educate the voting public about the integrity and secrecy of the vote.[6] As one of the leaders of this campaign related, the ACB became aware that poor people "would still take money" so "you can't tell them not to take it, but you can tell them to still vote their mind".[7] By 2007, and after realizing that the message was largely falling on deaf ears, the ACB changed the campaign name to "Tek di money, Vote yu mind".[8] The ACB leader added, "We just didn't see people understanding the 'don't take the money' line when poverty is so high and people need to survive."[9] Notwithstanding this rationale, the revised message encouraged deception and glossed over the illegal and indictable acts of bribery. One newspaper editorial did allude to this problem: "Buying and selling votes strike at the very heart of Belizean democracy" because "we cannot ask them [the voters] to do the right thing after we have entreated them to do something wrong".[10] The short-lived ACB campaign had no noticeable impact on the upward trajectory of vote trading as a preferred electoral tactic.

It is quite evident that political clientelism has contributed to blemishing the principle of ballot secrecy that is so intrinsic to electoral democracy. Although no exit polling data exist, pockets of doubt about ballot secrecy have long existed in the Belizean populace, and political clientelism has likely heightened the levels of distrust. The link to clientelism is straightforward: politicians try to find out if clients keep promises to vote for them, or simply make clients believe that there are ways to find out how they voted. Belizean politicians have used or attempted to use various tactics to achieve these ends, including having voters take photos of ballots or flash ballots to official party scrutinizers. Simply planting a seed of doubt in some voters' minds that politicians can find out is, sometimes, as effective as knowing for sure. Such tactics to monitor or seem to monitor voter compliance are effective in Belize, where a small constituency size means that few persons can be truly anonymous. Some have argued that if ballot secrecy is compromised or in doubt (because some voters feel obligated to prove that they voted for particular political patrons), then the very principle of voting by free will is tarnished.

After elections are over, some clientelist voters, who have already received some form of payment, may have to wait until the next major partisan event or the next election to play the game again. One politician referred to the latter category of clientelist voters as "election day people", meaning that they get a lot at election time and then are given less attention at day-to-day clinic operations after elections.[11] Another argued, "If you [the voters] take a handout, be it $50 or a sack of rice, some politicians believe that they don't have to work for you, that they already 'worked' for you and paid you. And you can only sell your vote once."[12] As Evan X Hyde posited, voters "can't be taking handouts from politicians and then expect them to be answerable after they are elected".[13]

Votes or political support "sold" in the informal game of clientelism may provide politicians – and, by extension, governments – with another excuse for not delivering resources to particular citizens or neighbourhoods. In this regard, the Belize case supports the finding that "vote buying may constrain the policy representation of some citizens relative to others because some prospective voters may express policy options contrary to their actual preferences to receive material inducements from politicians".[14] A related argument may also be relevant to the Belize case: "Vote buying keeps parties and governments from considering the policy interests of poor voters who sell their votes."[15] The rationale is that once politicians have secured votes of some of the poor through clientelism, the more difficult challenge of securing political support through successful poverty alleviation may become less urgent.

There are also indications that rates of voter turnout can increase due to clientelist inducements or decrease when fewer resources flow and when there is negative vote buying (paying targeted voters to abstain from voting).[16] In Belize's case, for example, is it only a coincidence that the 90.1 per cent record turnout for the 1998 election coincided with the largest inflow of private money into general elections up to that date? After the 2012 election there was widespread speculation in some UDP circles that the historically low voter turnout in some Belize City constituencies, averaging in the low 60s percentage range, was due both to a relative decrease in resources for vote buying and also to negative vote buying by the opposition.[17] As one informant put it, "Some UDP candidates on the south-side [Belize City] were alarmed that the people they have helped all these years were not coming out to vote."[18] In the Belize context of tiny constituencies and increasing poverty, clientelist exchanges do actually swing constituency elections and affect voter turnout.

Overall, the entrenchment of vote trading strips a degree of credibility and some lustre from the very act of voting as the primary means of conveying the free electoral will of Belizeans. In the process, elections increasingly became a competition between two clientelist parties seeking another turn at the powers of the state inclusive of the opportunity to further maximize clientelist options.

The PUP and UDP as Clientelist Machines

Intense clientelist competition between the PUP and the UDP, which was critical to the increased prevalence of clientelist politician–citizen relationships, has presented considerable institutional implications for the two-party system itself. Importantly, it has disincentivized the two parties and their candidates to develop and offer distinctive political philosophies and national visions. As Goetz argued, clientelist appeals "undermine the incentives to political parties to make broad programmatic appeals to the electorate, encouraging instead narrowly focused promise-making and clientelist resource distribution".[19] This is not to suggest that all national development appeals by political leaders ceased, but rather to emphasize that, as both parties further evolved to become more clientelist in the interest of competitive electoral advantage, they deprioritized programmatic appeals. Even when one of the parties takes what appears to be a principled or ideological position, such as the nationalization of public utilities by the UDP between 2008 and 2012, closer examination largely reveals motivations of political expediency rather than deep ideological or principled underpinnings. The fact that the PUP, after fiercely critiquing these nationalizations, had committed itself to maintaining majority government ownership if it had been elected in 2012 is another example of how clientelism has further pushed the parties towards being carbon copies of each other – or what some Belizeans sarcastically dub the PUDP (People's United Democratic Party).

The gradual, then rapid, shift of party electoral strategy towards clientelism has also contributed to both parties deprioritizing mass membership recruitments around national policy objectives. Instead, as each party has sought to outcompete the other with clientelist appeals, and as these appeals have proven electorally successful, there have been even more incentives to expand and fund larger constituency-based clientelist operations. At the constituency level, party membership is now based less on belief in national party visions for the common good and more on which party can deliver the most resources to citizens as individuals. As such, the primary focus of party organization at the constituency level has increasingly become that of building a client-membership base, rather than citizen-party membership based on programmatic appeals.

Also, the incentive to establish long-term support from non-party organizations has also diminished. In particular, the labour unions, on whose backs party politics had initially developed, have only short-term opportunistic value to the two dominant parties as clientelist approaches to individual citizens have proven successful. Just as the two parties have come to view constituents less as cause-inspired members and more as clients, constituents view the parties more as channels for individualized influence and less as a space for collective influence. In this regard, the Belize case is in line with Goetz's contention that clientelism discourages citizens, and especially poor citizens, from organizing "on the basis of shared interests in better service provision. Instead, the incentives are to 'fight' each other in order to be the privileged recipients of targeted transfers".[20] As Shoman argued, the optic of being seen to be with a political party, or having the parties so believe, is a survival strategy in Belize's small-state clientelism context: "People feel that they need to associate with a political party, even if it is in opposition, or they are not in play. They won't get jobs, help and protection. If you are totally independent, nobody [messes] with you. And this goes for all classes."[21] It is, therefore, misleading to deduce the breadth of the real membership bases of the PUP and UDP by their abilities to draw crowds or by their lists of card-carrying members because clientelism has transformed and diluted the meaning of party membership.

Whereas constituency party offices are constitutionally part of a party's organizational structure, the dominant clinic operations within them are de facto informal structures that have become increasingly independent from central party organs. Individual politicians organize themselves to seek resources for their clinic operations far beyond what the party can provide, and the party hierarchy has little interest in monitoring what their politicians do at their clinics, if this contributes to electoral victory. The dangers of this dynamic do not escape some political leaders. For example, in a public event in 2011, former prime minister Barrow, after praising politicians for helping to meet the everyday needs of their individual constituents through the distribution of assistance, confessed that "sometimes I am afraid to enquire how they [UDP representatives] do this . . . and I hope it is not at the price of selling their souls for financing".[22]

Just as the influx of money into the parties in the 1990s facilitated the rise of clientelism, expanding clientelism became the driving imperative behind the funding needs of the political parties. As illustrated, politicians need huge amounts to fund clientelist operations outside the immediate campaign period – including for the high costs of intra-party competition. The end result is an ever-growing competitive intensity to fund clientelist networks. This monetary snowball effect has been aptly and colourfully described by a broker: "If one politician gives people chicken for five years and then all of a sudden the opponent gives shrimp . . . then we all have to give shrimp to compete . . . and so on and so on."[23] This suggests that clientelism in Belize has had a self-perpetuating inflationary effect on the financing of political parties, which, in turn, has significant downstream implications for aspects of democratic governance and development.

Key among these are the diminishing calibre and the suspect motivations of politicians who decide to enter electoral politics and who are selected by the political parties. Some politicians themselves lament that the public service motive has been diluted by the "do it or lose" implications of handout politics. A former politician reflected: "It results in poor quality of candidates. In the first instance, in needy candidates who see it as a way to enrich themselves and, in the other, of well-to-do candidates for whom the salary is peanuts . . . but the other financial rewards are great."[24] A civil society leader was on point when he stated that politicians on a whole have less incentive "to learn the problems that affect their divisions and the nation since the focus is on delivering at the individual level".[25] He lamented that newcomers with little or no experience, no policy skills and no distinguishing policy positions can easily win elections by using handouts.[26]

The emerging picture is not pretty. Clientelist political parties that have few substantive differences are often shallow in the quality of political leadership. At the same time, electoral politics become less attractive to credible newcomers, and Belize is short-changed in accessing its best talent. When politicians do become candidates and get elected, most eventually complain about the distastefulness of the permanent need to "service" client demands and the never-ending need to seek more financing and other resources. As such, political clientelism becomes a catch-22 for both dominant parties and for their politicians – in that not playing means not winning and playing perpetuates the arduous and costly game even further.

Government Institutions Co-Opted: "Everything through Me"

Even though most public institutions with responsibilities for resource allocation have pre-existing limitations of coverage, these have been exacerbated by clientelist politics. Central to this impact is the ongoing clientelist imperative to increase partisan control over public institutions of resource allocation with the objective of expanding opportunities for handouts to individual constituents. One politician described the general approach succinctly: "In cabinet, ministers make it clear that they want to deal directly with their constituents. There is now an 'everything going through me' mentality so that [the politician] can benefit. Ministers do not want to use state institutions. These are seen as too slow, with too many rules and no sure political benefit. And remember that the people are impatient and want needs met now."[27]

The mechanisms that politicians in government use to maximize such clientelist opportunities from public institutions can be explored under two broad categories: directing resources to selected constituents through influence over existing institutions and creating new or "special" temporary allocation programmes. Taken collectively, the expansion of public resources going through politicians instead of the state institutions established for these purposes results in clientelist operations gradually supplementing or displacing some of the intended functions of these institutions – weakening and undermining them in the process.

To further demonstrate these worrying institutional implications, it is worth exploring the specific case of the Human Services Department (HSD) of the Ministry of Human Development, Social Transformation and Poverty Alleviation. Although departments in several other ministries have a social assistance role, the HSD is primarily designed and mandated to provide such services on behalf of the government. It is directly responsible for the government's limited social welfare and social safety-net interventions, including those for the most vulnerable children, families and older persons. Individual citizens can visit human development officers at the ministry's main office or its district offices to seek assistance. In the three fiscal years from 2009 through 2012, the HSD was allocated an annual average budget of some $3 million, one-third of the tiny budget of the entire ministry.[28] The entire ministry's annual budget averaged $9 million over this period – only 1.3 per cent of the total national budget. Most of the HSD's share of the ministry's budget is used for social assistance grants to the neediest, either for long-term social assistance (in the form of small weekly grants of $10 in 2010) or for immediate and emergency assistance, such as pauper funerals and help for fire victims.

As does the general public, politicians from both sides of the partisan fence identify the HSD as a grossly underfunded institution that is unable to meet the welfare needs of the population. Pre-existing institutional challenges apart, the limitations of the HSD to provide effective social welfare are made worse by the clientelist practices of successive parties in government. Despite the tiny budget, politicians have manoeuvred to target and compete for the HSD's grant funds for particular individual constituents. The most common approach involves ministers and area representatives making direct verbal or written requests for HSD assistance for particular constituents to the minister or the senior staff responsible.[29] Additionally, because the resources of the HSD are so limited, politicians have increasingly accessed non-HSD funds for social welfare assistance to constituents, including constituency stipends, the discretionary assistance budgets of other ministries and private sector donations. While some observers may see this simply as part of the normal process of politicians looking out for their constituents, it can trigger unintended negative consequences.

Indeed, the adverse institutional implications for the HSD are numerous. Staff members and regular operating procedures are often sidelined by well-connected partisans lobbying for assistance for "their" people.[30] As such, decisions on who receives the paltry assistance resources of the HSD have not always been made only on the strict imperatives of need and merit, as procedurally mandated, but sometimes based on clientelist interests. Over time, citizens have less confidence in the capacity of the HSD to address their needs and begin to view political clinic operations as a more responsive and dependable alternative. Consequently, more citizens go directly to politicians for personalized social assistance services. As more social assistance funds flow to constituents from clinic operations and from other public institutions, the HSD's inadequacies are exacerbated.

One politician referred to political clinics as "informal appellate courts" that provide social assistance to constituents who appeal to politicians for interventions because they do not get public assistance, or at least not quickly enough.[31] The public credibility of the state's institutions is further stained by the increased frequency of special and temporary programmes that pass through politicians and target specific groups with obvious clientelist purpose. A conspicuous example is the aforementioned Christmas Assistance Programme of December 2011, in which $40,000 was "distributed" to each of the thirty-one constituencies to allow UDP representatives and aspirants to deliver goodies of the season to constituents.[32] Another is the "special assistance" scheme three months later and before the March 2012 elections, in which each constituency received another $50,000 of public funds to be disbursed at the discretion of the UDP's thirty-one candidates.[33] A well-functioning HSD could easily have made good use of such funds and distributed them on merit-based and needs-based criteria.

This scenario plays out in institutions across the public service. For almost every resource and service provided by public institutions, politicians seek to exert enough discretionary control to have some disbursements go through them and around institutional processes so as to facilitate clientelist exchanges. The example of the Venezuela money, as detailed by the special audit, stands out as particularly egregious. Since the 1990s, even emergency humanitarian relief funds made available in the aftermath of natural disasters are not immune from the clientelist web.

The institutions that have responsibilities for the goods and services most traded in clientelist exchanges are the ones that are most targeted and therefore more affected. Apart from the HSD, these include those institutions responsible for education and health assistance, housing support, land distribution, immigration services, development-related loans and grants, trade licensing and tax concessions. Within existing discretionary procedures, or in spite of them, ministers and partisan employees in these institutions can make or influence decisions regarding which individuals receive goods and services, fee waivers and contracts. Such practices have become the modus operandi for a significant portion of the population, and one can understand why politicians have ever-diminishing incentives to strengthen public institutions such as the HSD. Indeed, the institutional weaknesses are viewed as advantageous and more conducive to the desired informality of the clientelist game.

As noted, incumbent politicians have also targeted funds of semi-autonomous statutory bodies to use as clientelist inducements. In the process, the institutional reputations of some services they provide have become tarnished. One case in point was the Non-Contributory Pension (NCP) programme of the Social Security Board. The NCP was launched in 2003, ostensibly as part of the PUP government's poverty alleviation initiative, with the goal of providing a small monthly pension to poor females (over sixty-five years of age) who had not contributed as workers in the past. In 2007, males (over sixty-seven years of age) were made eligible, and the $75 monthly stipend was increased to $100, and by 2010 there were some 3,900 recipients, 55 per cent of whom were female.[34] From the onset, constituency representatives and candidates attempted to influence who were selected as recipients. A review of the minutes of the NCP Committee for 2003 indicated that the NCP was hurriedly set up without clear criteria, and that these developed in reaction to problems as they arose.[35] The total annual cost of the NCP in 2010 was approximately $4.5 million[36] – more than the annual budget of the HSD for that year.

Even as the NCP's application process and eligibility criteria improved in subsequent years, the programme did not escape the tentacles of clientelism. Several citizens interviewed for this study confirmed this view. One citizen in Punta Gorda complained that he had lobbied his representative but had not gotten on the scheme because he was from the wrong party. Another from Belmopan claimed that recent immigrants, who were not yet official residents, were receiving NCP stipends.[37] This view was publicly expressed by a board member of a credible NGO set up to assist older persons:

> The NCP is a good idea – to get very poor older people some help – but it went bad. It began largely as a political gimmick in 2003 [an election year] and people have gotten on it due largely to partisan affiliation. There are stories about people getting on or off the list as parties change. Even recently arrived immigrants who are here for less than five years are said to be on the list. Unfortunately, it is not sustainable and a drain on those actually contributing. It is not a long-term solution to a real problem.[38]

The collective impact of clientelist intrusions on public institutions is well captured by the head of an inter-governmental social reform programme: "Handouts and the 'clinic syndrome' undermine government institutions, some of which are already limping. People have declining respect for them, and they break down even more as people get more from the informal system."[39] Similarly, a former politician argued, "Something has to give. For handout politics to increase; our national institutions fail and delivery through them declines."[40] In short, a parallel informal allocation system, based on clientelism, has become more normal and institutionalized at the expense of formally established institutions and procedures.

Blatant Job Patronage

The growth of job patronage associated with entrenched political clientelism presents other hard challenges for governance institutions. Even though governing parties already have majority appointment powers over most key public service posts, they still devise creative strategies to reward or attract partisan supporters with public service jobs. At the most senior level, the discontinuation of the Westminster tradition of permanent secretaries and their replacement with CEOs facilitated the politicization of public institutions. As contract officers serving at the pleasure of ministers over an election cycle, CEOs are expected to facilitate partisan clientelist requests from politicians. Also worrying is the institutional impact of job patronage on the lower ranks of the public service in relation to non-established workers on contract. For such hires, there is no requirement to use the formal employment process established for permanent established staff. Ministers have near total say, and, when in government, both major parties have engaged in the practice of hiring growing numbers of persons in non-established categories. As noted, the number of public officers in the open vote category jumped from miniscule numbers at independence to over a quarter of the public service (excluding teachers) in 2013. After every change of government, the losing political party lambasts the governing party with public accusations of patronage, job-based victimization, and paying workers to do little or no work.

The negative consequences of such highly politicized job patronage for the public service have been acknowledged by several governance assessments, including the reports of the Political Reform Commission (2000), the Public Sector Reform Council (2000) and the Management Audit (2004). These consequences included the hiring of ill-qualified persons, the dismissal of persons in whom training resources have been invested, the lack of institutional continuity, low morale among public officers, inaction brought on by fear of job victimization and low productivity. As such, the expansion of job patronage has contributed significantly to decreasing the effectiveness and fairness in the delivery of services to citizens by public service institutions.

Legislators or Welfare Agents?

Because political clientelism is no longer confined to election campaigns and because political support goes beyond voting, it is necessary to expand the analysis of its implications beyond formal democracy. From the viewpoint of citizens, clientelism can be viewed as "a part of citizenship practice, a means of engaging with the state in the person of the politician", and "through which citizens attempt to make politics and politicians, more representative and responsive".[41] In Belize's version of parliamentary democracy, this informal mode of citizen engagement transpires in the daily relationship of citizens with their representatives in spite of the fact that the formal constitutional role of these representatives is "to make laws for the peace, order and good government of Belize"[42] and to provide parliamentary oversight. Yet the unwritten and expected practice is that representatives look out for their respective constituencies, and constituents lobby representatives for attention and benefits.

As political clientelism has expanded since independence, representatives have come to self-identify and be viewed by a growing proportion of the electorate as problem-solvers and welfare agents of first resort. Constituents either play the game because they believe it delivers more quickly than formal channels or because they have come to expect that their representatives are responsible for satisfying individual needs and wants. The equation is similar for both the less needy and the higher-income constituents who play the clientelist game, except that more well-off clients view representatives less as welfare agents and more as facilitators of benefits. One indicator of the importance that representatives place on these roles is the proportion of their time they dedicate to them. The assessments of three politicians, who also have served as ministers, illuminate this point:

> Constituency work certainly takes more of my time than government work. My CEO and staff take care of the ministry work mostly, and I spend most of my time dealing with constituency needs . . . and mostly on a case-by-case basis. I am in the division an average of five days a week. The time I give to policy and ministry work is certainly affected.[43]

> After a while, politicians become hostages to the handout system. We end up spending most of our time on the business of delivering in the division and less time doing national work. We [representatives] have to run from the people sometimes or could spend all the time dealing with requests.[44]

> Handout politics messes up the concept and practice of representation as defined in the constitution. It should be to influence national policy, in the interest of people, in the House. But dealing with handouts becomes a major proportion of representatives' time and resources. We are judged by the amounts we deliver and not by how we vote in the House.[45]

Conversely, some representatives, who claim to devote significant time to ministerial responsibilities, see these ministerial responsibilities as constraints on their constituency time. One former minister reported that spending an average of three days per week on ministry work in Belmopan meant less time for constituents and that those representatives who have no ministerial role have a time advantage.[46] The time demands on political patrons to maintain an effective clientelist operation are not limited to one-on-one encounters with individuals in the constituency; they also include time needed to lobby minister colleagues for clinic resources, make deals with private donors, meet with brokers, manage the clinic staff, respond to written requests (texts, emails and letters) and see clients in ministerial offices. It is, by all accounts, a near full-time job for politicians and necessitates greater numbers of paid staff to operate the machinery.

The unwritten and unregulated functions of representatives as principal welfare agents and facilitators of handouts can often further marginalize their primary formal roles as policymakers, legislators and ministers. Apart from having less time to give to these roles, public policy programmes can be fleeced to facilitate the informal, immediate and short-term delivery of resources. In effect, these unwritten and informal roles of representatives result in different opportunities for constituents to negotiate resources from the government. Additionally, most citizens interviewed had no real knowledge of the constitutional legislative role of their area representatives, instead seeing them primarily as providers of personalized resources. This is not surprising given that clientelist relationships are facilitated by ministerial power and that citizens and politicians alike increasingly view elections as "running for minister". Overall, both the concept and the practice of constituency representation, whether from the viewpoint of the politician or the citizen, have been transformed by clientelism. From the viewpoint of a significant number of constituents, individual time with representatives or aspiring representatives is seen as an opportunity to influence the direction of specific resources in their favour.

As noted, most of the constituency-based community development activities provided by politicians operate out of party-constituency offices, are poorly organized, funded by government resources and disappear as soon as the politicians who operated them leave the constituency. One possible exception to this overall trend was the Samuel Haynes Institute for Excellence (SHIE) in the Pickstock constituency. Even though the then area representative operated his weekly political clinic from the complex, the SHIE received some positive reviews for the scope and quality of its community development and empowerment work. It is too early to assess how the SHIE will fare after the current area representative is no longer in the constituency and no longer has access to government resources to support its operations.[47] However, its relative initial success highlights the deep question of what role area representatives should indeed play in the provision of community development opportunities for constituents.

This question was broached by a visiting Jamaican academic and journalist who found the work of the SHIE impressive. Conceding that there are risks related to the SHIE's attachment to a partisan leader, she suggested that, in the context of the failure of formal institutions to address people's social and economic needs, the "question must not be whether, but how, the people's elected representative should contribute to the development process at the local level" in countries like Belize.[48] Pointing to the "destructive strategies of patronage and clientelism" that dominate the politician–constituent relationship, she argued for a comprehensive rethink of the role of representatives, with the SHIE as a possible model. Although the SHIE experience thus far suggests that a well-organized and well-funded community programme can, at least temporarily, operate side by side with clientelist operations, there is no evidence that the latter are decreasing as the dominant nodes through which constituents engage with their representatives.

"Paying" for Participation

At the same time political clientelism has expanded in Belize, there has been a precipitous decline of political party volunteerism – and there is a direct relationship. Up to the 1980s, constituency party operations were still largely based on volunteer labour from supporters who believed in their party. In the rampant phase of clientelism, most party workers at every level expect and receive payment, either in direct cash transfers or in some other kind of resource, favour or privileged treatment. This demise of party-based volunteerism, also linked to the lack of substantive differences between the PUP and the UDP, is yet another indicator that the size of a politician's cadre of workers is no longer a credible indicator of real political support. Additionally, some politicians indicate that switching parties, even at election time, is no longer a rare occurrence among street campaigners, based on which politician or party can offer more benefits at any one time.

The expectation of monetary or some other form of compensation for political support can extend to the attendance at party events such as conventions, rallies, civil protests and even public consultations. A useful example can be found in the House Committee public consultations in 2011 on the proposed constitutional amendment (of the then UDP government) to give the government guaranteed majority control of shares in specific public utility companies. A local television station reported that "both the PUP and UDP are mobilizing their supporters to swarm" the Belize City consultation.[49] In an interview with the station, the former UDP representative for the Port Loyola constituency in Belize City boasted that he would bring out one thousand supporters. When pressed on whether people were being paid to attend or being threatened with the withdrawal of patronage, the representative eventually conceded, "Those people remember the little house that they got. They remember the little help that they continue to get, including today. That's what they remember. The majority of people that are going out there in support of the [UDP] government and a lot of the people have gotten their 'deliverables'."[50]

Similar scenarios have played out increasingly across the country since the 1990s. Those constituents who are, in some way, "compensated" to attend such events are engaging in a form of informal political participation, which brings them some benefit.[51] At the same time, such exchanges, in the collective, can diminish the credibility of certain events and processes. The distaste and partisan labelling that can surround the "rented crowds" can repel those who genuinely want to freely express their considered views. The Belize case is replete with examples of how involvement in clientelist arrangements discourages other modes of participation due to fear that existing benefits may be lost. This effect is exacerbated by Belize's highly personalized small-state politics, which allows for a high degree of "compliance monitoring" by politicians. Politicians can easily keep an eye on constituents' actions and remove, or threaten to remove, benefits if they conclude that bargains are being broken. A colourful example relates again to the actions in 2011 of the former UDP representative for the Port Loyola constituency in Belize City, as reported in the local press. The opposition PUP was holding an intra-party divisional convention to select their candidate for the constituency. The UDP representative, then the minister of public works, stood with a few party workers in a private yard located next to the PUP convention voting area and directly in front of a queue of voters – ensuring the voters would know they were being monitored.[52] Some voters were apparently reminded about the benefits they were receiving – the implication being that they could be taken away.

That episode lucidly demonstrates how people can be intimidated from exercising a constitutional right. The term "perverse accountability" has been used to reference how "parties influence how people vote by threatening to punish them for voting for another party".[53] It should not be lost that the PUP aspirants in that Port Loyola party convention case were also offering monetary and other incentives for getting out the vote, illustrating how some voters can seek to maximize the value of their voting power by playing off competing politicians against each other. Rosberg captured this dynamic well:

> [T]here is a frantic organisation and re-organisation of social alliances as individuals attempt to get as close as possible to those who are able to provide them with scarce and badly needed resources. If possible, they make direct alliances with patrons or their gatekeepers. If this is not possible, they ally themselves to others who have better access. They engage in competition with other factions to reserve coveted resources for themselves, but if the alternative faction appears sufficiently successful, they might choose to abandon their own alliance and associate with the competing faction.[54]

Politicians also monitor constituents to gauge relative political support or opposition, especially with regard to promises bartered. In the Belize case, these actions include monitoring attendance at party rallies, positions taken on government actions, public statements to the media and involvement in independent advocacy campaigns. As a consequence, some citizens self-censor their activities so as to keep existing benefits or not jeopardize future benefits. The leader of the People's National Party (PNP), one of the tiny alternative parties, described this effect well: "There is a decrease in speaking out, speaking your mind, resisting, advocating . . . because it may end up meaning you will not get a handout or that special favour. It muzzles people, especially in a small society."[55] In short, clientelist politics discourages non-clientelist political participation and, in the words of Carl Stone, "inhibit[s] individual political freedom".[56] As such, even when people innocently engage in independent advocacy activities, there is often suspicion or mischief, created by partisans, that such involvement is as a result of clientelist inducements.

Locking Out Alternative Voices and Underrepresented Groups

The entrenchment of political clientelism also helps to explain why alternative or independent politicians and parties have failed so comprehensively to dent the electoral dominance of the PUP and UDP. In the elections of 2008 and 2012, independent and third-party candidates together polled only 2.8 per cent and 2.2 per cent of the vote, respectively.[57] Candidates of smaller parties and independents who choose to participate have either been unable to compete or have refused to compete with the established clientelist machines of the "big two" parties. Indeed, several smaller parties, such as the PNP and the Vision Inspired by the People, have made opposition to handout politics a part of their party platforms.[58] The PNP leader captured the challenges clientelism presented for his first election attempt in 2003:

> I did not expect that there would have been such demand for handouts. The PNP had resolved not to play that game but actually to try to fight it, to change it. But I was amazed at the actual extent of it. Clearly the culture of handouts was long entrenched by the blue [PUP] and the red [UDP]. The message was "if you got nothing for me, write me off".[59]

Whereas some past and current politicians spoke of the demands and distaste of clientelist politics as necessary evils or normal activities in a young state, some potential politicians were deterred from getting involved at all. One, who decided against running as a third-party candidate, explained his thinking by saying, "New people wanting to become politicians these days have a huge challenge . . . how to deal with and overcome this handout culture. I can't see how we can even begin without doing the same thing the two parties do. I can't do that."[60] Another former politician agreed: "Poor people cannot run for elections now. It's too expensive because of the handout game . . . unless you have a 'padrino' who owns you. It keeps out a lot of good people who want to run and makes contesting elections less egalitarian."[61]

There is also evidence that clientelism's disincentive effect on participation in electoral politics is one of the factors contributing to poor participation rates for women. Between 1981 and 2012 women made up only 5.6 per cent of all candidates seeking to become area representatives and only 2.9 per cent of all elected representatives.[62] In the 2008 and 2012 elections Belize had no women elected to parliament, and this placed it near the very bottom for women's representation not only in all of the Commonwealth Caribbean but also worldwide.[63] All the eight past and present female politicians interviewed agreed that clientelist politics, albeit but one of several barriers, affects the electoral participation of women more than men, and some pinpointed the use of handout politics by their male opponents as an insurmountable advantage.[64] In her comprehensive situational analysis of gender and politics, Lewis pointed to similar findings:

> It [handout politics] also makes it even more difficult to compete . . . women have fewer financial resources, less access to political donations, and less access to the powerful (and sometimes corrupt) networks that fuel political campaigns. Furthermore, there is some evidence that women have a greater distaste for feeding the system of handouts and patronage, while men more often see it as just part of the reality of political life. For all of these reasons, the ascent of a system of handout politics in Belize is one more barrier to women's political representation.[65]

Although participation rates for women as party candidates in elections have been very low, several studies have confirmed that women have higher rates of participation than men at most other levels of formal party activities, such as street campaigning, participation in rallies and general support work.[66] Interestingly, this pattern has also been observed in the informal activities of clientelism: women are hardly ever patrons or brokers but make up the majority of the clientele. Low rates of female participation in the higher levels of the hierarchy of clientelist networks at the constituency level, one of the training grounds for future political leaders, is, therefore, a critical cause of having fewer women as elected representatives in Belize's parliament.

Implications for Informal Participation through Civil Society

There is significant evidence that the expansion of clientelism has made the admirable work of CSOs in Belize significantly more challenging since the 1990s. Compared to clientelist flows, resources that come through CSOs (which have to be meticulously accounted for) are viewed by some citizens as overly tedious to access. Practised clients prefer political clientelism for its relative ease and predictability in satisfying their needs and wants. The "street" rationale for this preference is reflected in the sentiments of a female caller to a radio programme broadcast following Hurricane Richard, which struck the central Belize coast in October 2010. Complaining that the Belize Red Cross was in her neighbourhood but asking too many questions and slowing things down, the caller appealed to her area representative to come "take care of business" (distributing the food and building materials) because the "Red Cross da all Indians and no chief".[67] Of course, some citizens engage simultaneously in multiple informal modes of participation as part of a rational means of maximizing opportunities. This is the case, for example, with some members of CSOs in Belize City, such as the then Women's Circle. Several members attested to going to politicians for handouts, but they also sought out training and longer-term income-generating activities through membership in CSOs.[68]

The Belize case also suggests that entrenched political clientelism can complicate other aspects of the work of some CSOs. Those that seek to build membership bases or to mobilize support around a cause can have a difficult time attracting people who have come to expect short-term, personalized benefits from participation or who do not want to risk losing existing benefits by publicly affiliating with a contentious cause. With regard to the former, since the late 1990s, some CSOs have complained about the difficulty of attracting local volunteers.[69] This effect can be observed in a 2011 example in which a civil society group resorted to paying part-time workers to gather voter signatures for a petition aimed at triggering a referendum on the issue of the nationalization of major utilities. The Friends of Belize,[70] which organized the petition against nationalization, admitted to paying some workers $2 per signature collected and that this contributed to the success of collecting some twenty-one thousand signatures.[71] Furthermore, when CSOs are successful in organizing a particular advocacy activity, such as a protest march, there are sometimes hushed accusations or speculations, usually always false, that one or other political party assisted them by bringing out supporters with financial and other inducements. This was the case, for example, in the large union-led protests against public corruption in 2004–05.[72]

When governments make and implement policy decisions with a clientelist agenda, they can inadvertently complicate the programmes and advocacy messages of some CSOs. Instructive examples are found in the housing loan in 2011 and the mortgage write-offs of 2012, totalling some $77 million. In October 2011, five months before the 2012 election, the UDP government wrote off nine thousand and two hundred of what were described as non-performing loans valued at $60 million.[73] Then in January 2012, less than two months before the 2012 election, the government wrote off another seven hundred and eighty mortgages (each under $50,000) held by the Social Security Board and valued at $17 million.[74] Not surprisingly, many of these loans had been originally distributed through clientelist networks of several different governments. The director of a CSO, Help for Progress, contended that such write-offs "give our clients bad habits . . . some think that our small loans are gifts too, and we have trouble collecting".[75] The director of Belize Enterprise for Sustainable Technology, one of Belize's largest loan-making CSOs, provided a similar assessment:

> BEST is experiencing the negative effects of the actions of governments who gave loans as handouts, not following up on collecting loans and not taking those who don't pay to court. There are no repercussions. It's a culture now that a loan from government is a grant. This now extends to NGO projects. People don't expect to pay back. A huge part of the failure is this stupidity of not collecting or of writing off loans for partisan purposes. Yes, there are always cases of true inability to pay, but these are lumped with the ones who sometimes can pay. It creates conflict and tensions too when some get away and some have to still pay. I oppose this write-off of $60 million in non-performing housing loans. It will send the totally wrong message. But a big election is coming.[76]

CSOs can themselves contribute to the perception that they are not credible and effective alternative options for informal participation. As one CSO leader stated, "Quite a few CSOs depend on government support through subventions, exemptions, participation in internationally funded projects and other favours. Some CSO leaders are lured away with better government jobs."[77] Indeed, there is some evidence to support the contention that CSOs can themselves become clients of the state or be seen as such. In a small society in which most social relations are dominated or influenced by political parties and personal politics, it is not easy for CSOs to maintain their credibility as non-partisan actors. Both PUP and UDP governments have been known to use discretionary powers such as those of providing public grants and tax-exemption status to CSOs to curry favour or to punish.[78] An example of the latter phenomena was the elimination of the annual financial government subvention to the National Trade Union Congress of Belize just shortly after the union co-led the 2004–05 civil protests.[79]

Not surprisingly, politicians, who are generally intolerant of non-state actors, especially when in government, are among the most critical in their views of CSOs in relation to clientelism. A former PUP minister stated, "The social partners are not that much different from the people. At the same time, they protest and complain about some policy or other, they come to politicians asking for exemptions. It's hypocritical."[80] In a similar vein, former UDP prime minister Esquivel observed, "NGOs also began to act like the individual voters. They look out for what is good for 'my organisation', not the nation."[81] Esquivel also suggested that some churches seek to attract members in poor communities through inducements of food and other support. Even though such views must be taken in balance with the findings of several studies that CSOs have had significant successes in influencing public policy through advocacy and filling development gaps, the work of CSOs is significantly more challenging due to entrenched clientelism.

Politicized Social Welfare

Many politicians contend that their clinic-based assistance activities promote the distribution of resources in a way that is beneficial for Belizeans, especially lower-income citizens. This is an extension of the pre-independence "helping the people" justification. For example, the PUP leader of the opposition in 2011 defended his clinic work at the time in these terms: "Poor people in need do benefit. When I see needs, like mothers with sick kids with my own eyes, I can't ignore that."[82] A former UDP minister goes further: "Benefits politics is like a welfare system, and I know from experience that people get help. It is like a kind of conditional cash transfer programme. We may need to institutionalize it and bring it into the formal system. It works, and so giving more funds to representatives to use in their divisions will help more people."[83] Even those politicians who believe that handout politics can have negative consequences for the formal social welfare system share that they have had no choice but to assist needy constituents with other funds.

Although some citizens interviewed for this study stated that they would prefer not to depend on handouts, most agreed that people do benefit. In a social context that is itself supportive of political clientelism, such views are not surprising nor or are they unique to Belize.[84] In the words of George Price, there is "great social need".[85] A poor single woman with several children and with only a part-time job, even if lucky enough to receive a weekly $10 grant from the HSD, welcomes the assistance she can negotiate from her constituency representative. Poor immigrant parents who receive fast-track nationality and so can register to vote can better negotiate for benefits, such as educational assistance for their children.

A proportion of constituents justify bartering political support for needed resources with the argument that politicians "steal" and that what they get is, indirectly, the people's money anyway. From this viewpoint, the funds and resources received can be construed as an informal social welfare system in which political clinics are informal welfare entities, politicians are informal welfare agents and constituents are welfare recipients. As such, in the context of an ineffective social welfare system, clientelist relationships do help fill social welfare voids created by the failure of public institutions to adequately meet basic socio-economic needs.

This recognition that some people do indeed benefit from such informal modes of resource distribution comes with substantive caveats. First, although the majority of benefits are to meet immediate and short-term needs (such as the payment of utility bills, school fees and bus fares), not all clients are poor and some benefits are longer term, such as land, houses, education and productive inputs. Middle-class citizens who participate in clientelist relationships tend to request and receive more of these higher value resources. Thus, the "welfare" argument becomes more dubious for this set of clients as their motivations to play the game of clientelism are not generally aligned with the goal of meeting basic needs. Nevertheless, some middle-class and higher-income clients point to a broken social system and an unlevel playing field to access goods and services as their motivations for playing the game.

There are serious implications of political clientelism for the operations of the existing social welfare system itself. Some politician and citizen interviewees pointed to the lack of fairness inherent in distributing resources through informal clientelist operations. One politician summarized this consequence well: "The welfare system has been put into politicians' hands. The safety-net has become more and more partisan and so more based on subjective decision-making. It is less merit-based, less fair."[86] In short, the direction and volume of benefits in the informal welfare system are based, in significant part, on politicians' individual assessments of past or potential political support and on the street-smart bartering skills of citizens.

Without transparent guidelines and standards, the allocation decisions of politicians vary across constituencies and even within constituencies. The result is a skewed distribution process based less on merit and more on individual partisan assessments by politicians. Some citizens, who do have needs but are less well connected and tenacious, often fall through the cracks. Those who are more politically connected or bold tend to get more. There are also growing numbers of opportunistic clients who play the politicians at their own clientelist game. Such clients can easily manoeuvre to double-dip or freeload in a game with such informal rules. Without adequate standards, accountability and evaluation for the distribution of benefits given informally through politicians, measuring the real impact on people's livelihoods is difficult.

What is likely is that the expansion of welfare distribution through clinic operations has not effectively contributed to solving deeply entrenched social and economic problems, as some politicians believe. On the contrary, some problems may actually be exacerbated. Godfrey Smith's assessment here is very much on point: "The biggest downfall of handouts is that they promote short-term solutions to long-term problems. Much money is spent, but the problems remain. In the meantime, people grow to want short-term solutions at the expense of seeking real solutions."[87] Jones agreed: "People are getting assistance, but it is not sustainable and not solving key problems. For instance, the school non-participation rate is increasing, the income gap is increasing, poverty is increasing."[88]

For sure, clientelist politics, as demonstrated by the HSD case, weakens the very public institutions that are supposed to address the effects of social problems such as poverty. Smith contended, "Patronage politics have overturned government as the social provider . . . except perhaps in education."[89] As noted, even in education, an increasing percentage of the annual budget is allocated in a quota system for distribution on the recommendations of the thirty-one area representatives. Overall, what has transpired is akin to what Domínguez referred to as "the corruption of the welfare state".[90] This "corruption" is but collateral damage in the ongoing process of facilitating the clientelist politics that both major political parties deem necessary for winning elections.

A broader question is whether poverty, which was identified as a core-supporting condition for the expansion of political clientelism, is not itself exacerbated by entrenched political clientelism. Several studies point to at least two ways that political clientelism can contribute to poverty: clientelism encourages "declining relative productivity" and creates economic problems, which increase poverty; and clientelism contributes to poverty by providing short-term benefits to individuals at the expense of programmatic approaches.[91] The first is plausible, if difficult to verify, and is addressed later in this chapter. The second is also possible as even though some of the poor do benefit, what they receive are mostly band-aid solutions, and failing policies are perpetuated as systemic solutions are postponed.

Waste of Public Finances and Loss of Revenue

Since the 1990s, decisions and actions related to budgetary expenditure, revenue generation, public borrowing and the use of international grants have been increasingly influenced by the imperatives of keeping "clientelist machineries" oiled and clients minimally satisfied. Due to the informal, illicit and underground nature of most clientelist activity, it is especially difficult to calculate the proportion of public funds wasted and revenues lost due to clientelism. However, several clear links can be observed, especially with regard to the national budget.

In relation to the expenditure side of the budget, the assessment of a retired politician cannot be put much better: "The handout system is nothing but a form of irrational budget distribution because ministers now direct more and more of their ministries' budgets to their own constituencies at the expense of national programmes."[92] As illustrated, there has indeed been a trend towards increasing proportions of ministerial budgets being allocated through representatives and candidates of the ruling party, either under existing programmes or special projects. The 10 per cent of the education budget reserved for discretionary spending annually and the $2.7 million in special assistance funds granted for distribution by the UDP's thirty-one candidates before the 2012 elections are key examples.

More so, the example of the Venezuela money offers particularly poignant insights into the multi-layered nature of the linkages of clientelism to waste of public resources. The fiscal situation in the lead-up to the 2008 election, when Belize received the $40 million from Venezuela, was fragile. Fiscal belt-tightening and budgetary strain, largely due to one-quarter of the budget having to go to external debt payments, meant that the PUP had limited options to finance pre-election piñata projects and goodies. As demonstrated, only $20 million of the total Venezuela grant was made known initially, and the then government decided to expend this in a one-month period before the election.[93] As most of this money disappeared into the hands of politicians and voters, there were widespread allegations of election buying and voter bribery. Although it may have just been realpolitik from the standpoint of PUP politicians seeking a third term in office, this rushed clientelist spending of the Venezuela money was decidedly irrational in terms of the stated primary intent of helping to address the problem of insufficient and inadequate housing. In this regard, the fiasco also highlights another aspect of the waste problem: the ever-present temptation to use such financial windfalls for handouts and not for development programmes.

Another case in point here is the source of funds for the Christmas Assistance Programme in 2011: the $1.4 million was a portion of the proceeds received by the UDP government for shares held in the newly nationalized Belize Telemedia Limited.[94] These seemingly sudden bouts of reckless spending are seldom without upstream or downstream links to other activities related to clientelism. In the case of the Venezuela grant, the PUP government had attempted to divert half of the $40 million to service a loan from Ashcroft's Belize Bank, without informing the House of Representatives as was procedurally required.[95] The background to the attempted diversion of these funds is revealing. The Belize Bank had taken over the loan in question from the Development Finance Corporation, which had carried a sovereign guarantee from the government. However, the original loan had been made to a PUP-favoured business group and was part of a "loan for favours" scandal involving the Development Finance Corporation and the Social Security Board that came to a head in 2004. It is no secret that private donations, intended to influence such loan decisions, as well as portions of the loans themselves, can and do end up as kickbacks in party coffers and, by extension, in political clinics. This is to say that it is highly likely that the motive to find funds for pre-election clinic operations in 2003 played at least some role in the ensuing complicated and wasteful loan fiasco.[96] The scandal involving the Social Security Board and the Development Finance Corporation was the subject of two official public investigations – one by the Senate – and the revelations contributed to the public outrage and protests that were widely seen as factors in the PUP's defeat in the 2008 election.[97]

Cumulatively, fiscal decisions influenced by the need to fund clientelism contribute to a waste of public funds. The waste occurs on several levels, not the least of which is expending significant sums of money without advancing solutions to social and economic problems. Comparing the costs of some examples of clientelist spending to the budgets of some ministries throws light on the dimension of the problem. For example, the nearly $20 million of the Venezuela money expended in the four-week period before the 2008 election was more than the total annual budgets of eight of the then thirteen ministries of government in 2007–08.[98] In chapter 3, it was estimated that the total annual expenditures for clinic operations alone in a non-election year can be as high as $9.9 million. This is, for example, more than the total annual budgets of ten of the then nineteen ministries in 2010–11, including the ministries with responsibilities for human development, housing, economic development, public works and local government.[99] Also, the $2.7 million expended in the special assistance programmes leading up to the 2012 election was more than the annual budget of two ministries and one-third of the entire budget of the Ministry of Human Development.

On the public revenue side, some uncollected revenues are associated with incumbent politicians giving individual citizens financial waivers for which they may not otherwise be eligible. For example, when the UDP government decided to write off the mortgages of ten thousand individuals worth a total of $77 million in a five-month period before a national election, this not only deprived the treasury of needed income but also perpetuated a message to other mortgage holders and loan applicants that repayment will not be taken seriously. Similarly, the use of ministerial power to waive or lower import duties and fees for specified persons contributes to the overall revenue collection problem.

Most of the loss of revenue related to clientelism is a result of the favours bought or given to the business sector, not to the poor or most of the middle class. It is the local and international businesses that most reap the benefits in terms of lack of loan repayment by bigger debtors, investment concessions, fee waivers, bloated contracts and other special treatment afforded donors by politicians and political parties. A former politician made the links very well:

> For every dollar they give [to politicians], the donors can get back double, ten, up to a hundred times what was invested. And this indirectly means that government revenue is less and there is less money for the state to meet peoples' needs. Much of the non-payment of these loans, the lucrative concessions, the problems you saw at SSB and DFC that cost the state revenue can all be traced back to that dollar invested. Part of that dollar is to oil the wheels of patronage. If we include all such big and not so big party donors, the effect is less revenue for public coffers and for social spending.[100]

Although acknowledging the revenue-depleting effects, not all political actors assess "return on investments" as having an overall negative outcome. Such arguments are captured well by Smith:

> I do not see so huge a problem with the "return on investment" issue. Remember that the private sector is the engine of growth, and tax holidays and duty-free concessions assist this. For example, investments in shrimp and the tourism village have been made by campaign donors who did get breaks, but these

all added to economic activity and economic growth. If there is less money for the government budget, this is counterbalanced by the positive economic repercussions of major investments.[101]

This is indeed the point of view also held by Ralph Fonseca. He argued that the concessions given to businesses, which may have contributed to the PUP, have more benefits, such as transferring technology and boosting the economy, than costs, and that these are a "necessary part of the risks of doing business".[102] Former leader of the opposition John Briceño saw it as a matter of degree: "The 'return on investment' aspect can be a problem but does not have to be. I have no apologies for helping someone who helped my party to get a contract, but I do not condone that the contract is double the price. There is a line that should not be crossed."[103]

As challenging as it is to estimate the revenue lost due to clientelist businesses relationships, the evidence suggests that losses outweigh benefits. For example, it has long been argued that fiscal concessions to businesses contribute to under-taxation in Belize. One analysis of 2005 figures by Bulmer-Thomas and Bulmer-Thomas found that public revenue was nearly 30 per cent ($140 million) below what could have been expected and that this was double the entire education budget.[104] They also illustrated that gross national income (which adjusts gross national product to include income received and paid abroad) decreased as a ratio of GDP in the thirty years since independence to over 10 per cent in 2010 – meaning that over 10 per cent of GDP did not accrue to Belizeans. They refer to this as the "Ashcroft effect".[105] There is also urgent research that needs to be done on how much potential revenue is lost due to duty-free and other business promotion concessions awarded to investors that do not abide by the standards set and on which there is minimal follow-up to assess whether the promised jobs and economic benefits are indeed created.

Serious Challenges for Public Policy

A 2007 study of the policymaking process in Belize described it as top-down in approach, lacking in inter-ministerial coordination, not guided by national development goals, and hampered by weak implementation and monitoring practices, resulting in public policies that are largely "reactive, incremental, ad hoc and short-term".[106] The study pinpointed the two-party adversarial system and the imperatives of election timetables as key challenges for the policymaking process. Clientelist politics should be added to this list.

When informal resource distribution supersedes the formal functions of government, public institutions face added constraints in developing and implementing the policies needed to mitigate social ills. As Stokes argues, "Rather than using public policy to effect transfers from some classes of voters to others, parties deliver inducements to individual voters and thus bolster the parties' electoral prospects."[107] In Belize's case, the impact of clientelism on policy implementation in such ministries as education, health, housing and human development has been illustrated. The HSD example clearly showed ongoing interference and damage to social welfare policy implementation. In an attempt to influence individual voters before the 2008 election, a significant portion of the first tranche of the Venezuela funds was allocated outside of established policy guidelines and procedures. New policy initiatives of 2010–12, such as the CCT, struggled to escape the clientelist embrace. The cabinet had decided that the CCT scheme would be managed by the Ministry of Human Development and not by representatives because the government was required to demonstrate to international funders that the programme was effective and transparent.[108] While area representatives failed to get the CCT funds to pass through them, they still understood that they could influence who actually received CCT funds by sending recommendations and lists of names to the Ministry of Human Development. It will be important to independently assess the extent to which the Belize CCT has been able to maintain a firewall from clientelist politics. The central point here is that policy implementation is adversely affected when politicians succeed in influencing decisions on the allocation of public resources to favour selected constituents.

However, the more damaging impact of entrenched clientelism on the policymaking process lies in the financing demands for ongoing and growing costs of the clientelist operations of politicians. As illustrated, such costs are now year-round and represent the biggest portion of the financing needs of politicians in an election cycle. Two of the interrelated negative implications for the policy process are the promotion of short-term and individually targeted approaches to problem-solving, and the concurrent lack of incentives for long-term planning for national programmes. Politicians interviewed were generally open in their acknowledgement that political clientelism encourages ineffective policy approaches to societal problems:

> One of the biggest downfalls of this kind of politics is that it promotes short-term solutions without really fixing the problems. Over time people grow to want immediate solutions to their current problems.[109]

It's a vicious cycle. The party winning, and not the country, becomes the most important thing. The key is to get goods and services to the people in the short term and more and more this becomes the norm. It's hard to stop if you want to win.[110]

It [political clientelism] is a disincentive to long-term planning . . . and even for divisional and community planning. Ministers and area representatives focus less and less on collective and national development and more on needs of individual constituents. But this is also true for voters who want individual needs met and have decreasing interest in national programmes . . . these count for less in deciding who to support.[111]

Some politicians also spoke about a trend of constituents having waning interest in community goods and projects as they focus more on individual benefits. One politician expressed some frustration that the library, roads, sports field and park she had organized to build were but "minimally appreciated" by particular constituents who were looking out more for personal handouts.[112] Another added, "Some people can't see beyond their mouths and there is less interest in community projects that affect everyone. They say that those kinds of projects are OK but they don't put food on my table."[113] Former prime minister Barrow used a Kriol proverb to make the point 16: "While di grass di grow, di horse di starve" – in the time it takes to reform public institutions people still need help.[114]

A very small number of politicians interviewed objected to the view that their constituents are disinterested in collective projects. They contended that politicians who have this experience either use "overly paternalistic approaches"[115] or "take the easy road and go directly to only handouts".[116] The co-founder of the relatively successful SHIE agreed with this point of view: "It is not my experience that community-wide programmes have to be negatively affected. It is the calibre of the politician that matters. If you are a man of straw you will give in and be consumed fully by handout politics."[117] Nevertheless, the Belize case has illustrated that since the 1998 election, the vast majority of politicians have indeed opted to take the easy road.

On the whole, this discussion suggests that clientelist politics is a significant contributing factor to the "anti-planning trend". There has been decreasing interest in national development planning since independence and most macro-planning has been externally driven. Since the 1990s, governments have routinely ignored or given mostly lip service to long-term development plans, and the manifestos of the PUP and UDP have filled some of the vacuum created. Between 1990 and 2000, there were two attempts to develop five-year development plans and one to develop a longer-term plan. One of the five-year development plans was never completed and the other was mostly ignored. Even after a well-funded national consultation process between 1993 and 1994, the longer-term plan (the National Human Development Agenda) was never completed.[118] Several studies have emphasized that this lack of consistency in long-term national development planning is detrimental to the nation's development. For example, a 2006 United Nations Development Programme country assessment stated that "because there is no overall national development plan and corresponding centralized coordination strategy, individual planning efforts remain uncoordinated and non-strategic, thereby not systematically taking advantage of synergies and collective efforts".[119]

In 2007, after pressure from international organizations and local CSOs, a process to develop a twenty-five-year national development plan termed Vision 2025 was finally launched under the 2003–08 PUP government. It was renamed Horizon 2030 and completed in 2011, following nationwide consultations under the 2008–12 UDP government.[120] This impressive and comprehensive plan was only approved by the cabinet after the 2012 election – four years after the process began. A key player in the plan development process suggested at the time that the initial cool reception of Horizon 2030 at senior levels of political leadership is an example of the extent to which politicians focus on meeting immediate individual needs and are unmotivated to seek longer-term collective solutions: "Politicians have short-term visions – to the next election or even the next clinic day. There is little political interest at government level or in the opposition . . . just some rhetorical support. It does not bode well for the plan."[121]

Overall, entrenched clientelism represents a triple assault on long-term policy and collective development approaches: first, from political parties that have little incentive to offer distinctive national visions and policies to the electorate; second, from politicians who seek to deliver targeted goods and services directly to individuals and households; and third, from the growing numbers of citizens who demand immediate and individual delivery of benefits.

Private Money Calling the Shots

As has been illustrated, politicians receive a significant amount of their funds for campaigning and clinic operations from private sources, a fact that is widely acknowledged and corroborated. The 2008 SPEAR poll found that the largest proportion of respondents (33.3 per cent) believed that political parties get money to finance their campaigns from "big business", compared to 24.5 per cent saying "the government budget",

18.1 per cent saying "illegal sources", and 12.1 per cent saying "special interest groups".[122] The self-evident relationship between these private donations and public policy is not denied by most politicians: the larger the private donation, the more the donors can exert influence on policy decisions by cashing in on "returns on investments" from victorious politicians. The money trail of the linkages between clientelist politics and the policy influence of financial contributors in Belize is near impossible to follow due to the informal, shadowy and spaghetti-like transactions that occur and to the lack of regulation of campaign financing. Yet, there are some telling indications.

As noted (chapter 4), it is widely believed that donations from Sir Barry Bowen of Bowen & Bowen Ltd and Lord Ashcroft to both major political parties and to individual politicians were most substantive for the 1990-2010 period. It would, therefore, not be surprising if such donors attempted to influence particular policies and actions of government over time. In one instance of policy influence in 1993, Bowen was seeking a reduction of the tax on its locally produced beer and allegedly related this to facilitating a new investment it planned to make in milk production.[123] The tax cut was approved, but the beer prices remained the same at the time – even as the new investment did not materialize.[124] In another instance, when Bowen wanted to make major investments in the shrimp farming industry in 2007, he initiated a group of other investors to pen their own draft legislation and then to lobby the government for enactment. The draft bill contained favourable business concessions for the investors that could negatively impact government revenue.[125] The bill was eventually enacted and became the Aquaculture Development Act.

Few would disagree with the statement that "the influence on the political parties and governments of Belize by the British billionaire Lord Michael Ashcroft, former [Deputy] Chairman of the British Conservative Party, has been inordinate".[126] Some of the instances of policy influence related to Ashcroft's donations to both the PUP and UDP since the late 1980s have been referenced. As cited in chapter 5, the draft of the International Business Companies Act, which exempted Ashcroft's companies from various taxes for thirty years, was prepared by Ashcroft's lawyers in 1990. Ashcroft's companies have likely influenced the development of several other pieces of legislation including the Off-Shore Banking Act and the Telecommunications Act. With regard to telecommunications, and after negotiating a lucrative deal with the government in 1992 to purchase a majority share in the then Belize Telecommunication Limited, Ashcroft was also able to secure additional tax benefits, such as the controversial tax accommodation agreement granted by the PUP government of 2003–08. This guaranteed Ashcroft's telecommunication company 15 per cent minimum profits before business taxes were triggered.[127] It was largely such extensive influence on policy decisions procured by Ashcroft that led Bulmer-Thomas and Bulmer-Thomas to conclude, "No single person has been more assiduous in fighting for the fiscal concessions that have contributed to the failures of the growth model as well as leading to an oligopolistic banking system."[128]

Whether they are mega donors or somewhat smaller donors, their donations gain them influence over the development and the implementation of particular policies, and whether they acknowledge it or not, part of their donations end up oiling clientelist machines at the clinic level. The argument here is not that the policy influence of such donors would be non-existent without clientelism, but that the demand for funds for clientelist operations is a major and underestimated factor in influencing the entire policymaking and legislative process. This is especially the case for any governance reforms or enforcement of regulations that threaten the clientelist game.

Disincentives for Governance Reform

As Goetz contends, "The central dilemma that governance reforms pose to politicians inheres in their perceived high cost in terms of lost patronage resources, lost opportunities for private earnings, and an erosion of political support from public sector workers. Administrative reforms, in particular, decrease the ability of politicians to build political capital through the distribution of public sector appointments and jobs, or through the awarding of contracts."[129] In Belize, governance reform initiatives that place limits on the discretionary allocation of public resources face the most resistance from political parties in power. A review of government responses to the 103 recommendations of the Political Reform Commission reveals that there were high levels of resistance to those measures that would diminish existing powers to decide on targeted allocations and increase accountability around such allocations. Among the recommendations not implemented were two that sought to limit the arbitrary abuse of powers of ministers to waive fees and to regulate campaign financing, both of which are directly related to clientelist politics.

Since the 1993 election, both the PUP and UDP have repeatedly broken manifesto promises to develop and enact campaign financing legislation, notwithstanding ongoing advocacy in this regard by several CSOs. A

2006 SPEAR poll indicated significant public support for regulating campaign financing, with an overwhelming majority of 81.4 per cent saying that they would support a law requiring political parties to disclose their sources of campaign financing. In its 2003–08 term of office, elements of the PUP government actually drafted a campaign finance law, but it was squashed in the cabinet.[130] This bipartisan reluctance to regulate campaign financing exposes the absence of interest to enact legislative changes that may inhibit unregulated competition by political parties for private financing for campaigns and clientelist operations.

Similarly, recommendations from various public service reform commissions to fix the "open vote worker" problem have been ignored by both parties.[131] As noted, the practice of abusing the open vote option is attacked repeatedly by parties when in opposition, especially after huge staff turnovers in the public service when governments change. Despite repeated promises neither party has taken measures to address the issue through reform when in power. For example, in its 2012 Party Manifesto, the UDP promised to "transition open vote workers into the permanent establishment".[132] A task force set up after the 2012 election to advise on this matter actually determined that, due to levels of education and skills of open vote workers, it would not be possible to assimilate most into the permanent establishment and that a moratorium on future recruitment of open vote workers may be necessary.[133] However, as with governments before, the open vote workers problem was kicked down the road.

The same is true for reforms related to the election management machinery. As noted in chapter 3, amendments to the Representation of the People Act diluted the autonomy of the EBC by giving the party in power de facto majority (through the appointment process) and by transferring some EBC responsibilities to a government department. Both major parties have not acted on numerous recommendations to increase EBC independence. These include the recommendations of the Political Reform Commission to remove majority control from political parties, transfer the power to appoint the chief elections officer from the prime minister to a reformed EBC and give the reformed EBC priority budgetary treatment. In 2000, the governing PUP accepted the commission's recommendations on this matter but did not act to implement reforms. Similarly, in 2012 the UDP government announced that, due to lack of finances, it would not proceed with the legally mandated process of re-registering voters, which would clean up the voters' lists.[134] It is clearly not in the short-term interests of either party to have a more independent election management body with the authority and resources required to effectively perform such duties as re-registration and investigating allegations of voter bribery.[135]

Public Corruption and Corruption of the Public

The widespread presence of public corruption in Belize since the late 1990s is well established. In the first decade of the new millennium, Belize's ranking fell from 46 in 2003 to 109 in 2008 on the Corruption Perception Index, placing Belize in the category of states with "rampant corruption" on Transparency International's scale. A spate of national reports and studies pinpointed political corruption as one of the most challenging governance and development issues facing Belize, and it has been a priority campaign issue of parties in opposition in almost every election since independence. In a 2006 SPEAR poll, corruption was ranked as the national issue of highest concern, and even ahead of poverty. Yet a 2010 AmericasBarometer survey found that only 36 per cent of Belizeans believed that the government was confronting corruption.[136] The same survey suggested that this high level of concern about a poor record of fighting corruption helps to explain why more than half of Belizeans said they would support a more "authoritarian" approach to address such problems – more than any of all the twenty-three regional countries surveyed.

This increase in political corruption has occurred in the same post-1990 period of rampant clientelism in Belize, and there is a clear direct relationship. Political clientelism overlaps with public corruption when patrons use public office or access to office holders to extract favours related to state resources and services for use in clientelist transactions.[137] Rehren's observation on this link is worth repeating: "When political parties control the bureaucracy and behave as virtual patrons, dispensing public resources and positions in exchange for partisan allegiance, and eventually allow party members to enrich themselves, clientelism facilitates corruption."[138] In Belize too, the corrupting influence of clientelism is directly related to the relationships and opportunities created by the flow of public and private resources needed to oil the wheels of clientelism.

Clientelist exchanges between politicians and citizens when they involve public goods are, in effect, private gains for both politicians and clients. Politicians gain more votes from the electorate to attain or keep political power, and clients gain a wide variety of individualized benefits such as jobs, land or social assistance. The opportunity for abusing public funds inherent in these dyadic exchanges is a core reason why voter bribery is an illegal and indictable offence. Although there have been numerous informal allegations of political corruption in Belize, there have only been a handful of corruption-related court cases, and no politician or voter has ever been found guilty, fined or imprisoned as a result.

George Price, when asked to reflect on the post-1990s implications of political clientelism, maintained the "helping" justification, but also added a concern that no other politician interviewed mentioned: "It is a good thing that they [politicians] do. The problem is with those who get the money and keep some for themselves or their circle. They don't give it to the people."[139] Indeed, the opportunities for public funds to be siphoned off and to disappear into the black hole of clientelism abound, and a few illustrations make the point. There is absolutely no reporting done on the use of constituency stipends that go directly to area representatives.[140] Politicians confirm that this is only the "anchor money" for their clinic operations. One attempt by the Auditor General in 2011 to begin to follow the money trail of these funds was rebuffed by the Ministry of Finance.[141] There is no way to confirm how the money is spent and how many and which individual constituents may have received funds.

Similar accountability challenges afflict most of the short-term special assistance programmes that pass through the clinic operations of area representatives and party candidates. For instance, it is likely that much of the $7 million from the Venezuelan grant that was deemed "unaccounted" by the Auditor General ended up in the private hands of political operatives and voters alike.[142] In those cases when there is some paper trail, corruption is more directly implied. For example, the audit investigation into the 2003 education scandal found clear evidence that scholarship grants were being transferred to non-students.[143] In short, the characteristic lack of formality and rules governing clientelist operations present many opportunities for private gain from public money by politicians, brokers, party operatives and clients.

Another branch of the corruption trail is where private donations for clientelist operations lead to private gain for politicians and donors. The gain transpires when funds donated lead to eventual "returns on investment" for the donors through tax write-offs, duty-free concessions, discretionary fee waivers, bloated contracts, favourable legislation and the like. The long-term aggregate corruption impact of hundreds of donors getting some special favour from the government is incalculable. In the case of Lord Ashcroft, it is not unreasonable to ask if the returns on investments for financing both major political parties since the early 1990s have included the purchase of majority shares in the telecommunications monopoly, the drafting of favourable legislation and the receipt of concessions for his various businesses. Of note is that Ashcroft's returns have likely gone beyond investment-related concessions: shortly after the PUP's election victory in 1998, Ashcroft (who had procured Belizean citizenship) was appointed for a two-year year tenure as Belize's representative to the United Nations.

The Belize case also illustrates that clientelism plays a significant role in promoting the acceptance of corruption among the wider public. Because of the common justification given by politicians that such transfers "help" people, these links to corruption are sometimes defended, overlooked or ignored. Voters are generally aware that the clientelist game is being played, and most have little genuine respect for their politician patrons. Many perceive that their politicians are corrupt and enriching themselves, and they use this as an excuse for playing the game themselves. By extension, some people began to excuse or justify the corruption of their politicians and even to see it as normal. However, as Evan X Hyde argued, when "people do not ask where the money for handouts comes from", they can become "part of the whole process which involves dirty money and corruption".[144]

Political Culture: Horse or Carriage?

The analysis thus far suggests that political clientelism has not only transformed Belizean political culture, but is indeed now a defining feature of it. One political observer made the worryingly accurate observation that "the average 18 year old Belizean who has just become a voter may know little else about the political process other than selling votes for a favour. It is what they know and what they use".[145] Interviews with younger citizens and students, including a focus group with thirty-two students at the University of Belize, confirmed that there is indeed a high level of awareness of the clientelist game. For example, several interviewees pointed to the fact that their parents or guardians had to visit constituency representatives to get their children on lists for educational assistance.

The widespread acceptance of clientelism as political norm is reflected in the significant number of clientelist participants, in the open way in which constituents attend political clinics, in the blatant disregard of laws prohibiting voter bribery, and in the normality with which it is treated by most in the media and much of the public. A key indicator of the latter is the extent to which there is now "publicly negotiated clientelism" between individual citizens and politicians via the numerous live call-in talk shows. In relation to voter bribery, although allegations have skyrocketed, only three cases were successfully brought before the courts between 1981 and

2012. As before independence, these cases were all thrown out by the courts. This total absence of legal consequences and resulting impunity add to the "it's just part of our culture" justification. This thinking is evident in one opinion on the hard challenge of addressing vote buying in Belize: "At a minimum, Belize should be wary of importing regulations designed for countries that do not manifest the socio-cultural peculiarities – and realities – of Belize. A respected judge in the Caribbean once opined that vote buying was part of Caribbean culture and that therefore it could not effectively be outlawed."[146]

As an element of political culture, clientelism intertwines with other unpleasant aspects of Belizean political culture. Entrenched clientelism has made the "societal moral/legal divide" even more grey and nebulous, and attitudes "towards high risk" and "illicit activity" more nonchalant.[147] It has also encouraged the individualism inherent to the "me culture" at the expense of community approaches to political participation and development. As one CSO leader observed, "Handouts decrease the amount that people care about the community . . . instead, people care more about themselves."[148] The leader of the PNP went further: "You can't hold people's attention with real national issues. All they think about are handouts. It is damaging their minds."[149] In this regard, political clientelism plays a part in fostering a culture of dependency and of heightened expectations for immediate gratification among constituents.

Linkages to Conflict, Violence and the Drug Trade?

Especially since the late 1990s, Belize has witnessed a worrisome increase in overall violent criminal activity. Belize's homicide rate increased from 30 to 44 per 100,000 between 2002 and 2012, when it ranked sixth highest in the world, third in Central America and second in the Commonwealth Caribbean.[150] Some have linked aspects of this violence to the drug trade, because Belize has been a transhipment point for drugs, largely cocaine, since the 1990s, going from South America to North America, and traffickers are also located in Belize. In 2012, the US Department of State added Belize to its "Majors List" for drug transit for the first time and pointed to increasing concerns about the spread of money laundering activity. The 2012 US report estimated that ten metric tons of drugs were passing through Belize annually headed for the United States and expressed concerns related to the infiltration into Belize of major drug trafficking organizations (including Los Zetas of Mexico) and to the involvement of Belize's urban gangs in aspects of drug trafficking activities.[151]

Even though there is not enough evidence to make conclusive assessments about the relationship between clientelist politics and criminal activity, there are warning signs. Several interviewees observed that competition over clientelist resources has added a new dimension to party/political conflict and violence in Belize – beyond the usual tensions between partisan opponents and occasional acts of vandalism. There are two strands of this argument. The first is that there is now noticeable conflict emerging among clients competing for benefits, especially at times of heightened availability. Just as Belize's small size allows for a significant degree of client monitoring by politicians, clients can also monitor fellow clients. Several citizens spoke grudgingly about what others had received, and in some communities, tensions can run high. Some brokers informed that dealing with such tensions was one of the more challenging parts of their responsibilities. In 2008, when the distribution of the Venezuela money was in full swing, police, and even Belize Defence Force soldiers, had to be called in to some locations to keep the peace. For example, one news channel reported that "multiple teams of police and Belize Defence soldiers, armed with M16 rifles, stood guard outside" the office of the PUP candidate for the Port Loyola constituency.[152] The second strand of the argument centres on the contention that in times of scarcity of clientelist resources, especially after seasonal periods of high availability, the incidence of crime can spike. For example, one interviewee opined that higher levels of criminal activity can be directly related to periods of lower handout-politics activity, including periods after elections and after other spike points such as Christmas.[153]

Additionally, there is little doubt that "private" money related to the drug trade in Belize has been gradually entering clientelist politics. Although most politicians were reluctant to discuss drug operators as possible sources of clientelist resources in Belize, several agreed that this was indeed beginning to occur. One politician stated, "Drug money does enter the benefits politics machinery via some politicians. However, unlike Jamaica, it is more indirect."[154] Another politician revealed that he was approached by a person known to be deeply involved in the drug trade with an offer of an alliance to "assist" with his campaign.[155] The politician was quick to clarify that he refused because he knew there would be a catch, and the person gave his "support" to the other party's candidate. A representative in Belize City shared that a known drug dealer in his constituency had approached him with the information there was a hit on him – and had offered to provide "protection".[156]

Indeed, the quid pro quo inherent to a drug baron–politician relationship is no different than it is elsewhere in the region: in return for financial inducements to politicians and public officers, the transshipment of drugs by land, air and sea can be facilitated. Before Belize began to be used as a major transhipment point for cocaine, a former minister of government (he was already an ex-minister at the time) was arrested and imprisoned in the United States in 1985 for allegedly trafficking in the marijuana trade.[157] By 2012, news stories of incidents related to landings of small drug planes and the washing up of lost bales of cocaine – referred to colloquially as "sea lotto" – had become commonplace. The following assessment of drug relationships in the Caribbean is, indeed, apt for Belize: "Drug barons, dons ... and 'bigmen' and international entrepreneurs all have connections with government, commercial houses and party bosses. Overlapping, vertically integrated chains of patron–client relationships ripple throughout society, eventually connecting top to bottom."[158]

Not surprisingly, there are occasional allegations that particular Belize City gangs may have affiliations with particular politicians.[159] Some interviewees even named specific gangs they believed were associated with particular elements of a political party. One alleged that Belize City gang members have been used to provide "security" for particular politicians at party events.[160] A comprehensive study on male violence and gangs in Belize City reported claims by certain gang leaders that gangs have supported particular politicians at election time in return for certain favours later on.[161] The "garrison" experience of other countries such as Jamaica suggests that the red flags related to the linkages between clientelist politics, on the one hand, and violence and the drug trade, on the other, are too damaging to ignore. This is especially true for a number of constituencies in poorer areas in southside Belize City that have entrenched representatives and high levels of homogeneous voting, as well as high levels of criminal activity.

Conclusion

On balance, the aggregate and macro-level impact of political clientelism on both formal and social democracy in Belize is overwhelmingly negative. The entrenched nature of clientelism suggests that a significant portion of votes, which are freely and fairly counted, may not represent free will in the sense constitutionally intended. The small size of electoral constituencies has enhanced the prospect that entire elections can turn on the undemocratic act of buying political support. Clientelist politicians who purchase political support have diminishing interest in clientelist voters' positions on issues, and voters have less credibility once they have accepted some compensation for voting. The electoral success expedited by clientelist politics has incentivized Belizean politicians to exert even more discretionary control over state institutions of resource allocation, weakening these institutions in the process. As a result, the exercise of formal political power in the Belize version of Westminster government has become more politicized, more discretionary and less accountable, and the lines of power and function between the state and the political parties have blurred and converged. As the types and volume of public resources passing through politicians have expanded, Belizeans increasingly see their constituency politicians as problem-solvers of first resort.

Over time, as the two major parties have become increasingly clientelist and less differentiated by ideology and programmatic approaches, they have begun to compete mainly on their relative capacity to deliver targeted benefits to individuals and groups across all income levels. The official function of representatives as legislators has been diminished as their role as patrons to the poor and middle class has grown. Belizean parliamentarians and politicians have evolved into powerful "doctor politicians" who operate handout clinics and also make "house calls" to dispense resources to individual clients.

For clients of all income levels, these clientelist arrangements represent, in effect, another means of engaging with the state and influencing the allocation of public resources. As more Belizeans have come to participate informally through clientelism, other modes of participation are adversely affected. Belize's highly personalized, face-to-face politics, which facilitates monitoring voter compliance, has magnified this disincentive effect on participation. Both political parties and some CSOs have witnessed a decrease in volunteerism because of the spread of "compensation for participation". Moreover, under-resourced aspirants, independent candidates, smaller political parties, lower-income persons, women and other under-represented groups face yet another barrier to the doors of electoral politics.

In the context of poverty and fragile livelihoods, handouts from politicians mean survival for some and enhanced comfort for others. This widespread informal welfare function explains why a powerful broker, when asked about alternatives to handout politics, stated, "There will be chaos from people if there is nothing to replace it."[162] In a similar vein, a former politician warned, "Limit this [political clientelism] and there is disfigurement of a fully functioning welfare system relied upon by the majority of the citizenry."[163] Yet the distributive benefits of political clientelism are largely short term and are heavily outweighed by the overall damaging effect on most aspects of social democracy.

From the lack of transparent merit-based approaches for social welfare at political clinics, to the waste associated with "irrational" and reckless budgetary spending, the loss of public revenue, the disincentive effect on governance reform, the damaging favours given to donors, and the enablement of political corruption, the implications of rampant clientelism for social democracy are indeed overwhelmingly bleak. Simultaneously, the goal of finding alternatives and sustainable solutions to social-economic problems is undermined, in part, by clientelist imperatives.

Taken together, the implications of political clientelism for Belize put the grave warnings of a former politician in scary perspective: "If we don't stop [handout politics] we will end up a failed state . . . with more poverty, garrisons, more crime, drug barons running things . . . the state will lose control. It is just not sustainable."[164] Similarly, former prime minister Barrow assessed that "it [handout politics] is a hell of a conundrum because the more you try to address [social needs] via the area representatives the more you are ensuring that the already weak system becomes weaker – and obviously you are going to reach a point of no return".[165]

Ironically, the difficult challenges and the repercussions of sustaining the inflationary demand for material inducements for clients eventually contribute to electoral losses. There is a point of diminishing electoral returns for incumbent parties due to the macro-level social, economic and financial inefficiencies that are fuelled by high levels of political clientelism. Fiscal crises and political corruption scandals, both of which are fed by clientelism, have helped tip the electoral advantage to an eager opposition party. Yet this paradox of clientelism does not deter parties and politicians from clientelist politics. As one astute politician summarized, "Handouts won't always make you win, but not doing it can cost you the election."[166] By 2013, political clientelism had certainly become a distinguishing feature of Belize's political culture.

7.

Big Game, Small Town

Belize through Caribbean Lens

The potential value of any national case study lies not only in advancing the understanding of specific issues in a particular country context but also in facilitating comparisons with one or more other countries. In this chapter I explore, albeit preliminarily, how Belize's experience compares with that of other independent states of the Commonwealth Caribbean that share a common parliamentary political model and similar post-independence democratization experiences. I present this comparative analysis around the major issues highlighted by the Belize findings: the manifestations of the growth and prevalence of clientelism, the primary causal roles of competitive party politics and socio-economic inequality, the supporting causal roles of specific country-contextual variables and the key implications for the quality of democracy. My assessment, which is limited to secondary research, confirms that most studies of political clientelism in the region have focused, near exclusively, on Jamaica. However, using national studies, comparative governance texts and relevant newspaper articles, it is possible to identify insightful similarities and distinctions with the Belize findings beyond the case of Jamaica.

On the Prevalence of Clientelist Politics in the Region

Although the paucity of national case studies and national surveys of similar depth and breadth as the Jamaica and Belize studies limits extensive cross-national comparisons of the relative prevalence of political clientelism, it is clear that political clientelism has grown steadily across the region over the fifty-year-plus period since Jamaica and then Trinidad and Tobago became the first independent states of the Commonwealth Caribbean in 1962. Apart from the comprehensive works of Stone and Edie on Jamaica, the prevalence of clientelism has been referenced as one of several themes in national and regional studies on democratic governance.[1] National and regional reports on governance and a scan of newspaper articles also suggest that all the states of the region manifest noteworthy levels of clientelist politics.

The available material indicates that the incidence of political clientelism in Belize is likely closer to that in Jamaica, often perceived to have very high prevalence in the region, than it is to Barbados, which some perceive to have only moderate prevalence. In the case of Jamaica, Stone used survey data to estimate that 51 per cent of the Jamaican electorate in 1980 was predominantly engaged in electoral politics via clientelist ties.[2] Over three decades later in 2011, an independent survey found that over one-third of the Jamaican electorate sampled revealed that it had engaged in vote trading.[3] With regard to Barbados, and in absence of survey or other statistical information, the assessment of moderate prevalence is based largely on the general perceptions of political observers in the region. Indeed, Barbados, which has also led the region in overall human development indicators, is often viewed as the jewel in the crown of democratic governance. The highly respected Caribbean political scientist Selwyn Ryan is among those to suggest that Barbados has exhibited some, but less, clientelist tendencies than other states in the region.[4] However, as recent allegations of vote buying and party-based patronage in Barbados indicate, this may be more perception than reality and Barbados may be catching up with the rest of the region.[5]

In Belize by comparison, the 2005 SPEAR survey found 31.8 per cent of the electorate willing to engage in voting for money, and this book conservatively estimates that at least one-fifth of the Belizean electorate is involved in clientelist relationships. This implies that Belize is more similar to Jamaica with regard to the prevalence of clientelism in the Commonwealth Caribbean. Indeed, with specific regard to vote buying, the AmericasBarometer 2010 poll, which calculated the percentage reporting having been offered a material benefit in exchange for a vote, indicated that Belize at 17.6 per cent had a higher incidence than Jamaica (6 per cent), as well as than Guyana (5.9 per cent) and Trinidad and Tobago (5.3 per cent).[6] As in Belize, most clients across the region are poor, but elements of the middle class also participate as clients across the region.[7] For both Belize and Jamaica, rural and urban areas both participate in clientelist exchanges, but urban areas tend to feature concentrated areas of entrenched clientelism.[8]

The fluctuations of clientelist activity as observed in Belize in a typical year and over a five-year election cycle also transpire across the region. As in Belize, political clientelism is an ongoing, day-to-day political relationship that transcends election campaign periods and vote trading. Also, the kinds of resources and favours traded for political support appear to be very similar across the region to those identified for Belize, with minor differences based on context. For example, one 2011 study on Jamaica described clientelist resources as follows:

> Several persons in the inner cities received no more than J$500,[9] though the two modal receipts were J$2,000 and J$5,000. The poor were also very likely to be trapped with food. . . . There were a few, however, who received as much as 50 pounds of rice, along with (tinned) mackerel. The poor were also likely to receive phone cards and even mattresses. The rural poor were very likely to be baited with livestock, seeds and fertiliser. In a few cases, both rural and urban near-poor were drawn by construction material. A few received vouchers of J$20,000 and J$40,000 which they could take to specific hardware stores.[10]

Although the overall process of negotiating clientelist exchanges is similar across the region, there are subtle differences. For example, official party membership was an absolute prerequisite for gaining certain favours such as public service jobs in Guyana during the Forbes Burnham era.[11] In Jamaica, local government, community and civil society leaders have traditionally played key broker and liaison roles on behalf of Members of Parliament (MPs) and politicians much more than in Belize.[12] Apart from the fact that local and community leaders are valuable gatekeepers, local government bodies in Jamaica tend to have less authority than those in Belize, and clientelist relationships represent one way for local and community leaders to access resources and service for their communities. In contrast, the local government system in Belize has relatively more autonomy from central government, including some responsibilities for resource collection, and patron–client ties are relatively more independent from MPs.

On Competitive Party Politics as the Key Causal Variable

Although clientelism has seldom been used in the Caribbean as a primary analytic construct to examine the politics of the pre-independence period, the Belize experience is not unique in the region in relation to the colonial backdrop for the emergence of modern clientelist politics. Like Belize, all the countries of the region had some form of British-dominated state patronage well before independence. Generally, as colonial subjects, the citizens of the Caribbean colonies were allowed very limited and unequal access to resources and to political participation, and the colonial state was largely unresponsive to their needs and their requests. While the exposure of colonial subjects to Westminster-style politics differed across the region, histories of the road to independence demonstrate that the inadequate responses of the colonial authorities (in a context of limited formal political modes of participation) were key to catalysing the emergence of nationalist movements.[13] Token economic and social assistance from the colonial state came only after crises or to quell protests, and much of this appeared in the form of patronage. For example, the strategic use of work and relief programmes in pre-independence Belize had parallels in other British colonies, and as Duncan and Woods found, these were part of "an entrenched system of patronage administered through the welfare state".[14]

As it was for Belize, the general political–historical narrative is that of local elites across the region inheriting the power relationships and practices of British colonial authorities, including patronage practices, and adapting these to their political advantage in the post-independence context. For Jamaica, for example, Stone viewed party-based clientelism as a replacement for the "power base of capital and property ownership which gave the traditional planter-merchant ruling class" their controlling influence under colonialism.[15] Edie pinpointed the skewed power and social relationships of Jamaica's sugar-based plantation economy as the contextual background for the emergence of party-based clientelist relationships.[16] Belize did not have a plantation system, but its forestry-based economy exhibited similar skewed economic and political power relationships in the colonial period. Generally speaking, by the time of independence for most states across the region, informal politician–citizen relationships based on clientelism already existed to some degree in the vacuum of meaningful formal political participation in the colonial state. These relationships undoubtedly contributed to how those states that inherited the Westminster system adopted and transformed it to their political realities.

As political parties became established in the context of decolonization, as the Westminster system became consolidated and as nationalist Caribbean leaders gained political power after self-government and independence, the political ground was fertile for the consolidation of clientelist politics. In this regard, the Belize findings conform to the regional narrative of modern political clientelism emerging as a common element in the evolution and manifestations of competitive party politics after the onset of national elections under universal adult suffrage.[17] Indeed, there is evidence that competitive party politics is a primary driver for the rapid spread of clientelist politics after independence across the region. As Vaughan Lewis noted, "The transfer of power to local leaders . . . widened and deepened the connections between populace and government."[18] Comparative political scholars, examining the region's post-independence governance experience, have observed that "the political system became an arena [for parties and politicians] to outbid each other to dispense patronage to followers"[19] and "political parties have traditionally maintained the loyalty of their supporters in large part through patronage".[20] Even in the limited confines of the Commonwealth Caribbean, contextual differences, as well as the exact timing of independence for the colonies, have produced subtle but consequential distinctions in the development and manifestations of competitive party politics and, by extension, of clientelist politics.

At least three variants of party-based clientelism can be identified in the emergence of electoral democracy across the region: two-party dominant, multi-party (defined as having at least three parties that can credibly win seats in parliament) and one-party/authoritarian clientelism. The two-party dominant and multi-party types are similar to the extent that two or more competitive parties evolved, employing clientelism to more or less equal extents over time. The one-party/authoritarian category describes those states in which clientelism has been used for extended periods of time by authoritarian-style regimes as a key tool to maintain popular support and remain in power. This is not to suggest that other parties are absent or inactive, but rather to highlight the abuse of clientelism to ensure long periods of one-party rule within the context of the Westminster parliamentary model.

Like Belize, the majority of states in the region have been examples of competitive two-party dominant or multi-party clientelism. Even in those cases in which the first nationalist party won several consecutive elections at the onset, these regimes allowed for a significant degree of open competition from at least one other party in elections that were largely free and fair. Opposition parties, which railed against clientelism, embraced it when in power, eventually contributing to the aforementioned political snowball effect spurred on by electoral competition. Apart from Belize, Jamaica, the Bahamas and Barbados are key examples of states characterized by long-standing two-party dominant systems and the expansion of clientelism alongside party competition. Interestingly, it is in the smaller states of the Eastern Caribbean, such as St Vincent and the Grenadines, Dominica, and Grenada, that party competition has tended more to multi-party systems, at least for some time.[21] Although focused research on political clientelism is sparse for the Eastern Caribbean, several governance studies have referenced the existence of highly personalized "rum and roti" politics.[22] The intensity of electoral competition among multiple parties and the extent of party-based state patronage are magnified in these micro-island states.

The key examples of periods of one-party/authoritarian clientelism in the region include Guyana under Forbes Burnham's Peoples National Congress from 1964 to 1992,[23] Grenada under Eric Gairy's Grenada United Labour Party from 1967 to 1979,[24] and Antigua and Barbuda under the Antigua Labour Party between 1976 and 2004. In the case of Antigua and Barbuda, the Antigua Labour Party, under the leadership of Vere Bird, and then Lester Bird, governed during most of Antigua and Barbuda's modern politics, including the twenty-three years after independence in 1981. Paget Henry, who has judged the rule of the Birds as one of the most authoritarian in the region, argued that political clientelism emerged as a function of competitive party politics during Antigua and Barbuda's brief experience with two-party dominant politics between 1971 and 1976 when another party governed.[25] However, after the Antigua Labour Party was returned to power in 1976, competitive clientelism diminished and was replaced by almost thirty years of one-party patronage. Clifford Griffin has illustrated how the Antigua Labour Party used state patronage as a preferred tactic to maintain political support and power.[26] Paget Henry's analysis suggests that competitive clientelism "returned" to Antigua and Barbuda in 2004 only when the corruption-plagued Antigua Labour Party was defeated by the United Progressive Party.

Despite the unbroken electoral longevity of George Price and the PUP from 1954 to 1984, Belize's experience with the emergence and growth of political clientelism clearly fits the two-party model. Although it did not gain power until 1984, the UDP was not deterred from electoral participation, was increasingly competitive over time and had won a significant number of local government elections. Price, though hardly a political saint, did not tamper with the electoral process, suppress political opposition or govern in an authoritarian manner. In his authorized biography of Price, Godfrey Smith portrayed Price as a somewhat cunning, manipulative and sometimes vengeful leader, but without dictatorial or authoritarian tendencies.[27] Allowing for some contextual differences, the primary role played by competitive party politics in the emergence and take-off of political clientelism in Belize is likely more similar to the experiences of other states of the two-party dominant type, particularly to Barbados, Jamaica and the Bahamas. As opposition parties, such as the UDP in the Belize case, became better funded and more competitive, clientelism was increasingly used as a strategy to help secure competitive advantage.

The actual timing of political independence in the region is also a relevant factor in the development of party-based clientelism to the extent that states that achieved their independence and full political control over all the institutions of resource allocation earlier, such as Jamaica as well as Trinidad and Tobago in 1962, reached a point of entrenched clientelism before those that achieved independence later. In the case of Belize, delayed independence meant that the PUP and the UDP differentiated themselves primarily on how and when to achieve independence and on how to deal with the cause of the delay – the Guatemalan claim to Belize. Even as clientelism was creeping into the PUP's bag of tricks to help win elections before 1981, the PUP was able to maintain its identity as the progressive and programmatic party of national unity and independence, and to paint the opposition parties (NIP and then UDP) as anti-independence and, even, pro-British. In effect, party differentiation based on clientelism was also delayed. In contrast, Caribbean states that had negotiated their full sovereignty earlier no longer held the issue of independence as a source of political divergence.

Different experiences across the region in relation to the role of political ideology in the development of party politics also affected the trajectory of clientelism in particular states. In Belize, the diminishing and near-total disappearance of substantive differences between the PUP and the UDP after independence created a vacuum that was filled, in large part, by distinctions based on the relative capacity to provide clientelist inducements. In this regard, Belize's post-independence experience is likely more similar to that of states such as Barbados and the Bahamas, in which ideology has featured only marginally. However, Guyana, Grenada and Jamaica provide interesting insights into how clientelism may play out in states in which clear ideological distinctions feature for some time. This was the case in Jamaica from 1972 to 1989, when the People's National Party (PNP) under Michael Manley (1972–80) presented a distinct democratic socialist vision, in contrast to the pro-laissez-faire Jamaica Labour Party (JLP) under Edward Seaga (1980–89). After observing the PNP in power during its first term, Stone argued, "Shifts in policy issues and ideological directions . . . do not affect the dominant base of mass [clientelist] support unless these changes are associated with perceived increases or decreases in the capability to deliver material and social rewards."[28] Using examples of housing and employment programmes, Amanda Sives confirmed the findings of Stone and of Edie that clientelist politics persisted and actually expanded during Manley's first term.[29]

One key implication here is that competitive party clientelism may have already been so entrenched and systemic in Jamaica's modern politics that party distinctions based on ideology were insufficient to mitigate its rise. Against a backdrop of intense clientelism, Sives found that ideological distinctions added a new dimension of political conflict between supporters of the PNP and the JLP.[30] As such, "wearing" the PNP ideological label improved one's chances of receiving material and other inducements. Indeed, there is little evidence that the PNP treated clientelism as a significant problem to be dealt with as part of its socialist democracy platform. Widespread clientelist practices continued under Seaga's JLP when the party was returned to power in 1980. Whereas Grenada's experiment with socialism under the New Jewel Movement was too short-lived to provide much comparative insight, clientelism flourished under the long rule of the People's National Congress during the experiment with "co-operative socialism" in Guyana.[31] The region's experience reinforces the point that party-based clientelism, in a competitive electoral context, often transcends ideological platforms.

While not excluding the relevance of socio-economic inequality as a common causal variable, the type of competitive politics practised in the small-state context of the Caribbean's version of Westminster parliamentary democracy is at the heart of clientelist politics in the region. One study succinctly captures this argument for the region:

> Formal two-party democracy [deteriorated] into a collusive, cartel-based "gentleman's agreement" form of political party contestation. Over time, differences between parties become much more pronounced in personality and organisational culture than they do in terms of ideology and policy. This greatly disposes an otherwise competitive political system to act in clientelist ways, reinforcing, rather than undermining patronage and collusion. . . . A Westminster-style winner-take-all political system strengthens a two-party system, which works to the advantage of an already developed economy and society, but entrenches political patronage and clientelism in an emerging one.[32]

On Poverty and Economic Policies

Poverty and inequality have generally persisted or expanded in most states across the region since their independence.[33] National poverty rates (approximately 2010), measured as the percentage of persons below national poverty lines, were lower in Barbados, Antigua and Barbuda, and the Bahamas; higher in Jamaica, St Kitts and Nevis, Trinidad and Tobago, St Lucia, and Dominica; and highest in Belize, Guyana, Grenada, and St Vincent and Grenadines.[34] Only a few studies have discussed specific relationships of poverty to clientelism. As in Belize, these indicate the propensity for clientelism to be higher in poor, densely populated urban centres and constituencies. In the case of Jamaica, Obika Gray's powerful work supports the view that high rates of poverty in the capital city, Kingston, facilitated the entrenchment of clientelism as an alternative survival strategy for many.[35] Ryan et al. had similar findings for a poor urban constituency in Port of Spain, Trinidad.[36]

The available information in some countries in the region indicates some likely relationship between poverty rates and the prevalence of political clientelism. Barbados, which had the highest gross national income per head (US$12,660[37] in 2009) and the highest global Human Development Index rank (forty-seven in 2011) in the region, had a 2010 poverty rate of 19.3 per cent.[38] Jamaica, which had a much lower gross national income per head (US$4,980 in 2009) and a lower Human Development Index rank (seventy-nine in 2011), reported a poverty rate of 16.5 per cent and 17.6 per cent for 2009 and 2010, respectively.[39] Belize's gross national income per head was the lowest among the three at US$3,690 in 2009, its Human Development Index rank was worse at ninety-three in 2011, and its poverty rate was highest at 41.3 per cent in 2009. Although the lower prevalence of political clientelism in Barbados may bear some relation to its positive socio-economic and human development performance, other factors are clearly at play.

Apart from the few short-lived attempts at progressive alternatives in Jamaica, Grenada and Guyana, most states in the region, like Belize, have embraced neoliberal economic policies since the 1980s and 1990s. Several studies argue that, directly or indirectly, neoliberal policies have contributed to the perpetuation of skewed societal benefits and increased income inequality in the region. For example, Evelyne Huber found that in states with high-income inequality and poverty, neoliberal policies "have highly inegalitarian distributional consequences".[40] The fact that foreign investment, inherent to neoliberalism, has become a key additional source of private funding for clientelist operations is not limited to Belize. For example, Edie argued that the embrace of neoliberalism by the JLP in the 1980s expanded opportunities for local patrons to grease the wheels of clientelism through financial flows to official government programmes and private donations from foreign investors.[41] These funds helped to fill public spending shortfalls that occurred during the latter part of the Michael Manley years. However, such opportunities for funding clientelist activities decrease in times of reduced capital inflow and economic downturn. In the case of "co-operative socialist" Guyana in the 1980s, economic stagnation and IMF structural adjustment measures severely limited the state's ability to dispense state patronage.

For Belize, even as political clientelism has been on an upwards trajectory since 1981, macroeconomic hardships, such as in those in 1984 and 2008, limited the government's capacities to use certain public resources as clientelist inducements. Several studies on Jamaica also draw a similar link. It has been illustrated that party-based clientelism expanded in Jamaica in the post-independence period up to the 1980s, when there was an ebb. This decrease is generally attributed to the economic crunch and the structural adjustment medicine dished out by the IMF in the 1980s.[42] As Colin Clarke argued in relation to the belt-tightening policies, "As the state has withered away, so the capacity of politicians, and especially those in government, to offer patronage to their followers has declined."[43] Similarly, Huber Stephens and Stephens found that economic hardships, caused in part by the IMF agreed measures, also led to the loss of privileges for the middle class, which in turn contributed to the PNP's defeat in 1980.[44]

Even as the high incidence of party-based clientelism in Jamaica did diminish in the 1980s and 1990s, it remained a dominant feature of Jamaican political relations. As Sives argued, "[even] in the context of declining state resources, both political parties have sought to maintain the patron–client relationship".[45] Herbert Gayle's finding that one-third of Jamaicans experienced vote buying in 2011 supports this. As in Belize, political parties in Jamaica adapted to new economic and political realities and found alternative ways to thrive in periods when the state had less capacity to deliver resources. Clarke, for example, illustrated how "the shifting of some government resources directly to members of parliament has also given added life to clientelism in Kingston's politics through the 1980s and 1990s".[46]

There are also non-economic explanations for the persistence of clientelist relationships in Jamaica. Sives has argued that party loyalties survive during periods of low resource availability because there is also a "non-economic" benefit from being associated with the PNP or JLP – a sort of intangible sense of belonging.[47] For example, in periods of extensive party-linked violence in urban Jamaica, the provision of citizen security by political parties is in high demand by clients in "garrison" constituencies. Sives contends that such non-economic benefits help "explain why [clientelist] relations have fractured rather than broken down completely" when economic resources diminish.[48] The Belize findings do not dispute that there is a non-economic benefit to some clientelist relationships; however, such associations with a particular political party are often secondary to the motivation of having greater access to material resources.

On Demography, Culture and Small Size

In relation to the country-specific variables explored for the Belize case, interesting comparative insights emerge. The findings on the relationship between ethnicity and clientelism in Belize are particularly unique when compared to other multi-ethnic states in the region. In Guyana and in Trinidad and Tobago, dominant and competing ethnic-based political parties have employed clientelism as a tool to achieve and maintain the political support of the Afro or Indo populations. The 2002 census in Guyana indicated that there were 43.5 per cent Indo-Guyanese, 30.2 per cent Afro-Guyanese, 16.7 per cent mixed and 9.2 per cent Amerindian.[49] For Trinidad and Tobago, the 2000 census recorded that the ethnic breakdown of East Indian and African descendants was 40 per cent and 37.5 per cent, respectively, and that 20.5 per cent were of mixed heritage.[50] Once ethnic politics became established in both states, incumbent parties favoured and maintained ethnic supporters of all classes by preferential distribution of material and other inducements. Ethnic-based favouritism and victimization, or the perception thereof, are therefore ever-present sources of political tension in these states. In the case of Guyana, the People's National Congress with majority support from Afro-Guyanese governed from 1968 to 1992, and the People's Progressive Party with majority support from Indo-Guyanese governed from 1992 to 2015. Trinidad and Tobago has had a similar pattern with the Afro-dominant People's National Movement and the Indo-dominant United National Congress, broken by a short-lived Afro-Indo coalition party from 1986 to 1991.[51]

As with most political relationships in states with diverse ethnicity, those related to political clientelism are complex, and there are substantive differences in how they play out in Guyana and in Trinidad and Tobago versus Belize. In Guyana and in Trinidad and Tobago, ethnic-based clientelism, while dominant, is a matter of degree. For example, Steven Garner illustrated for Guyana under Burnham (1968–1992), that although the People's National Congress favoured the Afro-Guyanese in the dispensing of state patronage, it also minimized opposition through strategic clientelist inducements to elite Indo-Guyanese.[52] Unlike in Guyana and in Trinidad and Tobago, Belize's modern politics did not produce ethnic-based parties that overtly favoured one ethnic group over another. However, ethnicity factors in Belize did facilitate the expansion of political clientelism and colour its manifestations. Existing ethnic relationships and linkages, in particular ethnic-majority constituencies, provided politicians with ready-made communications and distribution networks. To remain competitive, Belizean politicians in multi-ethnic constituencies need to ensure that there is no perception that an ethnic group is favoured over another. Indeed, the lack of visible clientelist discrimination based on ethnicity in Belize, or at least the perception thereof, has contributed to the perpetuation of ethnically integrated political parties. In effect, the Belize case is unique in the region in illustrating that overt ethnic-partisan clientelism is not the only outcome in multi-ethnic societies with high incidences of clientelist politics.

There are also indications that immigration is becoming a relevant factor in the manifestations of political clientelism in other states in the region as it was demonstrated for Belize. Using 2005 United Nations population data, Belize's 15.3 per cent foreign-born population was second highest in the region, next to Antigua and Barbuda (22.1 per cent) and above third-ranking Bahamas (10 per cent).[33] Antigua and Barbuda has a history of immigration from the Dominican Republic and more recently from other Caribbean Community countries such as Guyana and Dominica. In the case of the Bahamas, some tens of thousands of Haitians are estimated to be among the population, with most having arrived since the fall of the Duvalier regime in 1980s.[54]

The Belize case clearly illustrated that in a competitive party clientelist context, the targeting of newer, and usually poorer, immigrant voters by political parties can become a common political strategy. Both the PUP and UDP have targeted new Central American immigrants as clients in equal measure, just as they have every other demographic group. In the absence of dedicated research on the relationship between clientelism and immigrant populations in the wider region, a review of newspaper reports suggested possible similar tactics in the case of the Bahamas. The Free National Movement, the losing incumbent party in the 2012 general elections, accused the Progressive Liberal Party of vote buying in poor Haitian–Bahamian communities in an attempt to decrease the Free National Movement's traditional advantage with this growing voting group.[55] After the election, the victorious Progressive Liberal Party levelled the same clientelist charge at the Free National Movement.[56] As for Belize, part of any new research into the relationship between clientelism and migration in the region should include investigations on if and how new immigrants from states with high prevalence of clientelist politics affect the incidence and features of political clientelism in receiving states.

In relation to the Belize finding that aspects of political culture may play a role in explaining the rapid spread of political clientelism, the available information on the region is also inconclusive. At the broader level, most studies have pointed to the region's common political-cultural history of British colonialism, which evolved into Westminster governance, as conducive to the development of democracy. Griffin, for example, contended that "because of this lengthy process of socialisation by which they have become habituated to democracy, Anglophone Caribbean countries are structurally and culturally disposed to consolidate the democratic process".[57] Others have also singled out the affinity for personalized politics and populist leaders. Only a few national-level studies have made linkages between clientelism and political culture. For the case of Jamaica, Stone argued that "underlying these clientelist structures are political values which show deep respect for the effective exercise of power, and place access to patronage benefits above the importance of citizens' rights, while accepting asymmetric and elitist power and authority relations as necessary to maintain the central institutions of government".[58]

Although the role of small-state scale in the expansion of political clientelism is readily acknowledged in the extant studies of clientelism in the region, the Belize findings suggest that more attention needs to be given to the "accelerator effect" of small size. Key here is the degree to which clientelism, and particularly vote buying, is more attractive and effective when only a small number of voters need to be induced to make a difference in constituency elections. For this reason, it would be interesting to explore whether the smallest states of the region, such as St Vincent and the Grenadines, Dominica, and Grenada, exhibit greater levels of clientelism and/or significantly different manifestations of the phenomenon.

On Implications for Electoral Democracy

The Belize case study is distinct in research on the modern politics of the Commonwealth Caribbean in its attempt to conduct a comprehensive analysis of the national implications of entrenched political clientelism for an emerging democratic state. The few assessments of the implications of clientelism in the region are often buried in wider discussions about democratic decay, political corruption, political conflict or ethnic politics. Additionally, the available assessments have the bias of focusing research attention more on the dyadic, constituency-level implications and less so on collective national impact. As noted, the positive democratic record of the Commonwealth Caribbean is mostly due to exemplary performance in the area of formal democracy. However, this positive record belies serious underlying questions about formal democracy in light of rampant political clientelism.

In particular, the questions raised by the Belize case about the meaning of the vote and of elections in a context of high levels of clientelism also have salience in the rest of the region. Michael Manley, who, as prime minister in 1972–80 and 1989–92, had one of the best seats from which to observe the operations of clientelism in his country of Jamaica, pinpointed some of the general concerns of the system of governances well:

> [T]he act of political choice involves the casting of a vote which is not commitment of the self to an activity. Instead, it is an act which expresses the expectation of a benefit, which will somehow come in spite of oneself, through the effort of a faceless authority known as the government. In due course, the expected package of benefits will be insufficiently realised. It will not occur to the voter that this may partly be the result of their own lack of involvement. However, it will be enough to guarantee that a rival set of promises will get the nod next time.[59]

In the Jamaica of the pre-independence period, when Manley's father, Norman Manley, was the leader of the PNP and served as chief minister (1955–62), voting in elections did involve commitment to a cause or to a personality, as much as it did in the pre-independence period in Belize and in other states in the region. However, by the 1990s, and except for the notable instances of ideological distinctions discussed earlier, governance assessments were increasingly pointing to elections as being contests between or among parties that had but minor differences. As such, parties increasingly used their relative ability to deliver clientelist inducements as a point of differentiation. Although the extent of this lack of partisan distinction varies over time and by state, the buying of votes in small constituencies challenges the principles of electoral democracy across the region. In short, it is debatable if elections can be fully free and fair when a large portion of the electorate engages in clientelist politics.

There is, moreover, some evidence that the concerns raised in the Belize case about the meaning of voter turnout figures and about the secrecy of the vote also have relevance in most of the region's states. One quantitative study of voter turnout trends in the Commonwealth Caribbean identified that there is a direct positive relationship between the extent of clientelist politics and voter turnout, and that this relationship transpires more in states with fewer political parties competing.[60] Even though there have been examples of outright election rigging,[61] the vast majority of elections in the region have generally tended to be free from direct vote tampering.

Yet the concerns that some expressed about ballot secrecy in Belize are not unique.

For example, until halted by electoral reform in the past decade, the "golden ballot" in Jamaica – where parties pay voters to switch ballots in the voting booth – was widely reported.[62] Additionally, the practice of taking photos of ballots with cell phones to prove that one voted as promised seems to transpire in other states across the region. For instance, former prime minister of the Bahamas, Hubert Ingraham, charged that the opposition party was planning to use cell phones to assist in vote buying, and the then opposition leader, Perry Christie, responded with similar claims.[63] The Belize case illustrates how the mere perception of lack of ballot secrecy can cast doubt on the credibility of elections and stoke fears that individuals could be discriminated against after an election. The related issue of influencing voter registration and voter transfer processes through clientelist inducements – and so influencing the voters' list – also resonates outside of Belize. This was the case, for instance, in the 2003 Grenada election in which there were numerous allegations of manipulating the voters' list in favour of the incumbent party, prompting the Organization of American States Electoral Mission to warn that the "key to people's trust in the elections is public acceptance of the voters' list. This is central to democracy".[64] While not the primary focus of this research, the relationship of political clientelism to voters' list manipulation and to gerrymandering in the region are also areas ripe for future research.

The shift in Belize from more programmatic and policy distinguishable parties to more clientelist parties is also in line with the experience of political parties across the region. When Ryan pointed to the decrease in the membership base of political parties in the Caribbean and to the failure of parties to maintain support based on substantive policy achievements, he related these more directly to the fallout from neoliberal policies across the region.[65] The Belize case suggests that party membership and union alliances decreased in importance partly because of the electoral success of constituency-based clientelist networks. Moreover, as in Belize, high levels of manipulation of state programmes and services for clientelist purposes have blurred the lines between public and party resources across the region.[66]

Belize's experience on how clientelism distorts people's participation outside of elections also resonates across much of the region. In their study of elections between 1994 and 2005, Barrow-Giles and Joseph found that the costs of financing elections limit the participation of third parties and of women.[67] In particular, the Belize finding on the changing role of constituency representatives rings true. Much more than MPs in the United Kingdom or in other developed states that have Westminster parliamentary systems, MPs in "Caribbeanized" Westminster systems are primary focal points for constituents to engage the state for individualized resources. Just twelve years after Jamaican independence, Michael Manley made this insightful observation about the evolving function of Caribbean MPs:

> [T]hey [MPs] tend to be under constant pressure to distribute favours not only to members of organizations, but also to supporters in the widest sense. In the Jamaican political system, which is based on geographical constituencies and is in other respects a fair approximation of the Westminster model, the Member of Parliament and, consequently, the constituency organisation becomes inextricably involved in things like provision of jobs, the distribution of houses, pressure for water supplies, streetlights and sidewalks, and indeed all the basic elements of the patterns of felt needs.[68]

As in Belize, the widespread nature of clientelism has redefined the role of MPs beyond that of legislators to that of key providers of needed resources directly to constituents. Reflecting on the Jamaican MP experience, Baker argued that this latter informal role becomes understandable in the context of an ineffective public service and lack of private sector opportunities.[69] As noted in chapter 5, Baker proposed a constitutional rethink of the role of MPs that goes beyond that of legislators and that accepts some degree of institutionalization of their role as development agents in constituencies. Because Baker accepts that clientelism is destructive in the long term, she suggested consideration of a community development approach akin to the experience of the Samuel Haynes Institute of Excellence in Belize. Indeed, this institute and other similar initiatives in the region should be assessed as a possible model for designing similar pilots both in Belize and the rest of the region. The important point here is that entrenched clientelist politics has significantly transformed the relationship between elected representatives and constituents in Caribbean parliamentary democracies. In Gray's analysis of clientelist relationships in poor areas of Kingston, Jamaica, a central argument is that the poor understand that this manner of engaging their politicians does deliver in accessing needs and that they have real power in this relationship.[70]

The gradual spread of homogeneous voting to more constituencies in Belize, due in large part to political clientelism, has long been evident in urban Jamaica. Figueroa and Sives pointed out that in the 1993 election, in one urban Kingston constituency 98 per cent of ballot boxes had no votes for the losing candidate, and in another 48 per cent of boxes had no votes for the losing candidate – which they attributed to the development of garrison communities.[71] Several studies have demonstrated how these garrisons evolved as a result of both individualized and communal clientelism, as governing political parties favoured their supporters in the distribution of public housing.[72] Over time, several of these exclusive party-based garrison communities became no-go zones for supporters of the other party. Indeed, it was these garrison communities that spawned much of Jamaica's reputation in the region for partisan political violence in the 1980s and 1990s. Sives pinpointed party-based clientelism as one of the major contributors to Jamaica's post-independence experience with political violence.[73] Once clientelism was entrenched, and with the encouragement of the PNP and the JLP, supporters used violence to protect the resources they had received and to maintain clientelist flows. As Sives argued, such party-based violence subsided in the 1990s largely because of the relative decrease in party-based clientelism related to the "shrinking" of the state and a vacuum that was partly filled by drug dons supporting and, in some cases, replacing politicians as patrons in certain urban constituencies.[74]

One of the most notorious examples of this phenomenon took place in 2010 in Tivoli Gardens, a housing project established by the JLP in West Kingston in the 1960s. Christopher "Dudus" Coke, a drug don, had established himself as the dominant patron in the community. When then prime minister Bruce Golding used the police to detain Dudus for extradition to the United States, it resulted in an unprecedented violent episode that left more than seventy people killed.[75] As such, the rise of drug-gang violence in garrison communities in Jamaica can be directly traced back to the origins of party-based clientelism in post-independence Jamaica. Anthropological research by Rivke Jaffe has illustrated how dons and their gangs functioned much like the state for some citizens in poor Kingston communities – changing the concept of citizenship in the process.[76]

Although the Jamaican experience of such high levels of political violence stands out in the region, the examples discussed in chapter 6 suggest that Belize must be on guard to avoid the phenomenon of competing drug gangs openly supporting a particular party or politician at the constituency level. Signs of the infiltration of drug money into party politics for campaigns and clientelist operations are also identifiable in the Eastern Caribbean since the 1990s.[77] Such experiences could signal the emergence of a new variant of drug-don clientelism alongside competitive party clientelism across the region. As Sives put it, this was one of "the ways in which clientelist patterns and partisan identity have been restructured following the adoption of neoliberal policies in the 1980s and 1990s".[78] It is also one additional illustration of the adaptive and opportunistic nature of clientelism.

On Implications for Social Democracy

Across the region, as in Belize, clientelist politics do provide some distributive benefits to citizens in the context of high levels of poverty and ineffective public welfare systems.[79] Although acknowledging negative impacts, several studies have highlighted this distributive function of political clientelism as a contributor to sustaining formal and liberal democracy in the region. For example, Stone found that "clientelism undermines the propensity for open-class antagonisms".[80] Duncan and Woods contended that clientelism helps to explain the longevity of democracy in the Commonwealth Caribbean because it has "contributed to the development of a redistributive political culture that has helped Caribbean governments mitigate poverty and social exclusion".[81] Domínguez argued that clientelism is "inherently distributive" and has benefited poor people with resources as well as elites with political power and economic opportunities. This, he contends, leads to a political equilibrium he termed "the statist bargain", which, in turn, helps to preserve the status quo of formal democracy.[82] In the case of Jamaica, Edie suggested that clientelism "prevents authoritarianism by dispensing resources" and that "democracy, as a result, survives by default".[83]

The implicit assumption of these arguments is that if the informal distributive benefits of political clientelism were to somehow disappear, then formal democracy stability could be severely threatened. The Belize case illustrated that although, in a context of increasing poverty and inequality, political clientelism has played an escape-valve function that contributes to the meeting of social needs for some, the preserving-democracy argument exaggerates the relative contributions of clientelism to political stability in the wider context of social democracy. Importantly, clientelism, however pervasive, is but one of several escape valves for unmet social needs. Others include emigration, remittances, civil society interventions and effective public sector programmes. The preserving-democracy argument also overstates the distributive benefit spin-off of clientelist relationships. The Belize case demonstrates that the benefits that accrue are often not based on transparent standards of merit and are overwhelmingly short term in nature. Although the poor can sometimes be empowered collectively by the successes of their clientelist negotiations for resources, the systemic causes of the inequality that breeds clientelism remain entrenched even longer and are more damaging than sustaining to democracy in the region's states.

In relation to the concerning implications for public institutions, the following assessments imply that the findings for Belize obtain in much of rest of the Commonwealth Caribbean.

> It [clientelism in Jamaica] promotes personalised authority and therefore weak, non-autonomous and partially bureaucratised institutions. It encourages low levels of accountability in political institutions and high concentrations of personal power. . . . It presents intimidating obstacles that stifle the free flow of public debate and discourages independent individual and group participation in public life.[84]
>
> Positive resources . . . have passed . . . to supporters via the patronage machine [in Antigua and Barbuda]. At the same time, negative resources such as the state's ability to repress, to fire, to deny civil rights, to weaken unions, etc., have passed to opponents through the victimisation machine.[85]
>
> Whenever elections herald changeovers of power [in the Caribbean], the incoming party generally rewards its supporters with civil service positions or government procurement contracts, with the result that bureaucratic neutrality cannot be assured, and neither can the effectiveness of the state apparatus. . . . Even where patronage is not explicit, longer-term developmental objectives regularly give way to short-termism.[86]

Although corruption has been a major issue of concern across the region over the past decade, precious few studies and reports make more than a superficial link to political clientelism. One 2008 assessment of corruption in Jamaica made the connection clearly: "Jamaican corruption has managed to develop in ways that permitted extended networks of diverse elites, together with certain elements of the mass public, to share major benefits among themselves while staving off political and economic competitors. The costs of such a Faustian bargain, however, were played out in terms of violence and the increasing degradation of non-partisan state power."[87] In addition to pinpointing entrenched party-based patronage and clientelism as a core cause of the high levels of corruption in Jamaica, the report found that people generally do not view themselves as part of the problem. As the Belize case illustrates, many clients look away when rules are broken by patrons as long as they keep receiving benefits.

Across the region, the expanding monetary costs of politicians to set up ever larger clientelist operations have also resulted in politicians and political parties becoming increasingly more creative and reckless in accessing resources. The usual narrative is that of incumbent parties devising ever more schemes to tap into public funds, including international loans and grants, for use as clientelist inducements. A common example concerns the abuse of the "constituency fund", as was demonstrated in Belize. In Jamaica, the roles of MP as primary problem-solver and welfare agent had become so established by 1985 that former prime minister Edward Seaga acted to formalize aspects of these roles by launching the Local Development Programme, which provided monies for direct transfer to MPs "so that an MP can exercise his own discretion as how he determines these funds should be employed".[88] By 2008, the new version of this programme, called the constituency development fund, was some 2.5 per cent of Jamaica's national budget.[89] In 2011, Jamaican MPs were receiving JA$20 million per year (approximately US$225,000) for direct constituency spending, with no requirement for needs assessments or accounting.[90] Over time, some form of constituency funding for MPs has been similarly legitimized throughout most states in the region. As Lyday, O'Donnell and Munroe contended for Jamaica, "In practice, it serves as a powerful backbone for maintaining the patronage system of [both] political parties."[91]

With regard to the disincentive effect that entrenched clientelism has on policy and reform processes, the Belize experience also has parallels elsewhere in the region. Edie argues that neither politicians nor clients in Jamaica have problems with policies or programmes such as the constituency development fund that give people resources even when they are openly clientelist in nature.[92] On the contrary, policies that are perceived to threaten access to giving and receiving clientelist inducements may find little support. One clear example is that of a region-wide failure to develop and implement legislation to regulate campaign financing. As the overall costs of electoral politics have expanded due to the high expenditures on elections and clientelist operations, and as the corrupting consequences of private donations become clearer, the imperative for regulation is hard to dispute. Yet, as is the case in Belize, the situation relating to disclosure and regulating of financing for political parties is similarly wanting across the region. With regard to the regulation of political parties, in particular Belize was one of only three states in the region (the others being Grenada and Dominica) in which there were no legal requirements for the registration of parties in 2006.[93]

An Organization of American States article on political parties in the region found that "with regard to political financing, the Caribbean is one of the least transparent regions in the world".[94] Indeed, various regional studies have pointed to weak or non-existent regulation of political parties and their financing.[95] Ryan illustrated that in 2005 only five of the twelve independent Caribbean states had some kind of candidate finance campaign disclosure legislation, and only in Barbados and in Trinidad and Tobago had there been attempts at enforcement.[96] Overall, there has been no requirement for party disclosure and no limits on the sizes of contributions, and of the four states that have spending limits, only Barbados had some degree of enforcement. The reluctance of governments in the region to address campaign finance regulation has continued even as the costs of campaigns continue to skyrocket, sources of funding are increasingly private and numerous allegations of clientelism-related corruption have arisen. It appears that neither governments nor most in the public seem genuinely interested in proposals for the enactment of party and campaign finance regulation.

Conclusion

Even if not openly discussed, the prevalence of clientelist politics in all states across the Commonwealth Caribbean is widely acknowledged. This introductory comparative analysis of the Belize findings suggests that the implications of entrenched political clientelism for formal and social democracy in the region are too troubling to ignore. As in Belize, clientelism has played a significant, and largely deleterious, role in the region's states, and the modern politics of the region cannot be fully comprehended without better understanding the causes and implications of political clientelism.

For sure, there is clear need for more research to determine country-specific manifestations and to inform more substantive comparisons within and outside the region. Cross-regional comparative studies on the origins, manifestations and interactions of political clientelism in the Caribbean and Central America could also be of particular usefulness. As microcosms of universal political behaviours, the small states of the Commonwealth Caribbean can provide meaningful insights into how clientelism affects democracy and development in similar developing states.

8.

Conclusions

Trapped in a Clientelist Web

Belize's seventh post-independence general election in March 2012, the first consecutive electoral victory for the UDP over the PUP, was further confirmation of the upward trajectory of political clientelism. For the first time since independence, the losing party had refused to accept the official results based, in part, on allegations of voter bribery. Of the various allegations of vote buying made by the PUP, only one was formally lodged in April 2012 and heard by the Supreme Court in May. It was brought by the PUP's candidate for Cayo North, Orlando Habet, who lost to the UDP's Elvin Penner by only seventeen votes. Penner was accused of bribing voters with money on election day and with citizenship papers in the lead-up to the election.[1] The case was dismissed by the court, confirming once again the hard challenge of legally proving voter bribery between politician and citizen. Interestingly, an election petition case alleging voter bribery was also lodged by the UDP's Lee Mark Chang, who lost to then PUP leader Francis Fonseca by 150 votes. That, too, was thrown out by the Supreme Court.[2]

During its 2008–12 administration, the UDP had further mastered the art of targeting more public resources as inducements to individual voters, and a larger number of UDP intra-party pre-election conventions and constituency contests were characterized by highly organized and well-resourced political machineries. In particular, the UDP and most of its politicians had upped their game at the critical level of operating effective day-to-day political clinics – further adding to the now consolidated narrative of the PUP and UDP having but superficial differences between them. In particular, the long-standing perception that the PUP, Belize's first political party, was more adept at clientelist politics than the UDP had evaporated. This achievement of "clientelist parity" between the two dominant parties was one further unambiguous indicator of the extent to which political clientelism, since its innocent beginnings in the 1950s, became an entrenched element of Belize's modern politics.

By employing the analytic lens of political clientelism to revisit Belize's modern political history, I have conceptualized political clientelism as a component of Belize's democratization and modern political relations in three phases: the "innocent'" phase from 1954 to 1981, the "bridging" phase from 1981 to 1991 and the current "rampant" phase since the 1990s. Over these periods, I have illustrated how political clientelism emerged in the formative and colonial period of Belize's modern politics, identified the principal manifestations of its expansion in the post-independence period, pinpointed the factors that contributed to its high rate of expansion (at the same time as formal democratic advances), examined the critical implications of widespread clientelism for Belize's democracy and then discussed how the Belize case compares to experiences of other independent parliamentary democracies in the Commonwealth Caribbean. In this final chapter, I synthesize my key findings and draw final conclusions.

Innocent Foundations: 1954–81

In characterizing this formative phase of modern political clientelism as innocent, I sought to capture the sharp contrast with the rampant and often nefarious expansion that followed after independence. It is clear, however, that not every aspect of this pre-independence experience with clientelism was innocent in intent – even as the overarching imperative was to "help the people". As Belize approached nationhood in 1981, party-based clientelist activity was indeed very minimal compared to 2013. Yet it was in this period that the foundation necessary for the expansion was laid. In 1954, when a new constitution gave the vote to all Belizeans and bestowed electoral relevance to the nascent political parties, the elements essential for the emergence of modern political clientelism were mostly in place. After a period in the 1960s and early 1970s characterized by genuine but inadequate attempts at programmatic approaches to address deep-seated social and economic problems, the dominant PUP gradually integrated more clientelist practices into its repertoire of strategies to appeal to voters. By 1981, handouts and favours in return for political support were more on offer and more needed, and the political pendulum was beginning to swing from still nascent programmatic politician–citizen relationships to one with increasing features of clientelist exchanges.

The primary and driving causal factor in this formative period was the introduction and consolidation of increasingly competitive party politics in a societal context of ongoing unmet livelihood needs and greater access to political power for locals in the nascent Westminster system. As the

UDP, still in opposition limbo, improved its electoral performance and slowly entered the handout game, the PUP stepped up its direct appeals to individual voters and communities through the emerging clinic system and targeted allocation of public goods. The public institutions of the emerging state were simply unable to meet most people's needs and high expectations. By the 1970s, weakened labour unions and decreased activity of social charity groups represented inadequate alternatives to the growing dominance of the political parties as social mediators. As such, the option of influencing distribution of public resources by bartering of political support became increasingly rational. As the tentacles of competitive party politics spread out from Belize City, political clientelism gradually took root in other parts of the country. The populist and paternalistic leadership style of George Price, Belize's "hero in the crowd", significantly textured the formative phase of clientelism. In the personalized politics of the small state, Price was not only the father of the nation but visibly its "grand patron". Additionally, Belize's diverse multi-ethnicity affected how politicians, communities and citizens used ethnicity as part of their negotiations of the distribution of resources.

In this pre-independence period, aptitude at clientelism was not yet a dominant indicator of difference between the two main parties. The incumbent PUP and the opposition NIP (later the UDP) presented distinctive national policies to the electorate, especially with regard to political independence, and the vast majority of party support was issue-based and voluntary. In the context of these times, the "helping the people" justification of Price and other early politicians was understandable and, for the most part, genuine. Yet in a poor emerging democracy with increasingly competitive party politics, the line between handouts and favours for "helping" versus for deliberately influencing voting decisions was getting thin. In aggregate, the ingredients required for the rapid and inevitable spread of clientelist politician–citizen relationships were taking root.

A Bridging Decade: 1981–91

I presented the transitional but formative decade of 1981–91 as one marked by a gradual increase in clientelist politics as politicians adapted to their new powers and confronted multiple economic and social challenges, including the settlement of tens of thousands of immigrants, of the newly independent state. Handouts were still mostly low in value, the use of public resources to target individuals was limited, party-based voluntarism was still significant and allegations of voter bribery were rare. Yet there were important developments relevant for the expansion of clientelist activity. Just three years after securing long-delayed independence for Belize, the Price-led PUP, dogged by a fiscal crisis, opted to succumb to the IMF – effectively launching Belize's embrace of neoliberalist prescriptions that would have significant downstream impact for the trajectory of political clientelism. Interestingly, it was around this time that the billionaire Lord Ashcroft made some of his first moves as a major financial player in Belize. Also central among the developments was the further intensification of competitive party politics as the UDP won its first general election in 1984 and the PUP regained power in 1989. These elections started a trend of successive peaceful alternations in government (up to 2003) and fully consolidated the competitive two-party system. For the UDP, the 1984–89 period represented its first real political tutelage in using the powers of government and incumbency to partisan advantage. Like the PUP before it, and to similar accusations of political victimization, the governing UDP began to engage in job patronage and to devise new ways of using public funds for targeted constituency-based programmes. In the 1980s, clientelist political strategies were no longer the sole domain of the PUP.

Key among other political precedents was the gradual diminishing of ideological and policy differences between the PUP and the UDP. As such, by the 1989 election, voters had fewer substantive distinctions around which to base voting decisions – opening the door to the further use of clientelist appeals by politicians. This in turn was facilitated by the flow of more private money and influence from big donors into the two main parties as both became more commercial party machines. Also, the legislative amendments relating to the Elections and Boundaries Commission in 1988 and 1989 gave any incumbent political party significant potential advantage in matters relating to election administration and registration. The large new immigrant population was about to become a significant voting bloc. The decade also demonstrated that a government's capacity to deliver and to increase clientelist inducements is often directly related to the developments in the macro economy. Even as severe economic hardships between 1981 and 1986 constrained both the PUP and UDP governments' potential to engage in clientelism, gradual improvements in the fiscal situation provided for more such opportunities in the remainder of the decade.

Entrenched Clientelist Politics: After 1992

By the time Belize commemorated its thirtieth anniversary as an independent state in 2011, the manifestations of entrenched political clientelism epitomized a colossal shift from its pre-independence beginnings. The PUP and UDP operated political clinics in almost every constituency, at least 20 per cent of the electorate was participating in the handout game, the types and value of resources exchanged had multiplied, volunteerism for political parties had virtually disappeared, and clientelist politics had spread to every municipality and village. Belize's politicians had become "equal opportunity" patrons across urban and rural communities, gender, ethnicity, and migratory status. Although the clear majority of clients at the constituency level have been poorer or lower-income Belizeans, representatives of the middle and business classes also play the game but for higher value exchanges. Women, who experience higher rates of unemployment and have headed the majority of single-parent households, outnumber men as clients but likely receive less in terms of monetary value of benefits.

My findings also demonstrated that the profile of the "client" in Belize is not all that straightforward. There is a core of "permanent clients" who, because of need or deliberate opportunistic intent, show no interest in changing their client status. Around this core is a shifting number of "transient clients" who move in and out of clientelist relationships based on an ongoing assessment of needs, of opportunities and of risks. Importantly, the absolute numbers of both types of clients have been growing as a proportion of the electorate since the 1990s – and is likely well above my cautious estimate of 20–25 per cent of the electorate.

The heightened intensity of party competition, within the Westminster model and FPTP electoral system, provided the overarching political framework for political clientelism to take root and expand. For sure, political clientelism would have emerged and grown to some extent without the intensity of party competition described, but this was the indispensable ingredient for the level of expansion witnessed. It was through party competition in constituencies that politicians and citizens interacted to establish the multiple personal relationships upon which the network of political clinics were constructed. As the PUP and UDP became even more alike in their policy positions and governing styles, aptitude at clientelist politics more heavily determined the outcome of their competition for votes. As such, the Belize case demonstrates that the rapid expansion and entrenchment of political clientelism can be conceptualized as a product of intensified competitive party politics and, subsequently, as a distinctive feature of such competition.

By far, the most significant of the other basic supporting factors that fuelled the expansion of clientelism has been the quantitative and qualitative shift in the nature of poverty. Although the incidence of poverty, in large part a legacy of colonialism, has been high since the 1950s and increased between 1995 and 2009, income disparities have also widened. This social context was ripe for more politicians to become patrons and for more Belizeans to become clients. The alternatives of formal social programmes and civil society interventions have not been sufficiently effective to dampen citizens' attraction to clientelist exchanges. As such, the relative failure of formal democracy to address social and economic inequalities contributed to a vacuum of unfulfilled needs for clientelism to enter, widen and embed itself. In short, poverty and inadequate alleviation responses made vote trading more cost-effective as an electoral strategy. Although occurring across Belize, this has been most visible in pockets of high poverty and deprivation in the densely populated constituencies in Belize City.

Besides contributing to the increase in poverty and inequality referenced to earlier, the further entrenchment of neoliberal socio-economic policies fuelled other developments that favoured clientelist relationships and behaviour. Implementation of neoliberal economic policies just after independence, especially generous fiscal concessions to investors, expanded opportunities for politicians to use both public resources and private donations for clientelist exchanges. As such, the Belize case exposes the clear linkages that clientelism has to international economic policy developments as well as to the disproportionate roles that very wealthy individual investors can play in funding clientelist politics and "commercial" political parties in small states. It also illustrates that at the same time neoliberalism facilitated the deepening of political clientelism in Belize; it also complicates and constrains the capacity of those who may seek to mitigate it through formal political action. This is not only because change through electoral processes is so tied to utilizing the very prohibitively expensive clientelist strategies or because the state's institutions are gutted, but also because small post-colonial states such as Belize (and in the rest of the Caribbean) have little real geopolitical power to counter the deep grip of neoliberalism on their societies even if they so wanted. George Monbiot summarized this straitjacket effect of neoliberalism well: "Perhaps the most dangerous impact of neoliberalism is not the economic crises it caused, but the political crises. As the domain of the state is reduced, our ability to change the course of our lives through voting also contracts. Instead, neoliberal theory asserts, people can exercise choice through spending. But some have more to spend than others: in the great consumer or shareholder democracy, votes are not equally distributed."[3]

The dominant level of control over resource allocation institutions, and the ease with which such control was increased in the context of Belize's Westminster system, provided local leaders with more options and means to dispense state resources to targeted groups and individuals. Once exercised, this power of control itself became the big prize and, therefore, a key impetus for the main parties to use clientelism to win elections. Belize's weak institutional frameworks for the management of elections, monitoring voter registration, pursuing allegations of voter bribery and regulating campaign contributions have fostered a permissive environment for clientelist activities.

I also explored how multi-ethnicity, small state size and migration have influenced the growth and manifestations of clientelism. Clientelist politics in Belize do not feature a significant ethnic-based divisive dimension; however, multi-ethnicity and the presence of a new bloc of mostly poor immigrant voters provided readily identifiable networks through which politicians and clients negotiate exchanges. Without doubt, Belize's small state size has accelerated the growth and coloured the manifestations of political clientelism across all phases of its trajectory. Belizean political clinic networks are small, highly personalized operations in which politicians and brokers, on the one hand, and clients, on the other, directly engage and monitor each other. In this regard, the Belize case illustrates that clientelism in states with tiny constituencies often disproportionately determines election outcomes due to the relative ease and affordability of influencing individual voters.

Although the PUP and the UDP initially drove political clientelism from the top, demand-driven motivations expanded during the 1990s as more Belizeans began to proactively engage politicians and improve their direct access to resources. More people began to view their votes as tradable commodities, and clientelism morphed into an alternative mode of political participation for a significant portion of the population. By the election of 2012, political clientelism in Belize had become a systemic and widely accepted political interdependency between people and politicians, and a prominent feature of Belize's political culture.

Grim Implications for the Quality of Democracy

From the perspective of social democracy, the distributive impact of clientelism has been deeply real for an increasing number of Belizeans. Given the limitations and failures of the state's social welfare system, a 41.3 per cent poverty rate (2009), high levels of income inequality and the general unevenness of the socio-economic playing field, handouts from politicians represent access to needed resources for a significant proportion of poor Belizeans. Since independence, clientelism has evolved into a de facto informal, if not semi-formal, welfare system that has helped to hold things together in a context of great social need exacerbated by neoliberal policies.

I argue, however, that the benefits to individuals that have been derived from clientelism's short-term distributive function are heavily outweighed by its overall damaging impact on most aspects of democracy, and that the aggregate and longer-term implications for socio-economic distribution and welfare are decidedly negative. The informal rules of the clinic system result in less means testing in social welfare programmes, more opportunists, waste of public funds and, in general, less focus on programmatic solutions to socio-economic needs. The spoils of the clientelist game are disproportionately enjoyed by those in the middle class and business class who are also aided and facilitated by politicians in return for favours. In particular, concessions given to party donors have contributed to a loss of public revenue and more political corruption. Importantly, clientelist activities undercut the urgent imperative to develop and implement alternative, sustainable and systemic solutions to socio-economic problems.

Moreover, the institutional implications of clientelism are highly detrimental to social democracy to the extent that they have further weakened the very public institutions that are supposed to address social problems. In order to fulfil bargains with clients and build up their voter base for the next election, clientelist politicians have exerted more discretionary control over Belize's formal institutions of resource allocation. Formal political power in Belize's version of Westminster government has become more concentrated, more personalized and more discretionary as clientelist practices became deeply entrenched. At the same time, lines of power and function between public institutions and political parties have become increasingly blurred.

Over time, as political parties became more clientelist, they placed even less emphasis on membership recruitment through ideological and policy distinctions. The fact that more citizens interact with the government through patron-politicians at the constituency level has worrying consequences for substantive participatory democracy. Generally, the formal function of representatives as legislators has become secondary to their informal role as patrons. As informal citizen participation through clientelism has expanded, participation through formal public institutions and civil society organizations has come to be perceived by more citizens as not as effective and responsive. Additionally, because of the high costs of competing based on clientelism, alternative political parties, poorer Belizeans, women and other under-represented groups have had even more difficulty getting a foothold in electoral politics.

These vexing implications for Belize's practice of democracy highlight three key paradoxes of political clientelism. First, even though electoral democracy within the Westminster system has provided the basic conditions for clientelism to expand, this expansion has shaken some of the very foundations of formal democracy itself. Even as elections remain formally free and fair, the portion of the votes cast based on clientelist transactions have increasingly determined election outcomes. When a significant number of votes have been bartered for resources, there is less guarantee that intra-party elections, local elections, constituency elections or general elections are reflective of issue-based distinctions. Additionally, the pervasiveness of the illegal activity of vote buying is a powerful indicator of growing disrespect for the rule of law among both politicians and people.

The second paradox has to do with the question of the degree of patron/client voluntarism in clientelist exchanges. The Belize case illustrates that although both clients and politician patrons, in theory, engaged in voluntary exchanges as clientelism took root and expanded, the obligation to so engage has become a part of the "practical" and rational equation for most politicians and for many citizens. As competitive clientelism has become entrenched in a societal context of growing inequality, a significant portion of citizens have become economically dependent on clientelist resources, and politicians believe they have no alternative but to become patron-politicians. In a very real sense, as clientelism has become rooted and systemic, more clients and patrons view their involvement as more necessary than voluntary. As such, the Belize case supports an approach to clientelism that, in practice, moves across a dynamic and, sometimes overlapping, voluntary–involuntary spectrum for both clients and patrons.

The third paradox is that clientelist activities eventually have diminishing returns for incumbent parties due to the inevitable social, economic and financial inefficiencies they breed. The inability to service the inflationary demand for material inducements by clients has been one reason why both PUP and UDP governments have lost elections. To feed the clientelist monster, politicians must expend much time and effort to procure money, including from undercover sources. Some of this money goes to assist constituents and some is pocketed. Rampant political corruption, ineffective fiscal management and public perceptions that politicians, many themselves clients of wealthy donors, are enriching themselves have sometimes shifted popular support to an eager opposition party. Many would argue that this explains the PUP's loss in the 2008 elections even when tens of millions, including the Venezuela money, was expended in the lead-up to the election. Yet these paradoxes do not deter parties and politicians from engaging in clientelist politics in a small state in which entire elections have turned on buying political support in selected constituencies.

In summary, most of the tens of thousands of dyadic clientelist transactions made annually at the constituency level in the Belize context are, on the surface, rational individual choices on the part of citizens, as well as politicians. Clientelism does represent an alternative mode of political participation and does have short-term distributive benefits for some Belizeans in a social context of poverty, unequal access to resources, broken social institutions and an unlevel playing field for commerce. However, when taken collectively and assessed in the longer term, these myriad rational transactions lead to irrational governance behaviour, poor civic practices and damaging consequences at macro-political and macro-economic levels. In the long term, the majority of people in Belize end up with the short end of the stick and the manifestations of the high incidence of political clientelism have predominantly negative consequences for both formal and social democracy.

Trapped in a Thorny Web

In its independence constitution, Belize defines itself as a "democratic state of Central America in the Caribbean region". Paraphrasing Carl Stone, the conclusions of this book suggest that "clientelist democratic state" may well be a more accurate denotation. From its emergence in the nascent period of political party development in the 1950s to its full consolidation as an entrenched feature of political relationships and political culture three decades later, the role of political clientelism in the modern politics of Belize has either been ignored or understated. This is due, in no small part, to the informal and often illegal nature of political clientelism itself, and to the challenges of researching it in a small society, where many see it as just normal behaviour.

I have demonstrated that the narrative of modern politics in Belize cannot be limited to the development and consolidation of formal political institutions. This narrative is incomplete without the story of the tens of thousands of informal relationships and multi-layered linkages that comprise political clientelism, and through which a growing number of Belizean, across class, gender and ethnicity, engage daily with their politicians and governments. It is also incomplete without an understanding of the micro- and macro-societal implications that entrenched political clientelism presents for Belize's democracy and development. In a very real sense, the expansion of clientelism is a symptom of the failure of democracy itself to progress to higher levels of social democracy. Documenting why clientelist politics emerged and expanded, how it operates, and its implications for Belizean society is important not only for filling gaps in the existing political narrative, but also because it contributes to understanding how the role of the constituency representative has changed; why so many citizens, across all income levels, prefer engaging with patron-politicians rather than government institutions; why some of these institutions are failing; how an informal welfare system has replaced much of the formal system; why politicians and governments shun longer-term programmatic reforms; how political corruption works; and why structural poverty persists.

This case study on political clientelism in Belize – the first country case study in the Commonwealth Caribbean since those on Jamaica – also demonstrates that a national, interview-rich country study can add relevant insights to the body of knowledge on political clientelism and can provide useful opportunities for revisiting and advancing analyses of this phenomenon for this set of states. The comparative discussion of the Belize findings in its Commonwealth Caribbean context indicated that, albeit with some unique contextual textures, clientelist democracy is more prevalent in states in the region than the paucity of dedicated studies suggests. Importantly, commonalities in most of these national experiences in the region give credence to a path-dependency perspective on the emergence and expansion of political clientelism, alongside the emergence and consolidation of party politics in the region.

As in Belize, competitive party politics and high levels of institutional control within the Westminster model, ongoing poverty and inequality, and small size dominate in the region as causal explanations for the high prevalence of clientelist politics. Ethnicity and migration have helped to determine the particular strategies of patrons and clients alike in several of the region's states. Although not indispensable for the emergence and expansion of clientelist politics, the personalities and actions of individual leaders, such as Belize's George Price, Jamaica's Michael Manley, Trinidad and Tobago's Eric Williams, and Barbados's Errol Barrow, and the behaviour of particular political parties have been significant factors in explaining differences in the development and in the textures of modern political clientelism in states across the region.

My findings on Belize also contain several analytical and methodological insights for the study of political clientelism beyond the Commonwealth Caribbean. Edie was percipient in arguing that clientelism, as an analytic concept, demonstrates "why and how the interests of the rich and poor manage to converge" in the democratic politics of some states.[4] The Belize results confirm that the politics of the poor feature much more in informal relationships at the dyadic and community levels than at the level of formal institutions of government. Even though those in higher-income brackets also exchange political support for resources and favours and though some rich donors help to grease the wheels of clientelism, the electoral support of poorer Belizeans is a politician's key to the doors of political power. It is the competition for this support, in a context of weak substantive party distinctions, that pushed the PUP, and then the UDP, to expand political clientelism.

Yet top-down conceptualizations of party-led clientelism are only part of the picture. For Belize, there was a critical pivot point in the trajectory of clientelism in the late 1990s when the collective weight of citizen demand began to drive clientelist relationships from the bottom up, as much as the dangling of material inducements from above. My conclusion here does not negate that poverty and inequality persist, or that the poor get the shorter end of the stick. Rather, my point is to emphasize that both politicians and clients have become politically dependent on the clientelist relationship. Reaching this stage of what might be denoted "mutual clientelist dependency" should be treated as a warning sign that political clientelism has reached dangerous levels of entrenchment.

Additionally, my findings strongly suggest that, within the broader academic research on democratization, studies of political clientelism should include more macro-political impact analysis at the national level than has been the case. This is not to deny the value of studies on the implications for sub-national political units, such as constituencies and towns, or of studies that focus on specific relationships between clientelism and other variables, such as political violence or voter turnout. Yet Belize's small size has facilitated both the research and the analysis of macro-implications for democracy in a way that would be more difficult to do for, say, Argentina or Brazil. Moreover, my findings show that the constructs of "clientelist democracy" and "patronage democracy" need conceptual refinement. Definitions cannot be limited simply to the high prevalence of clientelist and patronage practices in the formal institutions of a polity. It is equally important to consider the detrimental macro-political implications of political clientelism for the quality of democracy itself.

As damaging as political clientelism is for the quality of democracy and development in a developing state, the Belize case illustrates that the day-to-day engagement for many citizens in clientelist exchanges can be justifiably construed as rational choices aimed at influencing the allocation of needed resources in their favour. As a bona fide informal mode of participation, clientelism does not appear as anti-democratic or immoral from the viewpoint of some clients, as it is for many scholars and proponents of formal democracy. For some, it is itself a type of democracy. Yet, in the longer run, the high prevalence of political clientelism witnessed in Belize is deleterious to the difficult process of improving the quality of democracy for all Belizeans.

Poor Prospects for Early Change

What would Belize be like with less clientelism and how would it get there? At the conceptual level, Clapham outlined the logical prescription: diminishing the necessary conditions for political clientelism can result in the "decay of clientelism".[5] At a minimum, if party competition remains high, mitigating clientelism would entail decreasing poverty and inequality, improving resource allocation through the formal government welfare system and effective civil society interventions, enhancing party competition around non-clientelist distinctions, and giving teeth to punitive regulations. Indeed, decreases in blatant forms of clientelism in some developed states have been directly related to long-term improvements in economic opportunities and more effective enforcement of laws that regulate elections and politician–citizen relationships.[6] This trend of gradual decrease in political clientelism in some rich countries has not yet transpired in most post-colonial developing countries. Certainly, no concerted attempt has so far been made to arrest the prevalence of political clientelism in Belize, and there is little evidence that this will transpire soon.

The essence of the problem of mitigating political clientelism is found in a penetrating question posed by that Belize City broker: "What will replace it?"[7] Critical barriers to real change are further reflected in the highly pessimistic tenor of the vast majority of responses given by past and current politicians to my question of what to do about clientelist politics. Most responses were akin to "we can't do anything much, really. It's too far gone. It's now part of our culture"[8] and "neither the PUP nor UDP will stop because they would mess up their chances to win the next election".[9]

Some even suggested throwing in the towel and formalizing some aspects of political clientelism into public institutions and the budgetary system.

Belize's Assad Shoman, although conceding that change will be exceedingly difficult and unlikely in the near future, offers a recipe of radical systemic and programmatic change based on social democratic and anti-neoliberal principles.[10] Shoman's ideological nemesis, Ralph Fonseca, who does not see much wrong with political clientelism itself, believes that it is more a matter of better management of constituents' expectations, as funds available for "benefits politics" fluctuate across normal economic twists and turns in the market.[11] Even though some politicians and citizens find clientelist politics distasteful and question its sustainability, there is no evidence to suggest that the PUP and UDP will soon begin to compete more on the basis of ideological and programmatic distinctions, and less on clientelism. Rather, the two parties have become trapped in a thorny clientelist web largely of their own making. I liken this to a "clientelist cold war", in which neither party will independently seek to disarm its clientelist machine even when both parties are aware that clientelist practices are eventually destructive and do not always ensure victory. This clientelist web has also trapped significant portions of Belize's population, especially those who survive on the informal welfare system of handouts.

Once deeply institutionalized, mutual clientelist dependency between politicians and citizens is not easy to break. It is as Rosberg suggested, a problem of the "paradox of underdevelopment" in which "everybody wants the situation to be different, but nobody can afford to go first".[12] Critically, there is little indication that the prognosis for poverty and inequality will improve, that effective alternatives to informal social assistance institutions will appear, or that economic opportunities will significantly expand. A part of the difficulty is that too few of Belize's political leaders recognize and accept the situation as problematic, and all seem to believe and accept that the prevailing neoliberal economic policy framework is the only alternative. Even when political leaders attempt to use elections and the formal institutions of government to address the kind of poverty fuelled by neoliberalism, they find themselves straitjacketed by the very policy constraints of neoliberalism itself. Worse still, a significant proportion of Belizeans have grown to view handouts as entitlements and to believe that accepting them is rational in a political context where individualism reigns and in which they judge their political leaders as being corrupt. As Shoman highlighted about the imperatives of neoliberalism, "Democracy does not mean power to the people, but power of the market; everything conspires to undermine universal adult suffrage."[13]

Even if there was a concerted effort to curtail political clientelism, it would have to be based on a harsh reality: political clientelism has become a deeply systemic problem for Belize that will require systemic solutions and changes in power relationships that go far beyond isolated institutional reforms. Attacking political clientelism institutionally will likely be ineffective if politicians and political parties maintain such extensive decision-making power over the distribution of resources that Belizeans need, and if political parties have no strong incentives to disengage. The challenge is complicated even more by the fact that informal welfare practices, especially when they become a part of political culture and behaviour, are exceedingly difficult to alter. As the experience and aftermath of political and constitutional reform efforts in Belize indicate, there is little political will in the country for the deeper kinds of direct governance reforms that could help to mitigate clientelism, such as campaign finance regulation, curbing the abuse of the non-established workers category in the public service, curtailing discretionary spending and fee waivers, strengthening the Elections and Boundaries Commission, voter education, prosecuting voter bribery, and decreasing impunity. What does exist in large measure is deeply held cynicism among the political parties and people alike that even such changes will not make any substantive difference.

Overall, and notwithstanding occasional and temporary dips in clientelism's trajectory, high levels of political clientelism will persist and remain a characteristic feature of political relations in Belize for the foreseeable future. When the impetus for change does come, two conclusions from a historic 2010 gathering of the foremost international scholars of political clientelism in Quito, Ecuador, should be well heeded. The first, which addresses the challenge of sustainability of some clientelist activities, is that "patron–client relationships are inherently unstable and perhaps may contain the seeds of their own destruction".[14] The second is the sobering truism that political parties seldom initiate major change independently: "The solution cannot be left in the hands of the political system alone. Civil society has a key role to play; indeed, an indispensable one."[15] CSOs in Belize and the Caribbean already have rich experiences in initiating governance reform campaigns with occasional successes, and all the lessons from these must be brought to bear. Any actions by civil society or by new political leaders to mitigate rampant political clientelism must be sustained and must be informed by a comprehensive understanding of the linkages between the widespread, day-to-day practices of political clientelism, on the one hand, and its implications for the quality of democracy and people's long-term livelihoods, on the other. I trust this book will contribute towards this end.

Epilogue

The Next Tranche (Covering Selected Developments from 2014 to June 2021)

There has been, as a matter of course, significant change in aspects of Belize's national context since I completed the core research for this book some seven years ago. In November 2015, the UDP made post-independence political history by winning a third consecutive term in office, increasing its seat majority by two over 2012 with nineteen seats to the PUP's twelve. Five years later in the November 2020 general elections, the PUP finally succeeded in breaking the UDP's long hold on power with a landslide victory of twenty-six to five seats – a result surpassing the UDP's (twenty-five to six) sea-change victory in February 2008. John Briceño became Belize's fifth post-independence prime minister and led the PUP to a sweeping victory in municipal elections in March 2021, winning all but two of the sixty-seven city and town council seats. In between the 2015 and 2020 general elections, and after a long-delayed voter registration exercise, Belize held its first stand-alone national referendum in May 2019, sending the Guatemalan claim to the International Court of Justice.

Since 2018, and before the multi-sectoral blows of the Covid-19 pandemic, GDP growth had begun to slow and the public debt had continued to balloon. After the pandemic began in the first quarter of 2020, almost every macroeconomic and fiscal indicator plummeted in the year that followed: GDP decreased by 14 per cent, government revenue fell by 28 per cent, per capita income returned to 1992 levels, unemployment and underemployment rose to alarming rates, and the debt-to-GDP ratio jumped to 126 per cent.[1] Overall, the population of Belize, which surpassed four hundred twenty thousand in 2020, has continued to grapple with persistent and growing poverty (estimated at 52 per cent in 2018)[2] and worsening income inequality, ongoing citizen insecurity and multifaceted vulnerability – signalling that Belize's mix of fundamental development challenges has largely remained substantively constant. Entrenched political clientelism is, of course, one of those constants.

Nothing has transpired over the past seven years to cause me to substantively question the validity of my conclusions on political clientelism in this book. On the contrary, I assert that my principal findings on the deleterious implications of political clientelism have been further corroborated by recent societal developments as political clientelism continues to spread and tighten its tentacles around political parties and people alike. This is not to deny that some developments add texture to the basic narrative of political clientelism or that a few may even contain faint flickers of hope for taming aspects of rampant clientelist politics. Although the major PUP victories in general and local government elections in 2020 and 2021 marked a total swing of the pendulum of party-political power, the vast majority of developments I select to discuss about political clientelism after 2013 are, necessarily, from the periods of the UDP administrations that governed from 2012 to 2015 and from 2015 to 2020.

Venezuela Redux: PetroCaribe

After the 2015 national elections, the then opposition PUP accused the incumbent UDP government of winning the election through vote buying, just as it had after the 2012 election; but, this time, the PUP did not contest any constituency result. It was sobering political irony that the PUP's allegations in 2015 centred almost exclusively around a second incarnation of Venezuela money – the first being the $40 million which the PUP itself was accused of abusing when last in government in 2008.[3] This time around, the Venezuela money was made possible by the PetroCaribe programme. Launched by Venezuela in 2005, the regional programme allowed partner countries in the Caribbean and Latin America to purchase petroleum based on preferential financing terms. Although Belize signed on in 2005, it was not until September 2012 that it began to procure most petroleum products from Venezuela and was allowed to withhold a portion of the payments as a concessionary loan.[4] These withheld amounts eventually resulted in a windfall income of approximately $470 million[5] for the UDP government between 2012 and 2017, when the programme was suspended only due to political and economic developments within Venezuela.

In addition to using the proceeds from the PetroCaribe programme to finance a spate of nationwide road and infrastructure development projects, launch a national bank, top-up existing social assistance programmes, and respond to natural disasters, the UDP government also rolled out several one-off handout programmes. The latter continued and expanded on the strategies and examples of the seasonal clientelist allocations to constituencies discussed in this book.[6] For example, the Christmas Assistance Programme, which began in 2011 with $1.4 million for distribution among the thirty-one constituency representatives of the ruling party, was scaled up in 2013 with a \$2.2 million budget courtesy of PetroCaribe proceeds.[7] The same transpired in 2014 with a similar-sized budget. This programme became an annual fixture, albeit with decreasing budgets as PetroCaribe funds dwindled and then halted. Before it ended in 2017, the PetroCaribe loans also funded or co-funded other similar handout programmes, including the popular Mothers' Day events as well as party campaigning activities in the lead-up to local government elections and by-elections. As before, the middle class was not left out of the seasonal handouts. In December 2014, for example, alongside the "pro-poor" Christmas Assistance Programme, there was the Residential Mortgage Payment Programme in which PetroCaribe funds were used to pay one month's mortgage of anyone who applied with residential mortgages below \$100,000.[8]

Even as PetroCaribe was the dominant cash cow, it was not the only source of funds to oil the machinery of the UDP's political clinics after 2013. As before, money, goods and services in exchange for political support, or the promise thereof, also came from other public programmes and from private funding sources. Any comprehensive assessment of the latter remains a hard research challenge due to the lack of proper accounting and the total absence of campaign finance regulation. For sure, the PUP's own ability to remain competitive (in 2015 it won twelve seats with 47.28 per cent of the popular vote and lost seven seats by less than one hundred votes) is due, in no small part, to its own fundraising to grease the clientelist machine. However, the conventional wisdom is that the PUP could not manage to compete with the incumbent administration's PetroCaribe largesse, and that this was, at least, one of the core factors contributing to the spate of UDP victories in the national, local and by-elections between 2012 and 2017. Overall, this sequel of large sums of Venezuela money reinforced and further normalized the trend of political parties in power using public funds (in this case a soft loan) as targeted inducements for securing political support.

Indeed, over the last seven years, clientelist practices have continued to become more accepted and institutionalized as normal behaviour by more politicians and more citizens – indeed, by the wider society. Unsurprisingly, the UDP government defended its use of PetroCaribe loan funds for seasonal targeted-assistance programmes as an effective way of getting resources to people in need. After facing the seasonal allegations of vote buying and patronage from the opposition party, from smaller parties and from some pockets of the media about the Christmas Assistance Programme, the UDP government countered that a layer of transparency had been consolidated such that constituency representatives did not receive direct cash payments but had to use a version of the voucher system. Under this system, selected constituents receive vouchers for selected items that come from selected suppliers who are then reimbursed by the government.[9] While this added some level of accountability for the government departments which needed to report on expenditures, it was the constituency representatives, standard bearers or caretaker politicians who still subjectively influenced which names were on the much-prized lists to receive vouchers. Additionally, the "selected suppliers" are invariably either acquaintances, relatives, party supporters or party financiers – any of which could conceivably provide a kickback to a politician or partisan operative. In short, assistance programmes that use the voucher system become more formalized within the system without losing their true intent: seeking to maintain or solicit political support of individuals and households by influencing the direction of resources.

Another, if more subtle, manifestation of the normalization trend is that constituency representatives of the then opposition PUP were included in additional assistance programmes managed by the UDP government, a practice that had started cautiously under the 2008–12 UDP administration in relation to educational and housing assistance. For example, since 2013, elected representatives of the opposition were allowed to partake in the annual Christmas Assistance Programmes, albeit with lower allocations – usually one-quarter or one-third of what constituency representatives of the ruling party received. Except for the pre-election period in 2014, when the opposition sought to make political mileage points about UDP vote buying, PUP representatives generally accepted such constituency funds when on offer, and in some cases even lobbied for them.[10] It is not far-fetched to speculate that the then government's intentions may have been to muzzle or diminish criticism from the opposition PUP, particularly in the use of PetroCaribe funds. However, the PUP's participation in such handout programmes exposed its own urgent efforts to meet clients' demands and signalled a concurrence with the ongoing normalization of the practice. It is unlikely that the PUP government elected in 2020 will halt the practice of including opposition members of parliament in constituency funding programmes.

More Immigration and Nationality Woes

Predictably, the post-2013 years have witnessed their fair share of memorable political scandals and public accusations of corruption, some with direct or indirect links to political clientelism. One deserving of some scrutiny is yet another worrying chapter in the long-standing abuse of immigration and nationality services for political gain, and for securing political support. In May 2016, the Auditor General of Belize released the results of a special audit of the Immigration and Nationality Department for the period of 2011–13, covering issues related to visas, nationality and passports.[11] The special audit was triggered by information from the department regarding visas that had gone missing, but expanded to include nationality and passports based on initial findings. In short, the special audit found damning evidence of irregularities, abuse of procedures and apparent fraud, which, in turn, was the catalyst for a one-year investigation (October 2016–November 2017) by a Senate Special Select Committee that was broadcast live on national media. The report of the select committee, which was not completed until 14 July 2020, corroborated the findings of the special audit and added more layers of intriguing evidence about the widespread abuse.[12]

In summary, the 2016 special audit report found evidence of abuse of the nationality process, which further highlighted attempts by politicians to facilitate Belizean nationality (required for voter registration) for political support. The nationality rush that occurred before the March 2012 election (as detailed in chapter 4) was further ventilated, revealing that in the four months before the election 2,110 new nationalities were approved – a factor of twenty times the number for a normal quarter – of which some 1,000 was in the month before the election.[13] The Senate report verified that many of these nationality applications were fast-tracked and based on false or missing supporting documents, and also affirmed that the special audit's concerns about the interventions by politicians in the application process were warranted.[14] With regard to the latter, the special audit on nationality found that letters of recommendation and letters of follow-up from ministers of government and other politicians, although not required, accompanied many applications.[15] The special audit itemized seventy-two samples of such letters coming from fourteen different ministers of government for nationality and immigration applications,[16] many of which the Senate Select Committee found to be "riddled with irregularities and downright illegality".[17]

The Senate Select Committee struggled with how to assess this long-established practice of the ubiquitous "letters of recommendation" from ministers of government and other politicians to, in this case, senior officials at the Department Immigration and Nationality. With the agreement of the Auditor General, it eventually settled on the understanding that although irregular, the practice is not illegal per se.[18] However, the Senate report revealed that there were cases in which ministers of government, either knowingly or unknowingly, supported irregular applications. In short, the "letters of recommendation" tactic continue to be used by politicians to expand their pool of potential voters and to influence their votes, and this contributes to applicants believing that such letters are required to advance their cases. The politicians summoned to testify before the Senate Select Committee, several being sitting ministers, defended the letters as just "helping the people" – while denying clientelist intent. One notable exception was Elvin Penner, a former minister of immigration and nationality who was fired from cabinet in 2013 for a separate nationality scandal. He confirmed under oath that he paid a portion or sometimes all of the $300 nationality registration fee to help people in need of assistance so they could eventually register to vote in the election – in an effort to give him an edge over his opponent.[19] The Senate Select Committee also heard allegations that some ministers of government had received payments to write letters of recommendation and letters of follow-up for wealthier applicants (for visas, nationality and passports) as part of a wider immigration and nationality corruption scheme.[20] Those ministers questioned by the Senate Select Committee denied such allegations, and it was beyond the mandate of the committee to investigate further. If any of the allegations of such payments to politicians were to be confirmed in the future, it would be useful to explore if there were any links to the ever-present imperative to fund clientelist operations.

The Dermen Affair

Another political scandal worth highlighting is the sensational and revealing saga of a former UDP minister, John Saldivar, whose long-sought and hard-won victory to become the UDP party leader on 9 February 2020 lasted only seventy-two hours due to developments sparked by political corruption allegations. Saldivar, who continues to deny all such allegations against him, was serving as the minister of national security at the time he made his bid for party leadership to replace outgoing party leader and then prime minister Dean Barrow. Barrow, at the time in his third term as prime minister and so barred from seeking a fourth consecutive term by constitutional term limits, had indicated he planned to step aside before the 2020 election to allow a new UDP prime minister to gain some experience in the leadership post. In mid-January 2020, less than a month before the party leadership convention, news stories broke about a pending fraud case against a Mr Lev Dermen in a US federal court in Utah that promised to reveal that Dermen, who had links to Belize, gave a sitting UDP minister funds in return for favours. Saldivar's name was referenced in some news reports on the initial court depositions that were recounted in the Salt Lake City press.[21]

Despite the political maelstrom of rumours, suspicions, accusations, denials and new information that dominated the Belize news cycle and social media, Saldivar handily won the leadership convention by 342 to 227 party delegates votes over his key opponent, former minister of education Patrick Faber, and was sworn in as UDP party leader elect on the evening of 9 February 2020. Although the Utah court case had commenced before the UDP party convention of 9 February, it was not until the two days immediately after the convention on 10 and 11 February that the court heard testimony and received hard evidence about the allegations relating to a Belize ministerial connection. In short, Jacob Kingston, an associate of Dermen, provided testimony to the Utah court, supported by actual transcripts of text messages, suggesting that in 2014 Saldivar received a large sum of money from Dermen through him.[22] One of exchanges in the text transcript has Saldivar messaging Kingston that he needed "the February tranche", and then arranging with Kingston how the money could be best delivered.[23] By the evening of 12 February, Saldivar was forced by then prime minister Barrow to resign from his new post as UDP party leader elect and was suspended from the cabinet. On 13 February, Saldivar resigned from his post as minister of national security. As explained by Barrow in an address to the nation, the firing of Saldivar was not because of any evidence of guilt of fraud or bribery, but because there was proof that Saldivar had misled him and the cabinet in January 2020 about taking any money from Dermen.[24] The former prime minister also promised that there would be a thorough police investigation – which, at this writing, is still ongoing.

During the investigative news reporting on the Dermen affair, it was revealed that Dermen's name had appeared in the *Special Report – Immigration and Nationality Department: 2011–2013* as one of the individuals who had received a Belizean nationality certificate in September 2013 under possible irregular circumstances, including that the relevant nationality file with supporting documentation went missing from the Department of Nationality.[25] No allegations were made regarding Saldivar on this matter. However, news reports did reveal that Saldivar had supported an application in Las Vegas, United States, from Dermen to the Ministry of Foreign Affairs in mid-2013 for Dermen to become an honorary consul of

Belize. As revealed by the then minister of foreign affairs, Dermen failed the required vetting process due to a negative response on his suitability from US authorities.[26] Saldivar has denied any connection between his support for the honorary consul application and Dermen's contributions.

Indeed, Saldivar has vehemently and consistently denied that there was any bribery or quid pro quo related to his involvement in the Dermen affair. When Saldivar admitted that he had received funds from Dermen, he suggested that this was normal practice and insinuated that so did "many other politicians on both sides of the aisle who knew Lev Dermen".[27] Saldivar, who apologized on 14 February for the "mistake" and "poor judgement" for not disclosing his receipt of funds from Dermen, did publicly state that the funds from Dermen (through Kingston) were, indeed, campaign contributions.[28] In a House meeting on 5 March 2020, Saldivar also volunteered that the funds were for assisting his youth and sports programmes, stating, "I go out there on a daily basis to try to raise funds to help my youth, and that, Madam Speaker, can never be classed as corruption."[29]

What Saldivar was right about was that there is nothing illegal about receiving campaign funds in the laws of Belize, and there was no requirement to disclose any funds or their sources. Based, in part, on the argument that he did nothing wrong, Saldivar not only ran again for the high position of UDP party leader in the second national party convention of the UDP in July 2020, but, of three eventual candidates, only narrowly lost by nineteen delegate votes to Patrick Faber. The Dermen affair stands out only because there was an unintended but graphic public glimpse into how some politicians access funds – due only to the reporting on Dermen's legal troubles in Utah.[30] It illustrates how politicians, sometimes at great reputational risk, target wealthy, sometimes shady, private donors as key sources of campaign and constituency financing, which includes meeting the demanding expenses of the ubiquitous clinic operations.

Covid-19 Response Exposes Clientelist Thorns

That second July 2020 UDP national convention, likely to the financial relief of some candidates, had little of the glitz, bussing in of supporters, generous freebies and big spending as the one held five months earlier – due only to the measures for public health safety related to the Covid-19 pandemic. More substantively, the pandemic and Belize's urgent national response also exposed some existing and underlying conditions of policy and institutional weaknesses related to the influence of political clientelism over the very limited social welfare system. As Belize sought to provide urgent unemployment relief and additional food assistance to tens of thousands of affected citizens based on unbiased assessments of needs, it became clear that the existing social welfare mechanisms – both formal and informal – were not fit for purpose. Based on prior experience, many citizens went directly to their politicians in both political parties for assistance, but the demand, exacerbated by Covid-19 lockdowns, severely strained the informal clinic network. Also, several of the formal social assistance programmes were already tainted, to some degree, by clientelist elements – in that incumbent politicians had sought to exercise influence on the allocation of public resources needed by citizens. In the case of the Unemployment Relief Programme, an entirely new system had to be created from scratch not only to ensure the levels of transparency and accountability required from the international financial institutions that provided most of the loan funds but also because there was no suitable existing programme to just build on. A new Food Assistance Programme specific to Covid-19 was also launched. Importantly, in a rare effort at bipartisanship, the then opposition (PUP) agreed to sit on the National Oversight Committee that coordinated the development and implementation of Belize's initial Covid-19 response. Starting in March 2020, the opposition PUP, including at the level of the leader of the opposition, worked closely with the then UDP government to design and implement the launch of the Unemployment Relief Programme – until it decided to remove itself from the National Oversight Committee in June 2020 as general elections loomed.

Very early indications were that the Unemployment Relief Programme was being implemented effectively and mostly transparently in 2020 and was making real and immediate financial and livelihood difference for the unemployed and underemployed. Yet, as this new needs-based unemployment assistance scheme was rolled out, there were some mumblings of concerns from some incumbent representatives who could not exercise the influence they were used to direct allocations to constituents. It is also not far-fetched to speculate that some constituents, not accustomed to the detailed application process for accessing merit-based assistance directly from public institutions, found it strange that they could not go to straight to their politicians. Some aspects of other Covid-19-related assistance that built on existing pro-poor programmes did attract accusations of partisan bias in delivery, especially from the opposition PUP.[31] These include the existing BOOST cash transfer programme and the Food Pantry Programme, which as illustrated in chapter 6, were not fully shielded from clientelist influences. Shortly after the PUP took over the reins of government in November 2020, both the BOOST cash transfer programme and the Food Pantry Programme were suspended and then relaunched under new names.[32] Among the reasons suggested by the new government for the post-election review of these welfare programmes were that some recipients did not meet the agreed standards of need and that there was built-in bias towards supporters of the UDP.[33]

The More Things Change . . .

As with every post-independence general election before it, the November 2020 election featured allegations of voter bribery from elements of both dominant parties against the other. However, as was the case in 2015, none of these allegations were petitioned to a court. As with every post-independence election before it (that resulted in a change of administration), the 2020 election also triggered the expected personnel transition of contract officers and most appointees – including those on the boards of statutory bodies and on official commissions. I have argued (see chapter 4) that, even as Belize's winner-takes-all model grants political administrations near-total powers regarding such appointments, successive governments have sought and succeeded to expand these powers since independence, in part, to consolidate opportunities to transact and bestow patronage to those who contributed or may contribute to the parties' electoral victories. The cumulative collateral damage over time includes the erosion of the independence and impartiality that should underpin all public institutions. Early developments since the 2020 election in relation to both high-level appointees and to open vote workers indicate the continuation of this trend.

Well before the 2020 election, the evolving but unwritten practice has been for members of statutory bodies and of most official commissions to vacate their positions immediately after an election where there is a change of party in power – even if not legally required to do so. So, there was incredulity in high government quarters when the chairman of the Elections and Boundaries Commission (EBC), and the chairman and most members of the Public Services Commission (PSC), appointed under the previous UDP government, did not resign after the November 2020 elections.[34] Prime Minister Briceño himself weighed in: "They need to understand that there is a new government and as a new government it has been the practice from independence that when a new government comes in, everybody resigns, and so I am very disappointed that they have not resigned as yet."[35] The prime minister's statement accurately reflected the widespread acceptance by both the PUP and UDP of such across-the-board resignations after elections as customary political tradition from which they both benefit.

Notwithstanding the valid argument that any new government will want to have trusted and competent partisans in senior positions, the EBC and PSC situation and the government's reaction exposed several thorny issues. The EBC and PSC are constitutionally enshrined commissions originally construed to be independent bodies that are impartial in their functions regardless of which party is in power. Over time, these bodies also became part and parcel of the blanket narrative of winner takes all, and the members who did not resign were all appointed by the previous UDP administration. However, in Belize, there is no legal requirement for the chairpersons or members of constitutionally enshrined commissions to resign after elections if their appointment periods do not coincide with an election – as was, indeed, the case with the EBC and the PSC after the 2020 election.[36] To seek to fix and prevent a reoccurrence of what it perceived as unacceptable refusals to resign from such constitutionally enshrined commissions, the new PUP administration presented the Belize Constitution (Tenth Amendment) Bill to the House of Representatives in March 2021. If enacted, it would ensure that the posts of all members of the PSC and the ECB, as well as posts of all members of the Security Services Commission and the Belize Advisory Council, become vacant at the dissolution of the National Assembly just before a national election.[37] It would also force the current members of the PSC who did not resign to vacate office. Importantly, if the Tenth Amendment Bill is enacted, then the tenure of the members of the affected bodies would all be legally linked to election cycles and the tradition of "everyone resigns" would be further enshrined in the constitution itself.

In the first months after the November 2020 election, there were also the usual accusations that the new administration was engaging in nepotistic appointments and dismissing open vote workers. Indeed, several open vote workers (who are not established public officers) were dismissed shortly after the election, including from the Ministry of Transport, which prompted statements of concern from the Public Service Union.[38] When asked about these dismissals by the media, the new minister of transport gave a now very familiar reasoning: "It was not my intention. But if I did, I damned, if I don't, I damned, because my people are expecting me to provide for them."[39] The minister further sought to justify the dismissals by pointing back to the past UDP government doing the same thing. The minister of public service when questioned about the dismissals of open vote workers sought to ensure that the new government, especially in light of the fiscal challenges caused by the pandemic, would take a measured approach based on not filling redundant posts, on only engaging in new hires where necessary and on cutting compensation packages for the newly hired.[40] It is left to be seen whether, by proactive policy or pushed by circumstances, the new government will seek to address the deeper systemic patronage practice of over hiring "disposable" open vote workers.

One of the other notable evolving post-independence traditions that was perpetuated seamlessly by the new administration which assumed office in November 2020 was that of appointing almost every parliamentarian of the winning party to a ministerial or minister of state portfolio. Indeed, the cabinet of eighteen ministers (sixteen from the House, one from the Senate and one from outside the National Assembly) appointed in November 2020 is the largest cabinet in Belize's political history – even without adding the seven ministers of state who were also appointed (six from the House and one from the Senate).[41] With an additional minister of state appointed in 2021, twenty-three of the twenty-six PUP elected representatives were ministers (sixteen) or ministers of state (seven) at mid-2021 – equivalent to 88 per cent of the elected representatives of the majority party and to 74 per cent of the thirty-one elected members of the House of Representatives. As I have argued (see chapter 4), candidates of political parties in Belize see themselves and are seen by the electorate as competing for becoming ministers more than for becoming parliamentarians. This is in no small part because, apart from the additional income, ministers and ministers of state also enjoy much greater access to public resources and to influence for assisting constituents.

Overall, developments since 2013 indicate that the worst aspects of political clientelism remain deeply systemic, that the core drivers of poverty and viscerally competitive political parties persist, and that the deleterious impact on Belize's democracy and development goes on. In the examples I selected, we observed that a portion of the PetroCaribe loan funds was used to further institutionalize one-off handout programmes. The extent of further damage to the credibility of Belize's name and to the reputation of its passport caused by another immigration and nationality scandal is yet to be fully felt. The Dermen and Saldivar saga provided a disillusioning peek into the usually well-hidden transactional world of politicians who, in seeking funds to stay in the game, can become entangled with very shady characters. Nearly forty years after independence, Belize's Covid-19 response has exposed the inadequacies of the nation's still very limited social welfare system as well as the dangers of having large swathes of the citizenry viewing individual politicians as their welfare safety net of first preference. There is also no indication that governing parties have much interest in addressing issues related to blatant job patronage at all levels of government.

Not observing any critical mass of opposing forces to the deepening entrenchment of political clientelism, I concluded this book by stating that "overall, and notwithstanding occasional and temporary dips in clientelism's trajectory, high levels of entrenched political clientelism will persist and remain a characteristic feature of political relations in Belize for the foreseeable future".[42] Is there any reason for a more optimistic outlook beyond 2021? My considered assessment is that the odds remain decidedly bleak but that there may be just a few faint flickers of hope in the overall gloomy picture.

Flickers of Hope?

While part of the PetroCaribe proceeds was used to fuel clientelist politics, an attempt was made to add a layer of accountability to the targeted allocations as these became more institutionalized. Similar attempts were made with the Covid-19 relief programmes. In this regard, there should be data on some of these handout schemes and on the assistance programmes in government departments, including lists of names sent in by politicians, which constituents got what, which suppliers were selected (and why) and exactly how much was spent. An assessment of this data may not only generate further information on how these schemes operated, but could also provide further insights into that unsettling question: Should consideration be given to formalizing aspects of the practice of constituency representatives providing targeted resources and services to constituents? On the one hand, the findings of this book suggest that, in the interest of merit-based social assistance delivery by independent public institutions, politicians should be kept far away as possible from personally allocating public funds. On the other hand, patron–client relationships do not just wither away even after the implementation of governance reforms. Could some aspects of these constituency relationships be utilized while regulating their tendency to spurn corruption and bad governance? Based on the findings of this book, "enlightened clientelism" seems decidedly oxymoronic.

The latest rendition of the post-independence scandals related to immigration and nationality led to a few encouraging statutory and institutional reforms after 2014 that make it more difficult to abuse the visa, nationality, and passport processes and systems. These include revised guidelines for application processes, the establishment of a visa vetting committee, the launch of a nationality scrutinizing committee with multisectoral membership (unions, private sector and churches), and significant increases in fines and prison terms for persons found guilty of illegal activity. In the run up to the national elections in 2015 and 2020, it appears that the usual pre-election surge of new nationality approvals was largely avoided due to the additional scrutiny. The 2020 Report of the Senate Select Committee made several far-reaching recommendations for further reform, including the need to address the "culture of corruption" from the top ministerial levels to the public service level of immigration and nationality processes.[43] If and how these will be substantively acted upon remains to be seen.

In the immediate aftermath of the sensational Dermen–Saldivar episode in 2020, there was the usual spate of public calls for the enactment of laws to regulate campaign financing as a tool to address rampant corruption. There were early hopeful signs in the commencement of a concerted public advocacy led by the National Trade Union Congress of Belize (NTUCB) and the Belize Network of NGOs for national consultations that would lead to the enactment of campaign finance regulation.[44] A draft bill on financial disclosure by political parties, penned by the then president of the Senate, Darrell Bradley, was circulated and discussed in the local media.[45] Encouragingly, a section of the Bradley draft included proposals to add further legislative teeth to prohibit vote trading, which has direct links to unregulated private money in politics. However, it appears that limitations on gatherings caused by the Covid-19 crisis and the distractions of the campaign period leading up to the November 2020 national elections slowed the civil society-led momentum. True to usual practice prior to all post-independence elections, both major political parties again made bold manifesto commitments before the election to enact campaign financing regulations. It is left to be seen if the administration that took office in November 2020 will move on its promises in this regard or if civil society will sustain the advocacy pressure and generate the critical mass required to force action for meaningful reform.

Exactly how Covid-19 social assistance programmes have been impacted by entrenched clientelism and whether the experience of the pandemic leads to lasting improvements in social welfare delivery will be essential topics for future research and advocacy. Although the national response to Covid-19 has exposed weakness in the limited and ineffective social welfare system of Belize, the example of the Unemployment Assistance Programme also demonstrates how both major political parties, CSOs and the private sector can work together, albeit it was for a limited time, to design a programme that escapes undue partisan influence for some time. Even as the conditional requirements of international financial institutions were a part of the motivation, the fact that the UDP and PUP worked together on the programme during a national emergency provides a hopeful preview of what is possible when petty partisan and clientelist impulses are put aside in the nation's interest and for the common good. It may be politically naïve to believe that bipartisan and all-of-society approaches will become dominant, but the experience of the Covid-19 Unemployment Assistance Programme should provide some positive lessons on how social welfare programmes can be expanded and improved for the long term.

Some promising moments in the usually murky narrative of clientelist politics can also be found in Belize's recent experience of its first stand-alone national referendum in May 2019. The referendum, on whether Belize should take the Guatemalan claim of Belize to the International Court of Justice, presented voters with an existential and issue-based choice that had little to do with which party or constituency politicians could offer or pay an electricity bill, get you some land, or provide more handout money on election day. It was clear that supporters of the yes camp and the no camp transcended strict party lines. The yes camp, which the UDP supported, and no the camp, which the PUP supported, had to engage in real informational and educational campaigns on a scale not seen in Belize since the lead-up to independence. Although the full story of how the two main parties funded and operated their referendum campaigns (separate from the substantial non-partisan campaigns) has yet to be written, initial indications are that most resources were used for informational material, advertising and events, and for transportation for voters on referendum day. As such, there was little evidence of the well-oiled clientelist party machines that are omnipresent at election time. Instructively, an attempt by one UDP aspirant to put on a "Referendum Day Raffle" in his constituency to help get out the vote was roundly condemned by many, including the Citizens for the Defence of Sovereignty and by the opposition party (the PUP), and was quickly halted by former prime minister Barrow.[46] The experience of the referendum, which had a very respectable voter turnout of 67 per cent, begs an obvious question: Could there be less incentive for political clientelism if political parties and leaders were more differentiated by their visions, ideologies and substantive positions on key issues? My findings in this book allows no alternative but to answer this question in the affirmative – at least conceptually. However, we also observed that for some states in the Caribbean, ideological and policy differentiation without substantially addressing poverty and inequality may have little impact on the incidence of benefit politics.

It is, of course, much too early to speculate on if and how the PUP government elected in November 2020 may seek, through governance reform, to substantively address and mitigate some of the worst manifestations and consequences of entrenched political clientelism described in this book. With a supermajority in parliament of twenty-six to five seats, the electorate gave the PUP both the governance mandate and the constitutional amending power to become the potential champion of the most meaningful governance reform actions since independence. Like every party manifesto since independence, but perhaps even more substantively, the PUP's Plan Belize Manifesto (2020–25) promised comprehensive action to enhance good governance – some of which could help mitigate political clientelism if fully implemented. To a large degree, they reflect many of the demands and the proposals that civil society groups have been advocating since the SPEAR-led governance reform campaign of the mid-1990s to the most recent union-led efforts. Specifically, the PUP's manifesto included commitments to further empower the Integrity Commission, reduce discretionary power of ministers, reform the Public Accounts Committee to include social partners, enhance the independence of the Elections and Boundaries Commission, introduce campaign financing legislation, introduce a whistle-blowers act, and restore autonomy and impartiality in the public service.[47] Even as the new government sought to display seriousness about these commitments by passing a motion in the National Assembly in January 2021 to advance them, by moving quickly to reconstitute the Public Accounts Committee to include non-government senators, by presenting a bill for whistle-blower legislation and by announcing a constitutional review process, it faced deep-seated public cynicism about political parties and politicians built on layer upon layer of scandals and unfulfilled promises over the four decades since independence. Yet the opportunity for the PUP administration to act meaningfully on its commitments, made more urgent by the exigencies of the Covid-19 pandemic, is there for it to fully embrace.

Perhaps the brightest flicker of hope for tackling the worst manifestations and effects of political clientelism is that there may be signs of renewed life from elements of the civil society sector in Belize. In particular, the NTUCB, with the support of the Belize Network of NGOs and the Belize Chamber of Commerce and Industry, has over the last six years been spearheading advocacy efforts for good governance, and especially for anti-corruption and financial accountability. In 2016, this union-led "coalition" succeeded in lobbying for the Senate investigation of the immigration and nationality scandals and in pushing the UDP government to ratify the UN Convention Against Corruption. In 2018, after much resistance, the government finally caved to union-led civil society pressure and agreed to conduct the long-delayed voters re-registration exercise. In February 2020, the NTUCB put out a six-point set of demands, including for campaign finance regulation, speeding the process to ratify the UN Convention Against Corruption, finalization of the Senate report on immigration and nationality (which was completed in July 2020), and for an independent investigation around the Saldivar case.[48] These union demands were backed up by a large demonstration and energetic rally on 20 February 2020 with loud chants of "only the people can save the people".[49]

It appears that this newest spate of civil society efforts, while slowed by Covid-19 public health measures and sidelined by the intense pre-2020 election party campaigning, still have some life. Before the November 2020 elections, the NTUCB, the Belize Network of NGOs and the Belize Chamber of Commerce and Industry issued the joint "Declaration of Social Partners of Belize for Reform of Essential Oversight Mechanisms to Strengthen the Democratic Governance of Belize". The declaration repeated the civil society calls for key governance reforms, including of the electoral system. From the November 2020 election to May 2021, and with the Public Service Union and the Belize National Teacher's Union under heavy pressure to accept a 10 per cent salary cut for three years (as a primary approach to addressing the national fiscal crisis exacerbated by the pandemic), the unions were strident in maintaining their advocacy for governance reform through protests and strike actions.[50] In addition to the existing demands for the advancement of the UN Convention Against Corruption, campaign finance regulation and protection of whistle-blowers, the unions have lobbied for new laws to allow for the recovery of illicitly acquired assets, to prevent unlawful enrichment, and even for a full audit and review of that most scared of cash cows and dependable anchor for clientelist politicians – the constituency stipend provided monthly from public funds.[51]

Those chants of protest at that NTUCB rally of 20 February 2020 and the 2021 advocacy actions by civil society in Belize contain the elements of the only sure formula for transforming flickers of hope into real and lasting change. Combined with the substantive manifesto promises and early actions of the party in government and with the exigencies of the Covid-19 pandemic, could the recent spate of civil society actions signal that the stars are lining up for an inflection point for comprehensive and decolonizing constitutional overhaul in Belize over the coming five years? If, at some point, the organized civic demand does reach the critical and sustained mass that catalyses political leaders and citizens to engage in truly meaningful governance reform, the mitigation of the worst aspects of political clientelism must be one of its central targets.

Appendix 1

Electoral Map of Belize by Political Party Holding Each Constituency in 2008

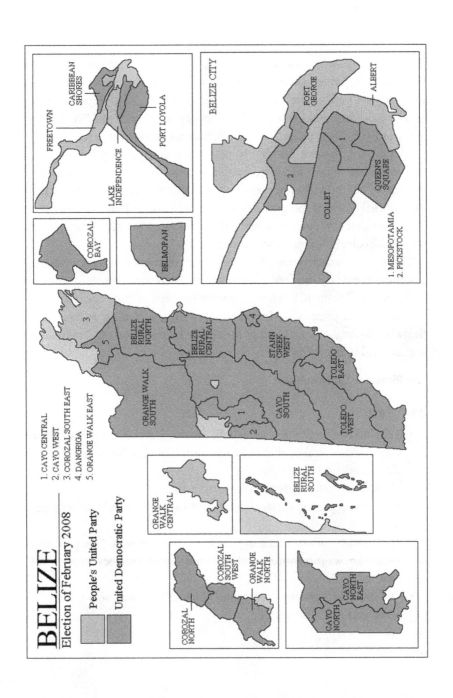

Appendix 2
Brief Description of the Four Constituencies Selected for Focused Research (2010 Data)

The four constituencies (representing 13 per cent of total electoral constituencies) were selected to generally reflect the proportional breakdown of twenty-six UDP to five PUP seats held in the House of Representatives in 2010. Consequently, three UDP (Pickstock, Belmopan and Toledo East) and one PUP constituency (Orange Walk Central) were selected.

Although it was not feasible to select one constituency from each of the six administrative districts, those selected cover the main geographic regions of the country and generally reflect the near fifty-fifty rural-to-urban breakdown of the population. They are also generally reflective of the ethnic demographics of Belize, with a focus on the four largest ethnic groups (Creole, Mestizo, Garifuna and Maya).

Three of the selected constituencies are in districts that have a range of (individual) poverty incidence below the national average of 41.3 per cent and Gini coefficients (GCs) just below the national average of 0.42.

A brief description of basic constituency information (as at the start of fieldwork in August 2010) and of the research conducted per constituency is presented in the following.

1. **Pickstock Constituency**

Basic Facts
- This urban constituency is on both the north and south side of Belize City in the central coastal Belize district. It is small in geographic size and densely populated.
- There were 3,168 registered voters in 2010.
- Pickstock is predominately Creole in ethnicity (approximately 65 per cent).
- The constituency is mixed in terms of income classes. However, most people are wage labourers and there are significant pockets of urban poverty.
- The individual poverty rate for the Belize district was 28.8 per cent in 2010, and its GC was 0.41.

- The constituency was held by the governing UDP (2008–12) in 2010.
- The incumbent representative was Minister Wilfred Elrington who is of Creole ethnicity.
- The PUP's candidate was Dr Francis Smith.
- Very few CSOs operate in the division.

Research Conducted

- **Elite interviews (4):** Minister Wilfred Elrington (UDP representative), Dr Francis Smith (current PUP candidate), Godfrey Smith (former PUP representative), Diane Haylock (former UDP candidate).
- **Brokers (3):** One current PUP, one current UDP and one past UDP.
- **Citizens/Clients (27):** Twelve males, fifteen females.
- **Other:** Street observation, collection of documents.

2. **Orange Walk Central Constituency**

Basic Facts

- This rural/urban constituency is in the northern district of Orange Walk. It includes Orange Walk Town but also several rural villages. Orange Walk Town proper is relatively small in geographic size and densely populated.
- There were 6,139 registered voters in 2010.
- It has been predominantly Mestizo in ethnicity, and most people are employed in the sugar cane industry.
- In 2010, the individual poverty rate for the Orange Walk district was 42.8 per cent and the GC was 0.36.
- The division was held by the opposition PUP (2008–12).
- The incumbent representative was John Briceño, who was also the leader of the PUP and of the opposition (2008–11). He is of Mestizo ethnicity.
- No UDP constituency candidate was selected at the time of fieldwork. There were two UDP aspirants.
- A small number of CSOs operate in the division.

Research Conducted

- **Elite interviews (3):** John Briceño (PUP representative), Damien Gough (constituency aspirant, UDP), Rueben Campus (former UDP representative).

- **Brokers (2):** One current PUP and one former UDP.
- **Citizens/Clients (26):** Fifteen males, eleven females.
- **Other:** Observation (including political clinics, neighbourhood meeting) and collection of documents.

3. **Toledo East Constituency**

Basic Facts

- This rural/urban constituency is in the most southern district of Toledo near the border with Guatemala. It includes the urban town of Punta Gorda but also twenty rural villages. It is one of the largest constituencies in geographic size. Although Punta Gorda Town is relatively densely populated, the villages are mostly small and spread out. It includes the large "new" village of Bella Vista, a predominately Latino immigrant community set up in the 1990s to house banana workers.
- There were 6,183 registered voters in 2010.
- It is of mixed ethnicity (Maya, Creole, Garifuna and East Indian), but also has several relatively new immigrant communities.
- Agriculture and tourism are the main industries in the district.
- In 2010, the Toledo district had the highest rate of individual poverty in Belize at 60.4 per cent and the highest GC at 0.46.
- The division was held by the ruling UDP.
- The incumbent representative was Minister Eden Martinez, who is of Garifuna ethnicity.
- The PUP constituency candidate was Mike Espat, a former representative and former minister, and a deputy leader of the PUP (2008–12).
- The People's National Party (PNP) has its base in Toledo and its leader, Wil Maheia, was the constituency candidate.
- A relatively large number of CSOs operate in the division.

Research Conducted

- **Elite interviews (4):** Minister Eden Martinez (UDP representative), Mike Espat (PUP candidate), Alejandro Vernon (former PUP representative), Wil Maheia (PNP candidate).
- **Brokers (1):** One UDP.
- **Citizens/Clients (35):** Twenty-five males, ten females.

- **Other:** Focus group with students at University of Belize (32), observation and collection of documents.

4. **Belmopan Constituency**

Basic Facts

- This urban constituency is in the capital city of Belmopan in the Cayo district and in the geographical centre of the country. The central part of the capital is small and densely populated. Several "new" semi-urban communities are on the immediate fringe of central Belmopan.
- There were 6,733 registered voters in 2010.
- It is an ethnically mixed division (Creole, Mestizo, Maya and Garinagu). As such it reflects the national ethnic breakdown.
- Most of the Mestizo population are recent immigrants from Guatemala and El Salvador. Most of the Maya residents are recent internal migrants. Most of the Mestizo/Maya population reside in the semi-urban communities outside the centre, which is made up of a majority Creole population.
- Most people are employed in the public service or agriculture.
- In 2010, the individual poverty rate for Cayo district was 40.6 per cent and the GC was 0.41.
- The constituency was held by the ruling UDP party (2008–12).
- The incumbent representative was Minister John Saldivar, who is of Creole ethnicity.
- The PUP did not have a candidate at the time of fieldwork, and four aspirants were vying for the seat. One of these was Dr Amin Hegar, who became the PUP candidate.
- The Vision Inspired by the People (an alternative party) has been active in this division.
- A significant number of CSOs operate in the division.

Research Conducted

- **Elite interviews (4):** Minister John Saldivar (UDP representative), Paul Morgan (VIP co-leader and candidate), Jennifer Arzu (VIP Deputy Chair). Personal communication conducted with Dr Amin Hegar (PUP aspirant).

- **Brokers (0):** However, interviews were conducted with key UDP party workers.
- **Citizens/Clients (26):** Sixteen males, ten females.
- **Other:** Observation (including of a political clinic), archival and library research, and collection of documents. An interview was also conducted with the mayor of Belmopan, Simeon Lopez (UDP).

Appendix 3

"Tek di money": Election Poster, December 2011

TEK di Money
TEK di Ham
TEK di Passport
TEK di Land

BUT stick to the plan

vote PUP

Notes

Preface

1. This matter of the "Venezuela money", which turned out to be $40 million not $20 million, developed into a major political scandal and is discussed in detail in chapter 4.

2. The author led a civil society political reform campaign in Belize from 1994 to 1998, served on all official commissions on political and constitutional reform between 1996 and 2008, and chaired Belize's first national Political Reform Commission from 1999 to 2000.

Chapter 1. Introduction: Belize, Democracy and Clientelism

1. "PUP Does Not Concede Defeat, Says Elections Not Free and Fair", 7 News, 8 March 2012. See chapter 8 for a full discussion of this matter.

2. I use the term "Commonwealth Caribbean" to refer specifically to the twelve independent states of the region that were once colonies of the United Kingdom: Belize, Jamaica, Trinidad and Tobago, Guyana, Barbados, St Lucia, St Vincent and the Grenadines, St Kitts and Nevis, Grenada, Dominica, Antigua and Barbuda, and the Bahamas.

3. Jorge Domínguez, "The Caribbean Question: Why Has Liberal Democracy (Surprisingly) Flourished?", in Democracy in the Caribbean: Political, Economic and Social Perspectives, ed. Jorge Dominguez, Robert A. Pastor and DeLisle Worrell (Baltimore, MD: Johns Hopkins University Press, 1993), 3.

4. See, for example, Dietrich Rueschemeyer, Evelyne Huber Stephens and John D. Stephens, Capitalist Development and Democracy (Chicago: University of Chicago Press, 1992), 227.

5. See, for example, Christopher Clague, Suzanne Gleason and Stephen Knack, "Determinants of Lasting Democracy in Poor Countries: Culture, Development, and Institutions", Annals of the American Academy of Political and Social Science 573 (January 2001): 16–41.

6. See, for example, Natasha T. Duncan and Dwayne Woods, "What About Us? The Anglo-Caribbean Democratic Experience", Commonwealth and Comparative Politics 45, no. 2 (2007): 202–18.

7. See, for example, David Hinds, "Beyond Formal Democracy: The Discourse on Democracy and Governance in the Anglophone Caribbean", Commonwealth and Comparative Politics 46, no. 3 (2008): 388–406; and Arend

Lijphart, *Patterns of Democracy: Government Forms and Performance in Thirty-Six Countries* (New Haven, CT: Yale University Press, 1999).

8. The Worldwide Governance Indicators of the World Bank incorporates a weighted average of 441 disaggregated indicators to compare 212 states across 6 broad aggregates of democracy beginning in 1996.

9. For favourable assessments of formal democracy in Belize, see Julio A. Fernandez, *Belize: A Case Study of Democracy in Central America* (Aldershot: Avebury, 1989); and Cedric Grant, *Governance in the Caribbean Community* (New York: United Nations Development Programme, 2004), 46 and 61–62.

10. As elaborated in chapter 2, Belize's major ethnic groups include Mestizo, Creole, Maya, Garifuna, East Indian and others.

11. Dylan Vernon, "A Synopsis of the Belize Political Reform Process since 1981" (working paper, Belize City, 2009).

12. Commonwealth Secretariat, *Belize General Election 7 February 2008: Report of the Commonwealth Expert Team* (London: Commonwealth Secretariat, 2008), 16.

13. Selwyn Ryan, "Democratic Governance in the Anglophone Caribbean: Threats to Sustainability", in *New Caribbean Thought: A Reader*, ed. Brian Meeks and Folke Lindahl (Kingston, Jamaica: University of the West Indies Press, 2001), 75.

14. See, for example, Simeon McIntosh, *Caribbean Constitutional Reform: Rethinking the West Indian Polity* (Kingston, Jamaica: Caribbean Law Publishing, 2002), 52–53.

15. See, for example, comprehensive assessments by Selwyn Ryan in *Winner Takes All: The Westminster Experience in the Caribbean* (St. Augustine, Trinidad: University of the West Indies, 1999); and Trevor Munroe, "Caribbean Democracy: Decay or Renewal?", in *Constructing Democratic Governance: Latin America and the Caribbean in the 1990s*, ed. Jorge Domínguez and A.F. Lowenthal (Baltimore: Johns Hopkins University Press, 1996).

16. Hinds, "Beyond Formal Democracy", 388.

17. The closer the Worldwide Governance Indicators score is to 100 per cent, the better the rank. The downward trend for control of corruption reflected the drop in the Transparency International Corruption Perception Index from number 46 in 2003 to 109 in 2008.

18. See, especially, the works of Assad Shoman, including *Party Politics in Belize* (Benque Viejo del Carmen: Cubola Productions, 1987) and "Belize: An Authoritarian Democratic State in Central America", in *Second Annual Studies on Belize Conference*, ed. Society for the Promotion of Education and Research (Belize City: Cubola Productions, 1990), 42–63. Also useful is Dylan Vernon, "The Political and Institutional Framework of Democratic Governance in Belize: Decay or Reform", in *Democratic Governance and Citizen Security in Central America: The Case of Belize*, ed. Coordinadora Regional de

Investigaciones Economicas y Sociales (Managua: Coordinadora Regional de Investigaciones Economicas y Sociales, 2000), 43–85.

19. Political Reform Commission, *Final Report of the Political Reform Commission–Belize* (Belmopan: Government of Belize, 2000), 11. This commission was Belize's most comprehensive attempt to assess and improve the performance of the political system since independence.

20. See, in particular, Carl Stone, *Democracy and Clientelism in Jamaica* (New Brunswick, NJ: Transaction Books, 1980); and Charlene Edie, *Democracy by Default: Dependency and Clientelism in Jamaica* (London and Kingston, Jamaica: Lynne Rienner and Ian Randle Publishers, 1991).

21. For example, clientelism has been used in the region to analyse political violence, for example, in Amanda Sives, *Elections, Violence and the Democratic Process on Jamaica: 1944–2007* (Kingston, Jamaica: Ian Randle Publishers, 2010); tribal politics, for example, in Mark Figueroa and Amanda Sives, "Homogenous Voting, Electoral Manipulation and the 'Garrison' Process in Post-Independence Jamaica", *Commonwealth and Comparative Politics* 40, no. 1 (2002): 81–108; and the political influence of the poor, for example, in Obika Gray, *Demeaned but Empowered: The Social Power of the Urban Poor in Jamaica* (Kingston, Jamaica: University of the West Indies Press, 2004).

22. Cynthia Barrow-Giles and Tennyson S.D. Joseph, *General Elections and Voting in the English-Speaking Caribbean, 1992–2005* (Kingston, Jamaica: Ian Randle Publishers, 2006), 146.

23. Mark Moberg, "Citrus and the State: Factions and Class Formation in Rural Belize", *American Ethnologist* 18, no. 2 (1991): 215–33.

24. Michael Rosberg, *The Power of Greed: Collective Action in International Development* (Edmonton: University of Alberta Press, 2005).

25. Political Reform Commission, *Final Report of the Political Reform Commission–Belize*, 119.

26. Commonwealth Secretariat, *Belize General Election 7 February 2008*, 6.

27. Brian Faughnan and Elizabeth Zechmeister, "Vote Buying in the Americas", *AmericasBarometer Insights* 57 (2011): 1–2.

28. Javier Auyero, "From the Client's Point(s) of View: How Poor People Perceive and Evaluate Political Clientelism", *Theory and Society* 28, no. 2 (1999): 298–99.

29. Derick Brinkerhoff and Arthur Goldsmith, *Clientelism, Patrimonialism and Democratic Governance: An Overview and Framework for Assessment and Programming* (Bethesda, MD: United States Aid for International Development, 2002), 4.

30. Classic examples of formal democracy scholars are Joseph A. Schumpeter, Robert A. Dahl and Samuel P. Huntington.

31. Juan J. Linz and Alfred C. Stepan, *Problems of Democratic Transition and Consolidation: Southern Europe, South America, and Post-Communist Europe* (Baltimore, MD: Johns Hopkins University Press, 1996), 3–7.

32. Guillermo O'Donnell, "Illusions about Consolidation", *Journal of Democracy* 7, no. 2 (1996): 40.

33. For noteworthy discussions of this approach, see the works of Guillermo O'Donnell and Laurence Whitehead.

34. Evelyne Huber, Dietrich Rueschemeyer and John D. Stephens, "The Paradoxes of Contemporary Democracy: Formal, Participatory, and Social Dimensions", *Comparative Politics* 29, no. 3 (1997): 324.

35. Hinds, "Beyond Formal Democracy", 404.

36. Laurence Whitehead, *Democratization: Theory and Experience* (Oxford: Oxford University Press, 2002), 7.

37. Jonathan Hopkin, "Conceptualizing Political Clientelism: Political Exchange and Democratic Theory" (paper presented at the Annual Meeting of the American Political Science Association, Philadelphia, August 2006).

38. Christopher Clapham, *Private Patronage and Public Power: Political Clientelism in the Modern State* (London: Pinter, 1982), 3.

39. Daniel Sabet, "Stuck in the Transition from Clientelism to Citizenship" (paper presented at the Annual Meeting of the American Political Science Association, Washington DC, September 2005), 3.

40. For a good example of the treatment of political parties as an institutional patron, see Petr Kopecky, Gerardo Scherlis and Maria Spirova, "Party Patronage in New Democracies: Concepts, Measures and the Design of Empirical Inquiry" (paper presented at Annual Meeting of the America Political Science Association, Chicago, August 2007).

41. Allen Hicken, "Clientelism", *Annual Review of Political Science* 14, no. 1 (2011): 292.

42. Kopecky, Scherlis and Spirova, "Party Patronage in New Democracies", 4.

43. Figueroa and Sives, "Homogenous Voting".

44. Javier Auyero, *Poor People's Politics: Peronist Survival Networks and the Legacy of Evita* (Durham, NC: Duke University Press, 2001), 14.

45. The term "clientelist politics" refers to party-based political activities that fit the definition of political clientelism used in this book. The terms "handout politics" (used in Belize) and "benefits politics" (often used in Jamaica) are assumed to have similar meanings.

46. Tina Hilgers, "Clientelism and Conceptual Stretching: Differentiating among Concepts and among Analytical Levels", *Theory and Society* 40, no. 5 (2011): 570.

47. Apart from the works of Javier Auyero, see Robert Gay, "Community Organization and Clientelist Politics in Contemporary Brazil: A Case Study from Suburban Rio de Janeiro", *International Journal of Urban and Regional Research* 14, no. 4 (1990): 648–66.

48. Hilgers, "Clientelism and Conceptual Stretching", 570.

49. John Booth and Mitchell Seligson, eds., *Political Participation in Latin America, Vol. 1: Citizen and the State* (New York and London: Holmes and Meier Publishers, 1978), 6.

50. Hans-Joachim Lauth, "Informal Institutions and Democracy", *Democratisation* 7, no. 4 (2000): 27.

51. Generally, rational choice theory holds that people choose to act based on assessments that their actions have more benefits than costs.

52. Studies that have applied a rational choice theory approach to research on political clientelism include Susan Stokes and Luis Medina, "Clientelism as Political Monopololy" (paper presented at the Annual Meeting of the American Political Science Association, Boston, 28 August 2002); Federico Estevez, Beatriz Magaloni and Alberto Diaz-Cayeros, "The Erosion of One-Party Rule: Clientelism, Portfolio Diversification and Electoral Strategy" (paper presented at the Annual Meeting of the American Political Science Association, Boston, August 2002); and Rebecca Weitz-Shapiro, "Clientelism and Social Welfare Policy in Argentine Municipalities" (paper presented at the Annual Meeting of the American Political Science Association, Chicago, August 2007).

53. Faughnan and Zechmeister, "Vote Buying in the Americas", 1.

54. Philip Keefer, "Clientelism, Credibility, and the Policy Choices of Young Democracies", *American Journal of Political Science* 51, no. 4 (2007): 804.

55. Auyero, *Poor People's Politics*.

56. Stone, *Democracy and Clientelism in Jamaica*, 102.

57. Stokes and Medina, "Clientelism as Political Monopololy", 17–18.

58. Domínguez, "The Caribbean Question", 13.

59. See, for example, Andreas Schedler, "My Vote? Not for Sale: How Mexicans Citizens View Electoral Clientelism" (paper presented at the Annual General Meeting of the American Political Science Association, Boston, August 2002), 32.

60. For a rich discussion of this point, see Christopher Clapham, *Private Patronage and Public Power: Political Clientelism in the Modern State* (London: Pinter, 1982), 7–8.

61. Susan Stokes, "Political Clientelism", in *The Oxford Handbook of Comparative Politics*, ed. Susan Stokes and Charles Boix (Oxford: Oxford University Press, 2007), 619.

62. Herbert Kitschelt and Steven Wilkinson, *Patrons, Clients and Policies: Patterns of Democratic Accountability and Political Corruption* (Cambridge: Cambridge University Press, 2007), 28.

63. For a sound discussion of this categorization, see Kitschelt and Wilkinson, *Patrons, Clients and Policies*, 7–11.

64. See the example of Jamaica in Evelyne Huber Stephens and John Stephens, "The Transition to Mass Parties and Ideological Politics in Jamaica", *Comparative Political Studies* 19, no. 4 (1987): 443–82; and Anthony Payne, "Multi-Party Politics in Jamaica", in *Political Parties in the Third World*, ed. Vicky Randal (London: SAGE Publications, 1988), 135–54.

65. See, for example, A.R. Menocal, *Why Electoral Systems Matter: An Analysis of Their Incentives and Effects on Key Areas of Governance* (London: Overseas Development Institute, 2009), 2–14.

66. For a useful discussion of this point, see Kitschelt and Wilkinson, *Patrons, Clients and Policies*, 42.

67. Fiona Mackay, Meryl Kenny,and Louise Chappell, "New Institutionalism through a Gender Lens: Towards a Feminist Institutionalism?", *International Political Science Review* 31, no. 5 (2010): 583.

68. Elin Bjarnegård, "Men in Politics: Revisiting Patterns of Gendered Parliamentary Representation in Thailand and Beyond" (PhD diss., Uppsala University, 2010); and *Gender, Informal Institutions and Political Recruitment: Explaining Male Dominance* (New York: Palgrave Macmillan, 2013).

69. Bjarnegård, "Men in Politics", 170–74.

70. For a discussion on this issue in Belize, see Debra Lewis, *A Situational Analysis of Gender and Politics in Belize* (Belize City: National Women's Commission and the United Nations Development Programme, 2012).

71. CCTs generally provide cash transfers to poor citizens based on compliance with specified educational and health responsibilities. A CCT was launched in Belize in 2010.

72. For a concise discussion, see Maxine Molyneau, "Conditional Cash Transfers: A 'Pathway to Women's Empowerment?'" (Pathways to Women's Empowerment Working Paper 5, Institute of Development Studies, Brighton, 2008).

73. Christian Gruenberg, "Genderized Clientelism in Conditional Cash Transfers" (discussion paper, International Council on Human Rights Policy Blog, ICHRP, Geneva, June 2011), 1–2.

74. Victoria Pereyra Iraola and Christian Gruenberg, "Clientelism, Poverty and Gender: Cash Conditional Transfers on the Loop" (paper presented at Gender and Corruption in Development Cooperation Workshop, Eschborn, Germany, November 2008), 8–10.

75. Paul Sutton, "Small States and the Commonwealth", *Commonwealth and Comparative Studies* 39, no. 3 (2001): 85.

76. Kitschelt and Wilkinson, *Patrons, Clients and Policies*, 15.

77. Stokes and Medina, "Clientelism as Political Monopololy", 17–18.

78. Kanchan Chandra, "Counting Heads: A Theory of Voter and Elite Behaviour in Patronage Democracies" (paper presented at the Annual Meeting of the American Political Association, Boston, August 2002): 2–3

79. Ralph Premdas, *Trinidad and Tobago: Ethnic Conflict and Public Sector Governance* (Basingstoke: Palgrave Macmillan, 2007).

80. For discussions of political clientelism with a focus on Central America, see, for example, Ezequiel Gonzalez-Ocantos et al., "Vote Buying and Social Desirability Bias: Experimental Evidence from Nicaragua", *American Journal of Political Science* 56, no. 1 (2012): 202–17; Ainhoa Montoya, "The Turn of the Offended: Clientelism in the Wake of El Salvador's 2009 Elections", *Social Analysis* 59, no. 4 (2015): 101–18; Joby Schaffer and Andy Baker, "Clientelism as Persuasion-Buying: Evidence from Latin America", *Comparative Political Studies* 48, no. 9 (2015): 1093–126; Esquiel Gonzalez-

Ocantos et al., "Carrots and Sticks: Experimental Evidence of Vote-Buying and Voter Intimidation in Guatemala", *Journal of Peace Research* 57, no 1 (2019): 46–61; and Daniel Altschuler, "How Patronage Politics Undermines Parental Participation and Accountability: Community-Managed Schools in Honduras and Guatemala", *Comparative Education Review* 57, no. 1 (2013): 117–44.

81. S.N. Eisenstadt and Louis Roniger, "Patron-Client Relations as a Model of Structuring Social Exchange", *Comparative Studies in Society and History* 22, no. 1 (1980): 49.

82. Anne Marie Goetz, "Manoeuvring Past Clientelism: Institutions and Incentives to Generate Constituencies in Support of Governance Reform", *Commonwealth and Comparative Politics* 45, no. 4 (2007): 404.

83. Ibid.

84. "Political corruption" is, herein, defined generally as the abuse of public norms, laws and/or resources for private gain.

85. Paul D. Hutchcroft, "The Politics of Privilege: Assessing the Impact of Rents, Corruption, and Clientelism on Third World Development", *Political Studies* 45, no. 3 (1997): 645.

86. Alfredo Rehren, "The Crisis of the Democratic State", in *Corruption and Democracy in Latin America*, ed. Charles H. Blake and Stephen D. Morris (Pittsburgh: University of Pittsburgh Press, 2009), 50.

87. Luigi Manzetti and Carole Wilson, "Why Do Corrupt Governments Maintain Public Support?", in *Corruption and Democracy in Latin America*, ed. Charles H. Blake and Stephen D. Morris (Pittsburgh: University of Pittsburgh Press, 2009), 77–78.

88. For example, for Bolivia, see Sian Lazar, "Personalist Politics, Clientelism and Citizenship: Local Elections in El Alto, Bolivia", *Bulletin of Latin American Research* 23, no. 2 (2004): 228–43; for Brazil, see Robert Gay, "Community Organization and Clientelist Politics in Contemporary Brazil: A Case Study from Suburban Rio de Janeiro", *International Journal of Urban and Regional Research* 14, no. 4 (1990): 648–66; and for Argentina, see the works of Javier Auyero.

89. Discussions on this implication can be found in Edie, *Democracy by Default*, 7; Domínguez, "Caribbean Question", 13; and Duncan and Woods, "What About Us?", 203.

90. Brinkerhoff and Goldsmith, *Clientelism, Patrimonialism and Democratic Governance*, 9.

91. Stone, *Democracy and Clientelism in Jamacia*, 93.

92. Chandra, "Counting Heads", 3.

93. Patronage can also include legally prescribed appointments (such as those to boards of statutory bodies and commissions) that tend to occur in the aftermath of changes of government in most political systems.

94. Stokes, "Political Clientelism", 650.

95. Luigi Graziano, "Introduction: Political Clientelism and Comparative Perspectives", *International Political Science Review* 4, no. 4 (1983): 426.

96. Electoral figures in this section are from the Elections and Boundaries Department of Belize.

97. The country of Belize is administratively divided into six districts: Belize, Cayo, Orange Walk, Corozal, Stann Creek and Toledo.

98. This was done not only to encourage natural discussions but also to protect respondents who may have concerns about possible retaliations related to sharing views about clientelist politics in a small society.

Chapter 2. Helping the People: 1954 to Independence

1. Apart from the key works by Nigel O. Bolland and by Assad Shoman, other authoritative studies on Belize's modern political history include Cedric Grant, *The Making of Modern Belize: Politics, Society and British Colonialism in Central America* (Cambridge: Cambridge University Press, 1976); and Anne Macpherson, *From Colony to Nation: Women Activists and the Gendering of Politics in Belize, 1912–1982* (Lincoln, NE: University of Nebraska Press, 2007).

2. Nigel O. Bolland, *Colonialism and Resistance in Belize: Essays in Historical Sociology* (Benque Viejo del Carmen, Belize: Cubola Productions and the Society for the Promotion of Education and Research, 1988), 184.

3. Anne Macpherson, "Citizens v. Clients: Working Women and Colonial Reform in Puerto Rico and Belize, 1932–1945", *Journal of Latin American Studies* 35, no. 2 (2003): 279.

4. Myrtle Palacio, *Selecting Our Leaders Past and Present: How the Election Process Developed* (Belize City: Elections and Boundaries Commission, 2002), 3–7.

5. W.H. Courtenay, *Courtenay Commission Report* (Belize: Government of Brtish Honduras, 1956), 26.

6. The NIP was itself the merger of two parties: the National Party and the Honduran Independence Party.

7. Figures from Myrtle Palacio, *Who and What in Belizean Elections: 1954 to 1993* (Belize City: Glessima Research and Services, 1993), 10.

8. Ibid., 75–87.

9. Guatemala has a long-standing territorial claim to Belize. See Assad Shoman, *Belize's Independence and Decolonization* (Hampshire: Palgrave Macmillan, 2010) for a comprehensive history of this claim.

10. The British were ready to grant Belize independence after 1961, but failed attempts to resolve the territorial claim by Guatemala before independence caused the delay.

11. Figures in this paragraph are calculated from statistics compiled by Palacio, *Who and What in Belizean Elections*, 75–87, and from Shoman, *Party Politics in Belize*, 38.

12. Shoman, *Party Politics in Belize*, 69.

13. Ibid., 24–25.

14. For histories of these progressive groups, see Evan X Hyde, *Communication: Selected Writings* (Belize City: Angelus Press, 1995); and Assad Shoman, *A History of Belize in Thirteen Chapters* (Belize City: Angelus Press, 2011).

15. For a compelling and critical revisionist history of the role of women in the pre-independence political history of Belize, see Macpherson, *From Colony to Nation*.

16. Victor Bulmer-Thomas and Barbara Bulmer-Thomas, *The Economic History of Belize: From 17th Century to Post-Independence* (Benque Viejo Del Carmen: Cubola, 2012), 116.

17. Ibid.

18. Bolland, *Colonialism and Resistance in Belize*, 184.

19. Figures for 1960 and 1970 are from Shoman, *History of Belize in Thirteen Chapters*, 71; and that for 1980 from the Statistical Institute of Belize, *Abstract of Statistics: 2007* (Belmopan: Statistical Institute of Belize, 2007), 13.

20. Figures calculated from election data compiled by Palacio, *Who and What in Belizean Elections*, 12.

21. Figures on ethnicity demographics come from the 1980 Population Census. In the Belize context, "Creole" refers to a mix predominantly of African and British; "Mestizo" to a mix of Maya and Spanish (mostly descendants of Maya and Mestizo refugees from the Guerra de Las Castas in Mexico in the late 1880s); and the "Garinagu" (the "Garifuna people"), previously called Black Caribs, who resettled in southern Belize after being relocated to Central America from the Eastern Caribbean by the British in the early 1800s.

22. For insightful discussions of ethnicity and party politics in Belize, see Nigel O. Bolland, *Struggles for Freedom: Essays on Slavery, Colonialism and Culture in the Caribbean and Central America* (Belize City: Angelus Press, 1997), 276–81; and Assad Shoman, "Reflections on Ethnicity and Nation in Belize", *Cuaderno de Trabajo* 9 (2010): 1–61.

23. People's United Part, *Constitution of the People's United Party* (Belize City: People's United Party, 1954), 2.

24. David Hanson, "Politics, Partisanship, and Social Position in Belize", *Journal of Interamerican Studies and World Affairs* 16, no. 4 (1974): 423.

25. For the only full-length authorized biography of Price, see Godfrey Smith, *George Price: A Life Revealed* (Kingston, Jamaica: Ian Randle Publishers, 2011).

26. Fredrick Hunter (former PUP minister before independence), interview by author, 5 November 2010, Belize City.

27. For a concise summary of this argument, see Martin Shefter, *Political Parties and the State: The American Historical Experience* (Princeton, NJ: Princeton University Press, 1994).

28. Shoman, *Party Politics in Belize*, 31.

29. Smith, *George Price*, 58. In the formative period of nationalist politics in the 1940s and 1950s, Robert Turton was one of Belize's first local donors of private funds to the new politicians, and especially to Price.

30. George Price [co-founder of the PUP, first premier (1964–81), and first and former prime minister (1981–84 and 1989–93)], interview by author, 17 November 2010, Belize City.

31. Ibid.

32. Ibid.

33. For personal recollections of these mobile clinics, see Rudolph Castillo, *Profile of Honourable George Price: Man of the People* (Belmopan: Government Printers, 2002).

34. V.S. Naipaul, *The Writer and the World: Essays* (London: Picador, 2002), 95–105.

35. Hector Silva (former PUP minister before independence), interview by author, 12 January 2011, San Ignacio Town.

36. Ibid.

37. Ibid.

38. Price kept copies of hundreds of these letters, which are now stored at the George Price Archival Collection.

39. Silva, interview; Hunter, interview.

40. Ibid.

41. Ibid.

42. Constituent OW20, interview by author, 23 March 2011, Orange Walk Town.

43. Grant, *The Making of Modern Belize*, 265–67.

44. Mark Moberg, "Continuity under Colonial Rule: The Alcalde System and the Garifuna in Belize, 1858–1969", *Ethnohistory* 39, no. 1 (1992): 14.

45. Moberg, "Citrus and the State", 222–23.

46. Rueben Campus (former UDP minister), interview by author, 17 March 2011, Orange Walk Town.

47. Ibid.

48. Hunter, interview.

49. This section of the original legislation (1953) has been revised only minimally over time. Revisions include increases in the monetary amounts of gifts allowed and of penalties. Up to the 1964 election, gifts to voters could be no more than 25 cents. This increased to $4 in 1978 and to $20 after independence.

50. Newspaper reports suggested that the British colonial authority, which was still attempting to undermine the Price-led PUP, instructed the police to gather the information required to bring the charges.

51. "Minister on Trial in Supreme Court, Sylvestre Charged with Bribery", *Daily Clarion*, 17 July 1961.

52. Ibid.

53. George Frazer, "Sylvestre Explains Give Away Scheme", *The Belize Billboard*, 27 July 1961, 1.

54. "Sylvestre Trial Today", *Belize Billboard*, 11 April 1961; "Sylvestre Case for Supreme Court", *Belize Times*, 26 April 1961; "Sylvestre Trial", *Daily Clarion*, 18 July 1961; and "Sylvestre Trial", *Daily Clarion*, 23 July 1961.

55. Ibid. Information on financial details supplemented with input from Silva, interview.

56. "Sylvestre Acquitted on All Nine Counts", *Belize Times*, 27 July 1961; and "Sylvestre Acquitted", *Belize Billboard*, 27 July 1961.

57. "PUPs Face UDP Election Petitions", *The Beacon*, 22 December 1979; and "Election Petition Case for January 21", *The Beacon*, 12 January 1981.

58. "UDP Loses Elections Case", *Amandala*, 21 December 1979; and "Supreme Court Squashes UDP Fraud Petitions", *Belize Sunday Times*, 20 January 1980.

59. "Rodríguez Accuses Usher of Corrupt Practice", *The Beacon*, 26 January 1980.

60. "Garcia Lied under Oath", *Amandala*, 25 January 1980.

61. Dean Lindo (first leader of the UDP and former minister), interview by author, 11 November 2010, Belize City.

62. Price, interview; Hunter, interview; and Silva, interview.

63. Price, interview. The terms "help the people" or "helping" appear in the Price interview dozens of times.

64. Ibid.

65. Henry Young Sr (former UDP minister), interview by author, 2 November 2010, Belize City.

66. Alejandro Vernon (former pre-independence parliamentarian), interview by author, 15 February 2011, Punta Gorda Town.

67. John Saldivar (UDP minister of public service and governance reform), interview by author, 30 November 2010, Belmopan.

68. Ibid.

69. Stuart Leslie (chief of staff for PUP leader of the opposition), 5 November 2010, Belize City.

70. Myrtle Palacio (former PUP constituency candidate and former chief elections officer), interview by author, 13 December 2010, Belize City.

71. Assad Shoman (former PUP minister, civil society leader and author), interview by author, 7 March 2011, Belize City.

72. Ibid.

73. Ibid.

74. Dean O. Barrow (prime minister under UDP, 2008–20), interview by author, 1 April 2011, Belize City. Barrow entered electoral politics with the UDP in 1984 and was prime minister in 2013 when this book concluded its coverage.

75. Ibid.

76. Duncan and Woods, "What About Us?", 209.

77. A. Vernon, interview. Vernon's quote "from my hands to yours" is the source of part of the title of this book.

78. Shoman, *Party Politics in Belize*, 32.

79. Lindo, interview.

80. Ibid.

81. Manuel Esquivel (former UDP prime minister 1984–89 and 1993–98), interview by author, 18 November 2010, Belmopan.

82. Ibid.

83. A review of Palacio, *Who and What in Belizean Elections*, 75–96, indicates (based on surnames) that the Maya of the Toledo district were the last ethnic group to follow this trend.

84. Premdas, "Belize Identity and Ethnicity in a Multi-Ethnic State" (2001, 26), has speculated that the one of the factors explaining the relative lack of ethnically based political formations in Belize is that "each of the major [ethnic] communities has pre-eminence in its own geographical sphere which limits inter-ethnic contests over power, recognition and resources".

85. For a useful discussion of the historical economic roles of the Creole population, see Grant, *The Making of Modern Belize*, 98–117 and 198.

86. Palacio, *Who and What in Belizean Elections*, 10.

87. For a sound analysis of the 1979 election results, see Shoman, *Party Politics in Belize*, 35–36.

88. This snapshot is based on the nine tracer markers selected in this study to track changes in clientelism from independence to 2012. See table 1.

89. Eamon Courtenay (PUP senator and former minister), interview by author, 23 November 2010, Belize City.

90. Hunter, interview.

91. Carlos Santos (former PUP constituency aspirant), interview by author, 1 March 2011, Belmopan; and Shoman, interview. "Constituency aspirant'" refers to a person seeking to represent a party in a general election by winning the constituency convention.

92. Courtenay, interview.

93. Silva, interview; Hunter, interview; A. Vernon, interview; and Shoman, interview.

94. Courtenay, interview.

95. Ministry of the Public Service, *Staff List of the Government of Belize, 1981* (Belmopan: Government of Belize, 1981), annex A. The figure of 1,736 did not include teachers who were supported by public resources but who were then considered "private" under Belize's church/state education system. The figure also does not include security personnel or contract officers.

96. Marian McNab, email message to the author, 6 February 2013.

Chapter 3. Fertile Ground: The First Post-Independence Decade

1. Dylan Vernon, "Ten Years of Independence in a Region in Crisis: Economic Dependency and Social Deterioration in Belize, 1981–1991", in

SPEA Reports 5: Fifth Annual Studies on Belize Conference, ed. Society for the Promotion of Education and Research (Belize City: Society for the Promotion of Education and Research, 1992), 44.

2. David Gomez, *Tilted Towards Unsustainable? Twenty-Five Years of Fiscal Policy in Belize: A Review of the Literature, Empirical Evidence, and Policy Considerations* (Belize City: Katalyst Institute for Public Policy and Research, 2007), 5.

3. See chapter 5 for a discussion of linkages of the rise of neoliberalism and political clientelism in Belize.

4. Statistical Institute of Belize, *Abstract of Statistics*, 13–15.

5. Dylan Vernon, "Belizean Exodus: For Better or for Worse?", in *SPEA Reports 4: Second Annual Studies on Belize Conference*, ed. Society for the Promotion of Education and Research (Belize City: Society for the Promotion of Education and Research, 1990), 8–9.

6. Joseph Palacio, "Frontiers Within and Without: The Case of Belize", *Caribbean Quarterly* 41, no. 3–4 (1995): 82.

7. Premdas, "Belize: Identity and Ethnicity in a Multi-Ethnic State", 201.

8. "Supermajority" refers to a greater than two-thirds or three-fourths majority in the House, which allows for constitutional amendments without the support of opposition members.

9. Evan X Hyde, "Behind the Political Parties", *Amandala*, 10 May 2011.

10. Herman Byrd, *Civil Society Organizations in Belize: A Rapid Assessment of Their Capacity to Influence and Monitor Public Policy* (Belize City: Association of National Development Agencies, 2003).

11. Price, interview; Hunter, interview.

12. Price to F. Marin, memorandum, Belmopan, 20 May 1982, GPAC, not coded.

13. Shoman to Price, memorandum, Belmopan, 5 June 1981, GPAC, not coded.

14. Price to J. Usher, memorandum, Belmopan, 29 January 1981, GPAC, 71.

15. Castillo to Price, letter, Belmopan, 3 October 1980, GPAC, not coded.

16. Bo to Price, letter, Belmopan, 1 October 1980, GPAC, not coded.

17. Price to Shoman, memorandum, Belmopan, 22 November 1984, GPAC, 102.

18. Price to E. Briceño, memorandum, Belmopan, 6 November 1984, GPAC, 82.

19. Price to V.H. Courtenay, memorandum, Belmopan, 8 November 1984, GPAC, 57.

20. Price to Musa, memorandum, Belmopan, 20 November 1984, GPAC, 74.

21. Price to Reconstruction and Development Corporation, memorandum, Belmopan, 10 December 1984, GPAC, 64.

22. Shoman, *Party Politics in Belize*, 36–37.

23. Esquivel, interview.

24. Ibid.

25. Ibid.

26. Robert Pennell (former constituency UDP campaign manager), interview by author, 5 February 2011, Punta Gorda Town.

27. Esquivel, interview.

28. Ibid. Deregulation of restrictive colonial broadcasting laws contributed to the rapid expansion of television and radio media in the 1980s.

29. Said Musa (parliamentarian, former PUP prime minister from 1998 to 2008 and former party leader), interview by author, 26 November 2010, Belize City.

30. Fonseca served as PUP campaign manager from 1987 to 2008 and had great influence on the financial management of the party and, when the PUP was in power, of the country.

31. Ralph Fonseca (former minister and former national campaign manager, PUP), interview by author, 31 March 2011, Belize City.

32. Musa, interview.

33. Leslie, interview.

34. Courtenay, interview.

35. Lindo, interview.

36. Joe Coye et al., *Executive Summary of Commission of Inquiry on Community Development Projects of 1989* (Belmopan: Government of Belize), 1990.

37. House of Representatives, *Hansard 1988–1989* (Belmopan: Government of Belize, 1989). This also is the amount that the then prime minister, Esquivel, recollected as accurate (personal communication with Manuel Esquivel, 2 May and 15 May 2012). At $1,800,000 the average total per constituency would have been approximately $65,000.

38. "UDP Uses Public Funds for Campaign", *Belize Times*, 6 April 1989.

39. Coye et al., *Executive Summary of Commission of Inquiry*.

40. Manuel Esquivel, email messages to author, 2 May and 15 May 2012.

41. Myrtle Palacio, "Belize at Crossroads 2003–2010: A Perspective on Electoral Matters" (working paper, Glessima Research and Services, Belize City, 2010), 4–7.

42. Ibid.

43. Michael Ashcroft, *Dirty Politics, Dirty Times: My Fight with Wapping and New Labour* (London: Biteback, 2009), 52. Ashcroft also stated that his "business interests in Belize began in 1987" when he bought this bank and renamed it the Belize Bank. However, it is not clear if he had other business investments in Belize at this time.

44. Ashcroft was appointed to the United Kingdom's House of Lords (as life peer) in 2000.

45. Smith, *George Price*, 289.

46. Palacio, *Who and What in Belizean Elections*, 10.

47. Saldivar, interview.

48. Musa, interview. "Bashments" refer to lavish partisan public events, usually with free food and drinks, raffles, and various kinds of handouts.

Chapter 4. Clientelism Entrenched: The 1990s and Beyond

1. Ann-Marie Williams (former constituency aspirant, UDP), interview by author, 14 December 2010, Belize City.

2. Jorge Espat (former minister, PUP), interview by author, 10 November 2010, Belize City.

3. Leslie, interview.

4. Courtenay, interview.

5. Francis Fonseca (PUP leader, parliamentarian and former minister), interview by author, 9 November 2010, Belize City. He had replaced John Briceño as PUP party leader in late 2011-16.

6. Esquivel, interview.

7. M. Palacio, *Electoral Politics in Belize: The Naked Truth* (Belize City: Glessima Research and Services, 2011), 176.

8. Douglas Singh (UDP senator and minister of the police), interview by author, 12 November 2010, Belize City. These figures refer only to funds from private sources.

9. Courtenay, interview.

10. NGO Consortium, *Report on the Granting of Belizean Nationality and Implications for Voter Registration* (Belize City: NGO Consortium, 1993).

11. Ibid., 13–14.

12. Ibid., 30–31.

13. Ibid., 1.

14. Details of this case are taken from the case file Court Registry (Action 388 of 1998/Election of Representative for Cayo West, 27 August, 1998/ Representation of the People Act).

15. Ibid.

16. Erwin Contreras (UDP minister of economic development), interview by author, 12 December 2010, Belmopan.

17. Name of source is withheld on mutual agreement on request for anonymity.

18. "UDP Accuses Education Officials of Scandal", *Channel 5 News*, 18 February 2003.

19. Ibid.

20. As cited in "7 News Unearths Report on Scholarship Scandal", *7 News*, 1 December 2004.

21. In this usage, a "government voucher" is itself de facto money in that it is traded for cash or a cheque at branches of the Treasury Department of the government.

22. Commonwealth Secretariat, *Belize General Election 7 February*, 6.

23. "Elections and Boundaries Says It Can't Ban Camera Phones", *Amandala*, 5 February 2008.

24. Office of the Auditor General, *Special Report on the Issuance of National Land Leases and Titles by the Ministry of Natural Resources and the Environment: September 2007 to February 2008* (Belmopan: Government of Belize, 2009).

25. "More Land Grab, More Patrimony Lost", *Guardian*, 25 February 2007.

26. "Where Is My Venezuela Money?", *7 News*, 11 January 2008.

27. Ibid.

28. "Desperate Fray at Housing Department", *7 News*, 6 February 2008.

29. Patrick Faber (minister of education, UDP), interview by author, 12 December 2010, Belize City.

30. Office of the Auditor General, *Special Report on the 2007 Venezuelan Grant Programme* (Belmopan: Government of Belize, 2009), 5–7 and 25.

31. The Belize Bank was formally the Royal Bank of Canada, which Ashcroft purchased in 1987.

32. This information is cited from a media interview with then prime minister Barrow reported on in "'Venezuela Money' Will Be Free Money", *7 News*, 15 October 2008.

33. For more on the breakdown of land in Belize by use, see J. Merman and R. Wilson, *Belize National Protected Areas System Plan – 2005* (Belmopan: Taskforce on Belize's Protected Areas Policy and Systems Plan, 2005).

34. "Honourable Penner Says He's Paying Half for 100 New Citizens", *7 News*, 18 January 2012.

35. "Citizenship for Votes in Belize City", *Channel 5 News*, 18 January 2012.

36. Ibid.

37. "PM Reports on Controversial Christmas Assistance Programme", *7 News*, 13 January 2012; and "Political Christmas Assistance Programme Is Vote Buying Says PUP and VIP", *Amandala*, 23 December 2011.

38. Ibid.

39. Ibid.

40. "Lavish Spending to Seduce the Electorate", *Channel 5 News*, 2 February 2012.

41. "Senator Questions Loan Write-Offs", *Channel 5 News*, 25 October 2011. These loans had been acquired through various "special" programmes of the Housing Department over a fifteen-year period under both PUP and UDP governments.

42. "Government Writes Off Mortgages, Opposition Says Piñata Politics", *7 News*, 13 February 2012.

43. Statistical Institute of Belize, *Main Results of 2010 Population and Housing Census* (Belmopan: Government of Belize, 2011).

44. Election and Boundaries Commission, *Electors by Division: August 2010* (Belize City: Elections and Boundaries Department, 2010).

45. Information on party organization and conventions is derived from the PUP (People's United Party 2010) and from UDP (United Democratic Party 2010) party constitutions.

46. Mark Espat (parliamentarian and former minister, PUP), interview by author, 11 November 2010, Belize City.

47. This number (fifty-five) refers to clientelist activities that have a fixed site of ongoing operation (a clinic office), as well as other less fixed and more informal operations that function with some regularity. This number was estimated in 2010–11 when intra-party conventions were just gearing up for the 2012 election.

48. Barrow, interview.

49. See the constituency map in appendix 1 for the location of these constituencies.

50. For example, while conducting fieldwork in Toledo, the author witnessed the UDP representative for Toledo West conducting a "clinic" from the cab of his official truck in Punta Gorda. Word quickly spread about his presence and a line of some twenty people formed.

51. For example, in 2011, the clinic of the representative for Orange Walk North (and minister of natural resources) is conducted from the office of the Ministry of Natural Resources in Orange Walk Town, and the clinic of the representative for Pickstock (to 2020) is conducted from a constituency community centre.

52. A "standard bearer" in the Belize context is a party candidate who has won an internal party convention at the constituency level to represent the party in the next election. "Constituency caretaker" refers to an aspirant seeking to represent a party in the general election and is given the nod by the party to be responsible for its affairs in the constituency before an internal party convention to select the standard bearer.

53. For those few politicians who still have a voluntary element in their operations, most volunteers are family members or close friends.

54. Juan Vildo Marin (former minister, PUP), interview by author, 22 March 2011, Corozal Town.

55. Saldivar, interview.

56. By prior agreement, the personal details of the six brokers interviewed are not revealed.

57. Broker Dan, interview by author, 1 February 2011.

58. Broker Jan, interview by author, 15 March 2011.

59. Broker John, interview by author, 31 March 2011.

60. Servelo Baeza (former minister, PUP), interview by author, 16 March 2011, Corozal Town.

61. "A Very Finny X-mas", 7 News, 16 December 2010.

62. Godfrey Smith (former minister, PUP), interview by author, 10 November 2010, Belize City.

63. Constituent P2, interview by author, 24 January 2011, Belize City. A "blue note" is a $100 bill in Belize.

64. Ibid.

65. Especially after the 1990s, politicians did keep records of specific assistance provided to specific constituents and citizens as an electoral tool of tracking voting pledges and compliance. However, given that voter bribery is illegal and the general handout game viewed as nefarious, secrecy around such records is not surprising.

66. SPEAR, *Voices of the People: Public Opinion Poll – December 2005* (Belize City: SPEAR, 2005). SPEAR was a pioneer in conducting opinion polls in Belize with some degree of regularity for several years.

67. Faughnan and Zechmeister, "Vote Buying in the Americas", 1–2.

68. Some politicians also target adolescents below the voting age (eighteen years) with the logic that some may become "their" voters by the time of the next election.

69. Statistical Institute of Belize, *Main Results of 2010 Population and Housing Census*, 53–54.

70. Joseph Palacio, "May the New Creole of Belize Please Rise", *SPEAR IDEAS* 6, no. 1 (2001): 3–6.

71. Faughnan and Zechmeister, "Vote Buying in the Americas", 5.

72. Singh, interview.

73. Constituent OW13, interview by author, 18 March 2011, Orange Walk Town.

74. This was shared by a constituent in the Orange Walk Central constituency.

75. Marin, interview.

76. Dolores Balderamos-Garcia (constituency aspirant and former minister, PUP), interview by author, 11 November 2011, Belize City.

77. G. Smith, interview.

78. Constituent P3, interview with the author, 24 January 2011, Belize City.

79. "Minister Boots' Opponent Claims Incumbent Is Padding List", 7 *News*, 7 September 2011.

80. Ibid.

81. "Public Consultation or Political Rally", 7 *News*, 8 August 2011.

82. Ibid.

83. Leslie, interview.

84. Singh, interview.

85. Constituent P3, interview with the author, 24 January 2011, Belize City.

86. Godfrey Smith, "Money, Politics and Democracy", *FlashPoint: Political Viewpoints of Godfrey Smith*, 3 May 2007, 2.

87. Stephen Griner and Daniel Zovatto, eds., *From Grassroots to the Airwaves: Paying for Political Parties and Campaigns in the Caribbean*, OAS Inter-American Forum on Political Parties (Washington, DC: Organization of American States, 2005), 13.

88. G. Smith, interview.

89. Young, interview.

90. G. Smith, interview.

91. The issue of drug trade linkages is discussed in chapter 5.

92. Griner and Zovatto, *From Grassroots to the Airwaves*, 13.

93. Esquivel, interview.

94. Yvette Alvarez, personal communication, 4 March 2012.

95. Ministry of Finance, *Approved Estimates of Revenue and Expenditure for Fiscal Year 2011–2012* (Belmopan: Government of Belize, 2011), 100.

96. Faith Babb (coordinator of Collet UDP constituency office and former UDP minister), interview by author, 31 January 2011, Belize City; and Faber, interview.

97. G. Smith, interview.

98. Ministry of Finance, *Approved Estimates of Revenue and Expenditure for Fiscal Year 2011–2012*, 27.

99. Ibid., 262.

100. Faber, interview.

101. Ibid.

102. For a full discussion of concerns about the extensive nature and the increasing abuse of such discretionary powers of ministers, see Political Reform Commission, *Final Report of the Political Reform Commission – Belize*, 65, 72 and 111.

103. Ibid., 50.

104. Statistical Institute of Belize, Main Results of 2010 Population and Housing Census, 15.

105. Although the salaries of most teachers are paid by government, most schools are church-managed schools and those so employed are not strictly considered as public service officers.

106. Management Audit Team, *Report of the Management Audit Team* (Belmopan: Government of Belize, 2004), 3. The Management Audit Team reported that an accurate total was not possible to determine due to poor record-keeping, especially in relation to non-established workers.

107. Government of Belize, *Government Open Work Voter Regulations, S.I. 145 of 1992* (Belmopan: Government of Belize, 1992), Section 2 (ii).

108. McNab, email message. McNab informed that no formal records of the open vote category were kept but that the numbers were determined from time to time for particular purposes.

109. Lawrence Sylvester (CEO, Ministry of Housing and Urban Development), interview by author, 2 March 2011, Belmopan.

110. The term "grassroots diplomacy" is borrowed from Patricia Fernández-Kelly and Jon Shefner, eds., *Out of the Shadows: Political Action and the Informal Economy in Latin America* (University Park, PA: Pennsylvania State University Press, 2006), 14.

111. Barrow, interview.

Chapter 5. Fuelling the Expansion: A Perfect Storm

1. Apart from governance assessments in the report of the Political Reform Commission, see Society for the Promotion of Education and Research, *Democracy in Crisis: Ten Proposals for Reform* (Belize City: SPEAR, 1996); and Public Sector Reform Council, *Public Sector Reform: Charting the Way Forward-2000 and Beyond* (Belmopan: Government of Belize, 2000).

2. Figures derived from the Elections and Boundaries Commission, http://www.elections.gov.bz/.

3. For analyses of the extent and causes of these emigration movements, see Vernon, "Belizean Exodus", 6–25; and Jerome Straughan, "Emigration from Belize since 1981", in *Taking Stock: Belize at 25 Years of Independence*, ed. Barbara Balboni and Joseph Palacio (Benque Viejo del Carmen: Cubola Productions, 2007). Straughan (p. 270) estimates that in 2007 between 110,000 and 120,000 Belizeans were in the United States, 30 per cent of whom were born there.

4. Statistical Institute of Belize, Main Results of 2010 Population and Housing Census, 20.

5. The statements here are based on a review of post-independence district census data by ethnicity, politician interviews and personal observation.

6. The normal naturalization process requires proof of legal residency status for five years, among other requirements.

7. "President-Elect of El Salvador Visits Belize", *Channel 5 News*, 31 March 2014.

8. Constitutionally, the leader of the opposition only has the authority to make minority appointments to a small number of public bodies. One of the very few circumstances in which an opposition party can wield some decision-making power is when the ruling party does not have the two-thirds or three-fourths majority in parliament required to amend the constitution without opposition member support.

9. After the 2012 election, all of the seventeen elected UDP representatives were appointed as ministers (eleven) and/or ministers of state (six). Four ministers were appointed through the Senate.

10. This two-thirds rule was one of the several constitutional amendments made by the PUP government in 2001.

11. Charles Gibson (CEO, Ministry of the Public Service), interview by author, 21 December 2010, Belmopan.

12. See Political Reform Commission, *Final Report of the Political Reform Commission – Belize*, 98–99. The PSC is appointed by the governor general on advice of the prime minister, after consultation with the leader of the opposition.

13. McNab, email message.

14. Ibid.

15. House of Representatives, "Transcript of Meeting of the House of Representatives, 25 July 2008", in *Hansard 2008* (Belmopan: Government of Belize, 2009).

16. As indicated, there are a small number of ministerial assistance programmes that can be accessed by opposition representatives, but these are not based on legislation and exist at the pleasure of the government in power.

17. Kay Menzies, "Keynote Address to Annual General Meeting of Belize Chamber of Commerce and Industry" (speech presented to the Annual General Meeting of the Belize Chamber of Commerce and Industry, Belize City, Belize, 13 May 2011).

18. Young, interview.

19. Balderamos-Garcia, interview.

20. R. Fonseca, interview.

21. Musa, interview.

22. Harold Young and Jeffery Lazarus, "Does Winning Matter? A Case Study of Belize" (unpublished paper, University of Georgia, Atlanta, December 2010), 19.

23. Unless stated otherwise, election data for this section are from the Elections and Boundaries Department's website.

24. This figure was calculated by the author based on a review of news reports.

25. Dylan Vernon, *Decentralization and Local Governance in Belize* (Belmopan: Government of Belize, 2008).

26. Figures calculated from data compiled by M. Palacio, *Who and What in Belizean Elections,*1993.

27. Vernon, *Decentralization and Local Governance in Belize*, 45.

28. Carla Barnett (consultant, former financial secretary and former deputy secretary-general to CARICOM), interview by author, 17 December 2010, Belize City

29. Palacio, *Electoral Politics in Belize: The Naked Truth*, 175.

30. Palacio, *Who and What in Belizean Elections*, 55.

31. Society for the Promotion of Education and Research, *SPEAR Pre-Election Poll 2008* (Belize: Society for the Promotion of Education and Research, 2008), 7.

32. "New Poll Shows Parties in Dead Heat", *The Independent*, 22 January 2012.

33. For solid discussions of such policy similarities, see Shoman, *History of Belize in Thirteen Chapters*; and Bulmer-Thomas and Bulmer-Thomas, *Economic History of Belize*, 2012.

34. As stated by then prime minister Dean Barrow in March 2010 in Ministry of Finance, "Recovery Today, Prosperity Tomorrow: Budget Presentation for Fiscal Year 2010 to 2011" (speech delivered on occasion of 2010 Budget Debate, Belmopan, March 2010), 2.

35. People's United Party, *Manifesto of the People's United Party, 2008* (Belize City: People's United Party, 2008), 2–4.

36. David A.K. Gibson and Joseph O. Palacio, *Belizean Strategic Culture* (Miami: Florida International University, 2011), 21.

37. Ibid.

38. Figures calculated from data compiled by Palacio, *Who and What in Belizean Elections*, 1993. The same pattern (of both the PUP and the UDP winning seats across elections) applies in the Mestizo dominant constituencies in the Orange Walk and Corozal districts, the Garifuna dominant constituencies in the Stann Creek district, and the Maya dominant constituencies in the Toledo district.

39. Shoman, *A History of Belize in Thirteen Chapters*, 319.

40. Dorothy Bradley (chief elections officer) and Francisco Zuniga (assistant chief elections officer), interview by author, 7 April 2011, Belize City.

41. Ibid.

42. Ibid.

43. Government of Belize, *Representation of the People Act, 2000* (Belmopan: Government of Belize, 2000), sections 32–36.

44. Mitchell Seligson and Pierre Zephyr, "The Political Culture of Belize: Preliminary Evidence", *AmericasBarometer Insights* 7 (2008): 4.

45. Katalyst Institute for Public Policy and Research, *The Policy-Making Process in Belize: Issues and Challenges for the New Millennium* (Belize City: Katalyst Institute for Public Policy and Research, 2007), 155.

46. Gibson and Palacio, *Belizean Strategic Culture*, 21.

47. F. Fonseca, interview.

48. Williams, interview.

49. Cited in Government of Belize, *2009 Country Poverty Assessment* (Bemopan: Ministry of Economic Development, 2010).

50. Ibid., 53–54.

51. Bulmer-Thomas and Bulmer-Thomas, *Economic History of Belize*, 147.

52. Government of Belize, *Country Poverty Assessment*, 59.

53. Ibid., 50.

54. Human Development Index figures are from http://www.undp.org/hdr2009.shtml.

55. See, for example, Caribbean Development Bank, *Final Report on Social Protection and Poverty Reduction in the Caribbean: Belize-Examining Practice and Experience* (Georgetown: Kari Consultants and Caribbean Development Bank, 2004).

56. Marin, interview.

57. Mark Espat, interview.

58. Saldivar, interview.

59. Singh, interview.

60. Diane Haylock (former UDP constituency candidate and former civil society leader), interview by author, 10 November 2010, Belize City.

61. Constituent P14, interview by author, 31 January 2011, Belize City.

62. Constituent P2, interview.

63. Constituent P21, interview by author, 4 February 2011, Belize City.

64. Constituent P8, interview by author, 27 January 2011, Belize City.

65. Source kept confidential by mutual agreement.

66. Ibid.

67. Government of Belize, *Country Poverty Assessment*, 64–65.

68. Ibid., 213.

69. Saldivar, interview.

70. Government of Belize, *Country Poverty Assessment*, 71.

71. Statistical Institute of Belize, Main Results of 2010 Population and Housing Census, 16.

72. Barnett, interview.

73. R. Fonseca, interview.

74. Ibid.

75. Shoman, interview. For more of his views on Belize's experience with neoliberal policies, also see Shoman, *A History of Belize in Thirteen Chapters*, 329.

76. For a concise summary assessment of Belize's economy from 1981 to 2011, see Ydahlia Metzgen, *Belize: 30 Year Retrospect and the Challenges Ahead* (Belize City: Central Bank of Belize, 2012).

77. Gomez, *Tilted Towards Unsustainable?*, 7–10.

78. Bulmer-Thomas and Bulmer-Thomas, *Economic History of Belize*, 139.

79. Ibid.

80. Ibid., 138.

81. Metzgen, *Belize*, 30–31.

82. Statistical Institute of Belize, *Abstract of Statistics, 2007 and 2012*.

83. Bulmer-Thomas and Bulmer-Thomas, *Economic History of Belize*, 163–64.

84. Economist Intelligence Unit, *Country Report: Belize, October 2007* (London: Economist Intelligence Unit, 2007), 12.

85. Central Bank of Belize, "Belize Debt Exchange Offer Successful", news release, 8 March 2013.

86. There has been little comprehensive analysis of these privatizations. One welcome exception is a study of the privatization of the water utility by Daanish Mustafa and Philip Reeder, "'People Is All That Is Left to Privatize': Water Supply Privatization, Globalization and Social Justice in Belize City, Belize", *International Journal of Urban and Regional Research* 33, no. 3 (2009): 789–808.

87. Gomez, *Tilted Towards Unsustainable?*, 13.

88. Bulmer-Thomas and Bulmer-Thomas, *Economic History of Belize*, 156.

89. Rosaleen Duffy, "Shadow Players: Ecotourism Development, Corruption and State Politics in Belize", *Third World Quarterly* 21, no. 3 (2000): 553.

90. "Lord Ashcroft of Belize Facing Eviction as Country Turns on Him", *The Observer*, 1 November 2009.

91. Smith, *George Price*, 289.

92. Dennis Jones (director, Belize Enterprise for Sustainable Technology), interview by author, 3 March 2011, Belmopan.

93. The term "piñata goodies" is also used in Belize to refer to handouts.

94. Belize has a semi-autonomous Public Utilities Commission with a mandate to regulate utilities and set fair rates; however, the government appoints the majority of commissioners.

95. "Water Rates Going Down", *Channel 5 News*, 24 January 2012; and "More on the Lowering of Electricity Rates", *Channel 5 News*, 26 January 2012.

96. People's United Party, *Deliverance for People: PUP Manifesto for 2012 to 2016* (Belize City: People's United Party, 2012), 11.

97. J. Espat, interview.

98. Barrow, interview.

99. "Pro-poor" is the label used by the UDP government to categorize various targeted relief programmes.

100. World Bank, "Belize 'Boosts' School Attendance and Access to Financial Services for the Poor", news release, 28 June 2012, https://www.worldbank.org/en/news/feature/2012/06/28/belize-boosts-schoool-attendance-and-acces-to-financial-services-for-the-poor.

101. Government of Belize, *Country Poverty Assessment*, 202–11.

102. For useful assessments of Belizean civil society organizations, see Dylan Vernon, "Six Claps, Six Slaps and Many Laps to Go: Some Reflections on Civil Society in Belize" (speech to the Annual Belize Civil Society Meeting, Punta Gorda, Belize, July 200); and Michael Witter, "Civil Society Participation in Governance in Jamaica and Belize", in *Assessing Caribbean Civil Society Participation in Regional Sustainable Development Processes, Report on the UNDP Commissioned Project*, ed. Dennis Pantin (Kingston, Jamaica: The Caribbean Sustainable Development Economic Development Network, 2004): 40–51.

103. Association of National Development Agencies, *Social Directory: 2005–2006* (Belmopan: Association of National Development Agencies, 2005).

104. Katalyst Institute for Public Policy and Research, *Policy Making Process in Belize*, 81.

105. For example, it was a six-year advocacy campaign by CSOs, led by the Society for the Promotion of Education and Research, that pushed the PUP government to commit to the national Political Reform Commission process in 1999. Several of the recommendations of the commission have been enacted by the government.

106. Haylock, interview.

107. Jones, interview.

108. Haylock, interview.

109. Esquivel, interview.

110. SPEAR, *Voices of the People*, 3.

111. SPEAR, *SPEAR Pre-Election Poll 2008*, 9.

Chapter 6. Tek di Money: Distorted Democracy

1. Evan X Hyde, "Behind the Political Parties", http://amandala.com.bz /news/behind-the-political-parties/.

2. Ibid.

3. The term "homogeneous voting" is used here to refer to voters in particular polling areas voting overwhelmingly for one candidate over an extended period of time.

4. Blue (the colour of a BZ$100 note) is also the official PUP party colour.

5. "Venezuela Millions Are Here but Not for Everyone", *Reporter*, 13 January 2008.

6. "ACB Launches Campaign against Vote Buying", *Channel 5 News*, 1 February 2006.

7. Allan Sharp (former executive member of ACB), interview by author, 11 April 2011.

8. Ibid.

9. Ibid.

10. Harry Lawrence, "Editorial", *Reporter*, 12 February 2006, 2.

11. Leslie, interview.

12. Pulcheria Teul (UDP senator and constituency aspirant), interview by author, 7 March 2011, Punta Gorda.

13. Evan X Hyde, "From the Publisher", *Amandala*, 15 July 2011, http://www .amandala.com.bz/newsadmin/preview.php?id=11448.

14. Mary Breeding, "Vote Buying: Is It a Threat to Democratic Policy Representation?", *Political Science & Politics* 40, no. 4 (2007): 821.

15. Susan Stokes, "Is Vote-Buying Undemocratic?" (paper presented at the Annual Meeting of the American Political Science Association, Chicago, August 2004), 16–17.

16. For comprehensive discussions of the tactics generally associated with vote buying and negative vote buying, see Frederic Charles Schaffer, *Elections for Sale: The Causes and Consequences of Vote Buying* (Boulder, CO: Lynne Rienner Publishers, 2006); John Morgan and Felix Várdy, "Negative Vote Buying and the Secret Ballot", *Journal of Law, Economics, and Organization* 28, no. 4 (2012): 818–49; and Chin-Shou Wang and Charles Kurzman, "The Logistics: How to Buy Votes", in *Elections for Sale: The Causes and Consequences of Vote-Buying*, ed. Frederic Charles Schaffer (Boulder, CO: Lynne Rienner Publications, 2007), 61–80.

17. This assessment is based on the author's confidential post-mortem discussions of the 2012 election with a UDP party operative in March 2012. The exact accusation was that PUP operatives were paying known UDP supporters not to vote.

18. Ibid.

19. Goetz, "Manoeuvring Past Clientelism", 408–09.

20. Ibid.

21. Shoman, interview.

22. Dean Barrow (presentation, Prime Ministers' Forum: Thirty Years of Independence, National Institute of Culture and History, Belize City, recorded 14 September 2011).

23. Broker Dan, interview.

24. Mark Espat, interview.

25. Jones, interview.

26. Ibid.

27. F. Fonseca, interview.

28. Figures calculated from a review of the annual budgets from 2009 to 2011.

29. Name of interviewee withheld on mutual agreement .

30. Ibid.

31. Marin, interview.

32. "PM Reports on Controversial Christmas Assistance Programme", 7 News, 13 January 2012; and "Political Christmas Assistance Programme Is Vote Buying Says PUP and VIP", Amandala, 23 December 2011.

33. "Lavish Spending to Seduce the Electorate", Channel 5 News, 2 February 2012.

34. Belize Social Security Board, 6th Annual Report of the National Non-Contributory Pension Programme (Belmopan City: Belize Social Security Board, 2010), 3.

35. Non-Contributory Pension Committee, Minutes of the 1st to 15th Meetings of the Non-Contributory Pension Committee, 2003 (Belmopan: Belize Social Security Board, 2003).

36. Jones, interview.

37. Constituent TE21, interview by author, 18 February 2011, Punta Gorda Town; and Constituent B2, interview by author, 2 March 2011, Belmopan.

38. Lindy Jeffery, board member of VOICE on Rise and Shine, 13 March 2011, Belize.

39. Mary Vasquez (director, Restore Belize), interview by author, 7 April 2011, Belize City.

40. Mark Espat, interview.

41. Lazar, "Personalist Politics, Clientelism and Citizenship: Local Elections in El Alto, Bolivia", 228.

42. Belize Constitution, Article 68.

43. Eden Martinez (UDP Minister of Human Development and Social Transformation), interview by author, 14 February 2011, Punta Gorda Town.

44. Melvin Hulse Jr (UDP minister of transport and communication), interview by author, 6 April 2011, Belmopan.

45. Saldivar, interview.

46. Marin, interview.

47. The SHIE did also receive some international development funding for its operations.

48. Peta-Anne Baker, "Constituency, Community Development – What Role for MPs?", *Jamaica Gleaner*, 23 August 2009, 1–3, https://jamaica -gleaner.com/gleaner/20090823/focus/focus7.html.

49. "Public Consultation or Political Rally", *7 News*, 8 August 2011.

50. Ibid.

51. As discussed in chapter 1, political clientelism can also be construed as a mode of political participation in that citizens barter their political support for benefits outside of the formal political system.

52. "UDP Resorts to Intimidation", *Belize Times*, 24 March 2011.

53. Susan Stokes, "Perverse Accountability: A Formal Model of Machine Politics with Evidence from Argentina", *The American Political Science Review* 99, no. 3 (2005): 315.

54. Rosberg, *The Power of Greed*, 133.

55. Wil Maheia (leader, People's National Party), interview by author, 8 February 2011, Punta Gorda.

56. Stone, *Democracy and Clientelism in Jamaica*, 229.

57. Palacio, *Electoral Politics in Belize*, 176; and Elections and Boundaries Department, *General Elections in Belize, 2012* (Belize City: Elections and Boundaries Department, 2012), 1–6.

58. Paul Morgan (co-leader, Vision Inspired by the People), interview by author, 24 February 2011, Belmopan.

59. Maheia, interview

60. Name of interviewee withheld on mutual agreement.

61. Marin, interview.

62. Lewis, *Situational Analysis of Gender and Politics in Belize*, 52.

63. John Roberts and Ibukunoluwa Ibitoye, *The Big Divide: The Ten Year Report of Small Island Developing States and the Millennium Development Goals* (London: Commonwealth Secretariat, 2012), 33.

64. Haylock, interview; Williams, interview.

65. Lewis, *Situational Analysis of Gender and Politics in Belize*, 44.

66. See, for example, Adele Catzim and Michael Rosberg, *Women in Politics: Seeking Opportunities for Leadership in Belize* (Belize: National Women's Commission, 2001).

67. Citizen Caller, "Wake Up Da Mawnin", *Krem Radio*, 29 October 2010, Belize City.

68. Debra Lewis, personal communication, 24 March 2012, Belize City.

69. Jones, interview.

70. It is assumed by many in Belize that Michael Ashcroft was one of the forces behind Friends of Belize.

71. "Friends of Belize Moves to Trigger Referendum", *7 News*, 12 October 2011.

72. See, for example, "Belizeans Revolt", *The Reporter*, 13 March 2005.

73. "Senator Questions Loan Write-Off", *Channel 5 News*, 25 October 2011. These loans had been acquired through various "special" programmes of the Housing Department under PUP and UDP governments.

74. "Government Writes Off Mortgages, Opposition Says Piñata Politics", *7 News*, 13 February 2012.

75. Elias Awe (director, Help for Progress), interview by author, 1 March 2011, Belmopan.

76. Jones, interview.

77. Ibid.

78. Jones, interview.

79. Adele Catzim, *An Assessment of the Status of Reform Initiatives* (Belize City: Society for the Promotion of Education and Research, 2006), 16–17.

80. Mark Espat, interview.

81. Esquivel, interview.

82. John Briceño (Leader of the Opposition for the PUP and former Deputy Prime Minister), interview by author, 23 November 2010, Belize City.

83. Saldivar, interview.

84. For example, for Bolivia, see Lazar, "Personalist Politics, Clientelism and Citizenship"; for Brazil, see Gay, "Community Organization and Clientelist Politics in Contemporary Brazil"; and for Argentina the works of Javier Auyero.

85. Price, interview.

86. Roger Espejo (city councillor for UDP), interview by author, 25 November 2010, Belize City.

87. G. Smith, interview.

88. Jones, interview.

89. G. Smith, interview.

90. Domínguez, "Caribbean Question", 13.

91. Stokes, "Political Clientelism", 618–19.

92. Hunter, interview.

93. Office of the Auditor General, *Special Report on the Venezuelan Grant Programme*, 5–7.

94. "SSB Earns $1 Million in Dividends, GOB $13 Mil, Central Bank $0", *Amandala*, 12 January 2012.

95. See further details on this story in "Belize Bank: A $10m Mystery, What Connects the Deputy-Chairman of the Conservative Party with Hugo Chávez?", *Economist*, 15 May 2008.

96. The Belize Bank took the Government of Belize to court to try to recover the original loan that was guaranteed by the PUP government. This resulted in further expenditure on legal fees.

97. For comprehensive reports on the episode, see Senate Select Committee, *Report of the Senate Select Committee Investigating the Social Security Board* (Belmopan: Government of Belize, 2008); and David Price, Herbert Lord and Merlene-Baily Martinez, *Report of the Commission of Inquiry into the Development Finance Corporation* (Belize City: Government of Belize, 2008).

98. This assessment derived from a review of Ministry of Finance Ministry of Finance, *Belize: Approved Estimates of Revenue and Expenditure, 2007–2008* (Belmopan: Government of Belize, 2007).

99. This assessment derived from a review of Ministry of Finance Ministry of Finance, *Belize: Approved Estimates of Revenue and Expenditure, 2010–2011* (Belmopan: Government of Belize, 2011).

100. Jose Coye (former PUP minister), interview by author, 11 November 2010, Belize City.

101. G. Smith, interview.

102. R. Fonseca, interview.

103. Briceño, interview.

104. Bulmer-Thomas and Bulmer-Thomas, *Economic History of Belize*, 144–45.

105. Ibid.

106. Katalyst Institute for Public Policy and Research, *Policy Making Process in Belize*, 166–67.

107. Stokes, "Political Clientelism", 611.

108. Contreras, interview.

109. G. Smith, interview.

110. F. Fonseca, interview.

111. Esquivel, interview.

112. Balderamos-Garcia, interview.

113. Hulse Jr, interview.

114. Barrow, interview.

115. Briceño, interview.

116. Mark Espat, interview.

117. Wilfred Elrington (UDP, minister of Foreign Affairs and Foreign Trade), interview by author, 30 November 2010, Belmopan.

118. Katalyst Institute for Public Policy and Research, *The Policy Making Process in Belize*, 99–100.

119. UNDP, *National Human Development Report* (Belmopan: United Nations Development Programme, 2006), 183.

120. Government of Belize, *Horizon 2030: Progress Report, 2011* (Belmopan: Government of Belize, 2011).

121. Barnett, interview.

122. SPEAR, *SPEAR Pre-Election Poll 2008*.

123. "Sick Government", *Belize Times*, 13 October 1996.

124. The milk factory was never constructed, apparently due to "complications" created by a change of government in 1993.

125. Mark Espat, interview.

126. Gibson and Palacio, *Belizean Strategic Culture*, 20.

127. "Lord Ashcroft of Belize Facing Eviction as Country Turns on Him", *The Observer*, 1 November 2009.

128. Bulmer-Thomas and Bulmer-Thomas, *Economic History of Belize*, 166.

129. Goetz, "Manoeuvring Past Clientelism", 406.

130. F. Fonseca, interview.

131. These include recommendations in the reports of the Political Reform Commission, *Final Report of the Political Reform Commission – Belize*; the Management Audit, *Report of the Management Audit Team*; and the Public Sector Reform Council, *Public Sector Reform*.

132. United Democratic Party, *Always for the People: Manifesto of the United Democratic Party, 2012–2017* (Belize City: United Democratic Party, 2012), 15.

133. McNab, personal communication.

134. "Re-registration Pushed Back Another Five Years", *7 News*, 29 June 2012. One of the biggest problems with the voters' list is that a significant number of voters do not reside in the constituencies they vote in. As noted, some voters are "compensated" for this. Re-registration was finally done in 2019 before a referendum on the Guatemala claim.

135. Bradley, interview.

136. Brandon Bell, "When Do High Levels of Corruption Justify a Military Coup?", *AmericasBarometer Insights* 79 (2012): 1–8, https://www.vanderbilt.edu/lapop/insights/IO879en.pdf.

137. Hutchcroft, " Politics of Privilege", 645.

138. Rehren, " Crisis of the Democratic State", 50.

139. Price, interview.

140. Alvarez, personal communication.

141. Edmund Zuniga (auditor general of Belize), interview by author, 24 February 2011, Belmopan.

142. Office of the Auditor General, *Special Report on the 2007 Venezuelan Grant Funding*, 25.

143. "UDP Accuses Education Officials of Scandal", *Channel 5 News*, 18 February 2003.

144. Evan X Hyde, "Corruption", *Amandala*, 27 August 2006, 5, https://amandala.com.bz/news/corruption/.

145. Courtenay, interview.

146. Smith, "Money, Politics and Democracy", 3.

147. These terms were used by Gibson and Palacio, *Belizean Strategic Culture*, 21.

148. Armando Chocó (director, Toledo Cacao Growers Association), interview by author, 15 February 2011, Punta Gorda.

149. Maheia, interview.

150. Julie López, "Organized Crime and Insecurity in Belize" (working paper presented in the Inter-American Dialogue, Washington, DC, 15 January 2013), 2–3.

151. United States Department of State, *International Narcotics Control Strategy Report* (Washington, DC: United States Department of State, 2012), 119–22.

152. "The Curse of the Venezuela Money", *7 News*, 11 January 2008.

153. Francis Smith (PUP constituency candidate), interview by author, 30 January 2011, Belize City.

154. Name of interviewee withheld on mutual agreement.

155. Name of interviewee withheld on mutual agreement.

156. Ibid.

157. Julie Marie Bunck and Michael Ross Fowler, *Bribes, Bullets, and Intimidation: Drug Trafficking and the Law in Central America* (University Oak, PA: Pennsylvania State University, 2012), 89.

158. Gary Brana-Shute, as cited in Bunck and Fowler, *Bribes, Bullets, and Intimidation*, 102.

159. See, for example, "Narco Money in the Politics of Belize", *Amandala*, 2 October 2007.

160. Name of interviewee withheld on mutual agreement.

161. Herbert Gayle and Nelma Mortis, *Male Social Participation and Violence in Urban Belize: An Examination of Their Experience with Goals, Guns, Gangs, Gender, God, and Governance* (Belize City: National Committee for Families and Children, 2010), 315–18.

162. Broker Dan, interview.

163. G. Smith, interview.

164. F. Smith, interview.

165. Barrow, interview.

166. Saldivar, interview.

Chapter 7. Big Game, Small Town: Belize through Caribbean Lens

1. See, for example, Selwyn Ryan and Gloria Gordon, *Trinidad and Tobago: The Independence Experience, 1962–1987* (St Augustine, Trinidad: University of the West Indies, 1988); Patrick Emmanuel, *Governance and Democracy in the Commonwealth Caribbean: An Introduction* (Cave Hill, Barbados: Institute of Social and Economic Research, University of the West Indies, 1993); Clifford Griffin, *Democracy and Neoliberalism in the Developing World: Lessons from the Anglophone Caribbean* (Aldershot: Ashgate Publishing, 1997); and Barrow-Giles and Joseph, *General Elections and Voting*.

2. Stone, *Democracy and Clientelism in Jamaica*, 96. Stone also found 25 per cent of the rest of the sample to be issue-driven and 24 per cent to be apathetic/not involved.

3. Janice Budd, "Vote-Buying Intensifies, Survey Finds: Some Jamaicans Selling Their Franchise for Mackerel and Rice", *Stabroek News*, 4 December 2011. The survey was conducted by Dr Herbert Gayle, social anthropologist at the University of the West Indies.

4. Ryan, *Winner Takes All*, 132.

5. See, for example, "The Evolution of Welfare", *Barbados Advocate*, 2 March 2012; and "Barbados Bans Camera Phones, Cameras from Voting Locations to Prevent Fraud", *The Daily Nation*, 11 January 2008.

6. Faughnan and Zechmeister, "Vote Buying in the Americas", 1.

7. Domínguez, "Caribbean Question", 13.

8. Gray, *Demeaned but Empowered*, 12–13.

9. US $1 = approximately $90 Jamaican dollars (July 2012).

10. Gayle, as cited in Budd, "Vote-Buying Intensifies, Survey Finds".

11. Steve Garner, *Ethnicity, Class and Gender: Guyana, 1838–1985* (Kingston, Jamaica: Ian Randle Publishers, 2008), 163.

12. For a discussion of this point, see Carlene J. Edie, "From Manley to Seaga: The Persistence of Clientelist Politics in Jamaica", *Social and Economic Studies* 38, no. 1 (1989): 6–12.

13. For a clear and convincing argument of this point from a gender perspective, see chapter 4 of Macpherson, *From Colony to Nation*, 2004.

14. Duncan and Woods, "What about Us", 211.

15. Stone, *Democracy and Clientelism in Jamaica*, 94.

16. Edie, *Democracy by Default*, 22–24.

17. Adult suffrage was granted by the United Kingdom to its Caribbean colonies at different dates in the 1940s and 1950s. Although the United Kingdom was ready to grant independence to most of its British colonies at the time, factors such as the extent of civil unrest generated by nationalist movements, fears of lack of economic viability and, in the case of Belize, a territorial dispute determined the exact timing.

18. Vaughan A. Lewis, *Size, Self-Determination, and International Relations: The Caribbean* (Mona: University of the West Indies, 1976), 7.

19. Selwyn Ryan, "Problems and Prospects for the Survival of Liberal Democracy in the Anglophone Caribbean", in *Democracy in the Caribbean: Myths and Realities*, ed. Charlene J. Edie (Westport, CT: Praeger, 1994), 236.

20. Evelyne Huber, "The Future of Democracy in the Caribbean", in *Democracy in the Caribbean: Political, Economic, and Social Perspectives*, ed. Jorge Dominguez, Robert A. Pastor and DeLisle Worrell (Baltimore, MD: Johns Hopkins University Press, 1993), 93.

21. For extremely useful election data that illustrate numbers and competitive performance of political parties in elections across the region between 1944 and 2006, see Patrick Emmanuel, *Elections and Party Systems in the Commonwealth Caribbean, 1944–1991* (St. Michael, Barbados: Caribbean Development Research Services, 1992); and Barrow-Giles and Joseph, *General Elections and Voting*.

22. "Rum and roti" (or "rum and corn beef") politics is among similar colloquial terms used in most countries in the region to describe the personal and populist style of politicians who give handouts to constituents.

23. For sound discussions of authoritarianism in Burnham's Guyana, see Clive Thomas, "State Capitalism in Guyana: An Assessment of Burnham's Co-Operative Socialist Republic", in *Crisis in the Caribbean*, ed. Fitzroy Ambursley and Robin Cohen (London: Heinemann, 1983), 27–48; and Ryan, *Winner Takes All*, 181–252.

24. For more information on the Gairy regime and its aftermath, see Paget Henry, "Grenada and the Theory of Peripheral Transformation", *Social and Economic Studies* 39, no. 2 (1990): 151–92; and Wendy Grenade, "Challenges to Democratization in the Anglophone Caribbean: An Analysis of the 2003 Elections in Grenada" (paper presented at 29th Annual Caribbean Studies Association Conference, St Kitts and Nevis, May 2004).

25. Henry, "Grenada and the Theory of Peripheral Transformation", 24–28.

26. Griffin, *Democracy and Neoliberalism in the Developing World*, 149–50. Other tactics used included abuse of voter registration lists, ballot tampering, control of broadcast media and refusal to comply with court-issued orders.

27. Smith, *George Price*.

28. Stone, *Democracy and Clientelism in Jamaica*, 95.

29. Amanda Sives, "Violence and Politics in Jamaica: An Analysis of Urban Violence in Kingston, 1944–1996" (PhD thesis, Department of Peace Studies, University of Bradford, 1998), 75–77.

30. Sives, *Elections, Violence and the Democratic Process in Jamaica*, 78.

31. See discussions of clientelism in Guyana in Thomas, "State Capitalism in Guyana", 47; Garner, *Ethnicity, Class and Gender*, 163; and Katherine Quinn, "Governing National Cultures in the Caribbean: Culture and the State in Castro's Cuba and Burnham's Guyana, c.1959–c.1989" (PhD thesis, University College London, 2005), 119.

32. C. Lyday, M. O'Donnell and Trevor Munroe, *Corruption Assessment for Jamaica* (Washington, DC: Management Systems International, 2008), 3–4.

33. United Nations Development Programme, *Caribbean Human Development Report 2012: Human Development and the Shift to Better Citizen Security* (New York: United Nations Development Programme, 2012).

34. This assessment is made on the basis of poverty figures from a variety of sources, including Ralph Henry, *Poverty in the Commonwealth Caribbean: Can We Break Its Persistence?* (Tunapuna, Trinidad and Tobago: Kairi Consultants, 2001); Government of Barbados, *Barbados Country Assessment of Living Conditions, 2010* (Bridgetown: National Assessment Team, 2011), 23; and from the World Bank database.

35. Gray, *Demeaned but Empowered*.

36. Selwyn Ryan, Roy McCree and Godfrey St. Bernard, *Behind the Bridge* (St Augustine, Trinidad: University of the West Indies, 1997).

37. Gross national income figures are from the World Development Indicators and Human Development Index figures from United Nations Development Programme, *Human Development Report 2011*.

38. Government of Barbados, *Barbados Country Assessment of Living Conditions, 2010*, 23.

39. World Bank, Country Data: Jamaica, http://data.worldbank.org /countryjamaica#cp_surv.

40. Huber, " Future of Democracy in the Caribbean", 81.

41. Edie, *Democracy by Default*, 115–45.

42. This argument is made, for example, in Colin Clarke, "Politics, Violence and Drugs in Kingston, Jamaica", *Bulletin of Latin American Research* 25, no. 3 (2006): 420–40; Edie, *Democracy by Default*; and Sives, *Elections, Violence and the Democratic Process in Jamaica*.

43. Clarke, "Politics, Violence and Drugs in Kingston, Jamaica", 431.

44. Evelyne Huber Stephens and John D. Stephens, *Democratic Socialism in Jamaica: The Political Movement and Social Transformation in Dependent Capitalism* (Basingstoke: Palgrave Macmillan, 1986), 212–13.

45. Sives, *Elections, Violence and the Democratic Process in Jamaica*, 132.

46. Clarke, "Politics, Violence and Drugs in Kingston, Jamaica", 431–32.

47. Sives, *Elections, Violence and the Democratic Process in Jamaica*, 118.

48. Sives, "Violence and Politics in Jamaica", 82.

49. Caribbean Community, *National Census Report 2002, Guyana* (Georgetown: Caribbean Community, 2002), 27.

50. Caribbean Community, *National Census Report 2000, Trinidad and Tobago* (Georgetown: Caribbean Community, 2009), 27.

51. The United National Congress was preceded by other Indo-based parties prior to its formation in 1989.

52. Garner, *Ethnicity, Class and Gender*, 282–85.

53. These figures are derived from the World Population Policies Database from 2005, https://esa.un.org/poppolicy/about_database.aspx.

54. "Bahamas Outlook Clouds for Haitians", *BBC News Channel*, 20 September 2009.

55. Information retrieved from "Bahamas PM Raises Vote Buying Concerns", *Caribbean News Now*, 4 May 2012; and "Bell Says He Witnessed FNM Vote Buying", *Nassau Guardian*, 5 June 2012.

56. Ibid.

57. Griffin, *Democracy and Neoliberalism in the Developing World*, 36.

58. Stone, *Democracy and Clientelism in Jamaica*, 109.

59. Michael N. Manley, *Up the Down Escalator: Development and the International Economy – A Jamaican Case Study* (London: Andre Deutsch, 1987), 268–69.

60. Scot Schraufnagel and Barbara Sgnouraki, "Voter Turnout in Caribbean Democracies", *Journal of Eastern Caribbean Studies* 31, no. 31 (2006): 18.

61. For example, it is fairly well established that the PNC under Burnham rigged elections through manipulation of voters' lists, ballot box stuffing and other acts of ballot tampering to maintain power.

62. The Carter Center, *Observing the 2002 Jamaica Parliamentary Elections* (Atlanta: The Carter Center, 2003), 56. A "golden vote": A voter is given a false ballot before entering the voting booth. This is swapped with an official ballot, which is given to party affiliates. Once the X is put in right place, the official ballot is given to another voter to place in the ballot box. This voter brings out another blank official ballot and the process continues.

63. Travis Cartwright-Carroll, "Bahamas PM Raises Vote Buying Concerns", *Caribbean News Now*, 4 May 2012.

64. As cited in Grenade, "Challenges to Democratization in the Anglophone Caribbean", 9.

65. Ryan, "Problems and Prospects".

66. See, for example, the analysis by the Organization of American States, *Report: Caribbean Meeting of the Inter-American Forum on Political Parties* (Montego Bay: Organization of American States, 2005), 19.

67. Barrow-Giles and Joseph, *General Elections and Voting*, 158–59.

68. Michael N. Manley, *The Politics of Change: A Jamaican Testament* (London: Andre Deutsch, 1974), 168.

69. Baker, "Constituency, Community Development", 1–3.

70. Gray, *Demeaned but Empowered*, 37–40.

71. Figueroa and Sives, "Homogenous Voting", 83.

72. In addition to the works of Figueroa and Sives, see also the study of the August Town garrison community by Christopher Charles, "Political Identity and Criminal Violence in Jamaica: The Garrison Community of August Town and the 2002 Election", *Social and Economic Studies* 53, no. 2 (2004): 31–73.

73. Sives, "Violence and Politics in Jamaica", 66.

74. Sives, *Elections, Violence and the Democratic Process in Jamaica*, 131–40.

75. "Jamaica Security Forces Storms 'Drugs Lord' Stronghold", *BBC News Channel*, 25 May 2010.

76. Rivke Jaffe, "Notes on the State of Chronic: Democracy and Difference after Dudus", *New West Indian Guide* 85, nos. 1 and 2 (2011): 69–76.

77. Tennyson Joseph, "Lessons from Jamaica", *The Nation News*, 28 May 2010. See also Ryan, *Winner Takes All*, 328–30, for a discussion of political violence and the drug trade in the region.

78. Sives, *Elections, Violence and the Democratic Process in Jamaica*, 118.

79. See, for example, Gray, *Demeaned but Empowered*, for Jamaica; and Ryan, McCree and St. Bernard, *Behind the Bridge*, for Trinidad and Tobago.

80. Stone, *Democracy and Clientelism in Jamaica*, 103.

81. Duncan and Woods, "What about Us", 211.

82. Domínguez, "Caribbean Question", 12–14.

83. Edie, *Democracy by Default*, 7.

84. Stone, *Democracy and Clientelism in Jamaica*, 109.

85. Henry, "Grenada and the Theory of Peripheral Transformation", 26.

86. M.L. Bishop, "Slaying the 'Westmonster' in the Caribbean? Constitutional Reform in St. Vincent and the Grenadines", *The British Journal of Politics and International Relations* 13, no. 3 (2011): 427.

87. Lyday, O'Donnell and Munroe, *Corruption Assessment for Jamaica*, 6–7.

88. As quoted in Edie, "From Manley to Seaga", 26.

89. Lyday, O'Donnell and Munroe, *Corruption Assessment for Jamaica*, 7.

90. Gary Spaulding, "Tear it Down: Researcher Says Political System Needs Re-Building", *Jamaica Gleaner*, 5 June 2010.

91. Lyday, O'Donnell and Munroe, *Corruption Assessment for Jamaica*, 7.

92. Edie, "From Manley to Seaga", 27.

93. Barrow-Giles and Joseph, *General Elections and Voting*, 151.

94. Stephen Griner, "Political Parties of the Caribbean: Changing the Rules inside and Out" (paper presented at Conference on Government and Opposition: Roles Rights and Responsibilities, Trinidad and Tobago, 2005), 25.

95. See, for example, Griner and Zovatto, *From Grassroots to the Airwaves*; and M. Pinto-Duschinsky, *Political Financing in the Commonwealth: Taking Democracy Seriously* (London: Commonwealth Secretariat, 2001).

96. Selwyn Ryan, "Disclosure and Enforcement of Political Party and Campaign Financing in the CARICOM State", in *From the Grassroots to the Airwaves: Paying for Political Parties and Campaigns in the Caribbean*, ed. Stephen Griner and Daniel Zovatto (Washington, DC: Organization of American States, 2005), 33–35.

Chapter 8. Conclusions: Trapped in a Clientelist Web

1. "Habet vs. Penner: Another Election Petition Is Struck Out", *Channel 5 News*, 24 May 2012.

2. "Election Petition against PUP Leader Fails", *Channel 5 News*, 23 May 2012.

3. George Monboit, "Neoliberalism – The Ideology at the Root of Our Problems", *The Guardian*, 5 April 5, 2016, 5–6.

4. Edie, *Democracy by Default*, 53.

5. Clapham, *Private Patronage and Public Power*, 8–14.

6. For an informative summary of the historical experience of the United States with prohibiting and mitigating vote buying through electoral laws and institutions, see Richard Hansen, "Vote Buying", *California Law Review* 88, no. 5 (2000): 1323–71.

7. Broker Dan, interview.

8. Lindo, interview.

9. Leslie, interview.

10. Shoman, interview.

11. R. Fonseca, interview.

12. Rosberg, *Power of Greed*, 134.

13. Assad Shoman, "Is This the Real Thing?", *Ideas* 8, no. 1 (December 2003): 3.

14. Network of Democracy Research Institutes, *Conference Report: Political Clientelism, Social Policy, and the Quality of Democracy: Evidence from Latin America, Lessons from Other Regions* (Quito: Network of Democracy Research Institutes, 2010), 6.

15. Ibid.

Epilogue: The Next Tranche (Covering Selected Developments from 2014 to June 2021)

1. Figures from Ministry of Finance, *Today's Sacrifice, Tomorrow's Triumph: Budget Speech for Fiscal Year 2021/2022* (Belmopan: Government of Belize, 2021); and from International Monetary Fund, *Belize: Staff Concluding Statement of the 2020 Article IV Mission* (Washington, DC: International Monetary Fund, 2021).

2. Statistical Institute of Belize, *Poverty Study 2018/2019* (Belmopan: Statistical Institute of Belize, 2021). The study also indicated that the Gini index had increased from 0.38 in 2009 to 0.49 in 2018 reflecting increased income inequality.

3. See chapter 4 for a discussion of the 2008 Venezuelan funds.

4. Under the scheme, Belize was required to pay 40 per cent up front for fuel imported and then settle the next 60 per cent as a loan at 1 per cent interest over twenty-five years.

5. Figure derived from Ministry of Finance, *Today's Sacrifice, Tomorrow's Triumph*, 15. The budget speech stated that 55 per cent of the $872 million in bilateral public debt was for the Venezuelan loan related to PetroCaribe.

6. See chapter 4 and chapter 6.

7. "PM Says Christmas Cheer Programme Is the Best the Opposition Has Ever Had It", *7 News*, 11 December 2013.

8. "PM Says You Can Wait to Get Reimbursed for December Mortgage", *7 News*, 9 December 2014.

9. This voucher system approach had been used before (see chapter 4); however, it expanded during the PetroCaribe period.

10. See, for example, "PM Says You Can Wait to Get Reimbursed for December Mortgage", *7 News*, 9 December 2014; and "PUP Accepting Christmas Cheer – Political Hypocrisy?", *7 News*, 8 December 2014.

11. Office of the Auditor General, *Special Report – Immigration and Nationality Department: 2011–2013* (Belmopan: Government of Belize, 2016). The report includes three volumes covering issues related to nationality, visas and passports for the 2011–13 period only. Additionally, the sampling done covered only some 25 per cent of the period reviewed.

12. Senate Select Committee, *Report of the Senate Select Committee on Special Audit on the Immigration and Nationality Department* (Belmopan: Government of Belize, 2020).

13. Office of the Auditor General, *Special Report – Immigration and Nationality Department: 2011–2013*, 358; and Senate Select Committee, *Report of the Senate Select Committee on Special Audit on the Immigration and Nationality Department*, 91–97.

14. Senate Select Committee, *Report of the Senate Select Committee on Special Audit on the Immigration and Nationality Department*, 102.

15. Ibid.

16. Office of the Auditor General, *Special Report – Immigration and Nationality Department: 2011–2013*, 471.

17. Senate Select Committee, *Report of the Senate Select Committee on Special Audit on the Immigration and Nationality Department*, III.

18. Ibid., 15.

19. Ibid., 87.

20. Ibid., 15–23.

21. See, for example, "Armenian Fraudster Sent Money Monthly to UDP Minister?", *7 News*, 13 January 2020; and "Who Is Lev Aslan Dermen? And Which UDP Minister Did He Bribe?", *Channel 5 News*, 14 January 2020.

22. See, for example, "Washakie Fraud Defendant Paid Thousands of Dollars to Man Next in Line to Lead Belize, Utah's Jacob Kingston Testifies", *Salt Lake Tribune*, 10 February 2020; and "Kingston Testifies Saldivar Texted about and Collected 50K USD", *7 News*, 11 February 2020.

23. "Kingston Testifies That Saldivar Texted about and Collected 50K USD", *7 News*, 11 February 2020.

24. "PM on Why He Moved against Saldivar", *7 News*, 12 February 2020.

25. Office of the Auditor General, *Special Report – Immigration and Nationality Department: 2011–2013* , 287.

26. "Hon. Saldivar Named as Bribe Recipient; He Denies, Says No Proof", *7 News*, 30 January 2020.

27. "John Saldivar, One Last Word", *7 News*, 14 February 2020.

28. Ibid.

29. As cited in "Disgraced John Saldivar Defends His 'Dutty' Money in Parliament from the Back Bench", *Amandala*, 18 March 2020.

30. Dermen was found guilty by the Utah jury on 16 March 2020 of mail fraud and money laundering in the case in which Saldivar's name was mentioned.

31. See, for example, "Is Party Politics Permeating Coronavirus Relief?", *Channel 5 News*, 21 April 2020.

32. The Food Pantry Programme was rebranded the Grocery Bag Programme in December 2020. In January 2021, the Grocery Bag Programme was merged with the Covid-19 Food Assistance Programme to become the Food Assistance Programme. In February 2021, the BOOST programme was rebranded the Belize COVID-19 Cash Transfer Programme.

33. See, for example, "Covid Cash Transfer Program Rolls Out Shortly", *Amandala*, 10 February 2021.

34. The chair of the EBC eventually resigned in February 2021.

35. "Members of the Public Service Commission Refuse to Resign", *Channel 5 News*, 26 January 2021.

36. In the case of the chair of the EBC, the former chairman had resigned before the November 2020 election, and his replacement was appointed under the former UDP government for five years, as is constitutionally stipulated. In the case of the chair and members of the PSC, the appointment period

stipulated by the constitution is up to three years and no less than two years. This, combined with the fact the UDP had been in power for three terms and had had two early elections, led to a situation in which the chair and members of the PSC had valid contracts at the time of the November 2020 election.

37. Government of Belize, *Belize Constitution (Tenth Amendment) Bill* (Belmopan: Government of Belize, 2020).

38. "Fired on George Price Day", *7 News*, 18 January 2021.

39. "Bus Terminal Workers Removed and Replaced", *Amandala*, 20 January 2021.

40. Excerpt from interview with minister of the public service, Henry Usher on *Love FM*, 19 March 2021. After reviewing a list of new open vote hires provided by the government, the Public Service Union has claimed that new open vote workers have been hired when this was not necessary.

41. In 2008, the UDP government had appointed a cabinet of sixteen ministries with twenty-one of its twenty-five representatives serving as ministers or ministers of state.

42. See end of chapter 8.

43. Senate Select Committee, *Report of the Senate Select Committee on Special Audit on the Immigration and Nationality Department*, 155–58.

44. See, for example, "Will the Government Enact Campaign Finance Legislation?", *Love FM*, 14 February 2020.

45. "Comprehensive, Practical Campaign Finance Laws Needed in Belize", *Channel 5 News*, 26 February 2020.

46. "Referendum Raffle Is Unlawful, Immoral and Unethical", *Channel 5 News*, 6 May 2016.

47. People's United Party, *Blu Plan Belize – A Belize That Works for Everyone: Manifesto 2020–2025* (Belize City: People's United Party, 2020).

48. "NTUCB Declares Their 6 Demands from Government", *Love FM*, 17 February 2020.

49. "NTUCB Holds Successful Demonstration in Belize City", *Channel 5 News*, 20 February 2020.

50. The government unilaterally imposed the 10 per cent salary cut in May 2021 but committed to advance action on several governance reform demands of the unions.

51. "P.S.U. Says Area Rep Funds Go Unchecked", *Channel 5 News*, 18 May 2021.

Selected Bibliography

Books, Articles and Reports

Altschuler, Daniel. "How Patronage Politics Undermines Parental Participation and Accountability: Community-Managed Schools in Honduras and Guatemala". *Comparative Education Review* 57, no. 1 (2013): 117–44.

Ashcroft, Michael A. *Dirty Politics, Dirty Times: My Fight with Wapping and New Labour*. London: Biteback, 2009.

Ashdown, Peter D. "Antonio Soberanis and the Disturbances in Belize 1934–37". *Caribbean Quarterly* 24, nos. 1 and 2 (1978): 61–74.

Association of National Development Agencies. *Social Directory: 2005–2006*. Belmopan: Association of National Development Agencies, 2005.

Auyero, Javier. "From the Client's Point(s) of View: How Poor People Perceive and Evaluate Political Clientelism". *Theory and Society* 28, no. 2 (1999): 297–334.

———. "The Logic of Clientelism in Argentina: An Ethnographic Account". *Latin American Research Review* 35, no. 3 (2000): 55–81.

———. *Poor People's Politics: Peronist Survival Networks and the Legacy of Evita*. Durham, NC: Duke University Press, 2001.

Avritzer, Leonardo. *Democracy and the Public Space in Latin America*. Princeton, NJ: Princeton University Press, 2002.

Baker, Peta-Anne. "Constituency, Community Development – What Role for MPs?" *Jamaica Gleaner*, 23 August 2009. https://jamaica-gleaner.com/gleaner/20090823/focus/focus7.html.

Barrow, Dean. Presentation at *Prime Ministers' Forum: Thirty Years of Independence*. Belize City: National Institute of Culture and History, recorded on 14 September 2011.

———. 2012. Speech delivered at *25th Anniversary of Belize Bank*. Belize City: Government of Belize, delivered 11 May 2012.

Barrow-Giles, Cynthia. *Women in Caribbean Politics*. Kingston, Jamaica: Ian Randle Publishers, 2011.

Barrow-Giles, Cynthia, and Tennyson S.D. Joseph. *General Elections and Voting in the English-Speaking Caribbean, 1992–2005*. Kingston, Jamaica: Ian Randle Publishers, 2006.

Belize Social Security Board. *6th Annual Report of the National Non-Contributory Pension Programme*. Belmopan: Belize Social Security Board, 2010.

Bell, Brandon. "When Do High Levels of Corruption Justify a Military Coup?" *AmericasBarometer Insights* 79 (2012): 1–8. https://www.vanderbilt.edu/lapop/insights/IO879en.pdf.

Benn, Denis, and Kenneth O. Hall. *Governance in the Age of Globalisation: Caribbean Perspectives.* Kingston, Jamaica: Ian Randle Publishers, 2003.

Bishop, M.L. "Slaying the Westmonster in the Caribbean? Constitutional Reform in St. Vincent and the Grenadines". *The British Journal of Politics and International Relations* 13, no. 3 (2011): 420–37.

Bjarnegård, Elin. "Men in Politics. Revisiting Patterns of Gendered Parliamentary Representation in Thailand and Beyond". PhD diss., Uppsala University, 2010.

———. *Gender, Informal Institutions and Political Recruitment: Explaining Male Dominance.* New York, NY: Palgrave Macmillan, 2013.

Bolland, O. Nigel. *The Formation of a Colonial Society: Belize, from Conquest to Crown Colony.* Baltimore, MD: Johns Hopkins University Press, 1977.

———. *Colonialism and Resistance in Belize: Essays in Historical Sociology.* Benque Viejo del Carmen, Belize: Cubola Productions and the Society for the Promotion of Education and Research, 1988.

———. "Society and Politics in Belize". In *Society and Politics in the Caribbean*, edited by Colin Clarke, 78–109. Oxford: Macmillan, 1991.

———. *Struggles for Freedom: Essays on Slavery, Colonialism and Culture in the Caribbean and Central America.* Belize City: Angelus Press, 1997.

Booth, John A., and Mitchell A. Seligson, eds. *Political Participation in Latin America: Citizen and the State.* 2 vols. Vol. 1. New York, NY and London: Holmes and Meier Publishers, 1978.

Breeding, Mary. "Vote-Buying: Is It a Threat to Democratic Policy Representation?" *Political Science & Politics* 40, no. 4 (2007): 821–24.

Brinkerhoff, Derick W., and Arthur A. Goldsmith. *Clientelism, Patrimonialism and Democratic Governance: An Overview and Framework for Assessment and Programming.* Bethesda, MD: United States Aid for International Development, 2002.

Budd, Janice. "Vote-Buying Intensifies, Survey Finds: Some Jamaicans Selling Their Franchise for Mackerel and Rice". *Stabroek News*, 4 December 2011. http://www.stabroeknews.com/2011/news/regional/12/05/jamaicavote-buying-intensifies-survey-finds/.

Bulmer-Thomas, Victor, and Barbara Bulmer-Thomas. *The Economic History of Belize: From 17th Century to Post-Independence.* Benque Viejo Del Carmen: Cubola, 2012.

Bunck, Julie Marie, and Michael Ross Fowler. *Bribes, Bullets, and Intimidation: Drug Trafficking and the Law in Central America.* University Oak, PA: Pennsylvania State University, 2012.

Byrd, Herman. *Civil Society Organizations in Belize: A Rapid Assessment of Their Capacity to Influence and Monitor Public Policy.* Belize City: Association of National Development Agencies, 2003.

Caribbean Community. *National Census Report 2002, Guyana.* Georgetown: Caribbean Community, 2002.

———. *National Census Report 2000, Trinidad and Tobago.* Georgetown: Caribbean Community, 2009.

Caribbean Development Bank. *Final Report on Social Protection and Poverty Reduction in the Caribbean: Belize-Examining Practice and Experience.* Georgetown: Kari Consultants and Caribbean Development Bank, 2004.

Carrillo, Fernando, and Christian Gruenberg, eds. *Fighting Clientelism: Transparency and Participation in Targeted Social Programs.* Washington, DC: Inter-American Development Bank, 2006.

Cartwright-Carroll, Travis. "Bahamas PM Raises Vote Buying Concerns". *Caribbean News Now,* 4 May 2012. http://www.caribbeannewsnow.com/news/newspublish/home.print.php.

Castillo, Rudolph. *Profile of Honourable George Price: Man of the People.* Belmopan: Government Printers, 2002.

Catzim, Adele. *An Assessment of the Status of Reform Initiatives.* Belize City: Society for the Promotion of Education and Research, 2006.

———. *The Amending of the Finance and Audit Act, 2005: A Snapshot of Public Policy Influence.* Belize City: Katalyst Institute for Public Policy and Research, 2006.

Catzim, Adele, and Michael Rosberg. *Women in Politics: Seeking Opportunities for Leadership in Belize.* Belize: National Women's Commission, 2001.

Central Bank of Belize. "Belize Debt Exchange Offer Successful". News release, 8 March 2013. http://centralbank.org.bz/docs/cbb_7.0_new_advisories/press-release———belize-debt-exchange-offer-successful-march-08-2013.pdf?sfvrsn=2.

Chandra, Kanchan. 2002. "Counting Heads: A Theory of Voter and Elite Behaviour in Patronage Democracies". Annual Meeting of the American Political Association, Boston, MA.

Charles, Christopher A.D. "Political Identity and Criminal Violence in Jamaica: The Garrison Community of August Town and the 2002 Election". *Social and Economic Studies* 53, no. 2 (2004): 31–73.

Chaves, Miguel Sobrado, and Richard Stoller. "Organizational Empowerment versus Clientelism". *Latin American Perspectives* 29, no. 5 (2002): 7–19.

Clague, Christopher, Suzanne Gleason, and Stephen Knack. "Determinants of Lasting Democracy in Poor Countries: Culture, Development, and Institutions". *Annals of the American Academy of Political and Social Science* 573 (January 2001): 16–41.

Clapham, Christopher. *Private Patronage and Public Power: Political Clientelism in the Modern State.* London: Pinter, 1982.

Clarke, Colin. "Politics, Violence and Drugs in Kingston, Jamaica". *Bulletin of Latin American Research* 25, no. 3 (2006): 420–40.

Commonwealth Secretariat. *Belize General Election 7 February 2008: Report of the Commonwealth Expert Team.* London: Commonwealth Secretariat, 2008.

Courtenay, W.H. *Courtenay Commission Report.* Belize: Government of British Honduras, 1956.

Coye, J., R. Swift, S. Ermeav, and L. Lopez. *Executive Summary of Commission of Inquiry on Community Development Projects of 1989.* Belmopan: Government of Belize, 1990.

Dahl, Robert Alan. *Polyarchy: Participation and Opposition.* New Haven, CT: Yale University Press, 1971.

———. *Democracy and Its Critics.* New Haven, CT: Yale University Press, 1979.

———. "Development and Democratic Culture". In *Consolidating the Third Wave Democracies,* edited by Larry Diamond, 34–39. Baltimore, MD: John Hopkins University Press, 1997.

Dobson, Narda. *A History of Belize.* Port of Spain: Longman Caribbean, 1973.

Domínguez, Jorge. "The Caribbean Question: Why Has Liberal Democracy (Surprisingly) Flourished". In *Democracy in the Caribbean: Political, Economic, and Social Perspectives,* edited by Jorge Dominguez, Robert A. Pastor, and DeLisle Worrell, 1–25. Baltimore, MD: Johns Hopkins University Press, 1993.

Domínguez, Jorge, Robert A. Pastor, and DeLisle Worrell, eds. *Democracy in the Caribbean: Political, Economic, and Social Perspectives, A World Peace Foundation Study.* Baltimore, MD: Johns Hopkins University Press, 1993.

Duffy, Rosaleen. "Shadow Players: Ecotourism Development, Corruption and State Politics in Belize". *Third World Quarterly* 21, no. 3 (2000): 549–65.

Duncan, Natasha T., and Dwayne Woods. "What about Us? The Anglo-Caribbean Democratic Experience". *Commonwealth and Comparative Politics* 45, no. 2 (2007): 202–18.

Economist Intelligence Unit. *Country Report: Belize, October 2007.* London: Economist Intelligence Unit, 2007.

Edie, Carlene J. "From Manley to Seaga: The Persistence of Clientelist Politics in Jamaica". *Social and Economic Studies* 38, no. 1 (1989): 1–36.

———. *Democracy by Default: Dependency and Clientelism in Jamaica.* London and Kingston, Jamaica: Lynne Rienner and Ian Randle Publishers, 1991.

———. "Jamaica: Clientelism, Dependency, and Democratic Stability". In *Democracy in the Caribbean: Myths and Realities,* edited by Carlene J. Edie, 25–41. Westport, CT: Praeger, 1994.

Eisenstadt, S.N., and Ren Lemarchand, eds. *Political Clientelism, Patronage, and Development, Contemporary Political Sociology.* London: Sage, 1981.

Eisenstadt, S.N., and L. Roniger. "Patron-Client Relations as a Model of Structuring Social Exchange". *Comparative Studies in Society and History* 22, no. 1 (1980): 42–77.

———. *Patrons, Clients and Friends: Interpersonal Relations and the Structure of Trust in Society.* Cambridge: Cambridge University Press, 1984.

Elections and Boundaries Department. *Electors by Division: August 2010.* Belize City: Elections and Boundaries Department, 2010.

———. *General Elections in Belize, 2012.* Belize City: Elections and Boundaries Department, 2012.

Emmanuel, Patrick. *General Elections in the Eastern Caribbean: A Handbook.* Cave Hill: University of the West Indies, 1979.

———. *Elections and Party Systems in the Commonwealth Caribbean, 1944–1991.* St. Michael, Barbados: Caribbean Development Research Services, 1992.

————. *Governance and Democracy in the Commonwealth Caribbean: An Introduction*. Cave Hill: Institute of Social and Economic Research, University of the West Indies, 1993.

Estevez, Federico, Beatriz Magaloni, and Alberto Diaz-Cayeros. "The Erosion of One-Party Rule: Clientelism, Portfolio Diversification and Electoral Strategy". Paper presented at the Annual Meeting of the American Political Science Association, Boston, MA, August 2002.

Faughnan, Brian, and Elizabeth Zechmeister. "Vote Buying in the Americas". *AmericasBarometer Insights* 57 (2011): 1–9. https://www.vanderbilt.edu/lapop/insights/I0857en.pdf.

Fernandez, Julio A. *Belize: A Case Study of Democracy in Central America*. Aldershot, England: Avebury, 1989.

Fernández-Kelly, Patricia, and Jon Shefner, eds. *Out of the Shadows: Political Action and the Informal Economy in Latin America*. University Park, PA: Pennsylvania State University Press, 2006.

Figueroa, Mark, and Amanda Sives. "Homogenous Voting, Electoral Manipulation and the 'Garrison' Process in Post-Independence Jamaica". *Commonwealth and Comparative Politics* 40, no. 1 (2002): 81–108.

————. "Garrison Politics and Criminality in Jamaica: Does the 1997 Election Represent a Turning Point?" In *Understanding Crime in Jamaica: New Challenges for Public Policy*, edited by Anthony Harriott. Kingston, Jamaica: University of the West Indies Press, 2003.

Flynn, Peter. "Class, Clientelism, and Coercion: Some Mechanisms of Internal Dependency and Control". *Journal of Commonwealth Political Studies* 12, no. 2 (1974): 133–56.

Fox, Jonathan A. *Accountability Politics: Power and Voice in Rural Mexico*. Oxford: Oxford University Press, 2007.

Frazer, George. "Sylvestre Explains Give Away Scheme". *The Belize Billboard*, 27 July 1961.

Garner, Steve. *Ethnicity, Class and Gender: Guyana, 1838–1985*. Kingston, Jamaica: Ian Randle Publishers, 2008.

Garriga, Ana Carolina. "Social Spending and Clientelism: The Case of the Argentinean 'Plan Jefes de Hogar Desocupados'". Paper presented at the Annual Meeting of the Southern Political Science Association, Atlanta, GA, January 2006.

Gay, Robert. "Community Organization and Clientelist Politics in Contemporary Brazil: A Case Study from Suburban Rio de Janeiro". *International Journal of Urban and Regional Research* 14, no. 4 (1990): 648–66.

————. "Neighborhood Associations and Political Change in Rio de Janeiro". *Latin American Research Review* 25, no. 1 (1990): 102–18.

————. *Popular Organization and Democracy in Rio de Janeiro: A Tale of Two Favelas*. Philadelphia, PA: Temple University Press, 1994.

————. "The Broker and the Thief: A Parable (Reflections on Popular Politics in Brazil)". *Luso-Brazilian Review* 36, no. 1 (1999): 49–70.

Gayle, Herbert, and Nelma Mortis. *Male Social Participation and Violence in Urban Belize: An Examination of Their Experience with Goals, Guns, Gangs, Gender, God, and Governance.* Belize City: National Committee for Families and Children, 2010.

Gibson, David A.K., and Joseph O. Palacio. *Belizean Strategic Culture.* Miami: Florida International University, 2011.

Goetz, Anne Marie. "Manoeuvring Past Clientelism: Institutions and Incentives to Generate Constituencies in Support of Governance Reforms". *Commonwealth and Comparative Politics* 45, no. 4 (2007): 403–24.

Gomez, David. *Tilted Towards Unsustainable? Twenty-Five Years of Fiscal Policy in Belize: A Review of the Literature, Empirical Evidence, and Policy Considerations.* Belize City: Katalyst Institute for Public Policy and Research, 2007.

Gonzalez-Ocantos, Ezequiel, Chad Kiewiet de Jonge, Carlos Meléndez, Javier Osorio, and David W. Nickerson. "Vote Buying and Social Desirability Bias: Experimental Evidence from Nicaragua". *American Journal of Political Science* 56, no. 1 (2012): 202–17.

———. "Carrots and Sticks: Experimental Evidence of Vote-Buying and Voter Intimidation in Guatemala". *Journal of Peace Research* 57, no. 1 (2019): 46–61.

Government of Barbados. *Barbados Country Assessment of Living Conditions, 2010.* Bridgetown: National Assessment Team, 2011.

Government of Belize. *Representation of the People Ordinance.* Belize City: Government of Belize, 1978.

———. *Belize 1980 Population Census.* Belmopan: Central Statistical Office, 1981.

———. *Government Open Work Voter Regulations, S.I. 145 of 1992.* Belmopan: Government of Belize, 1992.

———. *Representation of the People Act, 2000.* Belmopan: Government of Belize, 2000.

———. *The Belize Constitution.* Belmopan: Government of Belize, 2008.

———. *2009 Country Poverty Assessment.* Belmopan: Ministry of Economic Development, 2010.

———. *Horizon 2030: Progress Report, 2011.* Belmopan: Government of Belize, 2011.

———. *Belize Constitution (Tenth Amendment) Bill.* Belmopan: Government of Belize, 2020.

Government of British Honduras. *Representation of the People Ordinance, Laws of British Honduras.* Belize City: Government of British Honduras, 1953.

Grant, Cedric. *The Making of Modern Belize: Politics, Society and British Colonialism in Central America.* Cambridge: Cambridge University Press, 1976.

———. *Governance in the Caribbean Community.* New York, NY: United Nations Development Programme, 2004.

Gray, Obika. "Predation Politics and the Political Impasse in Jamaica". *Small Axe: A Caribbean Journal of Criticism* 7, no. 1 (2003): 72–94.

———. *Demeaned but Empowered: The Social Power of the Urban Poor in Jamaica.* Kingston, Jamaica: University of the West Indies Press, 2004.

Graziano, Luigi. "Introduction: Political Clientelism and Comparative Perspectives". *International Political Science Review* 4, no. 4 (1983): 425–34.

Grenade, Wendy. "Challenges to Democratization in the Anglophone Caribbean: An Analysis of the 2003 Elections in Grenada". Paper presented at 29th Annual Caribbean Studies Association Conference, St Kitts and Nevis, May 2004.

Griffin, Clifford. *Democracy and Neoliberalism in the Developing World: Lessons from the AngloPhone Caribbean*. Aldershot: Ashgate Publishing, 1997.

Griner, Stephen. "Political Parties of the Caribbean: Changing the Rules inside and Out". Paper presented at Conference on Government and Opposition: Roles Rights and Responsibilities, Trinidad and Tobago, 2005.

Griner, Stephen, and Daniel Zovatto, eds. *From Grassroots to the Airwaves: Paying for Political Parties and Campaigns in the Caribbean, OAS Inter-American Forum on Political Parties*. Washington, DC: Organisation of American States, 2005.

Gruenberg, Christian. "Genderized Clientelism in Conditional Cash Transfers". *International Council on Human Rights Policy Blog*, ICHRP, Geneva, June 2011. http://www.ichrpblog.org/2011/08/genderized-clientelism-in-conditional.html.

Hanson, David. "Politics, Partisanship, and Social Position in Belize". *Journal of Interamerican Studies and World Affairs* 16, no. 4 (1974): 409–35.

Hasen, Richard L. "Vote Buying". *California Law Review* 88, no. 5 (2000): 1323–71.

Henry, Paget. "Grenada and the Theory of Peripheral Transformation". *Social and Economic Studies* 39, no. 2 (1990): 151–92.

———. "Political Accumulation and Authoritarianism in the Caribbean: The Case of Antigua". *Social and Economic Studies* 40, no. 1 (1991): 1–38.

Henry, Ralph. *Poverty in the Commonwealth Caribbean: Can We Break Its Persistence?* Tunapuna, Trinidad and Tobago: Kairi Consultants Limited, 2001.

Hicken, Allen. "Clientelism". *Annual Review of Political Science* 14, no. 1 (2011): 289–310.

Hilgers, Tina. "Clientelism and Conceptual Stretching: Differentiating among Concepts and among Analytical Levels". *Theory and Society* 40, no. 5 (2011): 567–88.

———, ed. *Clientelism in Everyday Latin American Politics*. New York, NY: Palgrave Macmillan, 2012.

Hinds, David. "Beyond Formal Democracy: The Discourse on Democracy and Governance in the Anglophone Caribbean". *Commonwealth and Comparative Politics* 46, no. 3 (2008): 388–406.

Hintzen, Percy C. "Bases of Elite Support for a Regime: Race, Ideology, and Clientelism as Bases for Leaders in Guyana and Trinidad". *Comparative Political Studies* 16, no. 3 (1983): 363–91.

Hopkin, Jonathan. "Conceptualizing Political Clientelism: Political Exchange and Democratic Theory". Paper presented at the Annual Meeting of the American Political Science Association, Philadelphia, August 2006.

House of Representatives. *Hansard 1988-1989*. Belmopan: Government of Belize, 1989.

———. "Transcript of Meeting of the House of Representatives, 25 July 2008". In *Hansard 2008*. Belmopan: Government of Belize, 2009.

Huber, Evelyne. "The Future of Democracy in the Caribbean". In *Democracy in the Caribbean: Political, Economic, and Social Perspectives*, edited by Jorge Domínguez, Robert A. Pastor, and DeLisle Worrell, 74–98. Baltimore, MD: Johns Hopkins University Press, 1993.

Huber, Evelyne, Dietrich Rueschemeyer, and John D. Stephens. "The Paradoxes of Contemporary Democracy: Formal, Participatory, and Social Dimensions". *Comparative Politics* 29, no. 3 (1997): 323–42.

Huber Stephens, Evelyne, and John D. Stephens. "The Transition to Mass Parties and Ideological Politics in Jamaica". *Comparative Political Studies* 19, no. 4 (1987): 443–82.

Huber Stephens, Evelyne, and John D. Stephens. *Democratic Socialism in Jamaica: The Political Movement and Social Transformation in Dependent Capitalism*. Basingstoke: Palgrave Macmillan, 1986.

Huntington, Samuel P. *Political Order in Changing Societies*. New Haven, CT: Yale University Press, 1968.

———. *The Third Wave: Democratization in the Late Twentieth Century*. Norman, OK: University of Oklahoma Press, 1991.

———. "Democracy for the Long Haul". In *Consolidating the Third Wave Democracies*, edited by Larry Diamond, 3–13. Baltimore, MD: Johns Hopkins University Press, 1997.

Hutchcroft, Paul D. "The Politics of Privilege: Assessing the Impact of Rents, Corruption, and Clientelism on Third World Development". *Political Studies* 45, no. 3 (1997): 639–58.

Hyde, Evan X. *X Communication: Selected Writings*. Belize City: Angelus Press, 1995.

———. "Corruption". *Amandala*, 27 August 2006. https://amandala.com.bz /news/corruption/.

———. "Behind the Political Parties". *Amandala*, 10 May 2011. http://amandala .com.bz/news/behind-the-political-parties/.

———. "From the Publisher". *Amandala*, 15 July 2011. http://www.amandala.com .bz/newsadmin/preview.php?id=11448.

Ifill, Mellissa. "The Sphere of Governance in Developing Societies: Examining Guyana's Transformation". *Journal of Eastern Caribbean Studies* 33, no. 1 (2008): 54–84.

International Monetary Fund. *Belize: Staff Concluding Statement of the 2020 Article IV Mission*. Washington: International Monetary Fund, 2021.

Iraola, Victoria Pereyra, and Christian Gruenberg. "Clientelism, Poverty and Gender: Cash Conditional Transfers on the Loop". Paper presented at Gender and Corruption in Development Cooperation Workshop, Eschborn, Germany, November 2008.

Jaffe, Rivke. "Notes on the State of Chronic: Democracy and Difference after Dudus". *New West Indian Guide* 85, nos. 1 and 2 (2011): 69–76.

Joseph, Tennyson. "Lessons from Jamaica". *The Nation News*, 28 May 2010. http://www.nationnews.com/index.php/articles/view/jamaicas-lessons/.

Katalyst Institute for Public Policy and Research. *The Policy-Making Process in Belize: Issues and Challenges for the New Millennium*. Belize City: Katalyst Institute for Public Policy and Research, 2007.

Kaufmann, Daniel, Aart Kraay, and Massimo Mastruzzi. *Governance Matters VIII: Aggregate and Individual Governance Indicators, 1996–2008*. Washington: The World Bank, 2009.

Keefer, Philip. "Clientelism, Credibility, and the Policy Choices of Young Democracies". *American Journal of Political Science* 51, no. 4 (2007): 804–21.

Kettering, Sharon. "The Historical Development of Political Clientelism". *Journal of Interdisciplinary History* 18, no. 3 (1988): 419–47.

Kitschelt, Herbert, and Steven Wilkinson. *Patrons, Clients and Policies: Patterns of Democratic Accountability and Political Corruption*. Cambridge: Cambridge University Press, 2007.

Kopecky, Petr, Gerardo Scherlis, and Maria Spirova. "Party Patronage in New Democracies: Concepts, Measures and the Design of Empirical Inquiry". Paper presented at Annual Meeting of the America Political Science Association, Chicago, IL, August 2007.

Landé, Carl H. "Political Clientelism in Political Studies: Retrospect and Prospects". *International Political Science Review* 4, no. 4 (1983): 435–54.

Lauth, Hans-Joachim. "Informal Institution and Democracy". *Democratisation* 7, no. 4 (2000): 21–50.

Lawrence, Harry. "Editorial". *Reporter*, 12 February 2006.

Lazar, Sian. "Personalist Politics, Clientelism and Citizenship: Local Elections in El Alto, Bolivia". *Bulletin of Latin American Research* 23, no. 2 (2004): 228–43.

Lemarchand, Rene, and Keith Legg. "Political Clientelism and Development: A Preliminary Analysis". *Comparative Politics* 4, no. 2 (1972): 149–78.

Levitsky, Steven. "From Populism to Clientelism? The Transformation of Labour-Based Party Linkages in Latin America". In *Patrons, Clients, and Policies: Patterns of Democratic Accountability and Political Competition*, edited by Herbert Kitschelt and Stevens Wilkinson, 206–26. Cambridge: Cambridge University Press, 2007.

Levitsky, Steven, and Gretchen Helmke, eds. *Informal Institutions and Democracy: Lessons from Latin America*. Baltimore, MD: Johns Hopkins University Press, 2006.

Lewis, Debra. *A Situational Analysis of Gender and Politics in Belize*. Belize City: National Women's Commission and the United Nations Development Programme, 2012.

Lewis, Vaughan A. *Size, Self-Determination, and International Relations: The Caribbean*. Mona: University of the West Indies, 1976.

Lijphart, Arend. *Patterns of Democracy: Government Forms and Performance in Thirty-Six Countries*. New Haven, CT: Yale University Press, 1999.

Linz, Juan J., and Alfred C. Stepan. *Problems of Democratic Transition and Consolidation: Southern Europe, South America, and Post-Communist Europe.* Baltimore, MD: Johns Hopkins University Press, 1996.

———. "Toward Consolidated Democracies". In *Consolidating the Third Wave Democracies,* edited by Larry Diamond, 14–33. Baltimore, MD: John Hopkins University Press, 1997.

López, Julie. 2013. "Organized Crime and Insecurity in Belize". Working Paper presented in the Inter-American Dialogue, Washington, DC, 15 January 2013. http://archive.thedialogue.org/PublicationFiles/IAD9014_Belize_Lopez_Paper_FINAL.pdf.

Lyday, C. M O'Donnell, and Trevor Munroe. *Corruption Assessment for Jamaica.* Washington, DC: Management Systems International, 2008.

Mackay, Fiona, Meryl Kenny, and Louise Chappell. "New Institutionalism through a Gender Lens: Towards a Feminist Institutionalism?" *International Political Science Review* 31, no. 5 (2010): 573–88.

Macpherson, Anne S. "Citizens v. Clients: Working Women and Colonial Reform in Puerto Rico and Belize, 1932–45". *Journal of Latin American Studies* 35, no. 2 (2003): 279–310.

———. *From Colony to Nation: Women Activists and the Gendering of Politics of in Belize, 1912–1982.* Read in parts *Engendering Latin America.* Lincoln, NE: University of Nebraska Press, 2007.

Management Audit Team. *Report of the Management Audit Team.* Belmopan: Government of Belize, 2004.

Manley, Michael Norman. *The Politics of Change: A Jamaican Testament.* London: Andre Deutsch, 1974.

———. *Up the Down Escalator: Development and the International Economy – A Jamaican Case Study.* London: Andre Deutsch, 1987.

Manzetti, Luigi, and Carole Wilson. "Why Do Corrupt Governments Maintain Public Support?" In *Corruption and Democracy in Latin America,* edited by Charles H. Blake and Stephen D. Morris, 77–93. Pittsburgh, PA: University of Pittsburgh Press, 2009.

Markussen, Thomas. "Inequality and Political Clientelism: Evidence from South India". *The Journal of Development Studies* 47, no. 11 (2011): 1721–38.

McIntosh, Simeon C.R. *Caribbean Constitutional Reform: Rethinking the West Indian Polity.* Kingston, Jamaica: Caribbean Law Publishing Company Ltd, 2002.

Medina, Laurie Kroshus. *Negotiating Economic Development: Identity Formation and Collective Action in Belize.* Tucson, AZ: University of Arizona Press, 2004.

Menocal, A.R. *Why Electoral Systems Matter: An Analysis of Their Incentives and Effects on Key Areas of Governance.* London: Overseas Development Institute, 2009.

Menzies, Kay. "*Keynote Address to Annual General Meeting of Belize Chamber of Commerce and Industry*". Speech presented to the Annual General Meeting of the Belize Chamber of Commerce and Industry, Belize City, Belize, May 13 2011.

Merman, J., and R. Wilson. *Belize National Protected Areas System Plan – 2005.* Belmopan: Taskforce on Belize's Protected Areas Policy and Systems Plan, 2005.

Metzgen, Ydahlia. *Belize: 30 Year Retrospect and the Challenges Ahead.* Belize City: Central Bank of Belize, 2012.

Milbrath, Lester W., and Madan Lal Goel. *Political Participation: How and Why Do People Get Involved in Politics?* 2nd ed. Washington, DC: University Press of America, 1982.

Ministry of Finance. *Belize: Approved Estimates of Revenue and Expenditure, 2007–2008.* Belmopan: Government of Belize, 2007.

———. *Belize: Approved Estimates of Revenue and Expenditure, 2009–2010.* Belmopan: Government of Belize, 2009.

———. *Belize: Approved Estimates of Revenue and Expenditure, 2010–2011.* Belmopan: Government of Belize, 2010.

———. *Recovery Today, Prosperity Tomorrow: Budget Speech for Fiscal Year 2010 to 2011.* Belmopan: Government of Belize, 2010.

———. *Belize: Approved Estimates of Revenue and Expenditure for Fiscal Year 2011–2012.* Belmopan: Government of Belize, 2011.

———. *Today's Sacrifice, Tomorrow's Triumph: Budget Speech for Fiscal Year 2021/2022.* Belmopan: Government of Belize, 2021.

Ministry of the Public Service. *Staff List of the Government of Belize, 1981.* Belmopan: Government of Belize, 1981.

Moberg, Mark. "Citrus and the State: Factions and Class Formation in Rural Belize". *American Ethnologist* 18, no. 2 (1991): 215–33.

———. "Continuity under Colonial Rule: The Alcalde System and the Garifuna in Belize, 1858–1969". *Ethnohistory* 39, no. 1 (1992): 1–19.

Molyneau, Maxine. "Conditional Cash Transfers: A 'Pathway to Women's Empowerment?'" Pathways to Women's Empowerment Working Paper 5, Institute of Development Studies, Brighton, 2008.

Montoya, Ainhoa. "The Turn of the Offended: Clientelism in the Wake of El Salvador's 2009 Elections". *Social Analysis* 59, no. 4 (2015): 101–18.

Morgan, John, and Felix Várdy. "Negative Vote Buying and the Secret Ballot". *Journal of Law, Economics, and Organization* 28, no. 4 (2012): 818–49.

Munck, G.L. "Rational Choice Theory in Comparative Politics". In *New Directions in Comparative Politics*, edited by H.J. Wiarda. (Chapter 9). Boulder, CO: Westview, 2002.

Munroe, Trevor. "Caribbean Democracy: Decay or Renewal?" In *Constructing Democratic Governance: Latin America and the Caribbean in the 1990s*, edited by Jorge Domínguez and A.F. Lowenthal, 104–17. Baltimore, MD: Johns Hopkins University Press, 1996.

Mustafa, Daanish, and Philip Reeder. "'People Is All That Is Left to Privatize': Water Supply Privatization, Globalization and Social Justice in Belize City, Belize". *International Journal of Urban and Regional Research* 33, no. 3 (2009): 789–808.

Naipaul, V.S. *The Writer and the World: Essays*. London: Picador, 2002.

National Human Development Advisory Committee. *First National Report: Millennium Development Goals*. Belmopan: National Human Development Advisory Committee, Government of Belize, 2005.

———. *National Poverty Elimination Strategy and Action Plan: 2009–2013*. Belmopan: National Human Development Advisory Committee, Government of Belize, 2008.

Nazario, Olga. "A Strategy against Corruption". Paper presented at the CARICOM Conference on the Caribbean – 20/20 Vision, Washington, DC, June 2007.

Network of Democracy Research Institutes. *Conference Report: Political Clientelism, Social Policy, and the Quality of Democracy: Evidence from Latin America, Lessons from Other Regions*. Quito: Network of Democracy Research Institutes, 2010.

NGO Consortium. *Report on the Granting of Belizean Nationality and Implications for Voter Registration*. Belize City: NGO Consortium, 1993.

Non-Contributory Pension Committee. *Minutes of the 1st to 15th Meetings of the Non-Contributory Pension Committee, 2003*. Belmopan: Belize Social Security Board, 2003.

O'Donnell, Guillermo. "Delegative Democracy". *Journal of Democracy* 5, no. 1 (1994): 55–69.

———. "Illusions about Consolidation". *Journal of Democracy* 7, no. 2 (1996): 34–51.

———. "Democracy, Law, and Comparative Politics". *Studies in Comparative International Development* 36, no. 1 (2001): 7–36.

———. *Dissonances: Democratic Critiques of Democracy*. Notre Dame, IN: University of Notre Dame Press, 2007.

Office of the Auditor General. *Special Report on the 2007 Venezuelan Grant Programme*. Belmopan: Government of Belize, 2009.

———. *Special Report on the Issuance of National Land Leases and Titles by the Ministry of Natural Resources and the Environment: September 2007 to February 2008*. Belmopan: Government of Belize, 2009.

———. *Special Report-Immigration and Nationality Department: 2011–2013*. Belmopan: Government of Belize, 2016.

Organisation of American States. *Report: Caribbean Meeting of the Inter-American Forum on Political Parties*. Montego Bay: Organisation of American States, 2005.

Palacio, Joseph. "Frontiers Within and Without: The Case of Belize". *Caribbean Quarterly* 41, nos. 3–4 (1995): 78–84.

———. "May the New Creole of Belize Please Rise". *SPEAR IDEAS* 6, no. 1 (2001): 3–6.

Palacio, Myrtle. *Who and What in Belizean Elections: 1954 to 1993*. Belize City: Glessima Research and Services Ltd, 1993.

———. *Selecting Our Leaders Past and Present: How the Election Process Developed*. Belize City: Elections and Boundaries Commission, 2002.

———. "Belize at Crossroads 2003–2010: A Perspective on Electoral Matters". Working paper, Glessima Research and Services Ltd, Belize City, 2010.

―――. *Electoral Politics in Belize: The Naked Truth*. Belize City: Glessima Research and Services Ltd, 2011.

Pateman, Carole. *Participation and Democratic Theory*. Cambridge: Cambridge University Press, 1970.

Payne, Anthony. "Multi-Party Politics in Jamaica". In *Political Parties in the Third World*, edited by Vicky Randall, 135–54. London: SAGE Publications, 1988.

Payne, Anthony, and Paul K. Sutton. *Modern Caribbean Politics*. Baltimore, MD: Johns Hopkins University Press, 1993.

People's United Party. *Constitution of the People's United Party*. Belize City: People's United Party, 1954.

―――. *Manifesto of the People's United Party, 2008*. Belize City: People's United Party, 2008.

―――. *The Constitution of the People's United Party*. Belize City: People's United Party, 2010.

―――. *Deliverance for People: PUP Manifesto for 2012 to 2016*. Belize City: People's United Party, 2012.

―――. *Blu PlanBelize – A Belize That Works for Everyone: Manifesto 2020–2025*. Belize City: People's United Party, 2020.

Pinto-Duschinsky, M. *Political Financing in the Commonwealth: Taking Democracy Seriously*. London: Commonwealth Secretariat, 2001.

Political Reform Commission. *Final Report of the Political Reform Commission – Belize*. Belmopan: Government of Belize, 2000.

Premdas, Ralph R. "Belize: Identity and Ethnicity in a Multi-Ethnic State". Working paper, Belize City, 2001.

―――. *Trinidad and Tobago: Ethnic Conflict and Public Sector Governance*. Basingstoke: Palgrave Macmillan, 2007.

Price, David, Herbert Lord, and Merlene-Baily Martinez. *Report of the Commission of Inquiry into the Development Finance Corporation*. Belize City: Government of Belize, 2008.

Public Sector Reform Council. *Public Sector Reform: Charting the Way Forward – 2000 and Beyond*. Belmopan: Government of Belize, 2000.

Quinn, K.E. "Governing National Cultures in the Caribbean: Culture and the State in Castro's Cuba and Burnham's Guyana, c.1959–c.1989". PhD Thesis, University College London, 2005.

Ramsaran, Ramesh F. *Caribbean Survival and the Global Challenge*. Edited by University of the West Indies, Institute of International Relations. Kingston, Jamaica: Ian Randle Publishers, 2002.

Rehren, Alfredo. "The Crisis of the Democratic State". In *Corruption and Democracy in Latin America*, edited by Charles H. Blake and Stephen D. Morris, 46–59. Pittsburgh, PA: University of Pittsburgh Press, 2009.

Roberts, John, and Ibukunoluwa Ibitoye. *The Big Divide: The Ten Year Report of Small Island Developing States and the Millennium Development Goals*. London: Commonwealth Secretariat, 2012.

Robinson, James A., and Thierry Verdier. "The Political Economy of Clientelism". Discussion paper, Centre for Economic Policy Research, Harvard University, Cambridge, MA, 2003.

Rosberg, Michael. *The Power of Greed: Collective Action in International Development*. Edmonton: University of Alberta Press, 2005.

Rueschemeyer, Dietrich, Evelyne Huber Stephens, and John D. Stephens. *Capitalist Development and Democracy*. Chicago, IL: University of Chicago Press, 1992.

Ryan, Selwyn. *The Disillusioned Electorate: The Politics of Succession in Trinidad and Tobago*. Port of Spain: Imprint Caribbean Ltd, 1991.

———. "Problems and Prospects for the Survival of Liberal Democracy in the Anglophone Caribbean". In *Democracy in the Caribbean: Myths and Realities*, edited by Charlene J. Edie, 234–50. Westport, CT: Praeger, 1994.

———. *Winner Takes All: The Westminster Experience in the Caribbean*. St. Augustine: University of the West Indies, 1999.

———. "Democratic Governance in the Anglophone Caribbean: Threats to Sustainability". In *New Caribbean Thought: A Reader*, edited by Brian Meeks and Folke Lindahl, 73–103. Kingston, Jamaica: University of the West Indies Press, 2001.

———. "Disclosure and Enforcement of Political Party and Campaign Financing in the CARICOM States". In *From the Grassroots to the Airwaves: Paying for Political Parties and Campaigns in the Caribbean*, edited by Stephen Griner and Daniel Zovatto, 5–38. Washington, DC: Organisation of America States, 2005.

Ryan, Selwyn, and Gloria Gordon. *Trinidad and Tobago: The Independence Experience, 1962–1987*. St. Augustine: University of the West Indies, 1988.

Ryan, Selwyn, Roy McCree, and Godfrey St. Bernard. *Behind the Bridge*. St. Augustine: University of the West Indies, 1997.

Sabet, Daniel. "Stuck in the Transition from Clientelism to Citizenship". Paper presented at the Annual Meeting of the American Political Science Association, Washington, DC, September 2005.

Schaffer, Frederic Charles. *Elections for Sale: The Causes and Consequences of Vote Buying*. Boulder, CO: Lynne Rienner Publishers, 2006.

Schaffer, Frederic Charles, and Andreas Schedler. *What Is Vote Buying? The Limits of the Market Model*. México City: Centro de Investigación y Docencia Económicas, 2005

Schaffer, Joby, and Andy Baker. "Clientelism as Persuasion-Buying: Evidence from Latin America". *Comparative Political Studies* 48, no. 9 (2015): 1093–126.

Schedler, Andreas. "My Vote? Not for Sale: How Mexicans Citizens View Electoral Clientelism". Paper presented at the Annual General Meeting of the American Political Science Association, Boston, MA, August 2002.

Schraufnagel, Scot D., and Barbara Sgnouraki. "Voter Turnout in Caribbean Democracies". *Journal of Eastern Caribbean Studies* 31, no. 31 (2006): 1–29.

Schumpeter, Joseph A. *Capitalism, Socialism and Democracy*. London: Allen and Unwin, 1976.

Scott, James C. "Corruption, Machine Politics, and Political Change". *The American Political Science Review* 63, no. 4 (1969): 1142–58.

Scott, John. "Rational Choice Theory". In *Understanding Contemporary Society: Theories of the Present*, edited by G. Browning, H. Halcli, and F. Webster. London: Sage Publications, 2000.

Seligson, Mitchell A., and Pierre Zephyr. "The Political Culture of Belize: Preliminary Evidence". *AmericasBarometer Insights* 7 (2008): 1–4.

Senate Select Committee. *Report of the Senate Select Committee Investigating the Social Security Board*. Belmopan: Government of Belize, 2008.

———. *Report of the Senate Select Committee on Special Audit on the Immigration and Nationality Department*. Belmopan: Government of Belize, 2020.

Shefter, Martin. *Patronage and Its Opponents: A Theory and Some European Cases*. Ithaca, NY: Cornell University Press, 1977.

———. *Political Parties and the State: The American Historical Experience*. *Princeton Studies in American Politics*. Princeton, NJ: Princeton University Press, 1994.

Shoman, Assad. *The Birth of the Nationalist Movement in Belize 1950–1954*. Belize City: Belize Institute for Social Research Action, 1979.

———. *Party Politics in Belize*. Benque Viejo del Carmen: Cubola Productions, 1987.

———. "Belize: An Authoritarian Democratic State in Central America". In *Second Annual Studies on Belize Conference*, edited by Society for the Promotion of Education and Research, 42–63. Belize City: Cubola Productions, 1990.

———. "Governance and Our Political Institutions". In *Governance for Sustainable Development Conference Report*, edited by United Nations Development Programme, 16–29. Belize City: United Nations Development Programme, 1997.

———. "Is This the Real Thing". *Ideas* 8, no. 1 (December 2003): 1–4.

———. *Belize's Independence and Decolonization in Latin America: Guatemala, Britain, and the UN*. *Studies of the Americas*. Hampshire: Palgrave Macmillan, 2010.

———. "Reflections on Ethnicity and Nation in Belize". *Cuaderno de Trabajo* 9 (2010): 1–61.

———. *A History of Belize in Thirteen Chapters*. Belize City: Angelus Press, 2011.

Singham, A.W. *The Hero and the Crowd in a Colonial Polity*. New Haven, CT: Yale University Press, 1968.

Sives, Amanda. "Violence and Politics in Jamaica: An Analysis of Urban Violence in Kingston, 1944–1996". PhD Thesis, Department of Peace Studies, University of Bradford, 1998.

———. "Changing Patrons, from Politician to Drug Don: Clientelism in Downtown Kingston, Jamaica". *Latin American Perspectives* 29, no. 5 (2002): 66–89.

———. *Elections, Violence and the Democratic Process on Jamaica: 1944–2007*. Kingston, Jamaica: Ian Randle Publishers, 2010.

Smith, Godfrey. "Money, Politics and Democracy". *FlashPoint: Political Viewpoints of Godfrey Smith*, 3 May, 2007.

————. *George Price: A Life Revealed--The Authorised Biography*. Kingston, Jamaica: Ian Randle Publishers, 2011.

Society for the Promotion of Education and Research. *Democracy in Crisis: Ten Proposals for Reform*. Belize City: Society for the Promotion of Education and Research, 1996.

————. *Voices of the People: Pre-election Poll – December 2005*. Belize: Society for the Promotion of Education and Research, 2005.

————. *SPEAR Pre-Election Poll 2008*. Belize: Society for the Promotion of Education and Research, 2008.

Spaulding, Gary. "Tear it Down: Researcher Says Political System Needs Re-building". *Jamaica Gleaner*, 5 June 2010. http://jamaica-gleaner.com/gleaner/20100605/news/news1.html.

Statistical Institute of Belize. *Abstract of Statistics: 2007*. Belmopan: Statistical Institute of Belize, 2007.

————. *Main Results of 2010 Population and Housing Census*. Belmopan: Government of Belize, 2011.

————. *Abstract of Statistics: 2012, Volume 1*. Belmopan: Statistical Institute of Belize, 2012.

Stepan, Alfred, and Cindy Skach. "Constitutional Frameworks and Democratic Consolidation: Parliamentarianism versus Presidentialism". *World Politics* 46, no. 1 (1993): 1–22.

Stokes, Susan. *Cultures in Conflict: Social Movements and the State in Peru*. Berkeley, CA: University of California Press, 1995.

————. "Perverse Accountability: A Formal Model of Machine Politics with Evidence from Argentina". *The American Political Science Review* 99, no. 3 (2005): 315–25.

————. "Political Clientelism". In *The Oxford Handbook of Comparative Politics*, edited by Susan Stokes and Boix Charles. Oxford: Oxford University Press, 2007.

Stokes, Susan, and Luis Medina. "Clientelism as Political Monopoly". Paper presented at the Annual Meeting of the American Political Science Association, Boston, MA, 28 August 2002.

Stone, Carl. *Democracy and Clientelism in Jamaica*. New Brunswick, NJ: Transaction Books, 1980.

Straughan, Jerome. "Emigration from Belize since 1981". In *Taking Stock: Belize at 25 Years of Independence*, edited by Barbara Balboni and Joseph Palacio. Benque Viejo del Carmen: Cubola Productions, 2007.

Sutton, Paul. "Small States and the Commonwealth". *Commonwealth and Comparative Studies* 39, no. 3 (2001): 75–94.

The Carter Center. *Observing the 2002 Jamaica Parliamentary Elections*. Atlanta, GA: The Carter Center, 2003.

Thomas, Clive. "State Capitalism in Guyana: An Assessment of Burnham's Co-operative Socialist Republic". In *Crisis in the Caribbean*, edited by Fitzroy Ambursley and Robin Cohen, 27–48. London: Heinemann, 1983.

United Democratic Party. *The Constitution of the United Democratic Party*. Belize City: United Democratic Party, 2010.

———. *Always for the People: Manifesto of the United Democratic Party, 2012–2017*. Belize City: United Democratic Party, 2012.

United Nations Development Programme. *National Human Development Report*. Belmopan: United Nations Development Programme, 2006.

———. *Human Development Report 2011: Sustainability and Equity–A Better Future for All*. New York, NY: United Nations Development Programme, 2011.

———. *Caribbean Human Development Report 2012: Human Development and the Shift to Better Citizen Security*. New York, NY: United Nations Development Programme, 2012.

United States Department of State. *International Narcotics Control Strategy Report*. Washington, DC: United States Department of State, 2012.

Vernon, Dylan. "Belizean Exodus: For Better or for Worse?". In *SPEA Reports 4: Second Annual Studies on Belize Conference*, edited by Society for the Promotion of Education and Research, 8–38. Belize City: Society for the Promotion of Education and Research, 1990.

———. "Ten Years of Independence in a Region in Crisis: Economic Dependency and Social Deterioration in Belize, 1981–1991". In *SPEA Reports 5: Fifth Annual Studies on Belize Conference*, edited by Society for the Promotion of Education and Research, 38–54. Belize City: Society for the Promotion of Education and Research. 1992.

———. "Spear on Target?" In *Spitting in the Wind: Lessons in Empowerment for the Caribbean*, edited by Suzzanne Francis-Brown, 1–50. Kingston, Jamaica: Commonwealth Foundation and Ian Randle Publishers, 2000.

———. "The Political and Institutional Framework of Democratic Governance in Belize: Decay or Reform". In *Democratic Governance and Citizen Security in Central America: The Case of Belize*, edited by Coordinadora Regional de Investigaciones Económicas y Sociales, 43–85. Managua: Coordinadora Regional de Investigaciones Económicas y Sociales, 2000.

———. "Six Claps, Six Slaps and Many Laps to Go: Some Reflections on Civil Society in Belize". Speech to the Annual Belize Civil Society Meeting, Punta Gorda, Belize, July 2001.

———. *Decentralization and Local Governance in Belize*. Belmopan: Government of Belize, 2008.

———. "A Synopsis of the Belize Political Reform Process since 1981". Working paper, Belize City, 2009.

Wang, Chin-Shou, and Charles Kurzman. "The Logistics: How to Buy Votes". In *Elections for Sale: The Causes and Consequences of Vote-Buying*, edited by Frederic Charles Schaffer, 61–80. Boulder, CO: Lynne Rienner Publications, 2007.

Weingrod, Alex. "Patrons, Patronage, and Political Parties". *Comparative Studies in Society and History* 10, no. 4 (1968): 377–400.

Weitz-Shapiro, Rebecca. "Clientelism and Social Welfare Policy in Argentine Municipalities". Paper presented at the Annual Meeting of the American Political Science Association, Chicago, IL, August, 2007.

Whitehead, Laurence, ed. *The International Dimensions of Democratization: Europe and the Americas.* Expanded ed., *Oxford Studies in Democratization.* Oxford: Oxford University Press, 2001.

———. *Democratization: Theory and Experience.* Oxford: Oxford University Press, 2002.

Witter, Michael. 2004. "Civil Society Participation in Governance in Jamaica and Belize". In *Assessing Caribbean Civil Society Participation in Regional Sustainable Development Processes, Report on the UNDP Commissioned Project,* edited by Dennis Pantin, 40–51. Kingston, Jamaica: The Caribbean Sustainable Development Economic Development Network.

World Bank. "Belize 'Boosts' School Attendance and Access to Financial Services for the Poor". News release, 28 June 2012. https://www.worldbank.org/en/news/feature/2012/06/28/belize-boosts-schoool-attendance-and-acces-to-financial-services-for-the-poor.

Young, Harold, and Jeffery Lazarus. "Does Winning Matter? A Case Study of Belize". Unpublished Paper, University of Georgia, Atlanta, GA, December 2010.

Newspapers and Other Media

News stories that have named authors are referenced above under 'Books, Articles and Reports' by authors' names. News stories listed, herein, generally have unnamed authors and are listed chronologically under each category.

Newspapers

Belize Newspapers

Amandala
The Beacon
Belize Billboard
Belize Sunday Times
Belize Times
Daily Clarion
The Guardian
The Independent
Reporter
The Reporter

Commonwealth Caribbean Newspapers

Barbados Advocate
Caribbean News Now
Jamaica Gleaner
Nassau Guardian
The Daily Nation

Other Newspapers and Media

BBC News Channel
Salt Lake Tribune
The Economist
The Observer

Interviews with Key Actors

Important note: The positions/posts of the interviewees are as they were at the date of the interviews.

Judith Alpuche, chief executive officer, Ministry of Human Development and Social Transformation, 7 December 2010, Belmopan.

Jennifer Arzu, deputy chairperson, VIP, 24 February 2011, Belmopan.

Rick August, programme coordinator, Help for Progress, 1 March 2011, Belmopan.

Everisto Avella, former constituency aspirant (PUP) in Cayo district, 1 March 2011, Belmopan.

Elias Awe, director, Help for Progress, 1 March 2011, Belmopan.

Faith Babb, coordinator of Collet UDP constituency office and former minister (UDP), 31 January 2011, Belize City.

Servulo Baeza, former minister (PUP), 16 March 2011, Corozal Town.

Anna Dolores Balderamos-Garcia, constituency candidate and former minister (PUP), 11 November 2010, Belize City.

Carla Barnett, consultant, former financial secretary and former deputy SG-CARICOM, 17 December 2010, Belize City.

Dean O. Barrow, prime minister and minister of finance (UDP), 1 April 2011, Belize City.

Dorothy Bradley, Chief Elections Officer, 7 April 2011, Belize City.

John Briceño, leader of the opposition and former deputy prime minister (PUP), 23 November 2010, Belize City.

Rueben Campus, former minister (UDP), 17 March 2011, Orange Walk.

Armando Choco, director, Toledo Cacao Growers Association, 15 February 2011, Punta Gorda.

Erwin Contreras, minister of economic development (UDP), 12 December 2010, Belmopan.

Eamon Courtenay, senator and former minister (PUP), 11 November 2010, Belize City.

Juan Coy, minister of state for human development (UDP), 11 February 2011, Punta Gorda.

Jose Coye, former minister (PUP), 11 November 2010, Belize City.

Hubert Elrington, former minister (UDP-NABR), 16 November 2010, Belize City.

Wilfred Elrington, minister of foreign affairs and foreign trade (UDP), 30 November 2010, Belmopan.

Jorge Espat, former minister (PUP), 10 November 2010, Belize City.

Mark Espat, parliamentarian and former minister (PUP), 23 November 2010, Belize City.

Mike Espat, former minister (PUP), 21 February 2011, Belize City.

Roger Espejo, city councillor and former constituency aspirant (UDP), 25 November 2010, Belize City.

Sir Manuel Esquivel, former prime minister (1984-1989 and 1993-1998) (UDP), 18 November 2010, Belmopan.

Patrick Faber, minister of education (UDP), 12 December 2010, Belize City.

Francis Fonseca, parliamentarian and former minister (PUP), 9 November 2010, Belize City.

Ralph Fonseca, former minister and former national campaign manager (PUP), 31 March 2011, Belize City.

Charles Gibson, chief executive officer, Ministry of the Public Service, 21 December 2010, Belmopan.

Henry Gordon, senator (UDP), 14 December 2010, Belize City.

Damien Gough, constituency aspirant (UDP), 17 March 2011, Orange Walk.

Diane Haylock, former constituency candidate (UDP) and former civil society leader, 10 November 2010, Belize City.

Melvin Hulse, minister of transport and communication (UDP), 6 April 2011, Belmopan.

Fredrick Hunter, former minister (PUP), 5 November 2010, Belize City.

Lita Hunter-Krohn, former constituency candidate, 25 November 2011, Belize City.

Michael Hutchinson, minister of state for labour and local government (UDP), 6 April 2011, Belmopan.

Dennis Jones, director, Belize Enterprise for Sustainable Technology, 3 March 2011, Belmopan.

David Leacock, chief executive officer, Ministry of Education, 12 December 2010, Belize City.

Adrian Leivia, dean of Muffles Junior College, 23 March 2011, Orange Walk.

Stuart Leslie, chief of staff for leader of the opposition (PUP), 5 November 2010, Belize City.

Dean Lindo, first leader of the UDP and former minister (UDP), 3 November 2010, Belize City.

Simeon Lopez, mayor of Belmopan (UDP), 4 March 2011, Belmopan.

Wil Maheia, leader of the People's National Party, 8 February 2011, Punta Gorda Town.

Juan Vildo Marin, former minister (PUP), 22 March 2011, Corozal Town.

Eden Martinez, minister of human development and social transformation (UDP), 14 February 2011, Punta Gorda Town.

Paul Morgan, co-leader of the Vision Inspired by the People [Party], 24 February 2011, Belmopan.

Said Musa, former prime minister (1998-2008) and former party leader (PUP), 26 November 2011, Belize City.

Eugene Palacio, director of Local Government, 2 March 2011, Belmopan.

Myrtle Palacio, former constituency candidate (PUP) and former Chief Elections Officer, 13 December 2010, Belize City.

Robert Pennell, former constituency campaign manager (UDP), 8 February 2011

George Price, co-founder of the PUP, first premier (1964-1981), first and former prime minister (1981-1984 and 1989-1993), 17 November 2010, Belize City.

Osmany Salas, civil society leader and business owner, 10 March 2011, Orange Walk.

John Saldivar, minister of the public service and governance reform (UDP), 30 November 2010, Belmopan.

Carlos Santos, former constituency aspirant (PUP), 1 March 2011, Belmopan.

Allan Sharp, former board member of Association of Concerned Belizeans and former chairperson of Belize Trade and Investment Development Service, 11 April 2011, Belize City.

Assad Shoman, former minister (PUP) and former NGO leader, 7 March 2011, Belize City.

Douglas Singh, senator and minister of the police, 12 November 2010, Belize City.

Hector Silva, former minister (pre-independence, PUP), 1 December 2010, San Ignacio Town.

Francis Smith, constituency candidate (PUP), 30 January 2011, Belize City.

Godfrey Smith, former minister (PUP), 10 November 2010, Belize City.

Lawrence Sylvester, chief executive officer, Ministry of Housing and Urban Development, 2 March 2011, Belmopan.

Bartulo Teul, programme coordinator, Yaxache Conservation Trust, 15 February 2011, Punta Gorda Town.

Pulcheria Teul, Senator and constituency aspirant (UDP), 17 March 2011, Punta Gorda Town.

Mary Vasquez, director, Restore Belize, 7 April 2011, Belize City.

Alejandro Vernon, former parliamentarian (pre-independence, various parties), 15 March 2011, Punta Gorda Town.

Anne-Marie Williams, director of National Women's Commission and former constituency aspirant (UDP), 14 December 2010, Belize City.

Henry Young Sr., former minister (UDP), 2 November 2010, Belize City.

Edmund Zuniga, auditor general of Belize, 24 February 2011, Belmopan.

Francisco Zuniga, assistant chief elections officer, 7 April 2011, Belize City.

Index

Note: Page locators in italics refer to tables and figures.